War in the Early Modern World

Edited by Jeremy Black
University of Exeter

D0103373

Westview Press
A Member of the Perseus Books Group

First published in 1999 by UCL Press

UCL Press Limited
1 Gunpowder Square
London EC4A 3DE
UK

Published in 1999 in the United States of America
by Westview Press, 5500 Central Avenue, Boulder, Colorado 80301-2877.

A CIP catalog record for this book is available from the Library of Congress.

ISBNs:
0-8133-3612-0 HB
0-8133-3611-2 PB

Typeset by Best-set Typesetter Ltd., Hong Kong
Printed by T. J. International Ltd., Padstow, England

Contents

CONTENTS

For Carole Kaplan and Peter Saunders

Contributors notes

Jeremy Black is Professor of History at the University of Exeter and was formerly Professor at the University of Durham. His 27 books include *A military revolution? Military change and European society 1550–1800* (1991), *Culloden and the '45* (1991), *War for America. The fight for independence 1775–1783* (1992), *European warfare 1660–1815* (1994), *Warfare; renaissance to revolution 1492–1792* (1996), *Maps and history* (1997) and *War and the world 1450–2000* (1998). His five edited books include *The origins of war in early modern Europe* (1987), and his six co-edited volumes include *The British navy and the use of naval power in the eighteenth century* (1988).

Jan Glete is Senior Lecturer of History at Stockholm University, Sweden. He has published several studies of Swedish industrial and financial history of the nineteenth and twentieth centuries, as well as studies of Swedish naval and military history from the sixteenth to the twentieth century. In English he has published *Navies and nations: warships, navies and state building in Europe and America*, 1500–1860 (1993).

Jos J. L. Gommans, PhD (1993), University of Leiden, teaches Indian history at the Kern Institute of the University of Leiden. Previously he published *The rise of the Indo–Afghan empire, c. 1710–1780* (Leiden: E. J. Brill, 1995) as well as several articles on medieval Indian history. Currently he is working on a UCL volume on Mughal warfare.

Ross Hassig is currently Professor of Anthropology at the University of Oklahoma. His publications include *Trade, tribute, and transportation: the sixteenth century political economy of the Valley of Mexico* (1985), *Aztec warfare: imperial expansion and political control* (1988), *War and society in ancient Mesoamerica* (1992), and *Mexico and the Spanish conquest* (1994).

Peter Lorge graduated from the University of Pennsylvania in 1996 with a doctorate on *War and the creation of the Northern Song*. He is Adjunct Faculty at the Philadelphia College of Textiles and Science.

John Thornton was educated at the University of Michigan and the University of California at Los Angeles where he received his doctorate in 1979. He has taught at the University of Zambia, Allegheny College and the University of Virginia before coming to Millersville University where he is Professor of History. His special interest is in the history of pre-colonial Africa and the African Diaspora.

Armstrong Starkey is a Professor of History and Provost at Adelphi University in New York. He has published articles on a variety of subjects in eighteenth-century history. Most recently he has written on the values of British officers participating in the War of American Independence.

Paul Varley is Senior Professor of Japanese Cultural History at the University of Hawaii and Professor Emeritus of Japanese History at Columbia University. He has written a number of books on Japanese history, the most recent of which is *Warriors of Japan, as portrayed in the war tales* (University of Hawaii Press, 1994)

Peter H. Wilson is Lecturer in Early Modern European History at the University of Newcastle-Upon-Tyne. His publications include *War, state and society in Württemberg, 1677–1793* (1995) and a number of articles on war, politics and society in Central Europe 1500–1800. He is currently writing on absolutism, war and German politics.

Preface

Conflict is central to human history and is frequently the cause, course and consequence of change. Yet the study of war, especially prior to the modern period, is a subject that has received insufficient attention in academic circles over the past four decades. Furthermore, most of that attention has been devoted to warfare in Europe. When the rest of the world has been considered, it has generally been with reference to the expansion of European military power.

This volume seeks to redress this emphasis. Europe is deliberately only allocated one chapter and that is not placed first. A team of distinguished international scholars offer accounts designed to limit the Eurocentric perspective, and in the Introduction an attempt is made to discuss the "rise of the West" in the light of the volume's emphasis on the vitality of non-Western military systems. Because of limitations of length, it has been necessary to omit consideration of systems in several parts of the world. It is hoped that they will be covered in succeeding volumes.

I am most grateful to Jan Glete, Cliff Rogers and Peter Wilson for commenting on earlier drafts of parts of the Introduction, and to Wendy Duery for her secretarial support. I have benefited from the opportunity to develop themes outlined in the Introduction in papers delivered at Temple University and the Anglo-American Conference.

Chapter One

Introduction

Jeremy Black

How wars are won is the central question in military history. However, as with the question of why wars break out, where it is easier to account for one war starting than for a number, it is difficult to provide a general account of success. In part, this reflects the multifaceted cultural assumptions, both past and present, in which notions of success are embedded. Success, like victory, defeat and loss, is culturally conditioned, and it is as dangerous to assume a Eurocentric definition of these concepts as it is to offer a Eurocentric account of world history.

Three interrelated issues will receive particular attention in the Introduction. First, the global dimension of power and, specifically, the "rise of the West"; secondly, the nature and role of technological change; and, thirdly, the relationship between military developments and state-building.

The rise of the West

The early modern period was one which saw both greater interaction between different parts of the world and the rise of European influence and power. The two were linked. It was through the projection of European power that the "Old World" and the "New World" were connected, and indeed that the "New World" was created as an idea as, first, Spain and Portugal and, later, England, France and the Dutch conquered and settled important portions of North and South America. It was through the projection of Portuguese naval power from the 1490s that European trade and military strength began to make its impact in the Indian Ocean.

The result was a major shift in global power. For much of the fifteenth century the Europeans had been relatively inconsequential on the world stage; indeed, they were unable to prevent the advances of the Ottoman Turks into the Balkans, a process that led to the dramatic fall of Constantinople, the capital of the Byzantine empire, to Mehmed II in 1453. No European state matched Mehmed's power, and the Ottoman empire became the most important state in Europe. At the same time, it was the Chinese, not the Europeans, who were the leading power in Asian waters; indeed, in the first half of the century, the Chinese sent fleets into the Indian Ocean that were far larger than any European fleet.

By the late sixteenth century the situation was very different. The Ottomans had made significant advances in Europe and the Mediterranean, capturing Belgrade in 1521, defeating Hungary in 1526 and conquering Cyprus in 1570–1, although their invasion of southern Italy in 1480 had been repelled in 1481 and they had been held at Vienna (1529), Corfu (1537) and Malta (1565). It was further afield, however, that the shift was dramatic. When Spanish forces began to take control of the Philippines in the 1560s, Philip II of Spain, after whom the islands were renamed, became the first ruler with an empire on which the sun never set. Spanish forces had already overthrown the Aztecs of Mexico and the Incas of Peru, a process greatly aided by divisions among Spain's opponents and by the impact of European diseases. Portuguese warships in the Indian Ocean had destroyed the leading Indian fleets of Calicut and Gujarat – and also those of Egypt and Turkey.

However, over most of Asia the European impact was far more limited. In East Asia the crucial struggle was between Japan and China for control of the continental littoral, a struggle that focused on Korea in the 1590s. Although European adventurers had an impact in coastal Southeast Asia, especially in Burma and Cambodia, they played little role in the ebb and flow of power in such states as Siam. In India, the decisive political change was the destruction of Lodi power by that of the Mughals in the 1520s, and the subsequent defence, consolidation and expansion of Mughal power in northern and central India. In Persia, another dynasty relying on cavalry, the Safavids, successfully invaded and established control in the 1500s. Although they were affected by the Portuguese presence in the Persian gulf, their foreign policy, and methods of warfare, were dominated by repeated wars with their neighbours, the Ottomans and the Uzbeks.

The dynamic of transoceanic European maritime activity and territorial control was to be maintained throughout the period. In the seventeenth century the English and French took over much of the eastern seaboard of North America, while the Dutch, defeated there by the English, had already taken over some of the crucial spice-producing regions of the East Indies. Meanwhile, Russian power spread across Siberia to the Pacific, ensuring that China acquired a land frontier with a European state.

In the first three-quarters of the eighteenth century, European power continued to expand in the New World, with the Portuguese pressing into the interior of Brazil, the Spaniards expanding into coastal California and the English and French competing for supremacy in the Great Lakes region. Native American resistance was frequently successful in individual engagements, as in the case of Pontiac's War against the British in 1763, but it proved difficult to sustain military operations. This reflected the nature of native American society, politics and economic practices. In addition, the British were greatly helped by their growing demographic weight, a product both of emigration and of the impact of disease on the natives.[1] This was not only a general preponderance, but also a preponderance at the point of contact. Natives, such as the Apaches, had greater success in stemming Spanish expansion north from Mexico, although such expansion was not central to the purposes of Spanish power in Mexico.[2] In India, the British took over Bengal and became the leading power on the Carnatic (southeast) coast, although in each case not until the 1750s, and in mid-century the most important challengers for control of northern India were not European, but, rather, Nadir Shah of Persia, who invaded in 1739, the Afghans, who invaded in 1761, and the Marathas of western India.

The only serious and lasting defeat that the Europeans were to experience occurred in North America, where the Thirteen Colonies fought their way into independence from Britain in 1775–83. Yet, it is significant that this defeat was at the hands of people of European descent, armed with European weapons and fighting with the direct land and sea assistance of a European state – France – while they also benefited from Britain's conflict with two other European states: Spain (1779–83) and the Dutch (1780–3).

It would be misleading to imply that the Europeans were everywhere victorious. Their impact in Africa and the Pacific was very limited, and in East Asia the most expansive state in the eighteenth century was China. In the eighteenth century, the Russians found it difficult to make lasting headway against the Persians, while, after major defeats in 1683–1717, the Ottomans displayed great resilience against Austria, regaining Belgrade in 1739.

However, the world was increasingly one where the crucial links between distant parts were controlled or created by Europeans. This helped to ensure that a "world economy" developed and that distant regions traded, so that the British shipped Indian tea to North America or the Dutch moved Chinese porcelain to Europe. This trade was to the profit of the European maritime powers that controlled it, and helped to ensure that Britain was well placed for rapid economic growth in the eighteenth century.

European maritime control also had crucial demographic consequences. It made possible a major emigration of Europeans and of African slaves to the New World, and permanently altered the demography of the latter. The population of

3

Europe expanded in the sixteenth century, and, after a period of protracted stagnation, from the 1740s, and this provided the people to settle Pennsylvania and to move the frontier of settled agriculture south across the Russian steppes.

An emphasis on European expansion might appear misplaced. Much of the world had never seen a European. European maps of central Asia or of inland Africa were either blanks or full of errors, and remained so until the nineteenth century. To talk of European power would have been curious in Tibet, conquered by China in 1720, or in Mombasa, whence the Omani Arabs had expelled the Portuguese in 1698, or in West Africa, where the Kingdom of Dahomey dominated European coastal trading posts from the 1720s, or in Angola and Mozambique, where Portuguese expansion was held in the sixteenth and seventeenth centuries.

Nevertheless, however limited their political or military impact might have been, it was a case of Europeans off the coast of Asia, not Asians off the coast of Europe. It was Europeans who charted the oceans, who explored their dark side of the world – the Pacific – and thus acquired the knowledge that helped them to profit from their strength.[3] The world was increasingly renamed by the Europeans, its spaces organized in and by their maps and projections[4]; although the consequences of this were not to be apparent in much of the world until the nineteenth century. European products became sought after, and European self-confidence was enhanced. Many of the consequences of European ambition were unattractive, most obviously the slave trade, a process that reflected an ability to plan and execute long-range economic exchanges. We can now consider the rise of Europe without applauding its consequences. Yet, it is difficult to challenge its importance. The Europeans remoulded the world, creating new political, economic, demographic, religious and cultural spaces and links that still greatly affect the world in which we live.

Technological change

Across most of the world in the early-modern period, explanations of success in periods of warfare focused on leadership, individual bravery, collective prowess in the use of weaponry and discipline. An emphasis on technology as the motor of military change and success developed most of all in Europe. It can be seen in the writings of commentators such as Edward Gibbon[5], although the emphasis became most pronounced from the nineteenth century, as the pace of technological change grew. Gunpowder was also seen as instrumental in the demise of medieval feudalism, and thus as crucial to the onset of modernity.[6] Robert Fulton, a pioneer of submarine warfare, placed past, present, and future change in a continuum: "It does not require much depth of thought to trace that science by discovering gunpowder changed the whole art of war by land and sea; and by future combination may sweep military marines from the ocean".[7] Differences in weaponry were seen as crucial to operational effectiveness and success, and weaponry thus became the central issue in military capability. This was especially the case if the warfare in question was between different types of society, particularly between Western and non-Western societies.

Weaponry serves as an obvious indicator of military capability. It is where soldiers, tactics, organization and economic strength intersect. Weapons appeal to military enthusiasts. Furthermore, there are major attractions concentrating scholarly and popular attention on weapons. They appear to exist outside cultures and to offer ready comparisons across space and time: it is not necessary to know the language of a society in order to measure the thickness of its town walls, the length of its spears, or the calibre of its guns. It is attractive to see capability and success in military history as a function of weaponry, not least because discussion of contemporary warfare often concentrates on such questions as the ability of one plane to outfly another. The atomic bomb is a potent symbol of the ability of technology to create weaponry that decisively altered the course of events. Although only used twice in actual warfare, atomic weapons have had a huge impact on preparations for war, deployments, force structure, etc., and have indeed revolutionized the role of the military and of war itself. There is also an extremely vigorous discussion of the current RMA (Revolution in Military Affairs) based on stealth, "smart", space and computer weaponry.

Nonetheless, the emphasis on weaponry can be misleading. The atom bomb draws attention to the crucial dimension of contexts, the role of political, cultural, social and economic assumptions and requirements in affecting the use of weapons. Indeed, it is at this point of assumptions and requirements that the notion of measuring weapons across societies and outside their contexts is least helpful. At the very basic level, the length of a spear or the calibre of a gun provides little information about tactics – still less about strategy. It also tells little about the willingness to take and to inflict casualties. The possession of the atom bomb did not enable the USA to secure victory for its allies in the Chinese Civil War of 1945–9, when no other power had such a bomb.

These introductory points are of importance because of the role that military technology takes in explanations of the rise of the West, and specifically in the question of why a minority of the world's population was able to take control of so much population and territory, and to do so as a continuous process for over 400 years. The standard answer has been presented in terms of weaponry on both land and sea. Ocean-going, cannon-firing warships are seen as giving Europeans a decisive advantage at sea from the 1490s onwards. One very important result of the introduction of efficient gunpowder weapons at sea was that capital was, in part, substituted for manpower. This increased dramatically the operational radius of seaborne fighting forces, as only a limited number of men had to be fed on long travels. On land, the European utilization of steel and gunpowder weapons against societies that knew nothing of them are generally seen as playing a crucial role in the Spanish overthrow of the Incas and Aztecs in the early sixteenth century, and in the Russian conquest of Siberia starting in the 1560s.

Thus, firepower at land and sea, including major gaps in capability among forces armed with firearms, can be seen as the crucial multiplier that allowed relatively small numbers of Europeans to defeat and conquer far larger numbers of non-Europeans; in general, the Europeans deployed only a small portion of their military resources outside Europe. The argument from the specific case of European success to the general can thus provide an explanation that can be used to account for other specific cases.

However, this explanation has to be qualified by noting European numerical superiority in particular areas, such as the zone of contact in North America, and, more generally, the ability of Europeans to gain local allies. Furthermore, the account can be modified in a number of other respects. First, the European advantage in military technique and infrastructure should not be exaggerated, although, in comparison with many other societies, there was such an advantage, especially in naval terms, from the start of the sixteenth century. It rested on the foundations of centuries of European economic, technological, social and institutional change. Secondly, technology can be seen not as an independent variable, but, in part, as the product of a more wide-ranging set of developments. Thirdly, it is important when discussing the rise and fall of powers to move from a concentration on warfare. In many respects, the most interesting battles were those that did not actually take place.

This was certainly the case with naval warfare. In the 1430s the state with the greatest global-reach capability, in terms of the distant deployment of substantial naval forces, was China. A century later, especially after its victory over the Ottoman fleet off India in 1538, it was Portugal. It is all too easy in drawing attention to Portuguese victories in the Indian Ocean to neglect the battles that did not occur, in particular major engagements with the naval powers of East Asia: China, Japan and Korea. None of these states challenged Portuguese maritime expansion, in large part because none had distant naval interests in the sixteenth century, while the Portuguese sensibly accommodated themselves to the regional powers, pursuing trade at Macao and Nagasaki, rather than territory. Whereas the Spaniards had exploited local divisions in Mesoamerica, and the Portuguese likewise in India, there was no comparable intervention in the divided politics of Japan.

Similarly, Spanish expansion in the Philippines from the 1560s and Russian along the Sea of Okhotsk from the 1630s were not contested by any of the major East Asian naval powers. This did not reflect any lack of naval strength, although, without heavy guns, Far Eastern ships might have fared badly had the Portuguese been able to deploy a sizeable fleet. Indeed, the Japanese mounted a major and sustained amphibious assault on Korea in the 1590s, an operation that, at least initially, was more successful than the Turkish attack on Malta in 1565 or the Spanish on England in 1588, both of which commonly attract far more attention in naval history.

Early modern East Asian maritime history demonstrates three problems with military history as commonly presented. First, there is the downplaying or ignoring of any occurrence that did not involve Europeans. This is true of the Japanese invasion of Korea in 1592. Another good, non-maritime example comes from eighteenth-century India. Major battles, such as Karnal (1739), when Nadir Shah of Persia defeated the Mughals north of Delhi, and the third battle of Panipat (1761), when the Afghans, under Ahmad Shah Abdali, defeated the Marathas nearby, receive far less attention than Robert Clive's victory at the head of British East India Company troops over Surajah Dowla, the Nawab of Bengal, at Plassey (1757), a shorter struggle in which fewer troops were engaged and total casualties were less than 600, and one in which dissension among the Nawab's forces was crucial.

The second point to emerge from East Asian maritime history is the lack of attention devoted to struggles involving Europeans, if the latter failed. Thus, in 1661 the Dutch were driven from Formosa (Taiwan) by the Ming loyalist Cheng Ch'eng-Kung (known to Europeans as Coxinga). This is not a struggle that receives much attention, any more than the Russian failure in the 1680s to retain their positions in the Amur valley against Chinese pressure. More generally, an account of military history that focuses on the rise of the "West" commonly devotes insufficient attention to contra-indications, or explains them by reference to the failings of the particular Western force – for example, poor generalship, rather than more general Western deficiencies and the strengths of their opponents.[8]

Thirdly, there is a general failure to consider the implications of clashes that did not occur, and to ask how far they indicated differences in military priorities. The Chinese were scarcely pacific in the sixteenth century: they fought against the Mongols, sent a large army into Korea, fought off Japanese pirates and launched campaigns against indigenous people in Southwest China. However, there was no war with Portugal. Had there been so, the Chinese would have had large numbers of warships, although they were lightly gunned. Nevertheless, a Chinese naval squadron, employing cannon, defeated a Portuguese force off

Tunmên in 1522. Chinese ships were more strongly constructed than their Indian counterparts. Yet, this defeat simply highlights the issue, for Tunmên is near Macao. There was no attempt to challenge the Portuguese at a greater distance, for example off Malacca. The Chinese had an inshore naval capability, but they no longer deployed distant fleets.

Battles, campaigns and wars that did not occur are important both in counter-factual terms and in trying to assess relative capability. They, therefore, help to complicate any emphasis on weaponry which, by its very nature, concentrates on clashes that did occur. A consideration of conflicts that did not occur, and in which territory did not, therefore, change hands, also limits the temptation to treat military activity in terms of a zero-sum game in which European transoceanic activity was the central theme and territorial expansion was at the expense of non-Westerners.

The reality was far more complex. First, most transoceanic European military activity between 1550 and 1815 was directed not against non-Europeans, but against other Europeans – for example, the first "world war", the struggle between the Portuguese and the Dutch in the seventeenth century in Brazil, West Africa, India, Sri Lanka and the East Indies. Secondly, most non-European military activity was at the expense of other non-Europeans. Thirdly, so much was this the case that the group of expanding states was not restricted to European and European-American until the late nineteenth century, and even then Ethiopia expanded considerably after its victory over the Italians at Adowa in 1898.

Thus, in 1680–1795 China made significant territorial gains, especially in Mongolia and Xinkiang, as well as acquiring Formosa (Taiwan), driving the Russians from the Amur and sending expeditions to Burma and Nepal. To neglect these gains, and the successes for the Chinese military system that they represented, is to adopt a misleading perspective. By 1870 China was clearly less successful militarily than the European powers, but this is not necessarily a helpful perspective to employ when considering the situation which existed over a hundred years earlier. The same argument can be made in the case of the Ottomans. It can be argued that the roots of later problems can and should be traced back, but such an approach can be teleological and lead to a failure to understand a given period on its own terms.

By focusing attention on the issue of what should receive attention, the military historian emphasizes the role of choice in the selection of battles, campaigns, wars and topics for discussion. There is, however, no clear basis for choice. To take battles as an example: are the most important those with the most advanced weaponry, the greatest number of combatants or casualties, or the most significant consequences, and how is the last to be assessed? Does this vary between different spheres of military activity, not least between land and sea conflict? Plassey can be seen as more important than the third battle of Panipat in the long run – simply because the British, not the Afghans, became the rulers of India, but it is understandable that many Indian rulers were concerned about how best to resist invasions from the northwest.

A similar problem confronts the discussion of warfare within Europe. The French defeat of the Spaniards at Rocroi in 1643 receives far more attention than subsequent Spanish victories at Pavia (1655) and Valenciennes (1656), because the "Decline of Spain" and the "Rise of France" are central themes in seventeenth-century historiography, and Rocroi, misleadingly, appears to be both an appropriate military indication of a trend and a turning-point.

Thus, military history cannot evade the problems that, more generally, affect historical analysis and exposition, specifically those of perspective: what is the temporal distance by which things are being judged as important? If the goal is to view events at a distance of ten years, many events may seem important; but if the historian's viewing distance is to be measured in centuries, some events will indeed seem more important than others which at the time – meaning, say, within a fifty-year perspective – would have appeared just as important. However, the identification and explanation of "long-range issues" can privilege hindsight so much as to be teleological.

Methodological questions aside, it is possible to turn to the impact of technology and to query some of the claims made on its behalf. Ross Hassig looks at the Spanish success in overthrowing the Aztec empire, one of the essential first steps in making much of America "Latin", and shows that it is important to look at non-technological factors. The battle superiority of the Spaniards, which owed much to steel helmets and swords, promised those who allied with them a good chance of victory, but the availability and willingness of Mesoamericans to co-operate against the Aztecs reflected the nature of the Aztec empire, in particular the absence of a practice and theory of assimilation. Jos Gommans emphasizes the limited role of hand-held firearms and infantry in India prior to the eighteenth century.

The naval situation is also ripe for re-examination. Portuguese capability on the high seas in the early sixteenth century did not necessarily extend to inshore, estuarine and riverine waters where deep-draught sailing ships found it difficult to operate, and the Europeans only achieved technological superiority and capability with the development of shallow-draught steamships from the 1820s onwards.[9] In addition, a number of Southeast Asian states, such as Johor in Malaya and 'Aceh in Sumatra, developed naval forces which were able to challenge the Portuguese. Eurocentric accounts of the Portuguese Indian Ocean empire present it as being brought low by the Dutch and, indeed, in the seventeenth century the Dutch captured many of the Portuguese bases. Yet, in addition, the Portuguese had been put under great pressure – in the Persian

Gulf, on the Swahili coast of East Africa, in the Bay of Bengal and in the East Indies – by non-European states, such as Persia, Oman and various Indian and Indonesian principalities.[10]

The Portuguese military experience in the sixteenth century exemplified, more generally, the problems facing the Europeans overseas, and the variety of military tasks they confronted. In some areas, such as India, the Red Sea and Abyssinia, the Portuguese faced non-European states armed with gunpowder weapons. One such state, Morocco, was to destroy King Sebastian of Portugal and his army in 1578.

In other areas, such as Brazil, opposition came from peoples whose state organization was limited and who lacked such weapons. Elsewhere, for example in Angola, opposition came from more developed polities lacking gunpowder weaponry, at least initially, although, as John Thornton shows, that did not mean that they were militarily weak, while, as Armstrong Starkey indicates for North America, such weapons were frequently rapidly diffused. This was also the case in India. The Portuguese also faced the problem of hostility on the part of other European states, and Portugal rapidly succumbed to Spanish invasion in 1580.

Thus, the Portuguese had to develop a military capability to operate in very different military environments. This was to be a characteristic of the military systems of European powers that developed transoceanic capability, and also of Russia. However, it was not only true of such states. Powers such as Ming and Manchu China, Mughal India and Ottoman Turkey similarly fought a number of opponents in very different military environments. In the sixteenth century the Ottomans fought the Europeans on land in Europe, North Africa and Abyssinia, and at sea in the Mediterranean, Red Sea, Persian Gulf and Indian Ocean, attacked Persia and Egypt, developed Islamic states deploying large cavalry armies, and also a series of less powerful polities ranging from Bedouin Arabs to opponents in the Caucasus. Furthermore, as Virginia Aksan shows, these opponents were engaged using a military system that required a considerable measure of organization, especially in logistics.

Organizational factors, both structural and cultural, offer another approach to the question of possible contrasts between European and non-European military societies. Enhanced organizational capability was not simply a matter of financing, supplying or moving the military – of the military from outside–but was also interactive with the specific organizational nature and operational effectiveness of military units.

The Europeans moved most towards a large-scale "rationalization" of such units: they were to have uniform size, armaments, clothing, command strategies, etc. Such developments made it easier to implement drill techniques that maximized firepower. They were not dependent on a particular political mechanism, for allied and subsidized units could be expected to fight in an identical fashion with "national" units, a marked contrast to the situation in the Asiatic empires where there was a major difference between core and ancillary troops. There was an obvious contrast between the Allied forces in battles in the War of the Spanish Succession, such as Blenheim (1704), and the situation in major engagements in Asia. In the former case, Austrian, British and Dutch forces fought in a similar fashion and combined with little difficulty. The Europeans extended this model to India, training local units to fight as they did. This ensured that the Indian military labour market could be utilized to maximum effect.

Captain Robert Stuart, commander of a *sepoy* battalion in 1773, was convinced that only discipline, or rather his firepower-linked definition of it, would allow his unit to prevail:

> As the superiority of English sepoys over their enemies, as likewise their own safety consist entirely in their steadiness, and attentiveness, to the commands of their officers, it is ordered, that no black officer or sepoy pretend to act, or quit his post without positive orders to that purpose from an European officer . . . should any man fire without orders, he is to be put to death upon the spot . . . regularity and obedience to orders are our grand and only superiority.[11]

Nevertheless, even if there thus was an organizational superiority, its impact in terms of European control over much of the world was limited by a number of factors. European organizational developments were in part diffused, especially with the formation of "new type" units, as in eighteenth-century Turkey and India and nineteenth-century Egypt. Thus, in 1882 when the British attacked Alexandria, they fought Egyptians equipped and deployed in a very different fashion to the Egyptians who had been beaten by Napoleon at the Battle of the Pyramids (1798). This process of diffusion was not easy, however, as the last Khan of the Crimean Tatars in the 1770s and Selim III of Turkey in the 1800s discovered. This was true both of specific instances and more generally, because the adoption of European-style military organization and weaponry depended in part on a wider process of Europeanization that encompassed social practices, ideological assumptions and administrative conventions. Such a process was difficult to graft on to non-European societies, although Japan in the late nineteenth century was to be a spectacularly successful example. European-style use of firearms depended on types of drill that relied on patterns of constrained behaviour that in part reflected an ethic of self-constraint and a mechanistic aesthetic that were particularly developed in European culture.[12] Apart from the issue of diffusion, European units were not always able to defeat non-European forces, whether they fought in a fashion that the Europeans were accustomed to, or not. Spectacular defeats, such as that of the British by the Afghans in 1842, exemplified this.

Even if we allow that organizational advances cannot serve as a *deux ex machina*, it is, nevertheless, the case that such advances did play a major role in European successes and success. This was specifically the case with the organization and control of transoceanic deployment. This depended on technology, but the latter was not a sufficient cause. What was crucial was the allocation *and* utilisation of resources, so that European forces could be deployed and maintained successfully. Technical and administrative developments helped encourage a separation of European interests and commitments between an Atlantic world, with, increasingly, a struggle about transoceanic trade and colonies, and a Continental world focused on rivalry over European territories. By the eighteenth century, the major Continental states were able to deploy rapidly increasing armies over wide distances, particularly so in the case of Russia. In the Atlantic world, it was a case of expanding navies, larger fleets and army forces deployed overseas, and increasing European interest in colonies and zones of *future* expansion, visible in the crises over the Falkland Islands (1770) and Nootka Sound on Vancouver Island (1790).

In the sixteenth century the quantity of force thus deployed had been extraordinarily low in manpower terms. This reflected a number of factors, including the absence of extensive European migration to provide a local manpower basis, although by the late seventeenth century there was the basis for raising substantial local forces of "Europeans" in North and South America. European troops were most effective in co-operation with large numbers of local allies, as in Angola and Mexico in the sixteenth century and in India from the mid-eighteenth century. Otherwise, whatever the technological relationship, in the face of a major demographic imbalance the Europeans could achieve relatively little in terms of conquering large areas.

As far as South and East Asia and West Africa were concerned, however, such conquest was not the European objective. The profits of trade were sought, and this objective was seen in coercive terms, as a product of naval power and accompanying bases, but not as requiring large-scale territorial conquest. There were of course other purposes. One of the most interesting in geopolitical and military terms was the Portuguese attempt to challenge Ottoman power in the Red Sea and Persian Gulf, and associated support for Christian Abyssinia. Again, this did not entail a policy of extensive territorial conquest. Instead, the Portuguese relied on warships, bases and the dispatch of a small force to assist Abyssinia against the Islamic Sultanate of Adal. Success was, however, mixed. In particular, Aden was incorporated in the Ottoman (1538), not the Portuguese, system, thus ensuring that the Portuguese lacked both a base near the Red Sea and one able to challenge Ottoman naval moves towards the Persian Gulf, India or the Swahili coast of East Africa.

There is little reason to believe that the result would have been very different had the Portuguese made more of a military effort in the region. However much of an effort had been made, the Portuguese would have been greatly outnumbered by the Ottomans once they had conquered Egypt. Ottoman strength was only in part countered by superior Portuguese military capability, as seen in the naval Portuguese victory at Diu in 1538. Instead, the Portuguese presence in the region owed more to alternative Ottoman commitments and, specifically, to the Portuguese role in the Ottoman–Safavid rivalry. In the sixteenth century the Portuguese provided cannon to the Safavids of Persia (as did Ivan IV, "the Terrible", of Russia), and the latter accepted their position in Ormuz. As often, in face of the demographic weight of South Asia, it is necessary to think not in terms of the West versus the Rest, but of specific Western initiatives and their interaction with the complex rivalries and relationships of local states.

This interaction generally played a smaller role in the great outburst of imperial expansion that took place in the late nineteenth century. Then the theme was not solely conquest, but, insofar as states were left outside European political control, they often played the role of buffers (Afghanistan, Persia, Siam), were brought under a measure of economic control (China), and had their frontiers defined by European imperial power.

Transoceanic territorial conquest was much more important in the late nineteenth century than hitherto, and this set new requirements and, thus, parameters for the military. The subjugation of established polities in Africa and Asia was, largely, a new task in this period, as indeed was the conquest of large areas inhabited by acephalous peoples. The conquest of the Aztecs and the Incas was not a relevant experience for the nineteenth century. The qualification "largely" above reflects some important exceptions, such as Britain and Mysore in the 1790s, and Russia and Siberia.

The campaigns of the 1790s indicate some of the major themes of European transoceanic conflict in the nineteenth century, not least the primary importance of achieving the deployment of troops where they were initially required, and then moving them as needed in accordance with strategic plans. Logistics was transformed as part of an organizational–industrial–technological nexus that was inherent to the process of European change in this period. For the military, this was compounded by the sustained demographic expansion that began in the mid-eighteenth century, ensuring that there were more young men, and that soldiers and sailors could be raised in greater numbers without restricting the labour force, and that at a time when economic demands for labour were rising significantly.

The bulk of this enhanced military capability was maintained and used, not in the cause of transoceanic expansion, but against other European states. This process of "internal" rivalry was taken further in the USA, where the Civil War was the major military commitment of the century and the Mexican War was the second. There was no comparable projection of American power outside the American mainland until the 1890s.

This "internal" rivalry between European and also between European–American powers led to a process of competitive military improvement that provided a basis for the projection of force at the expense of non-Europeans, although subsequent conflict in 1914–45 was gravely to weaken the psychological capability (though not the technology) for such power projection. Thus, the nineteenth century exemplifies Gibbon's observation that Europe's power *vis-à-vis* non-European polities was enhanced by the competitive military emulation of a multipolar system within Europe.[13] The rifled weapons developed, manufactured and distributed to contest the European wars of nationalism in 1858–71 were to be employed outside Europe. So also were weapons developed later in the century. That does not mean, however, that firepower alone was responsible for European conquests, nor that the European enhancement was mainly directly military. For example, the development of steam-engine railway technology within Europe enabled the European powers to operate more effectively elsewhere.

To take the argument from the technological to the cultural dimension, it is clear that in the period of European expansion there were strong cultural imperatives that facilitated the major effort that was made. The character and context of these imperatives varied: for example, the extension of the *Reconquista*, which was important to Spain and Portugal in the sixteenth century, was different to the Social Darwinism of the nineteenth. The perception of other cultures, and thus of the acceptable parameters of the European response to them, also varied. The presentation of China as decadent and deserving of conquest, or at least control, widely advanced in the nineteenth century, was not widespread earlier. There had been Spanish suggestions of conquest in the sixteenth century, but they were implausible in terms of cultural suppositions as well as military strength.

Cultural suppositions operated in a number of ways, but the most significant were to encourage bellicosity, offensive war and territorial conquest. Such tendencies are not organic, and they need to be taken into account when discussing military history, especially the history of military relations between different cultures. The variety of European suppositions in this field is readily apparent. The emphasis on territorial conquest that played such a major role in the New World was far less apparent in the Indian Ocean. There trade played the leading role, but "trade" as a factor in military activity was not without its variations.

14

The political and military contexts and connotations of trade in Siberia were different from those near Hudson's Bay, another fur source, let alone the Indian Ocean.

Emphasis on different constructions of the pursuit of trade serves as a reminder of the problems of reification and subsequent analysis. This is true not only of the search for causation, but also of consideration of comparative strengths. The comparison, for example, of European infantry and non-European forces in the sixteenth and subsequent centuries is more dependent on the specific context than is generally appreciated. For example, in eighteenth-century India British infantry was more effective in operations on the Carnatic coast near their base at Madras and in the marshy Lower Ganges valley than in conflict against the Marathas and Mysore in regions that favoured their light cavalry. This led to Britain's defeat by Haidar Ali of Mysore in 1769.[14]

To outline methodological and empirical drawbacks with general theses of military development and power does not, however, address the general question of explaining the military rise of the West. It is clear that technological factors do play a major role, although technology has to be understood in the widest of senses, not least to include technological factors that helped to provide Europe with a flexible economy able to utilize its natural resources and to trade widely. It is also clear that technological factors were initially more important at sea than on land. They were crucial to the ability of Europeans to deploy their power.

On land, it was arguably fortifications that were most important. Geoffrey Parker closes the second edition of his justifiably influential *The Military Revolution. Military innovation and the rise of the West 1500–1800* (Cambridge, 1996) by arguing that:

> until the late eighteenth century, thanks to their ability to mobilize and maintain enormous armies, the major Islamic states – like the empires of East Asia – proved able to keep the West at bay . . . in 1683 . . . it was the Turks at the gates of Vienna and not the Europeans at the gates of Istanbul. This perception brings us back to the true significance of the "military revolution" of early modern Europe. The sixteenth century saw a strong phase of Islamic expansion . . . so many states and societies were overwhelmed that the resistance of the West to this Islamic tide stands out as unusual . . . Only military resilience and technological innovation – especially the capital ship, infantry firepower and the artillery fortress: the three vital components of the military revolution of the sixteenth century – allowed the West to make the most of its smaller resources in order to resist and, eventually, to expand to global dominance.[15]

This is an overly schematic view, not least because it fails to position the Ottomans within their multiple commitments, including warfare with Persia, which for many years was more important than conflict with Christian Europe. Furthermore, infantry firepower and fortresses did not save Ming China from the Manchu. However, Parker is instructive in that he directs attention to a defensive character of European military activity with regard to the outside world that it is easy to neglect if attention is devoted to naval warfare and to success against Aztecs and Incas. From this defensive perspective the role of fortifications, whether Vienna, Corfu, Malta or less famous positions, such as the Russian lines constructed to resist Tatar attacks, was certainly important. However, Parker's focus is too narrow, not least because it assumes that states will and have to expand until stopped – a questionable notion and one that underrates the constraints affecting land expansion in the sixteenth century.

A concentration on the Ottomans is, nevertheless, valuable because it serves as a reminder that gunpowder weaponry was not only possessed by the Europeans, indeed the term "gunpowder empires" was coined to describe Muslim states: those created by the Ottomans, Safavids, Mughals, and Sa'dids of Morocco.[16] Recent work has corrected the earlier view that the Ottomans concentrated on large cannon, rather than larger numbers of more manoeuvrable, smaller cannon, and has, instead, emphasized that their ordnance was dominated by small and medium-sized cannon.[17] The ability of the Ottomans to manufacture an adequate supply of gunpowder has also been emphasized.[18] The same range of use was also true of sophisticated fortifications. The Ottomans built fortresses – for example, a large one in Tabriz when they seized it from the Safavids in 1585. Major Skelly of the British army, campaigning against Tipu Sultan of Mysore in 1791, recorded of the fortress of Nundadroog:

two complete ramparts . . . each flanked with ample circular bastions, well furnished with artillery, and a projecting work, which forms a reentering angle at the north extremity, flanks all the approaches to the front wall . . . the rampart was of such excellent materials[19]

that it took a while for the British cannon to breach it. Another British commentator, however, was less complimentary about Tipu's artillery:

old fashioned things taken from the enemy's works, and mounted on their crazy carriages, they are European made it is true, but in the style, and hardly to be trusted. There is no certainty of hitting with these pieces, cast with the vacant cylinder, and not bored solid. We had a 24 pounder of this description in the battery against Bangalore, and no skill could make it throw twice the same way.[20]

Similarly, the Safavids had relatively few cannon and displayed limited skill in their use. More generally, the Safavids failed to match Ottoman use of muskets and cannon. The widespread availability of gunpowder weaponry underlines the need to contextualize "technology" in order to understand why "advances" were made in particular societies and what factors affected patterns and practices of military diffusion.[21] The importance of differences in military ethos in the various "zones of military entrepreneurship" in India[22] is of wider applicability.

Military developments and state-building

Peter Wilson's essay directs attention to the role of states, specifically to their ability to consolidate and legitimate monopolies of violence and taxation. These spheres were clearly related. Military forces and war were expensive, whether or not they involved military–technological change, such as the European developments of the *trace italienne* system of fortification and of fleets of ocean-going warships, or the acquisition of European weaponry by non-Europeans. These costs could be borne in a variety of ways. Standing (permanent) forces involved continuous expenditure and this could not be provided by the fruits of offensive warfare – land and plunder – because such forces were not always engaged in war. On the other hand, societies and states that relied, in whole or part, on forces that only served during campaigns did not have to adopt the financial and governmental techniques necessary to provide for standing forces. This divide was more like a continuum; nevertheless, there were significant sociological and operational consequences. These were revealed where different military systems clashed, as in North America, which is discussed by Armstrong Starkey.

A common military theme and sociology of power underlay many of the wars of the period – for example, those between China and the Mongols in the sixteenth century and the 1690s: the struggle between the forces of relatively organized, settled agrarian societies and nomadic or semi-nomadic peoples. The agriculture of the former supported larger populations and, thus, the resources for substantial armed forces and also, thanks to taxation, for developed governmental structures. The North American Thirteen Colonies that rebelled against Britain in 1775 created a standing force, the Continental Army, funded by taxation. This army, and its needs, served as a centralizing element in the political debates and governmental problems of the fissiparous state.

Nomadic and semi-nomadic peoples generally relied on pastoral agriculture, were less populous and their governmental structures less developed. They did not therefore tend to develop comparable military specialization, especially in fortification and siegecraft. While the agricultural surplus and taxation base of settled agrarian societies permitted the development of logistical mechanisms to

17

support permanent specialized military units, nomadic peoples generally lacked such units and had a far less organized logistical system: in war they often relied on raiding their opponents.

This organizational divide, which owed much to factors of terrain and climate, was linked to one in methods of warfare. Nomadic and semi-nomadic people exploited mobility and generally relied on cavalry, whereas their opponents placed more stress on numbers, infantry, and fortifications.

These cavalry forces could be devastating. The early sixteenth century is generally seen in terms of the triumph of gunpowder forces, most obviously with the Spanish and Portuguese victories, but also with a series of spectacular Ottoman victories over Persia, Egypt and Hungary in 1514–26. Yet, it is also, necessary to give due weight to the triumphs of cavalry forces. Cavalry provided mobility, and that was crucial for strategic, logistical and tactical reasons. It enabled forces to overcome the constraints of distance, to create equations of numbers, supplies and rate of movement that were very different to those of infantry, and also to form the battlefield in a very different fashion. Cavalry was not incompatible with firepower. The horse archers of Central Asian origin had shown this effectively in the twelfth and thirteenth centuries in combating the Crusades and the Mongols. Mounted archers remained important in the sixteenth century, as in the Mughal victory over a larger insurrectionary force at the Second Battle of Panipat in 1556.[23] Mounted archers were also effective in co-operation with foot musketeers and artillery, as at the Ottoman victories of Chaldiran (1514) and Mohacs (1526), that of the Mughals at First Panipat (1526), Kanua (1527) and Haldighati (1576), and of the Safavids at Jam (1528). As Peter Lorge shows, Ming Chinese advances against both Mongols and Manchus were defeated by the mobile mounted archers of their opponents. Jos Gommans also demonstrates the continued role of horse archers.

It is all too easy to concentrate on infantry gunpowder weaponry and to ignore the continued role of cavalry, whether armed with bows or with muskets. Such forces could make the transition to gunpowder weaponry, although that was not necessary to their power in the sixteenth and seventeenth centuries. At Alcazarquivir (1578), Abd al-Malik of Morocco defeated the Portuguese in part by making effective use of arquebusiers trained to fire from horseback.[24] The Baluchis used firearms from the early eighteenth century. Mounted musketeers played a major role in the Afghan victory at Third Panipat (1761), as did their heavy cavalry.[25] Cavalry also continued to be important in large areas of Africa, especially the savanna belt to the south of the Sahara.[26]

It is, therefore, misleading to see cavalry as anachronistic and likely to fail. Such a reading reflects twentieth-century assumptions about cavalry and also, in part, a Eurocentric extension of the situation, for, indeed, although it could still be decisive in battle, as in the Anglo-Austrian victory over the French at

Blenheim (1704), cavalry became proportionately less numerous in European armies in the seventeenth and eighteenth centuries. In contrast, north Indian rulers had to remain able to repel cavalry forces invading from Persia or Afghanistan, while on their northern and eastern borders the Safavids of Persia faced opponents in the sixteenth and seventeenth centuries whose cavalry made little use of firearms, ensuring that there was little pressure for any development in weaponry or tactics. This was even more the case because of a protracted period of peace with the Ottomans after the Peace of Zuhab of 1639.[27]

If cavalry is not seen as necessarily anachronistic, this has consequences for assumptions about whether particular governmental–social systems were better suited to military success. These issues and, more generally, the military dimensions of state-building and the governmental and social contexts of military change[28] again return us to the question of military purpose. Clearly, some systems were not suited to the maintenance of substantial standing forces. Such systems succumbed in the eighteenth and, still more, nineteenth century, most obviously with the Russian conquest of peoples such as Crimean Tatars, Kazakhs and Uzbeks. Yet, to read back from that failure to the early modern period is problematic. It is not simply that it entails a nineteenth-century perception of infantry and artillery firepower, and of the attendant relationship between disciplined, well-drilled and well-armed permanent firepower forces and those that were not so armed. There is also the related perception of the governmental dimension – namely, the increased effectiveness of states able to mobilize and direct resources, and to support permanent forces. In the European context, this is seen most clearly with the arguments employed to explain the partitioning of Poland in 1772–95: Poland lacked the strong government of the partitioning powers, Austria, Prussia and Russia. Thus those states that were able to organize, control and direct their populations appear more potent.

Again, this approach faces problems. Methodologically, it fails to address adequately the controverted and contingent nature of governmental strength. There is also the problem of extrapolation: the degree of organization required to create and support a large, permanent, long-range navy, or large, permanent armies, was not required to maintain military forces fit for purpose across most of the world. In addition, there is a problematic empirical dimension. In the early modern period administrative sophistication did not suffice, as the Chinese discovered with their defeats at Mongol and Manchu hands.

Fit for purpose was a matter not only of military success but also of the internal dynamics of sociopolitical systems. If war was a forcing house of change, it was also designed to prevent it, both in terms of changes in territorial power and the prevailing political, social and ideological practices and norms. Armies suppressed rebellions and maintained or strengthened social and spatial patterns of control.[29] Thus, in Europe, states came to monopolize organized, large-scale violence, but with the co-operation of their social elites who monopolized command positions. The social elite was willing to co-operate with military change, including the organization of armies around a state-directed structure, and the downgrading of cavalry, processes that elites elsewhere were more reluctant to accept.[30] Such a monopolization of violence could not be sustained in the Ottoman or Mughal empires. The former was as much weakened by internal warfare as by foreign attack, and control over Egypt proved an intractable problem.[31] However, comparison with the situation in individual European states has to make allowance for the very great difference in scales. Christian Europe in, for example, 1580–1604, 1618–59, 1688–1714, 1739–63 and 1792–1815 was more violent and wracked by as much, if not more, warfare, than was the case with the Ottoman and Mughal empires, but the multipolar nature of Europe ensured that this warfare was largely controlled by reasonably well-established states, rather than directed to their overthrow. The comparable polities within the Ottoman and Mughal empires were more inchoate.

Political–social revolutions in Europe, most obviously the English republic (1649–60) and the French Revolution (1789–95), were, in part, characterized by substantial changes in the composition and ethos of the officer corps, and this helped to make them threatening forces. In general, however, armies did not act as revolutionary forces; instead, it was the need to provide for them and to retain their capacity to resist territorial, political and social change that caused political pressures and governmental change. This was not only true of Europe. Indeed, insofar as land warfare is concerned, it would be misleading to suggest that the relationship between military demands and governmental change was restricted to Europe, although much of the literature has been about that continent.[32] Other important examples include the Songhay Empire on the middle Niger under Askia Muhammad (1493–1528), Persia under Abbas I (1587–1629) and the kingdom of Dahomey in the eighteenth century.[33]

However, only European powers had to decide how best to organize, control and support transoceanic land and sea operations, and these became more important in the mid-eighteenth century as Britain and France developed *sepoy* forces in India, that were larger, more effective and more dynamic than those of Portugal, and also sent appreciable numbers of regulars to North America. This led to a range of multiple military capability that no non-European power possessed, a range that was to be of great importance in helping to channel the products of nineteenth-century technological change and economic and demographic growth to European military and political advantage elsewhere in the world.

The unique European experience of creating a global network of empires and trade was based on an equally unique type of interaction between economy, technology and state formation. China, Korea and Japan were relatively centralized states; they knew how to build large ships and manufacture guns and their economies and levels of culture were not obviously below early-modern European standards; they wished to import little from Europe. However, there was hardly any interaction between these three factors which might create development and change. Economic gain was a very important factor behind European maritime power projection: the possibility of profit acted as a powerful stimulus to technological development and improved organization for war, trade and colonization. These were to frame the nineteenth-century world.

Notes

1. I. Steele, *Warpaths. Invasions of North America* (Oxford, 1994).
2. D. J. Weber, *The Spanish frontier in North America* (New Haven, 1992).
3. D. Howse (ed.), *Background to discovery. Pacific exploration from Dampier to Cook* (Berkeley, 1990).
4. J. B. Harley, Silences and secrecy: the hidden agenda of cartography in early modern Europe, *Imago Mundi*, 40, 1988, pp. 58–9.
5. E. Gibbon, *The history of the decline and fall of the Roman empire*, J. B. Bury (ed.) (7 vols, London, 1897–1901), IV, p. 167.
6. J. R. Hale, Gunpowder and the Renaissance: An essay in the history of ideas, in his *Renaissance War Studies* (London, 1983), pp. 389–90.
7. Fulton to Lord Grenville, 2 Sept. 1806, London, British Library, Additional Manuscripts (hereafter BL. Add.), 71593 fol. 134.
8. A useful exception is P. Marshall, Western arms in maritime Asia in the early phases of expansion, *Modern Asian Studies*, 14, 1980, pp. 13–28. See also R. J. Barendse, The Portuguese army in the Arabian seas in the seventeenth century, paper given at conference on military history of South Asia, Wolfson College, Cambridge, 15 July 1997.
9. A. Deshpande, Limitations of military technology. Naval warfare on the west coast [of India], 1650–1800, *Economic and Political Weekly*, 25 April 1992, p. 902.
10. C. R. Boxer and C. de Azevedo, *Fort Jesus and the Portuguese in Mombasa 1593–1729* (London, 1960); E. Winius, Portugal's "Shadowy empire in the Bay of Bengal", *Camões Center Quarterly*, 3, nos. 1 and 2, 1991, pp. 40–1.
11. D. Kolff, *Naukar, Rajput and Sepoy: the ethnohistory of the military labour market in Hindustan, 1450–1850* (Cambridge, 1990); S. Alavi, *The Sepoys and the Company. Tradition and transition in Northern India 1770–1830* (Delhi, 1995); Stuart, orders, BL. Add. 29198 fol. 120, 123.
12. H. Kleinschmidt, Using the gun. Manual drill and the proliferation of portable firearms, paper given at Anglo-American Conference of Historians, London, 3 July 1997.
13. Gibbon, *Decline and fall*, I, 109, IV, p. 166.
14. G. J. Bryant, The cavalry problem in the early British Indian Army, 1750–1785, *War in History*, 2, 1995, pp. 13–14. See also his The Military imperative in early British expansion in India, 1750–1785, *Indo-British Review*, 21, 1996, pp. 18–35.
15. Parker, *Military Revolution*, pp. 174–5. See also Geoffrey Parker's *Military Revolution*: Three reviews of the second edition . . . with a response, *Journal of Military History*, 61, 1997, pp. 347–54.

16. M. G. S. Hodgson, *The venture of Islam. III. The gunpowder empires and modern times* (Chicago, 1974).

17. G. Ágoston, Ottoman artillery and European military technology in the fifteenth and seventeenth centuries, *Acta Orientalia Academiae Scientiarum Hungaricae*, 47, 1994, pp. 32–47.

18. Ágoston, Gunpowder for the Sultan's army, *Turcica*, 25, 1993, pp. 75–96.

19. Skelly, narrative, BL. Add. 9872 fol. 114–15.

20. Anon. narrative, BL. Add. 36747 C fol. 42.

21. D. Ayalon, *Gunpowder and firearms in the Mamluk kingdom: a challenge to a mediaeval society* (London, 1956); R. Murphey, The Ottoman attitude towards the adoption of western technology: The role of the Efrencî technicians in civil and military applications, in J. Bacqué (ed.), *Contributions à l'histoire économique et sociale de l'Empire ottoman* (Paris, 1983), pp. 287–98; Ágoston, Ottoman artillery.

22. S. Gordon, *Marathas, marauders, and state formation in eighteenth-century India* (Delhi, 1994), pp. 182–208.

23. D. E. Streusand, *The formation of the Mughal empire* (Delhi, 1989). +

24. E. W. Bovil, *The Battle of Alcazar* (London, 1952); W. Cook, *The Hundred Years War for Morocco. Gunpowder and the military revolution in the early modern Muslim world* (Boulder, 1994).

25. T. S. Shejwalkar, *Panipat: 1761* (Poona, 1946); H. R. Gupta (ed.), *Marathas and Panipat* (Chandigarh, 1961). See, more generally, J. Gommans, *The rise of the Indo-Afghan empire c. 1710–1780* (Leiden, 1995).

26. H. J. Fisher, The central Sahara and Sudan, in R. Gray (ed.), *The Cambridge History of Africa IV* (Cambridge, 1975), p. 73; R. Law, *The Oyo Empire c. 1600–c. 1836: A West African imperialism in the era of Atlantic slave trade* (Oxford, 1977).

27. R. Matthee, Unwalled cities and restless nomads: firearms and artillery in Safavid Iran in C. Melville (ed.), *Safavid Persia. The History and Politics of an Islamic Society* (London, 1996), pp. 406–7, 410.

28. S. Morillo, Guns and government: A comparative study of Europe and Japan, *Journal of World History*, 6, 1995, p. 103.

29. R. Hellie, *Enserfment and military change in Muscovy* (Chicago, 1971).

30. J. E. Woods, *The Aqquyunlu, clan, confederation, empire. A study in 15th/9th century Turko-Iranian politics* (Minneapolis, 1976), p. 122.

31. H. Inalcik, The socio-political effects of the diffusion of firearms in the Middle East, in V. J. Parry and M. E. Yapp (eds), *War, technology and society in the Middle East* (London, 1975), pp. 195–217; R. C. Hess, Firearms, bandits and guncontrol, *Archivum Ottomanicum*, 6, 1980, pp. 339–80.

32. Important recent work includes S. A. Nilsson, Imperial Sweden. Nation-building, war and social change, in Nilsson (ed.), *The Age of New Sweden* (Stockholm, 1988), pp. 8–39; T. Ertman, *Birth of the Leviathan. Building states and regimes in medieval and early modern Europe* (Cambridge, 1997).

33. For the relationship between force and state development see M. Haneda, The evolution of the Safavid royal guard, *Iranian Studies*, 21, 1989, pp. 57–86; I. A. Akingogbin, *Dahomey and its neighbors, 1700–1828* (London, 1966); S. Subrahmaniyam, Aspects of state formation in South India and Southeast Asia, 1500–1650, *The Indian Economic and Social History Review* 23, 1986; V. J. Cornell, Socioeconomic dimensions of reconquista and jihad in Morocco: Portuguese Dukkala and the Sa'did Sus, 1450–1557, *International Journal of Middle East Studies*, 22, 1990; Morillo, Guns and government. A comparative study of Europe and Japan, *Journal of World History*, 6, 1995, pp. 75–105.

Further reading

It is difficult to choose from among the wealth of fine studies on the period. For reasons of space this list is very selective and concentrates on recent works in English and books, as these are more accessible. Details of other relevant material can be found in the bibliographies of the works cited.

General

M. S. Anderson, *War and society in Europe of the old regime 1618–1789* (London, 1988).

J. M. Black, *War and the world 1450–2000* (New Haven, 1998).

C. M. Cipolla, *Guns and sails in the early phase of European expansion 1400–1700* (London, 1965).

M. van Creveld, *Supplying war. Logistics from Wallenstein to Patton* (Cambridge, 1977).

M. van Creveld, *Technology and war from 2000 B.C. to the present* (New York, 1989).

B. P. Hughes, *Firepower. Weapons' effectiveness on the battlefield 1630–1850* (London, 1974).

A. Jones, *The Art of war in the Western world* (Oxford, 1987).

J. Keegan, *A History of warfare* (London, 1993).

J. A. Lynn (ed.), *Tools of war. Instruments, ideas and institutions of warfare, 1445–1871* (Urbana, 1990).

J. A. Lynn (ed.), *Feeding Mars. Logistics in Western warfare from the middle ages to the present* (Boulder, 1993).

W. H. McNeill, *The Pursuit of power. Technology, armed force and society since A.D. 1000* (Oxford, 1982).

G. Parker, *The military revolution. Military innovation and the rise of the West* 2nd edn (Cambridge, 1996).

Important works not covered in other lists include

S. Arasaratnam, *Dutch power in Ceylon, 1658–87* (Amsterdam, 1958).

W. F. Cook, *The Hundred Years' War for Morocco. Gunpowder and the military revolution in the early modern Muslim world* (Boulder, 1994).

A. S. Donnelly, *The Russian conquest of Bashkiria, 1552–1740* (New Haven, 1968).

R. D. Edmunds and J. L. Peyser, *The Fox wars. The Mesquakie challenge to New France* (Norman, 1993).

J. Forsyth, *A History of the peoples of Siberia* (Cambridge, 1992).

A. C. Hess, *The forgotten frontier. A history of the sixteenth century Ibero-African frontier* (Chicago, 1978).

W. J. Koenig, *The Burmese polity, 1752–1819* (Ann Arbor, 1990).

J. R. McNeill, *Atlantic empires of France and Spain. Louisbourg and Havanna, 1700–1763* (Chapel Hill, 1986).

P. W. Powell, *Soldiers, Indians and silver. The northward advance of New Spain 1550–1600* (Berkeley, 1969).

M. C. Ricklef, *War, culture and economy in Java, 1677–1726* (The Hague, 1990).

D. J. Weber, *The Spanish frontier in North America* (New Haven, 1992).

Chapter Two

Warfare at sea 1450–1815

Jan Glete

The sea is not the natural element of man. It is not the property of individuals or states. The sea connects and separates land. Warfare at sea is not only a special branch of war but also a special form of human activity at sea. Its setting is determined by political and economic conditions, technology, geography and climate, which all influence man's ability to live, work and fight on the sea. In this chapter a brief outline will be made of the changing conditions for sea warfare from the late Middle Ages to the advent of industrial society.

Maritime trade, state formation and warfare at sea

Warfare at sea is essentially a contest about the sea lines of communication. They are used for commercial trade, power projection and as a source of wealth extracted by violence or through protection from violence. Consequently, wars at sea are fought in the interest of those who use the sea for trade, power projection and resource extraction. Wars are also fought by those who feel threatened if competing groups are given free access to the sea for such activities. During the early modern period (1500–1800), the sea lines of communication increased in importance. Growing seaborne trade and European expansion around the world created a network of contacts and an international economy where the flow of merchandise became essential for the dynamic development of production and consumption. The sea was also a potential highway for military power projection, but for the defender it was an area for naval operations aiming at delaying and preventing such actions.

From a modern perspective, maritime trade is the occupation of mercantile groups, power projection, protection and legitimate resource extraction (taxes and custom duties) are state monopolies, while illegal plunder at sea is labelled "piracy". This neat division of activities is the result of centuries of changing institutions and the integration of various interests behind the modern state. It also presumes the existence of an organized navy as an instrument of state policy. In medieval and renaissance Europe much warfare at sea was waged by mercantile groups centred in autonomous trading cities. They coerced competing groups by embargoes and attacks on trade and even by power projection (invasions or military support to allied interests in other countries). Merchants acted as peaceful traders if that was profitable or as users of violence against competitors, if that suited their interest. Protection of trade at sea was normally not organized by territorial rulers, but by the merchants themselves. Coastal defence relied on local militias and fortifications rather than on navies. In areas where the sea connected territories, non-mercantile rulers might be interested in using it for invasions and transfer of armed forces from one area to another, but the ships were often provided by the merchants. The limit between war and peace at sea was diffuse, as was the concept of sovereignty. Activities labelled "piracy" by the victims were often a form of unofficial or limited warfare. The means of coercion at sea were predominantly private or locally owned, and used for offensive and defensive actions by those who could afford to do so. Up to the late fifteenth century few states possessed any means of coercion which might be called a permanent navy.

Gradually the institutional and organizational framework around warfare at sea changed towards growing specialization and a concentration of the use of violence to centralized states. The aggregation of interests behind centrally-controlled armed efforts grew considerably during the early modern period. As a part of the general state-formation process in early modern Europe, states developed navies as increasingly bureaucraticized organizations, financed by taxes and custom duties and subordinated to the general policy of territorial states. Independent trading communities nearly always surrendered their rights to use violence at sea to territorial states, or chose a low profile as neutral carriers of trade without any naval ambitions. When states became efficient protectors and controllers of violence, the diffuse use of violence as a mean of competition diminished, as did piracy in Europe and in the growing European empires overseas. Merchantmen might sail more or less unarmed and the crews might be reduced to the minimum necessary for ship-handling, a development which was very noticeable in the eighteenth century. The reduced cost of protection at sea has been used by economic historians (especially Frederick C. Lane and Douglass C. North) as a striking example of the degree to which states might promote economic development by reducing transaction costs, and provide institutional frameworks which decreased the risk for investments in entrepreneurial activities.

The growth of state power also made navies into instruments of policies which in themselves had little to do with the sea lines of communication or the private users of the sea. Wars were fought on land and at sea for important territories, for hegemony on the European continent, and for power within states, as rulers often tried to improve their prestige by victories in wars. Whatever the ultimate goal of the war, trade was affected by the struggle at sea. The influence of war and politically-determined blockades and regulations upon trade in the sixteenth and seventeenth century has been a matter of dispute: historians like Fernand Braudel have argued that they had little effect, while others, in recent years especially Jonathan Israel, have argued the opposite. For the eighteenth century it is less difficult to see that the great maritime wars affected trade and European empires. The power that dominated the sea might seriously interrupt enemy trade and conquer colonies.

The development of permanent navies, centralized state power and gunpowder and warship technology were radical changes which occurred in the same period. They were also contemporary with similar changes in warfare on land. It is natural to assume a causal interconnection, but its existence and direction are far from obvious. Was it the rise of centralized states, which created permanent armed forces and the systematic development of technology, or was it the opposite causal relationship that determined the development?

A few partial answers are possible. First, the general development of centralized states and permanent armed forces took much longer than the spread of new weapons and their efficient use in war. It may indicate that the latter development was partly independent of the other two, and it also reflects the extent to which guns and gun-carrying ships were developed and used by both private groups and governments. Secondly, the European development of gun-carrying warships and permanent armed forces was unique in its time. In connection with the expansion of well-armed European trade and colonization they provided the Europeans with a temporary hegemony over large parts of the world. The use and development of military and naval technology to gain profit and power is the causal connection best supported by empirical evidence. It might be used both by private entrepreneurs active in trade, violence and colonization, and by entrepreneurs in state-building. The latter are usually known to history as the early modern princes and statesmen who created the national states.

The fact that both commercial interests and political power were involved in warfare at sea has frequently made the ultimate aims of the wars a question of historical debate. Were they fought in the interests of political rulers, national security or the profits of merchants? Various interpretations along these lines have been given to, for example, the Dutch–Hispanic conflict in the seventeenth century (especially the maritime war period 1621–48) and the three Anglo-Dutch wars 1652–74. The Swedish expansion in the Baltic (1561–1660) has also been explained either as a struggle for national security or for the ports and river estuaries where custom duties might be found. The creation of a large French navy in the 1660s has been interpreted as a part both of Colbert's efforts to promote French trade and of Louis XIV's to dominate Europe. The great naval and colonial wars between Great Britain, France and Spain in the eighteenth century have been less debated, as there seems to be rather more consensus that they were wars about rapidly expanding transoceanic trade and colonial empires which contemporary decision-makers were aware would have important effects on the balance of power in Europe.

The debates reflect the degree to which early modern wars at sea were increasingly fought by agents and national organizations, and not by those who were immediately interested in the results of violence. It is important to focus more interest on the fact that political and mercantile war aims were usually not in conflict, and that this may have been important in persuading the various interests involved to unite behind the establishment of permanent navies. Merchants, rulers and various interest groups found that this type of organization was important for them and, consequently, they were willing to pay for it even in times of peace. Compared to earlier periods in European history this integration behind a permanent state organization for war at sea was an important change.

A Eurocentric form of warfare

Throughout the period Europe was the dominating centre of advanced naval warfare. The Amerindians and the Africans (outside the Arabian sphere of influence) did not develop indigenous shipping or navies. In the Indian Ocean a network of usually peaceful trade existed before the European entry into the area around 1500, and early types of guns were already in use. European technology was rapidly adopted by local shipbuilders and various rulers built minor naval forces of the European type, but no serious threat against European dominion at sea ever arose from an indigenous power. The Europeans were remarkably free to create their own networks of trade and even to control much of the indigenous shipping.

In the Chinese sphere of culture state navies were employed for coastal protection and suppression of piracy throughout the 1450–1815 period. For most of the time the states in this area were able to control the use of violence at sea and restrict European trade at will. However, the Chinese, Japanese and Korean rulers were uninterested in developing naval forces for foreign deployment in spite of having the necessary technology and centralized state power.

The famous Chinese expeditions into the Indian Ocean in the first half of the fifteenth century were never repeated and the fairly advanced types of gun-armed warships used by the Koreans against the Japanese in archipelago warfare in the 1590s were not developed further. Japan, which in the sixteenth century had been active at sea, launching piratical attacks into Chinese waters and invading Korea in the 1590s, became a closed society from the early seventeenth century onwards.

In spite of the fact that European ability to project seaborne power all around the world was the most spectacular aspect of warfare at sea in this period, most of the actual warfare did take place in waters close to Europe. Europe is a large peninsula on the great Asian continent with several important peninsulas (Scandinavia, the Iberian peninsula, Italy, Balkans) and islands: the British Isles and the large islands and archipelagos in the Mediterranean and the Baltic. A large part of the European population lives within short distances from the sea. Large-scale wars in Europe were often a combination of contests on land and at sea where sea routes of supply and amphibious operations were important or decisive. The seas adjacent to the European continent were essential for long- and short-distance trade, and the growing network of worldwide trade had its centres in the great European trading ports.

Consequently, warfare at sea had a bipolar character. Attacks on and protection of trade were routine operations usually carried out by small groups of ships, whereas power projection in order to occupy enemy territory from the sea were major operations requiring careful preparation. Large-scale invasions by major armies supported by concentrated navies on an enemy mainland in Europe (such as Normandy in 1944) were rare, but the fact that such operations were possible often determined the grand strategy of the contending navies and armies. The classical case was the threat of a large-scale Spanish (1588) or French invasion of England across the Channel. This remained a threat only, but in the Baltic there were repeated seaborne invasions by major field armies against the Stockholm area (1471, 1497, 1517, 1518), against Copenhagen (1523, 1658, 1700, 1807) and southern Sweden (1676, 1709). The Swedish expansion in the Baltic (1561–1660) saw several large-scale, seaborne invasions: Riga and Livonia (1621), Prussia (1626) and Pomerania (1630).

Normally seaborne power projection took other forms. One form was the eccentric operation against a peripheral enemy area such as a transoceanic colony or a European island or peninsula. The rich colonies in the West Indies were tempting targets for such attacks, and in Europe islands such as Sicily and Ireland were frequently regarded as suitable targets for seaborne operations. The Mediterranean galley fleet operations often aimed at the capture of a city or an island: the Spanish attacks against Tunis in 1535 and Algiers in 1541, the Ottoman landings on Rhodes 1522, Malta 1565, Cyprus 1571, Tunis 1574 and

Crete 1645. Napoleon's invasion of Egypt in 1798 is an example of an eccentric form of power projection where the fleet was rapidly destroyed, while the British intervention in Portugal and Spain from 1808 was based on undisputed command of the sea. Another form was the temporary attack against a vital enemy port or coastal area in order to destroy or capture as much as possible before enemy forces had been concentrated to rescue the attacked area. British (or Anglo-Dutch) attacks of this type against Spanish and French ports were common in most wars throughout this period.

A third form of power projection was flank support and supply over the sea of army units operating near a coast or in a territory across the sea. Such operations often had the character of help to an allied power. Classical examples are English, Dutch and French support of their own or allied forces operating in Spain or Italy during various wars from the Italian wars (1494–1559) to the Napoleonic wars. Failures in seaborne logistic support might have decisive importance. The most obvious example is, perhaps, the British failure to break the French naval blockade of the Chesapeake in 1781 which resulted in the British army's capitulation at Yorktown and the independence of the American colonies. The Dutch fleet's breaking of the Swedish naval blockade of Copenhagen in 1658 might have saved both the city and the independence of Denmark–Norway. In the Baltic, sailing fleets and oared flotillas often supported armies operating along a coast.

The difference between trade warfare and power projection was often diminished by the overriding aim of reducing or neutralizing enemy armed force at sea. If successful, this might facilitate both attack and defence in the war on trade and naval support of military operations. The enemy force might be reduced through decisive battles, but that could only be achieved against enemies which exposed their ships at sea. Normally an inferior fleet only took that risk if it had important missions to fulfil or if it was under pressure from political decision-makers without information on the real situation at sea. Some of the most spectacular decisive naval battles in the European history were the results of fleets that had been dispatched against the better judgements of their commanders: the Spanish Armada in 1588, the Anglo-Dutch fleet defeated by the French at Beachy Head in 1690, the French fleet defeated by the Anglo-Dutch at Barfleur and la Hogue in 1692 and the French–Spanish fleet defeated by the British at Trafalgar in 1805. An enemy might be neutralized by blockade of his naval bases, but it was generally difficult to make such blockades effective. The blockading fleet must have a considerable superiority and it must be kept on constant guard in adverse weather conditions. In spite of that, darkness, fogs and winds might favour the blockaded fleet and give it opportunities to escape. Seventeenth-century Dutch and British attempts to bottle up Spanish or French forces in the port of Dunkirk are a well-known example. Groups of fast cruisers were often able to slip out of this harbour, and in 1713 the maritime powers found it necessary to enforce the permanent demilitarization of Dunkirk as part of the peace treaty with France.

If close blockades were difficult, strategic blockades of enemy trade through narrow straits were often important. The fact that stores essential for early modern warfare at sea – timber, masts, hemp, tar, high-quality iron – were concentrated on the Baltic gave powers in this area and those in control of the Channel opportunities to enforce strategic blockades of their enemies. This was mainly used by the English and the Dutch, first from the 1580s to 1648 against Spain, and later (during wars from 1689 to 1815) against France and Spain. France, with considerable domestic resources in timber and iron, was less vulnerable than Spain to such blockades, but they imposed a considerable handicap on sea powers south of the Channel.

Constraints on early modern naval warfare: climate, human endurance and technology

Apart from economic incentives and the growth of state power, warfare at sea, its aims, strategies and tactics, were determined by climate, human endurance and technology. Of these factors, climate and human endurance were fairly stable constraints, while the development of technology reflected human efforts to reduce their effects. This was achieved from the fifteenth to the early nineteenth century, but the changes were evolutionary and gradual compared to the revolutionary changes in technology, medical science and food preservation that took place during the nineteenth century. Economics and state-formation were the general framework of human activity that formed warfare at sea, but the development of this framework must not be seen as disconnected from the development of technology. The unique European experience in these centuries – the creation of a global network of empires and trade almost entirely connected by the sea – was based on an equally unique type of interaction between the three forces: economy, technology and state-formation.

The climate was largely a constant factor, although the "Little Ice Age" from the last decades of the sixteenth century to the early eighteenth century made wind conditions in western Europe somewhat different and gales more frequent compared to earlier and later periods. Climatic conditions had a determining influence on operational seasons and strategy. This has often been forgotten in naval history, especially as much of it was written around 1900 when the

31

advanced sailing warships of the nineteenth century were fresh in memory. In the sixteenth and seventeenth centuries the safe operational season for large warships was limited to the summer months. Attempts to send major fleets to sea in late autumns frequently ended in disasters caused by gales in combination with cold which dramatically increased the risk of diseases. During the eighteenth century improvements in ship design and more efficient rigs gradually made battle-fleet operations during autumn, and even winter, a practical possibility.

The adverse weather conditions on the North Atlantic acted as a shield against major European power projections into this area far into the eighteenth century. At the same time, the direction of the winds made the passage from Europe to the West Indies easy, and this, in combination with the attraction of treasure and rich colonial trade, is reflected in a large number of major operations directed to this area. The Channel, the North Sea and the Bay of Biscay were dangerous for most of the year. In spite of the great strategic importance of the sea lines of communication along the Atlantic seaboard, major naval operations in this area were often restricted or prevented by bad weather. Continuous blockade of enemy bases, often supposed to be a traditional British naval activity in this area, was in reality only possible from the latter half of the eighteenth century, and even then it was an activity that strained the blockading force to the utmost. In the Baltic the operational season was surprisingly extended even in the sixteenth and seventeenth centuries. It is not clear if this was due to less severe weather conditions or the fact that Baltic naval operations often were part of an amphibious strategy, where operations on land determined the length of the campaign season at sea.

On more southerly latitudes, such as in the West Indies, winter was no problem, but the hurricane season (late summer) had to be avoided. In the Indian Ocean the pattern of the monsoon winds did much to determine naval strategy. In areas with generally calm weather, such as the Mediterranean and the northern parts of the Indian Ocean, oared warships were realistic alternatives to sailing ships. As the wind was the only available source of propulsion power for major warships, its direction and strength was important for strategy and tactics. Lee coasts (coasts to which the wind usually blows), were difficult to blockade as gales might force the blockading fleet ashore. On the other hand it was difficult for fleets based on lee coasts to leave the port. Improvements in hull design and rigs gradually increased the seaworthiness and the weatherliness (ability to sail close to the wind) of the warship, but problems with heavy weather and adverse winds could not be eliminated with sailing technology. But the wind was also an inexhaustible source of propulsive power for the sailing warships. Their endurance was determined by human ability to stay at sea and the possibility of storing provisions. If water and food could be supplied regularly and the crew remain in good health, the ship might operate far from its bases for two or three years until a thorough refit of the hull became necessary.

However, the preservation of the health of the crew was a major problem. Naval history may be rewritten as campaigns of human endurance under adverse conditions. The main threats were epidemics, difficulties with food preservation and unbalanced food supply. Epidemics were the same as those which struck civilian society, but in the cramped conditions on a warship they spread with greater speed. The early phase of a war, when sailors were recruited from various areas and from ships which had sailed in different parts of the world, was often critical. The sailors brought with them various infections to which men from other areas lacked immunity, and the result was often that warships sailed with a large number of the crew struck by disease. The survivors became seasoned and much more resistant to infections. Naval operations in tropical waters brought special problems if the men had not acquired immunity to tropical diseases. Defending forces, such as the Spaniards in the West Indies, often had an advantage in that their soldiers and sailors were used to the climate and the local diseases.

Preservation of food was another problem which was solved only slowly and gradually. Over the centuries, navies learnt how to prepare food for long-distance operations, various types of barrels and packing were developed and store facilities below deck were improved. This did not solve the problem of unbalanced food, especially the lack of vitamin C. This could only be helped by a regular supply of fresh food, especially vegetables and citrus fruits, which was often difficult to organize. Even in the eighteenth century scurvy was a major problem during extended operations at sea. Well-organized logistics and an awareness of the importance of fresh vegetables and fruit were the best solutions until the nineteenth-century revolutions in food preservation radically changed the situation.

The design of a gun-carrying warship was a complicated process, possibly the most demanding task undertaken in pre-industrial Europe. Warships had to be able to fight with their guns in adverse weather, survive gales and extended periods at sea (even after battle damage), move in the desired direction at the best possible speed and provide shelter for the crew. Continuous progress in technology was one of the chief elements behind European supremacy at sea during this period. However, this progress took place within the framework of certain basic constants. Ships were built of wood and they were powered by sails or oars. The ships were armed with smoothbore guns firing solid shots whose size was limited by the fact that guns must be loaded by hand. Close combat with infantry weapons gradually declined in importance, but it was never abolished and remained common in duels between smaller ships. Within these constraints marked progress took place. Hull designs were much improved, the sail area was increased and the rig developed to enhance safety and sailing qualities. By the end of the period advanced theoretical and mathematical methods had been developed to optimize warship design.

Gunnery made great progress in the latter half of the fifteenth century, when guns cast in copper (bronze) began to replace the early type of guns made up of bars of wrought iron. Cast guns could be made thick enough to withstand the pressure from large powder charges and this type of gun might be used with good effect against large ships. The next great step forward was the development of cast-iron guns, first successfully produced in England in the 1540s. However, it was not until the latter half of the seventeenth century that cast-iron guns became sufficiently dependable to replace the larger types of copper guns. Cast iron was much cheaper than copper and this reduced the cost of mass use of artillery at sea. Gun foundry technology and the manufacture of gunpowder improved. This increased the reliability of guns and the effects of hits.

To improve the staying power of warships in combat, hulls had to be built with thick planking and strong internal fastenings. Improved gunnery increased the size of ships able to serve in main-fleet contests. In the mid-seventeenth century ships with a displacement of around 500 tonnes armed with guns firing 12-pounder shots were regarded as ships-of-the-line or battleships. A century later, ships of 1,500 to 2,000 tonnes armed with 24-pounders were regarded as the smallest units suited for a battle line. By 1815 ships of around 3,000 tonnes with 32- or 36-pounders in the main battery had become the normal battleship. When the ships suited for the battle line became larger and more expensive, they also became less suited for many routine naval tasks such as reconnaissance, escort of convoys and the control and policing of large areas of the ocean. At the same time the growth of the European empires and networks of trade throughout the world dramatically increased the areas and networks of sea communication that required the presence of naval force. This development is reflected in a large increase in the number of smaller units suited for tasks, such as cruisers.

Changing frameworks and maritime expansion: warfare at sea, 1450–1650

During these two centuries European warfare at sea developed from its medieval setting into an early modern framework. The main changes were maritime expansion outside Europe, the introduction of guns and specialized, gun-carrying warships and the foundations of navies as permanent state organizations. Within Europe the centre of maritime activities and warfare at sea shifted from the Mediterranean to western and northern Europe.

The introduction of artillery as a main weapon at sea meant that manpower (infantry) was replaced by capital (guns). This increased the ability of sailing warships to operate on long distances, even across oceans, or during extended periods at sea without massive supplies of food and water. The change from hand weapons to artillery also meant an important change in strategic doctrines. Earlier, the fighting power of a navy carrying an invading army was the army itself. A defender might organize his own naval force and send it to sea with the army in order to stop the invasion by a decisive battle at sea, but this was only one alternative. It was often not the best for a defender who preferred to use the terrain conditions, and the attacker's logistical difficulties during an extended operation, to beat off an attack. The defender often found it a better alternative to concentrate his army in defensive positions on land rather than exposing it in a forward position at sea. With gun-armed warships a defender with an inferior army might prefer to meet the enemy at sea and try to defeat the invader when the superior army could not act. As the infantry in the same period became the dominating force in the armies, its reduced importance at sea meant that armies and navies became sharply distinctive organizations. Even inferior navies were often effective as anti-invasion deterrents, since army commanders were normally reluctant to expose their forces to attacks at sea until the enemy fleet was decisively beaten or effectively neutralized by blockade. With gun-armed ships the sea had become an excellent terrain for stopping or delaying an invading army.

The development of a specialized type of gun-armed sailing warship made the creation of specialized organizations for violence at sea – navies – an attractive idea for ambitious state-builders. Navies might break and enforce blockades, support power projection and defy invaders, escort merchantmen and attack enemy trade, and they might do so as part of a policy of the state. A permanent navy was a new way to give rulers an edge over competitors both within their nations and in the international competition for power. Earlier, the sea power of a state meant the ability to hire or requisition merchantmen and convert them into warships with high castles fore and aft from which infantry could fire missile weapons. However, the development of permanent navies was uneven, and the two greatest powers in western Europe, Spain and France, were for long periods more or less without permanent sailing navies. When they existed, they were to a considerable extent organized by regional interests in co-operation with the crown. Permanent and centralized navies with sailing warships were first organized by medium-sized monarchies: Portugal, England, Denmark–Norway and Sweden. At the same time, violence and armed protection at sea as private enterprises thrived and made full use of the development of guns and gun-armed ships.

European maritime activities expanded from the littoral regions of Europe to the Indian Ocean, the entire Atlantic area and to some extent also into the Pacific.

The Portuguese crown was the pioneer in this activity, and for a century after Vasco da Gama's arrival in Indian waters in 1498, Portuguese gun-carrying ships and fortified trading stations were the sole European presence in the Indian Ocean area. This activity had two aims: as an attempt to use violence to channel the trade in valuable Asian commodities (primarily spices) around Africa; and as a protection-selling enterprise where Portuguese warships refrained from attacks on indigenous shipping in exchange for money. Around 1600 well-armed English and Dutch traders arrived in the Indian Ocean in order to buy Asian products. This defiance of Portugal's monopoly claims on trade and maritime violence required a new and more efficient combination of trade, protection and aggressiveness and the Dutch East India Company proved to be able to achieve this. In the 1620s and 1630s it was able to defeat the Portuguese both commercially and in naval combats. Until overtaken by the British in the eighteenth century, the Dutch remained dominant in the European trade with the East Indies.

The new Spanish empire in America soon attracted competitors in trade, predators and enemies of the Spanish state. During the sixteenth century French, English and Dutch traders, privateers, and freebooters sailed to the West Indies, looking for trade or plunder. In the early seventeenth century they also began to settle in the area, mainly on the islands, which became bases for intensified attacks on Spanish colonies and trade. The attractions were the treasure which every year was sent to Spain and the opportunity to break the Spanish trade monopoly which was far from popular among the Spanish settlers. Spain had to organize most of her trans-Atlantic trade in a convoy system, and in the last decades of the sixteenth century intensified attacks from English privateers and royal warships made it necessary to provide these convoys with strong naval escort. Fortifications were built in the West Indies as protection against seaborne attacks. On the whole the system worked as a protection for the trade routes – only one treasure fleet was captured before 1650 (by the Dutch at Matanzas, Cuba in 1628) – but the cost of imperial protection became a heavy burden.

During the sixteenth century the Mediterranean was still the centre for large-scale European warfare at sea. In earlier centuries galley fleets, especially those of Venice and Genoa, had fought wars about trade and territories. As an inheritance from this period Venice retained a permanent galley fleet with its infrastructure of bases. Early gunpowder weapons did not make the galleys obsolete. In fact, the permanent Mediterranean galley navies, powered by slaves and prisoners chained to the oars, were mainly a creation of the early gunpowder period. Earlier galley fleets had usually been organized during wars and often powered by free oarsmen. The gun gave the low-hulled galley a weapon with which it could attack large sailing ships with high sides. It was only gradually, with the spread of cheap iron guns as a mass weapon, that galleys became an uneconomical weapon carrier. In the sixteenth century one heavy gun and an infantry force on every galley made a galley fleet into a formidable striking force against enemy sailing ships and the large number of thin-walled, pre-gunnery fortifications which provided the main defence in large parts of the Mediterranean. The sudden obsolescence of this local defence system is one explanation for the rapid appearance of the Spanish and Ottoman Mediterranean empires in the decades around 1500. In a maritime perspective they were based on the new offensive and defensive power of the gun-armed galley which could offer protection and deterrence over wide areas. It lacked the endurance of the sailing-ship, but in the Mediterranean a galley fleet with an extensive regional-base system was an efficient force.

The Mediterranean maritime power struggle reached imperial and, for its time, grand proportions from the 1490s to the 1570s. Before that, during the great contests, and after that (up to the early nineteenth century) there was also a constant state of irregular and limited warfare: privateering, piracy, coastal raids and small-scale extortion of wealth from trade. Much of this violence was connected with the conflicts between Christians and Muslims, with the Muslims in Algiers, Tunis and Tripoli and the Christian order of St John (Malta) as the most persistent contenders. However, there was also rather more non-state violence between Christians. The Uskok attacks against Venetian trade in the Upper Adriatic is one example, as were attacks against Christian trade with the Muslims by Christian privateers. Violence and extortion of wealth by the threat of violence was a way of life for some Mediterranean coastal communities, even after most Europeans had turned such activities away from Europe, directing it towards the rest of the world.

The regular Mediterranean wars were fought by four powers: the Habsburg empire in Spain and Italy, the Ottoman empire, France and Venice, and some small Italian navies and the Order of St John (until 1522 at Rhodes and from 1530 at Malta) usually allied with the Habsburgs. Italian entrepreneurs in galley warfare, of which the Dorias of Genoa were the most important, also served the Habsburg rulers. In the western Mediterranean the war for imperial power started in the 1490s with the unification of Spain, the Spanish conquest of Granada (1492), the Spanish expansion in North Africa and the Spanish expedition to fight French expansion in Italy (1494–95). This set the agenda for the period up to 1559, when Spain and France often fought each other in great European wars and Spain at the same time had to fight Ottoman empire-building in North Africa. The centre of this activity was Algiers, conquered by Turkish adventurers in 1516 and turned into a naval base by the formidable Kheir-ed-Din Barbarossa. The main Ottoman fleet, from 1534 to 1546 under the command of Barbarossa, often operated in the western Mediterranean, in the early 1540s and in the 1550s in alliance with France against the Habsburgs. There were few large naval battles in the area, but several large amphibious assaults.

In the eastern Mediterranean (the Levant) the Ottoman conquest of Constantinople in 1453 was followed by decades of low-level wars and gradual Ottoman conquests of Christian territories. The rapid growth of Ottoman power from 1499 to 1517 (conquest of Venetian positions in Greece 1499–1503, of Egypt 1517 and of Rhodes 1522) created greater stability than in the west. Venice, still with a reputation as a leading naval power, was very much dependent on trade with the by now Ottoman-controlled ports in the Levant and attempted to live in peace with the Muslim empire, only fighting in defence when attacked. The war from 1499 to 1503 was a Turkish victory. One action of tactical interest is the battle of Navarino (or Zonchio) in 1499, which showed the great difficulties in co-ordinating galleys and gun-armed sailing warships. In 1537–40 Venice again had to fight the Ottomans and they allied with the Habsburgs. A large galley-fleet contest off western Greece (Prevesa) in 1538 was a Muslim victory in spite of the fact that the Spanish–Italian–Venetian fleet had a considerable quantitative superiority. The Ottoman ability to operate in the western Mediterranean was not only based on Christian internal wars but also on a superiority in tactical skill and seamanship.

After the peace with France in 1559 Habsburg Spain could concentrate on naval and amphibious warfare in the Mediterranean. It started with an expedition to Tripoli in 1560 which ended in a disastrous defeat off the island of Djerba (southern Tunisia) where the main Ottoman fleet attacked. From a strategic perspective it was an early example of an amphibious expedition intercepted by the defender at sea. The next major move was an Ottoman assault on Malta in 1565 which failed after an epic siege and a last-minute relief by Habsburg forces. In 1570, the Ottomans occupied Venice-controlled Cyprus. This led to the formation of a Christian league of Venice, Spain and its Italian territories, the Pope and minor Christian powers under Habsburg command. The two fleets joined in combat at Lepanto in western Greece. Around 150,000 men took part in this battle (about half on each side), making it the largest battle on land or at sea in Europe before the late seventeenth century. Most of the participants might have been chained oarsmen, but as a demonstration of the sophistication of sixteenth-century logistics and organization in the Mediterranean the concentration of forces was impressive. The result was a great Christian victory, although the strategic results were small. Venice accepted the loss of Cyprus and concluded a separate peace in 1573. Habsburg forces captured Tunis in that year, but in 1574 an Ottoman fleet, larger than that destroyed at Lepanto, retook the city.

After this, the Spanish–Ottoman conflict was shelved. In fact, it was never restarted. Spanish aid to the Austrian Habsburgs during their war with the Ottomans in the 1590s turned out to be mainly naval demonstrations. The central role of the galley fleets in the sixteenth-century confrontation is obvious if we consider that Spain and the Ottoman empire, the two leading military powers of this period, never met in a large battle on land. The confrontation may be described as a contest between two amphibious navies or seaborne armies. Its nature has been rather difficult to understand for later naval and military historians, used to the preconditions of sailing or continental warfare.

In the Baltic and the North Sea areas the German Hanse gradually dissolved as a mercantile cartel and an alliance for the mutual protection of trading cities. The cities began to rely on agreements with and protection from the crowns of England, Denmark–Norway and Sweden. Lübeck, which had usually been the leader of Hanseatic warfare at sea, was the last Hanse city which attempted to act as a major power with the aim of retaining her control of trade in the Baltic area. In the early sixteenth century the city was still able to send out fleets which might determine the power struggle in Scandinavia. In the 1530s Lübeck's attempt to control the entrance to the Baltic by an intervention in a Danish civil war failed. During the Swedish–Danish war in the 1560s Lübeck fought as a junior naval partner to Denmark but without achieving any of her mercantile war aims. This was the last major German naval effort for three centuries. The Baltic became a sea open to foreign mercantile shipping, protected by the two Scandinavian powers who claimed that they had the sole right to maintain navies in the area.

In the Baltic, the Danish kings had developed a navy during the fifteenth century and superiority at sea was a major asset in the intermittent wars with Sweden. From the 1520s a new royal dynasty in Sweden also created a gun-armed navy which gained control of the sea lines of communication in the northern Baltic. It intervened in the Danish civil war 1534–36 where at least one battle against a Lübeck-controlled fleet was won by gunfire (Bornholm, 1535). In the war against Denmark and Lübeck from 1563 to 1570 the Swedish navy was successful in blockade-breaking, invasion-prevention and control of sea lines of communication within the fledgling Swedish Baltic empire. This war may be described as the first "modern" war at sea. It was fought by permanent sailing navies, guns were the main weapon in seven main fleet battles from 1563 to 1566, and the operations of concentrated battle fleets against each other were the dominant feature of the war at sea. In two further Danish–Swedish wars, 1611–13 and 1643–45, operations at sea also proved important. In the first the Danes took the initiative from the beginning and eliminated several Swedish warships in port. In the second a Swedish naval victory in 1644 against a reduced Danish autumn fleet gave Sweden control of Danish waters.

From a European perspective naval warfare in western Europe was on a low level until the last part of the sixteenth century. France, Spain (Castile), England, Scotland and Burgundy Netherlands (from 1477 part of the Habsburg dominion and from 1516 unified with Spain) fought several wars about territories and political power. Spain and the Netherlands were usually allied with England, and Scotland with France. The naval operations connected with them were surprisingly uneventful and fought within a largely medieval framework of strategic mentality: transports of troops, devastation of coastal areas and more or less uncontrolled warfare against trade. English intervention in Brittany around 1489 and large-scale troop transports to France (usually through English-controlled Calais) in 1475, 1492, 1512, 1513, 1523 and 1544 did not lead to any contests at sea. An army at sea was still regarded as invincible if not met by a superior army. In 1545 the French and English naval and military strength balanced each other evenly in the Channel area. Both coasts were raided, but repeated attempts to bring the fleets into serious combats were frustrated by winds and the difficulties of tactical co-operation between sailing ships and galleys. Both England and France (the coastal provinces) had developed permanent gun-armed navies and they experimented with various ideas about how to combine oared and sailing warships, but the inconclusive fights in the Channel area during the first half of the sixteenth century showed the problems of such co-operation.

The Dutch struggle against Spain from the late 1560s was from its start fought at sea, and the Dutch soon gained local control of their inland waterways and the adjacent sea. Attempts to send fleets from Spain were frustrated by other commitments (Mediterranean, the conquest of Portugal and the Azores 1580–83), a lack of preparation (no permanent sailing navy), lack of a deep-water base in the Netherlands and by the increasing hostility shown by England with its well-prepared navy. When the Spanish superpower finally launched its enterprise towards the north it was with a combination of permanent forces (the Portuguese navy and the Atlantic convoy force) and a collection of large, armed merchantmen. Principally it was an invasion fleet against England, a medieval (pre-gunnery) enterprise organized by the most bureaucratically-developed, early-modern power. The Armada of 1588 was defeated by superior English gunnery, lack of a local Channel deep-water base and unusually severe summer gales. A gun-armed navy had defeated an army with great superiority of manpower before it landed. But Spanish seapower increased in the following decade and further English attempts at inflicting defeats on Spanish trade and colonies were largely frustrated. The English state and maritime community were at this time too weak and weakly co-ordinated to fight a sustained offensive war or to challenge the Iberian trading empires overseas.

Instead, the first half of the seventeenth century did see the world's first global maritime war between Habsburg Spain (including Portugal up to 1640) and the Dutch "rebels" against Spain. The second Dutch–Spanish war period 1621–1648 was, especially, very much a fight about trade and hegemony over Europe's contacts with Asia and America. The Netherlands had become Europe's leading merchant nation, and Spain hoped to reduce her economic ability to fight by embargoes and intensive attacks on Dutch shipping in the North Sea and Channel area, around the Iberian peninsula and even, if possible, in the Baltic. The Dutch responded with convoys in Europe, but also with large-scale expeditions to the East and West Indies. These were launched by commercial companies which looked for valuable trade and fought maritime wars. They attacked enemy seaborne trade and colonies and attempted to replace them with trading networks and settlements of their own. Spain and Portugal had to send major naval and military expeditions to the West Indies and Brazil to protect their interests. The 1630s was a particularly disastrous period for the Habsburg overseas empires, and the losses suffered by the Portuguese in this period were probably a major cause for their defection from Spain in 1640.

The overall result of this long war was that Dutch trade in Europe suffered (how much is debated by the historians), but was not seriously hurt in the long run. Overseas the Dutch won in the East Indies, while the Portuguese were able to recover after 1640 in the Atlantic area, retaking Brazil. Spain's American empire and trade suffered from high protection costs and this must have contributed to the growing crisis in the Spanish hemisphere. In Europe the naval war reached a climax in the late 1630s. France, which had recently created a navy, joined the war against Spain in 1635. Unlike the Dutch, the French aimed to defeat the Spaniards in fleet contests and won a victory against an inferior Spanish squadron at Guetaria in northern Spain in 1638. In an attempt to defeat both the French and the Dutch with a concentrated battle fleet Spain decided to gamble on a new major enterprise to the Channel area in 1639. The large Spanish–Portuguese fleet first failed to defeat an inferior Dutch force in a running battle. It then took protection in the Downs, which gave the Dutch time to concentrate their forces and launch a devastating attack. It turned out to be one of the most decisive battles of the sailing-ship period, as most of the Hispanic fleet was captured or destroyed. The Spaniards seem to have been lacking in firepower, seamanship and the imaginative use of a large force in offensive warfare. The defeat was much more total and definite than the more famous catastrophe in 1588, and it contributed to the growing sense of despair which caused a deep political crisis within Habsburg Spain in the 1640s.

Bureaucratic battle fleets: warfare at sea, 1650–1720

The dominant trend during this period was the rapid growth of bureaucratically-organized, permanent navies. In 1650 England, the Netherlands, France, Denmark–Norway, Sweden, Spain and Portugal had sailing navies with a total displacement of around 200,000 tonnes. Half a century later the total size of European fleets had increased almost fourfold. This increase included Venice, the Ottoman empire and Russia which had joined or were about to join the league of major sailing-ship powers. The increase in naval strength enabled the European states definitely to enforce their monopoly on violence in European waters, and the leading sea powers in western Europe acquired the ability to deploy major naval forces to the Baltic and the Mediterranean in order to deter enemies, support allies and protect trade. The foundation of great battle fleets meant the end of the practice of hiring of temporary warships from the merchant communities. It also meant the formalization of tactics into a line-of-battle system suitable for the bureaucratic war machines controlled by centralized states. Bureaucratic navies also developed permanent officer corps and various systems for the mass recruitment of sailors during wars. Privateering remained important, but it was strictly regulated by the states. Piracy and unofficial warfare at sea were gradually eliminated, although the threat from non-Europeans remained in some areas.

The vastly increased navies (and armies) and the stabilization of centralized states were based on interaction and competition between states. Repeated wars and mutual suspicion between nations increased the political integration behind strong, permanent, armed forces. At sea the first obvious case of an armament race without subsequent retrenchment took place between the English and the Dutch during their three intense maritime wars. The first (1652–54) was a clash between two republics in internal political turmoil. It was a war about mercantilistic regulations and shares in trade, but also about the ability of new regimes to assert their positions. The second (1664–67) was the result of the restored Stuart dynasty's attempt to increase its popularity and power at home through a successful and profitable war. The third (1672–74) was fought for much the same reason, but England was now a junior partner in Louis XIVs first large-scale use of his new large army and recently created battle fleet.

The Anglo-Dutch wars were dominated by intense battle fleet actions in the North Sea and the Channel: about fifteen major actions (and some minor) in seven campaign seasons. The intensity of the short wars reflected the fact that they were fought in what was now the centre of European and world trade where great wealth was at stake with every convoy and even with short periods of blockades. In the first war the English navy won, thanks to massive superiority in firepower and larger, purpose-built warships. In the second the Dutch were better prepared, and after initial setbacks, their financial strength began to tell. In 1667 the Dutch fleet was able to raid the Thames estuary and inflict losses on an English fleet which was laid up due to lack of money. The third war was a successful Dutch struggle for national survival, as a defeat at sea would have meant trade blockade and the military invasion of Holland. With strategic and tactical skill the Dutch made use of the shallow waters along their coast, and the combined Anglo-French fleet repeatedly failed to defeat their quantitatively inferior enemy. The English withdrew, frustrated, from a profitless war. Fifteen years later, the Glorious Revolution of 1688–89 turned the two maritime powers into close allies.

The rise of a great French navy in the 1660s was the result of the French monarchy's increased ability to assert its power at home. Louis XIV converted domestic peace into the means of power assertion abroad. His prime target for that up to 1700 was Habsburg Spain, whose territories in the Netherlands and Italy might be separated by French seapower. In the war which ended in 1659 Spain and France had increasingly become unable to fight at sea, but from the 1660s Spain was helpless at sea against the growing French navy. This was serious for those who wished to block French rise to dominance in western Europe. During the war with France in 1674–78, Spain received Dutch support at sea. During the next great war period in western Europe (1688–1697), England and the Netherlands co-operated in order to preserve the political results of the English Revolution, their trade and the Spanish empire in Europe. France started with ambitions to restore James II on the British Isles, efforts which resulted in three large naval battles between 1689 and 1692. The strategy then changed to trade warfare: French naval squadrons and privateers were sent out to attack the vast enemy trade. The two maritime powers penetrated the Mediterranean with battle fleets in order to support their Spanish and Austrian allies. Much of the war was fought on land with the navies supporting the military logistical systems. The war ended in a stalemate and France was still a great power at sea.

In the War of the Spanish Succession (1701/2–1713/14) the situation changed as a French Bourbon prince inherited the Spanish empire which an Austrian Habsburg prince contested. The war on land was fought in the southern Netherlands and Germany, in Italy and in Spain with the navies of the two maritime powers in support of a vast system of military logistics and of military operations in coastal areas. At first, France attempted to control the Mediterranean, but after the inconclusive battle fleet action at Malaga (1704) France abandoned its battle fleet. Trade war became the dominant French effort at sea, a war fought with determination. France (paid by Spain) was also able to protect the vital transfer of Spanish bullion from America to Europe. The trade war was a part of a general tendency towards attrition warfare between the, by now, very large armies and navies of western Europe. The war ended in a compromise peace, with the Bourbon dynasty in control of Spain and the Habsburgs of former Spanish possessions in Italy and the Netherlands. The French navy was in ruins, a fact which reflected the decline of Louis XIV's power and which made peace attractive for the two maritime powers. The war had its aftermath in the

Mediterranean in 1717–20 when Bourbon Spain with a recreated navy tried in vain to restore Spanish power in Italy. A British squadron defeated the Spanish fleet off Sicily in 1718.

Little research has been done on the long wars fought between Venice and the Ottoman empire in this period. The manning, administration and infrastructure of the two navies are unknown. The fact that Venice now – by contrast with the sixteenth century – was able to fight extended wars with the Ottomans was a somewhat paradoxical effect of the republic's no longer being a great maritime power. Much of the trade between Europe and the Levant had passed into the hands of the Dutch, English and French. Venice was now predominantly a regional power in the Adriatic, and a great part of the resources with which the wars were fought must have been extracted from land. The wars were mainly about territories in Greece and Dalmatia, not about trade. It seems that both sides were motivated by a desire to hold as many strategic positions in Greece as possible in order to defend their centres of power: Constantinople and the Adriatic. As the positions were mainly islands and coastal fortresses, the wars naturally became highly amphibious. Venice no longer had a large seafaring population from which to recruit her crews, and, in this respect, the republic did not much differ from the Turks.

The first war 1645–69 was mainly fought over Crete, which the Ottomans in the end were able to conquer. Most of the naval operations took place in the Greek archipelago and the Venetians were periodically able to blockade the Dardanelles. The galley fleets were supplemented by sailing warships, on the Venetian side mainly Dutch and English, armed merchantmen chartered with their crews. In the next war, 1684–99, Venice fought as the maritime partner in an alliance with Austria, Poland and Russia. Both navies now used conventional sailing battle fleets with galleys as auxiliaries. The Venetians were able to occupy the Peloponnese and keep it at the peace. The contests between the battle fleets resulted in draws. In the third war (1715–18) the Ottomans were able to concentrate on the Venetians and recovered the losses of the earlier war. There were again a number of large-scale battle fleet actions with indecisive results. In all three wars the Venetians were able to deploy their main fleet to the Greek archipelago, close to Constantinople, but it seems to have been difficult to convert this strength into an effective blockade or a serious threat. However, it might have been enough to motivate the Turks to fight long wars for the control of Greece.

Sweden and Denmark repeatedly clashed in their traditional struggle for domination in the Baltic. The wars started with Danish attempts to use Swedish entanglements in continental wars to reconquer territories earlier lost to Sweden. Warfare at sea and on land were always closely interconnected in these wars which in terms of naval strategy were fought about the lines of communication between Jutland, the Danish isles, Scania (Swedish from 1658) and northern Germany, dominated by Sweden since the Thirty Years' War. The battle fleet that gained control of these lines could protect the transfer of troops and military logistics between these areas, which were strategically decisive in contests for the Baltic and large parts of Germany. In order to gain a base in this strategic area the Swedish fleet was permanently moved from Stockholm to the new city of Karlskrona in the 1680s.

The war period 1657–60 saw the first intervention of Dutch and English battle fleets in the Baltic. In the early phase of the war, Sweden (helped by a severe winter in 1658 which made the Danish isles accessible over the ice) made large conquests of Danish–Norwegian territory. In the second phase, active Dutch support of the Danes stopped further Swedish expansion. In the war of 1675–79 the Swedish fleet was repeatedly defeated by the Danes, initially supported by the Dutch. French support of Sweden and the threat of intervention by the French fleet in the Baltic nullified the Danish success. In 1700 the Danes took part in the alliance with Russia and Saxony–Poland which attacked Sweden, but, together with a Dutch–English squadron, the Swedish navy achieved overwhelming superiority and succeeded in landing the Swedish army close to Copenhagen. Denmark quickly withdrew from the war and did not rejoin it until 1709 when the Swedish main army was defeated in Ukraine. Until 1716 the Swedish and Danish fleets fought each other for the last time as the main adversaries in a Baltic war. They met in two inconclusive actions, but by 1716 their ability to make offensive strikes alone had disappeared.

Russia's development as a sea power started during the war against the Ottomans in the 1690s and a considerable fleet was built in the sea of Azov. It had to be abolished and dismantled in 1711 as a result of Russian defeat in another Ottoman war. The more spectacular Russian advance to the sea was made in the Baltic where Tsar Peter I joined the anti-Swedish alliance with the aim of establishing a Baltic port and a navy as part of his ambition to modernize Russia. After initial setbacks he was able to gain a foothold on the Baltic where St Petersburg was able to be founded. From 1710 he launched an ambitious programme of battleship acquisition, and by 1720 he possessed the largest battle fleet in the Baltic. The sailors were inexperienced, the officers were to a large extent foreigners and the tsar had a realistic and cautious attitude to the capability of his fleet in comparison with more seasoned adversaries, but the achievement was impressive. The European model of bureaucratic battle fleet had for the first time been implemented in a purely continental state without maritime traditions and without maritime interest groups. It was a demonstration of what early modern state power might achieve if used with determination.

In actual warfare against Sweden in the 1710s the Russian galley fleet made a greater contribution, as it was the key to the conquest of Finland. The battle fleet avoided combat alone, but in 1716 it joined the Danish and the British fleets (serving the interest of Hanover which took part in the anti-Swedish coalition) in an attempt to invade Scania. However, the action was called off by Tsar Peter. In the last years of the war (1719–21) he sent his galleys on raids on the Swedish coast. The British and Swedish fleets joined to fight Russia, but in the absence of superior army forces to send ashore little could be achieved. Russia had established a Baltic empire.

Oceanic and continental power struggles: warfare at sea, 1720–1815

This was the century that saw the apogee of warfare under sail. It also saw the rise of Great Britain from a position as a recently-established, European great power to the status of a global superpower, based upon economic and naval supremacy. The battle fleets matured into increasingly effective instruments for transoceanic warfare and for efficient control of European sea lines of communication. Major European naval and army forces were deployed overseas to fight for the control of the American continent and the Indian subcontinent. Control over non-European territories (not only trade) became a major issue in European power politics and this increased the importance of maritime strategies and presence in areas which might be of interest for future expansion. Not until the Second World War was global maritime strategy of the same importance. The political interest aggregation behind great increases in European naval strength is impressive, although it was helped by an economic development which was more favourable than in the preceding century, due not least to rapidly increasing maritime trade.

During this century, European power politics was increasingly separated into an oceanic and a continental hemisphere. In the latter Austria, Prussia and Russia were the great contenders (and dividers of Poland) with Sweden and the Ottoman empire acting on the flanks. It was the conflicts of the latter two powers with Russia that generated warfare at sea in the continental power struggle, as the Baltic, the Black Sea and the Mediterranean could be used for maritime strategies. The Turks were at war with Russia and Austria in 1736–39. Russian efforts to gain access to the Black Sea failed in spite of the creation of a large riverine flotilla to support the army. A Swedish attempt at reconquering lost territory in a war against Russia in 1741–43 ended in a new defeat, caused to a considerable extent by widespread sickness in the fleet and unwillingness to support the army flank in Finland during the campaign of 1742. An Ottoman attack on Russia in 1768 met the unexpected response of a long-distance Russian naval expedition from the Baltic to the Mediterranean where the Ottoman fleet was defeated in 1770. Russia conquered the Crimea and re-created a Black Sea fleet. In the 1780s Russia drastically increased her naval strength in order to attack the Turks both from the Levant and the Black Sea in a new war which was expected to result in an Austro-Russian division of the Balkans.

An Ottoman declaration of war in 1787 was followed by four campaign seasons in the Black Sea where the Russian fleet was successful, although not markedly superior to the Ottomans. Sweden unexpectedly decided to attack Russia in 1788, partly with the hope that England and Prussia were about to join the war. The Swedish intervention prevented the Russians from the planned expedition to the Mediterranean, as the battle fleet had instead to defend St Petersburg from Swedish amphibious assaults. In this it was successful in a series of actions from 1788 to 1790, of which those in the last year led to considerable losses for the Swedish battle fleet. A Russian counterattack on the Swedish oared flotilla in the Finnish archipelago was repulsed with severe Russian losses. It was the last large combat involving oared warships in the world.

In the oceanic (Atlantic–East Indies) hemisphere, Great Britain, France and Spain were the main contenders, while Portugal and the Netherlands attempted to stay neutral. The three competing powers increased their battle fleets in order to protect and expand their transoceanic interest spheres. The first conflicts arose between the increasingly dynamic and expansive Great Britain and Spain, still the largest colonial power in the world. In 1739 Britain launched a war against Spain to avenge alleged harassment of her trade. Large British expeditions were sent against the West Indies but with only limited success. In 1744 France also went to war against Britain. Britain and her colonists were successful against the French colonies in North America and the British fleet, much increased by new construction, was able to inflict losses on French squadrons protecting convoys, but, thanks to French successes on the European continent, the war ended as a draw in 1748. After 1754 colonial wars escalated into an Anglo-French war (1756–63) connected politically with the contemporary war on the continent. Britain and Prussia fought as allies, but the maritime power concentrated her resources on assaults on French colonies in Canada, the West Indies and India. Britain's navy was already superior to France at the beginning of the war, and a major new programme of construction in combination with victories at sea, most importantly at Quiberon Bay in 1759, reduced France to impotence overseas. Isolated by British seapower, French colonies were captured and North America and India disappeared from the French sphere of interest. Spain joined the war in 1762, only to suffer defeats at Havana and Manila resulting from the now well-developed British capability for rapid strikes with seaborne military power.

France and Spain had in 1761 formed an alliance and launched ambitious programmes of naval expansion. When the British colonies in North America revolted in 1775, the two Bourbon powers had ample time to prepare their navies, and when they joined the war for American independence in 1778–79 they proved to be a formidable combination. In 1779 their fleets gained temporary command of the Channel. In 1780 the Netherlands was forced to join the anti-British alliance, as her rights as a neutral trader were not respected. The French fleet seriously challenged the British in the West Indies and North America: a number of inconclusive actions were fought and colonies taken and lost. The British were unable to stop French reinforcement of the rebellious Americans and, when the French fleet and the French–American army in 1781 were able to isolate the main British field army at Yorktown, the British will to continue the fight against her colonists was at an end. At sea the new British construction capability began to tell, however, and in 1782 the French fleet in the West Indies was defeated, thus destroying its ability to support further conquests.

The peace concluded in 1783 was not regarded as an end to the maritime contest. On the contrary, the European powers were preparing for great, new naval wars. France and Spain continued to expand their navies with a view to future power struggles about trade and colonies in America and Asia. In fact, the sailing battle fleets reached their quantitative peak in the early 1790s, a total displacement of around 1.7 million tonnes. Britain, by now established as a great power in the Indian Ocean area, prepared for the same struggle but was also considering how the navy could be used to stop further Russian expansion to the south. This was the beginning of the nineteenth-century, Asian "great game" between these two powers. Smaller navies expanded for regional wars (the Ottomans, Sweden, Denmark–Norway, Naples) or for the protection of old empires (the Netherlands, Portugal).

But, unexpectedly, the decades from 1792 to 1815 was dominated by a gigantic struggle for European hegemony, a development initiated by the French Revolution. On the continent France took the initiative and with a much increased and reinvigorated army defeated all major continental powers. On the sea the British gained an early advantage over the temporarily disorganized French navy, which it retained, and it was also able to defeat new naval adversaries added by French victories on land. British naval organization, financial strength and growing technological superiority (for example the better foundry technology that enabled the British to produce guns with increased hitting power), showed themselves in combat and in the ability to stay at sea under adverse conditions. The French Mediterranean fleet was to a large extent annihilated in Toulon in 1793 (due to a Royalist revolt) and again at Aboukir in Egypt in 1798. The Spanish fleet was diminished by defeats in 1797, as was the Dutch which also suffered from unwillingness to fight for French interests. British expeditions to the West Indies could not be countered by the French, and the British also showed their naval superiority by breaking up an alliance in 1801 between the three neutral powers – Russia, Denmark–Norway and Sweden.

Peace was concluded in 1802, but Napoleon's ambitions to re-create a naval threat against Britain caused the latter power to declare war again in 1803. French ports were blockaded and Napoleon's attempt in 1805 to bring together a French–Spanish fleet temporarily strong enough to clear the way for his army across the Channel was unsuccessful. The battle of Trafalgar reduced French and Spanish naval strength to such a degree that a new attempt would prove to be impossible. The decade after 1805 was uneventful in terms of great naval actions, but the contest at sea took other forms. Napoleon launched a great programme of new construction which, if fulfilled, would have created a huge French battle fleet. Britain had to counter this with a similar programme, and at the same time the British fleet had to deploy huge forces to blockade ports around Europe and to protect a large system of convoys. The competition in fleet strength led to extraordinary actions, notably the British attack on neutral Denmark–Norway in 1807 when the whole Danish fleet was captured, because the British feared that it might fall under Napoleon's control. Britain was also able to eliminate the French and Dutch colonial empires. In American waters the small American navy had some successes in cruiser contests with the British during the war 1812–1815, but the overall picture is that Britain was by now a superpower fully able to regard fighting the Americans as a small sideshow to the great European war.

In the Baltic and Black Sea/Levant regions several large naval operations took place in this war period. The Russians deployed battle squadrons in the Baltic, the North Sea and the Mediterranean in support of various operations on land (the partition of Poland in 1792–5, operations against France in various coalitions) and their Mediterranean fleet defeated the Ottomans when the latter joined France in 1807. The Russian conquest of Finland in 1808 was a winter campaign, but the fact that the Russians gained control over the main Swedish base in Finland (Sveaborg) with the archipelago flotilla made it difficult for the Swedish battle fleet to support amphibious expeditions to retake southern Finland.

The wars 1792–1815 had resulted in a very marked British superiority at sea. The contest about the future domination of world trade and the lion's share of future colonial expansion for which the navies had prepared in the 1780s had in fact been settled in European waters. Together with financial, commercial and, increasingly, industrial strength, British ability to control the sea lines of communication around the European coasts and from Europe to the rest of the world was the base upon which her position as a superpower in world politics was to last for a century. Economical, technological and naval leadership were interrelated phenomena, but it had taken centuries to achieve it.

Further reading

Much of our knowledge of naval history is based on multi-volumes studies of different navies, usually written in the late nineteenth and early twentieth century. Older literature as well as more recent studies are listed in J. Glete, *Navies and nations: Warships, navies and state building in Europe and America, 1500–1860*, 2 vols (Stockholm, Almqvist & Wiksell International, 1993).

This list concentrates on recent studies in English and a few important works in French and Spanish. The Anglo-Saxon literature on warfare at sea is concentrated on the Atlantic hemisphere. For other areas there are some useful broad surveys in English which remain indispensable for those who do not read Russian, Italian and the Nordic languages: R. C. Anderson, *Naval wars in the Baltic, 1522–1850* (London, Francis Edwards, 1910, 1969) and *Naval wars in the Levant, 1559–1853* (Liverpool, Liverpool University Press, 1953), Recent surveys on wars in the Baltic: G. Rystad *et al.*, *In quest of trade and security: The Baltic in power politics, 1500–1990, vol. 1: 1500–1890* (Lund, Lund University Press, 1994); S. P. Oakley, *War and peace in the Baltic, 1560–1790* (London, Routledge, 1992).

Economic theory and historical syntheses relevant to studies on war, violence and protection, especially at sea: F. C. Lane, *Profits from power: readings in protection rent and violence-controlling enterprises* (Albany, State University of New York Press, 1979); W. H. McNeill, *The Pursuit of power: technology, armed force, and society since A.D. 1000* (Oxford, Basil Blackwell, 1983); I. Wallerstein, *The modern world-system, 3 vols* (New York & San Diego, Academic Press, 1974–89). Navies in an international relation theory perspective: G. Modelski, G. and W. R. Thompson, *Seapower in global politics, 1494–1993* (Seattle, University of Washington Press, 1988).

Individual navies: England and Great Britain: J. R. Hill (ed.), *The Oxford illustrated history of the Royal Navy* (Oxford, Oxford University Press, 1995), P. M. Kennedy, *The rise and fall of British naval mastery* (London, Allen Lane, 1976); R. Harding, *The evolution of the sailing navy, 1509–1815* (London, Macmillan, 1995); D. Loades, *The Tudor navy: an administrative, political and military history* (Aldershot, Scolar Press, 1992); D. Lyon, *The sailing navy list* (London, Conway, 1993). France: E. H. Jenkins, *A history of the French navy: from its beginnings to the present day* (London, MacDonald, 1973); M. Acerra, *Rochefort et la construction navale francaise, 1661–1815*, 4 vols (Paris, Libraire de l'Inde, 1993); P. Villiers, *Marine royale, corsaires et trafic dans l'Atlantique de Louis XIV à Louis XVI*, 2 vols (Dunkirk, 1991). The Netherlands: J. R. Bruijn, *The Dutch navy of the seventeenth and eighteenth centuries* (Columbia, University of South Carolina Press, 1993). Spain: R. Cerezo Martinez, *Las armadas de Felipe II* (San Martin, Madrid, 1988); J. P. Merino Navarro, *La armada espanola en el siglo XVIII* (Madrid, Fundacion Universitaria Espanola, 1981).

Naval technology: R. Gardiner (series ed.), *Conway's history of the ship*: the volumes *The age of the galley* (London, 1995), *Cogs, caravels and galleons* (London, 1994) and *The line of battle* (London, 1992); H. I. Chapelle, *The American sailing navy: The ships and their development* (New York, Crown, 1949); B. Lavery, *The ship of the line, 2 vols* (London, Conway, 1983–4).

Climate, health, naval manning and provisions: J. H. Pryor, *Geography, technology and war, studies in the maritime history of the Mediterranean, 649–1571* (Cambridge, Cambridge University Press, 1988); N. A. M. Rodger, *The wooden world: An anatomy of the Georgian navy* (London, Collins, 1986); C. Buchet, *La lutte pour l'espace caraïbe et le facade Atlantique de l'Amérique central et du sud, 1672–1763*, 2 vols (Paris, Libraire de l'Inde, 1991); J. Pritchard, *Anatomy of a naval disaster: the 1746 French naval expedition to North America* (Montreal, McGill-Queen's University Press, 1995); P. W. Bamford, *Fighting ships and prisons: The Mediterranean galleys of France in the age of Louis XIV* (Minneapolis, University of Minnesota Press, 1973). Officers: G. Teitler, *The genesis of the modern officer corps* (London, Sage, 1977), M. Vergé-Francheschi, *Marine et éducation sous l'ancien régime* (Paris, CNRS, 1991); J. D. Davies, *Gentlemen and tarpaulins: the officers and men of the Restoration navy*

(Oxford, Oxford University Press, 1992). Administration: D. A. Baugh, *British naval administration in the age of Walpole* (Princeton, Princeton University Press, 1965); I. A. A. Thompson, *War and government in Habsburg Spain, 1560–1620* (London, Athlone, 1976); J. Pritchard, *Louis XV's navy: A study of organization and administration, 1748–1762* (Kingston, McGill-Queen's University Press, 1987); P. W. Bamford, *Forests and French sea power, 1660–1789* (Toronto, University of Toronto Press, 1956). Tactics: J. Creswell, *British admirals of the eighteenth century: tactics in battle* (London, Allen & Unwin, 1972): Dockyards: J. G. Coad, *The royal dockyards, 1690–1850* (Aldershot, Scolar Press, 1989); R. C. Davies, *Shipbuilders of the Venetian arsenal: workers and workplace in the preindustrial city* (Baltimore, Johns Hopkins, 1991). Privateering: E. Otero Lana, *Los corsarios españoles durante la decadencia de los Austrias: El corso español del Atlantico peninsular en el siglo XVII, 1621–1697* (Madrid, Editorial naval, 1992); J. S. Bromley, *Corsairs and navies, 1760–1660* (London, Hambledon, 1987); D. J. Starkey, *British privateering enterprise in the eighteenth century* (Exeter, University of Exeter Press, 1990).

1450–1650: Several of the best studies of navies and naval warfare in this period are parts of more general studies of political and economic history. Late medieval period: J. Paviot, *La politique navale des ducs de Bourgogne, 1384–1482* (Lille, Presses Universitaires de Lille, 1995); J. D. Fudge, *Cargoes, embargoes, and emissaries: the commercial and political interaction of England and the German Hanse, 1450–1510* (Toronto, University of Toronto Press, 1995). The Mediterranean: J. F. Guilmartin, *Gunpowder and galleys: changing technology and Mediterranean warfare at sea in the sixteenth century* (Cambridge, Cambridge University Press, 1974); P. Brummett, *Ottoman seapower and Levantine diplomacy in the age of discoveries* (Albany, State University of New York Press, 1994). Spain: M. Pi Corrales, *Felipe II y la lucha por el dominio del mar* (Madrid, San Martin, 1989); R. A. Stradling, *The armada of Flanders: Spanish maritime policy and European war, 1568–1668* (Cambridge, Cambridge University Press, 1992); C. Rahn Phillips, *Six galleons for the king of Spain: Imperial defense in the early seventeenth century* (Baltimore, Johns Hopkins, 1986). The enormous literature about the Armada and 1588 is discussed in E. L. Rasor, *The Spanish armada of 1588: Historiography and annotated bibliography* (Westport, Greenwood Press, 1993). England: D. D. Hebb, *Piracy and the English government, 1616–1642* (Aldershot, Scolar Press, 1994). The Hispano-Dutch conflict: J. Alcala-Zamora, *Espana, Flandes y el Mar del Norte, 1618–1639* (Barcelona, Planeta, 1975); J. I. Israel, *The Dutch republic and the Hispanic world, 1606–1661* (Oxford, Clarendon Press, 1982). The Baltic: A. Attman, *The Russian and Polish markets in international trade, 1500–1650* (Gothenburg, Ekonomisk-historiska institutionen, 1973). Warfare at sea in America: P. E. Hoffman, *The Spanish crown and the defense of the Caribbean, 1535–1585: precedent, patrimonialism and royal parsimony* (Baton Rouge, Louisiana State University Press, 1980); D. B. Quinn and A. N. Ryan, *England's sea empire, 1550–1642* (London, Allen & Unwin, 1983). The Portuguese and their competitors in the East Indies: B. W. Diffie and G. D. Winius, *Foundations of the Portuguese empire, 1415–1580* (St Paul, University of Minnesota, 1977); N. Steensgaard, *The Asian trade revolution of the seventeenth century* (Chicago, Chicago University Press, 1974); J. C. Boyajian, *Portuguese trade in Asia under the Habsburgs, 1580–1640* (Baltimore, Johns Hopkins, 1993).

1650–1720: There are few studies focused on the special problem of this period: the breakthrough for large battle fleets and bureaucratic navies. J. R. Jones, *The Anglo-Dutch wars of the seventeenth century* (London, Longman, 1996); B. Capp, *Cromwell's navy: The fleet and the English revolution, 1648–1660* (Oxford, Oxford University Press, 1989); D. Dessert, *La Royale: vaisseaux et marins du Roi-Soleil* (Paris, Fayard, 1996), S. Hornstein, *The Restoration navy and English foreign trade, 1674–1688* (Aldershot, Scolar Press, 1991); J. Ehrman, *The navy in the war of William III, 1689–1697: Its state and direction* (Cambridge, Cambridge University Press, 1953); *Guerres maritimes, 1688–1713* (Vincennes, Service historique de la marine, 1996); G. Symcox, *The crisis of French sea power, 1688–1697: From the guerre d'escadre to the guerre de course* (The Hague, Nijhoff, 1974); P. E. Pérez-Mallaina, *Politica naval española en el Atlantico, 1700–1715* (Sevilla, Escuela de Estudios Hispano-Americanos, 1982); E. J. Phillips, *The founding of Russia's navy: Peter the Great and the Azov fleet, 1688–1714* (Westport, Greenwood Press, 1995); J. H. Barfod, *Niels Juel: A Danish admiral of the 17th century* (Copenhagen, Marinehistorisk Selskab, 1977).

1720–1815: There are few modern general studies on naval operations and naval strategy in this period of global warfare at sea. Some examples are N. Tracy, *Navies, deterrence and American independence: Britain and seapower in the 1760s and 1770s* (Vancouver, University of British Columbia Press, 1988); J. R. Dull, *The French navy and American independence: A study of arms and diplomacy, 1774–1787* (Princeton, Princeton University Press, 1975); P. Mackesy, *The war in the Mediterranean, 1803–1810* (London, Longmans, Green, 1957). European naval warfare in America: R. Harding, *Amphibious warfare in the eighteenth century: The British expedition to the West Indies, 1740–1742* (Woodbridge, Boydell Press, 1991); M. Duffy, *Soldiers, sugar and seapower* (Oxford, Clarendon Press, 1987); J. R. McNeill, *Atlantic empires of France and Spain: Louisbourg and Havana, 1700–1763* (Chapel Hill, University of North Carolina Press, 1985); War and Revolution: M. Acerra and J. Meyer, *Marines et revolution* (Rennes, Ouest-France, 1988); W. S. Cormack, *Revolution and political conflict in the French navy, 1789–1794* (Cambridge, Cambridge University Press, 1995). Trade warfare: R. P. Crowhurst, *The French war on trade: privateering, 1793–1815* (Aldershot, Scolar Press, 1989). Russia: A. Bode, *Die Flottenpolitik Katharinas II und die Konflikte mit Schweden* (Wiesbaden, Harrassowitz, 1979); N. Saul, *Russia and the Mediterranean, 1797–1807* (Chicago, University of Chicago Press, 1970). The early American navy: W. M. Fowler Jr, *Rebels under sail: The American navy during the Revolution* (New York, Scribners, 1976); S. C. Tucker, *The Jeffersonian gunboat navy* (Columbia, University of South Carolina Press, 1993); C. L. Symonds, *Navalists and antinavalists: The naval policy debate in the United States, 1785–1827* (Newark, University of Delaware Press, 1980).

Chapter Three

Warfare in Japan 1467–1600

Paul Varley

Japan in the mid-fifteenth century was a country on the verge of disintegration. Its emperor, whose court was located in Kyoto, had not exercised real authority for centuries, but was a "sacred legitimizer" of the rule of others. From the late twelfth century, when the first warrior – samurai – government was established at Kamakura in the Kantō or eastern provinces (a government known in English as "shogunate", because its head was the shogun or "generalissimo"), the effective rulers of the land were warrior chiefs. The Kamakura Shogunate spanned the years 1185–1333, and was replaced, after a brief hiatus, by the Ashikaga Shogunate, 1336–1573, which was situated in Kyoto in proximity to the emperor and his court and headed by shoguns of the Ashikaga family.

The Ashikaga Shogunate came into existence in 1336 at the commencement of a sanguinary conflict, known as the War Between the Courts, that was not settled until 1392. Even after this war the Shogunate was able to exercise only limited control of the country. Its leader, the shogun, presided as hegemon over semi-independent warrior chiefs invested by him as constables (*shugo*) of the various provinces (66 in all) into which Japan was divided. But distant areas of the country, especially the island of Kyushu in the west and the northern reaches of the main island of Honshu, were largely beyond effective Shogunate administration, and in the early fifteenth century the vital Kantō region, heartland of the warrior class, also slipped from Shogunate control and lapsed into disunion. During the Ōnin War, 1467–77, the Ashikaga Shogunate was reduced to near-impotence, and Japan itself was plunged into the age of *Sengoku* or "The Country at War", 1467–1568.[1]

The origins of the Ōnin War, named after the Ōnin calendrical period that began in 1467, were complex, but lay primarily in the failure of the balance of power that had been established between the Ashikaga shogun and his constables, at least those constables in regions where Ashikaga authority still prevailed (on the eve of the Ōnin War, roughly central and western Honshu and the island of Shikoku).[2] Many of the constables had been appointed by the Shogunate to provinces – in some cases, two or more provinces – with which they had no traditional ties: in other words, they were outsiders who sought to impose their control from above. As outsiders, most constables had weak economic bases in the agricultural lands of their provinces (Japan in this age and indeed throughout pre-modern times was overwhelmingly an agricultural, especially rice-producing, country), and in nearly all cases had difficulty managing the local warrior leaders whom they had to enlist as vassals if they were to build the military forces necessary to support their governance.

By the mid-fifteenth century, many constable families were in trouble, if not in outright turmoil. This trouble assumed the form primarily of succession disputes in which local warriors, as vassals or would-be vassals, backed rival contenders to the offices vacated by the deaths of constables. Of the three leading constable families in the service of the Ashikaga – the Hosokawa, Hatakeyama, and Shiba – two, the Hatakeyama and Shiba, were by mid-century divided by succession disputes that had degenerated into open warfare. Then, in the mid-1460s a quarrel over succession erupted in the Ashikaga house itself. The shogun, Ashikaga Yoshimasa, who, according to the records, was more interested in the arts than politics, had wearied of his office and wished to retire, even though he was only in his late twenties. Lacking a son to follow him, Yoshimasa persuaded his brother to stand in line to become the next shogun. Meanwhile, in 1465, Yoshimasa's wife gave birth to a boy, and she immediately formed a faction backing this son, instead of Yoshimasa's brother, to be the shogunal successor. The two most powerful constables at that time, Hosokawa Katsumoto and Yamana Sōzen, each seeking to outdo the other in their rivalry for power, began taking sides not only in the Ashikaga dispute but also in those of the Hatakeyama and Shiba. Yoshimasa, who might at least have solved the issue of shogunal succession by taking a firm stand, only made matters worse by vacillating. In the first month of 1467 fighting broke out north of Kyoto between the two Hatakeyama contenders. Yamana Sōzen and Hosokawa Katsumata each backed a different contender, and the Ōnin War, which in its protracted violence nearly destroyed Kyoto and ultimately rent the country asunder, was launched, almost willy-nilly.

At least one scholar has suggested that it is misleading to apply the designation "Ōnin War" only to the decade 1467–77.[3] The convention of regarding the war as only a decade-long conflict derives from the fact that the principal contending armies, the eastern army of Hosokawa Katsumoto and the western army of Yamana Sōzen ("eastern" and "western" refer to the locations of the armies' base camps in Kyoto), concentrated their main fighting in the imperial capital – thus making the war in this phase primarily an urban conflict – and that the last units of these armies departed Kyoto in 1477. But from the beginning the war spread to other parts of the country, and after 1477 it simply merged with the local and regional warfare that continued countrywide throughout the Sengoku age. Hence it may be more accurate to think of the Ōnin War not as a conflict limited to ten years, but as a Japanese Hundred Years' War.

Before commenting on warfare during the 1467–77 phase of the Ōnin War (which will lead directly into a discussion of Sengoku warfare in general), let me summarize how war was conducted in earlier times in Japan.[4] With the rise of a warrior class in the provinces in the late ninth and tenth centuries warfare became almost exclusively the preserve of this class. Although most warriors continued to engage in the management of their agricultural lands and hence, in that sense, still belonged to the peasantry, they increasingly formed an identifiable elite of professional fighters. Their elitism was guaranteed by two basic conditions: fighting was conducted almost entirely from horseback, and the bow and arrow was the warrior's principal weapon. In order to become a warrior, a man needed: first, the wherewithal to purchase armour, weapons, and horse, and to provide for the horse's maintenance; and, secondly, the skill necessary to shoot arrows from horseback, which could only be acquired through years of training and practice. Although, as we will see, other kinds of fighters appeared in later centuries, the ideal of the warrior as an equestrian archer prevailed throughout pre-modern times. This is reflected, for example, in the continuing use through the centuries of the phrase "the way of the bow and horse" (*kyūba no michi*) to mean "the way of the warrior".

The rise of a warrior class was accompanied by the development of a Japanese version of feudalism.[5] At the heart of Japanese feudalism, as at the heart of its European counterpart, was the lord–vassal relationship. In the war tales (*gunkimono*), a genre of literature dating from the tenth century that deal with warriors and their battles and which are part-history and part-fiction,[6] the lord–vassal relationship is idealized by analogy to that of parent and child: the lord loves his vassal as a father loves his son, and the son is prepared to serve his father-like lord in a spirit of "absolute self-sacrifice" (*kenshin*), even to the death. Although there are treacherous and disloyal vassals in the war tales, they are few, and they do not significantly diminish the dominant portrayal of the vassal in these writings as utterly faithful and self-abnegating. Yet, as we will see, there came to be an enormous difference, especially by the Sengoku age, between how vassals *ought* to behave, according to the idealism of the war tales, and how they actually behaved. In Sengoku, for reasons that will be discussed later, acts of vassal disloyalty became so common and so widespread that they threatened to tear apart the very fabric of warrior society.

Warfare, as it evolved in the ancient age, was highly individualistic. In open-field battling, armies, which probably seldom exceeded a thousand and were usually much smaller, typically confronted each other separated by a distance of about a hundred yards. A general exchange of arrows marked the commencement of fighting, and was sustained as the armies rode forward. Once the armies came together, warriors tended to pair off, riding back and forth past each other and firing arrows. Small in stature, the warrior rode a horse that was probably not much larger than a pony. Since the principal weapon was the bow and arrow, the warrior did not have an arm free to carry a shield. Instead, he wore armour, composed primarily of horizontal strips of leather and metal lames tied together by cloth lacing, that incorporated a number of shield-like features, including: a box-shaped skirt of four tasses that settled around the warrior's saddle and protected his waist and thighs; a curved neck shield of lame strips that hung from the helmet down to the shoulders; and so-called "great sleeves" (ō-sode) that were like flexible boards draped over the shoulders and upper arms and, along with the neck shield, provided cover from the front when the warrior crouched over the pommel of his saddle.

When the warriors in a battle ran out of arrows (each had about 24 in his quiver), they fought, one-against-one, with swords. The aim of the warrior was not so much to deal a mortal blow, which was difficult from horseback, but to unseat the enemy, then leap down and kill him with a dirk. As a trophy of victory the warrior took his enemy's head. After the battle, the winning side held an "inspection of heads" (kubi jikken) to determine how rewards should be distributed. Since warriors fought primarily for rewards, usually in lands taken from the defeated, there was a premium in battle on individual heroics, especially those leading to the acquisition of the heads of prominent enemies.

Scholars dispute whether foot soldiers, recruited from the peasantry, were employed in battles in the ancient age. The mounted warrior was usually accompanied into battle by one or two grooms on foot. But did these grooms merely perform such services as caring for the master's horse, looking after his armour and weapons, and collecting the enemy heads he took in battle, or did they also participate in the fighting? Although some scholars claim that the grooms did not fight,[7] there are frequent references in the sources to weapons used in battle that were especially suitable for foot soldiers, such as the naginata, a pole with a large, curved blade at one end, and the kumade or "bear claw" rake. In later narrative picture scrolls (emakimono) depicting ancient warfare we often see men on foot in battle scenes, some wearing only loin cloths and straw sandals, others equipped with helmets and various pieces of armour, who carry not only naginata and bear claw rakes but also bows and arrows and swords.

Whether or not foot soldiers participated in battles during ancient times, they certainly became prominent fighters in the medieval age, which was ushered in by a five-year war, 1180–85, that led to the founding of the Kamakura Shogunate.[8] I will not attempt to give the details of this war, called the Genpei or Minamoto-Taira War because it centered on fighting between branches of the powerful Minamoto and Taira warrior clans for national hegemony (the Minamoto were victorious and founded the Kamakura Shogunate). Suffice it to say that the conflict brought significant changes in warfare. These changes resulted primarily from the vast expansion in fighting caused by the war. Although the struggle for national hegemony between Minamoto and Taira held centre stage, there were uprisings throughout the country, many of which were unrelated to the main Minamoto–Taira contest.

Although armies in the ancient age, as noted above, probably seldom exceeded 1,000 and were usually much smaller, during the Genpei War 1,000-man, 10,000-man, and even larger armies took the field.[9] The records, including the war tales, continue to describe warfare as almost exclusively the pursuit of mounted warriors, but armies numbering thousands or more could not have been staffed exclusively or even mainly by these warriors because the elite class was not large enough. Foot soldiers were undoubtedly used in ever-increasing numbers, although they were not formed into orderly units. They fought individualistically, like their mounted superiors.

The changes in warfare brought by the Genpei War involved not simply a great expansion in the sizes of armies and the incorporation into these of large numbers of foot soldiers, but also the results of violations of the traditionally recognized rules of warfare. If we are to believe some of the more romantically-inspired writings of the ancient age, warfare – or at least some of it – was conducted according to exacting standards of behaviour, including prior consultation between belligerent forces to decide upon the place, day, and time for battle, and the exchange of envoys to mark its start. But even in the ancient age surprise attacks and ambushes were common; and one of the most terrifying and destructive tools in all subsequent warfare in pre-modern times – arson – was already common. I will discuss the particular uses of arson in warfare later. Let me simply note here that it was a readily accessible and very effective method of fighting because almost all buildings in Japan until modern times were made of wood.

The violations of the traditional rules of warfare that contemporary writers pointed out and deplored were committed mainly by foot soldiers. The traditional rules (to the extent that there really were such rules) were concerned mainly with equestrian fighting. They meant little if anything to foot soldiers, and hence we see these soldiers engaging in such "deplorable" practices as shooting at horses instead of their riders, pulling riders off their horses with bear claw rakes and other weapons, and erecting barricades on roads to stop horses and enable the soldiers to shoot at stationary targets.[10]

Despite the incorporation of large numbers of foot soldiers into armies during the Genpei War, the mounted warriors or cavalry units of armies continued to be the decisive forces in battle. It was not until the fourteenth century and the period of more than 60 years of fighting, 1331–92, which began with the overthrow of the Kamakura Shogunate and was resumed during the War Between the Courts, that armies began to be formed around masses of foot soldiers. A new weapon, the spear (*yari*), became especially popular among foot soldiers, although they also continued to use *naginata*, bows and arrows, and swords.

The warrior-led armies of the fourteenth century maintained at least fairly firm control over their foot soldiers, even if they did not organize them into trained infantry units. But the age also witnessed the participation in battles of groups of outlaws – some on foot, some on horseback – who, because of their lawless behaviour and, often, total disregard for any rules of warfare, were labelled "evil bands" (*akutō*) by contemporary diarists and other recorders of the events of the time.[11] Especially common in the central and western provinces, the *akutō* were primarily guerrillas. They specialized in hit-and-run tactics, indiscriminate arson, and pillage, fighting with particular effectiveness in mountainous and other difficult terrain. *Akutō* were also among the leaders in this age in developing mountain-top forts (*jōkaku*) capable of withstanding lengthy sieges by large armies.

There will be much to say about forts later. But let us note that the mighty castles we see in Japan today, which were greatly admired by the European Christian missionaries who visited the country in the late sixteenth and early seventeenth centuries,[12] did not appear until the late 1500s, after the Sengoku age and just a few decades before the Tokugawa Shogunate was founded (in 1600) and warfare ceased. Earlier forts, even during most of Sengoku, comprised fairly simple, sometimes makeshift layouts and structures, whose builders often took advantage of terrain, as in the case of the fourteenth-century mountain-top forts mentioned above.

The siege warfare of the fourteenth century was, however, an exception. Forts (that is, the predecessors of the great castles of the late sixteenth century) were for the most part not regarded by medieval Japanese warriors as places where they intended to make last-ditch stands, or that they wished to defend until reaching some decisive conclusion in battle. The construction of a fort was, for example, usually undertaken with an eye to providing a route of escape. When the fighting went against him, a warrior chief was quick to abandon a fort. If possible, he sought a truce that allowed him to open the fort and depart safely. But even if he had no way to retreat or escape, the lord of a fort was unlikely to fight to the end or to surrender. The warrior's code of honour dictated that he commit suicide, usually by disembowelment (*seppuku*).

Let us return to the Ōnin War, which, as we have seen, began as a decade-long, urban conflict in Kyoto, 1467–77, but can also be regarded as a Japanese Hundred Years' War that spanned the entire Sengoku age, 1467–1568. The most active part of the war as a decade-long conflict was the period 1467–73. After 1473, the year in which the commanders of both armies, Hosokawa Katsumoto and Yamana Sōzen, died of natural causes, the war settled into a near stalement in Kyoto, with the armies camped behind formidable barricades.

Rather than attempt to discuss the countless skirmishes and pitched battles of the Ōnin War, let me instead describe the new kind of fighter, the *ashigaru* or "lightfoot", who emerged at this time and became one of the war's principal scourges. The *ashigaru* were in part the successors to the *akutō*, the "evil bands". *Akutō*, it will be recalled, was a term broadly applied by the Ashikaga Shogunate and other authorities to armed groups whom they regarded as outlaws, groups that included mounted warriors as well as foot soldiers. *Ashigaru*, on the other hand, were exclusively fighters on foot, as their name implies; and inasmuch as they were employed by both the eastern and western armies during the Ōnin War, they could not so readily be labelled outlaws. What they inherited from the *akutō* was their rampaging fighting style, and in this regard they were considered by many in Kyoto – for example, members of the effete courtier class – not only as outlaws but also as subhuman and a threat to civilization itself.[13] Eventually, during later Sengoku times, *ashigaru* became a respectable term, applied to members of the trained infantry units that warrior commanders developed. But during the Ōnin War the *ashigaru* were the perpetrators of many, if not most, of the worst horrors of that devastating conflict.

The *ashigaru* were recruited from among the common folk of Kyoto and the surrounding countryside. They are described in the records as "fleet of foot" and as capable of "flying" through the streets of the city. Sometimes they possessed partial suits of armour, but more often lacked all armour and were scantily dressed, often even in cold weather wearing only loincloths and straw sandals. Although they horrified many Kyoto residents, the *ashigaru* were seen as dashing figures by others, and as the war progressed young men eagerly sought to join their ranks.[14]

The *ashigaru* used a variety of weapons, including the *naginata* and spear (*yari*). They fought as urban guerrillas, sparing nothing that got in their way. But they inflicted their greatest damage through arson, not hesitating to torch even the venerable Buddhist temples and Shinto shrines that were among the greatest treasures of Kyoto, the "flowery capital", which from the late eighth century had been the cradle of higher culture and civilization in Japan. In mid-1467, the first year of the war, a court diarist dolefully noted: "From Funaoka Mountain in the north to Second Avenue in the south, the fires blaze day and night".[15] By the end of the first year, most of the upper half of the city and a substantial part of the lower half had been reduced to ashes. When the war reached its conclusion in 1477, the damage was so extensive that Kyoto almost literally lay in ruins. Although the *ashigaru* were not responsible for all the damage, they inflicted much of it. A prominent courtier wrote: "Although there have been periods of strife in the country since earliest times, the term '*ashigaru*' cannot be found in any of the ancient records . . . The *ashigaru* who have appeared for the first time now have exceeded [in evilness?] even the *akutō*. The destruction of shrines, temples, and courtier residences inside and outside the city has been their doing".[16]

The decade-long, Kyoto-centred Ōnin War did not so much end as peter out. The ostensible cause of the war, the dispute over succession to the office of shogun, was settled as early as 1473, when Yoshimasa's son, rather than his brother, succeeded him. After 1473, the war had no central purpose, but became a jumble of private disputes among the combatants, with warrior chieftains and their families, including the divided Shiba and Hatakeyama, frequently changing sides, breaking pacts, and concluding new alliances. Gradually, units of warriors began to leave the city, and finally, in 1477, the last of them departed.

After 1477 the Ashikaga Shogunate, which derived most of its strength from its network of provincial constables, became little more than a nominal government, as the constable network itself collapsed. Even those constable families that survived the 1467–77 war and its aftermath retained only tenuous ties with the Shogunate. Much of the country lapsed into disunion, and fighting raged everywhere. The upheaval that occurred at all levels of society during this age, from peasants rising against estate proprietors to warrior vassals betraying their lords, has been aptly described as *gekokujō*, "those below overthrow those above".

Beginning in the last years of the fifteenth century, a new class of warrior chieftains gradually emerged in the provinces to carve out domains which they proceeded to rule as virtually independent states. Historians call these chieftains Sengoku daimyos, employing a term, *daimyō*, that literally means "big name" and can be traced back to the ancient age as a designation for warriors with many followers. In some cases, pre-Ōnin constables made the transition to become Sengoku daimyos; in other cases, men emerged from obscurity to achieve daimyo status. But most Sengoku daimyos rose from the ranks of local warrior leaders, many of whom were former vassals of constables.[17] The Sengoku daimyos as a whole ruled smaller domains than the pre-Ōnin constables, but they ruled them far more firmly and, as mentioned above, independently of Shogunate authority.

In warrior society during the Sengoku age family status meant little. Even those Sengoku daimyos who inherited their offices had to prove themselves by their ability, especially the ability to lead their vassals in war. In an age of pervasive militarism, many vassals were ready to abandon or even rebel against their daimyo lords if the lords proved incompetent. Vassals thirsted for additional lands, and since these could only be provided through "foreign" conquest (that is, the conquest of lands outside one's own domain), many Sengoku daimyos were obliged to fight year after year beyond their borders, in some cases leading their armies on two or more campaigns a year into other domains. This is not to suggest that the daimyos themselves were loath to undertake such campaigns. In the violent, predatory world of Sengoku, the successful daimyo was by definition a man of vigorous military action.

As an example of the great appetite for war-making of some Sengoku daimyos, let us look at the rivalry for supremacy that was enacted in east-central and eastern Honshu in the mid-sixteenth century between two of the most prominent and belligerent daimyos, Takeda Shingen and Uesugi Kenshin.

The Takeda family had held the constableship of Kai, a mountainous, land-locked province (containing Mt. Fuji) immediately to the west of the Kantō, since the Kamakura period. Shingen's father, Takeda Nobutora, who assumed the family headship in 1507, became one of the few constables to make the transition to Sengoku daimyo. In 1541, as part of his campaigning outside Kai, Nobutora led his army into Shinano, a large province directly to the north of Kai that was agriculturally rich but lacked a strong overall ruler (that is, a Sengoku daimyo). Ruggedly-featured like Kai, Shinano was blanketed with mountains and valleys in which petty warrior families constantly feuded among themselves. Nobutora's intrusion into Shinano had no grand purpose, such as the conquest of the province. Like the vast majority of Sengoku daimyo military campaigns it was a brief operation whose duration was governed in part by the need for the members of Nobutora's army to maintain supervision of their agricultural lands back in Kai during the planting and harvesting seasons. Nobutora simply wished to seize some lands over the border from Kai, and did so successfully after decisively defeating one of the local warrior chiefs in battle.

A scant ten days after Nobutora returned victoriously to Kai, he was abruptly and unceremoniously driven from the province by his oldest son, Shingen. Historians are at a loss to explain this startling act of *gekokujō*, although son turning against father was hardly unusual in the Sengoku age. If a Sengoku daimyo had to be constantly alert to the possibility of rebellion by his vassals, he needed to be doubly attentive to traitorous behavior by kin, since fratricide, parricide, and the like were commonplace in daimyo families as well as those of lesser chieftains.

Leadership was of such importance in the Sengoku age that many daimyos sought to envelop themselves in cults of personality. None was more successful at this than Takeda Shingen, who adopted for himself the motto, taken from Sun-Tzu, "Swift as the wind, silent as the forest, aggressive as fire, immovable as a mountain",[18] and established the myth that he was an "ever victorious" commander, incapable of being defeated. Both contemporaries and people of later ages have celebrated Shingen as the epitome, both personally and symboli-cally, of the martial spirit of Sengoku.

In 1542, following his banished father's lead, Shingen led an army into

61

Shinano to defeat another petty chieftain just over the Kai border and to seize more land. For more than a decade thereafter he campaigned annually in Shinano, sometimes entering it twice in a year, until he had asserted his control over nearly the entire province. Meanwhile, as Shingen penetrated ever northward through Shinano, he inevitably came into confrontation with Uesugi Kenshin, daimyo of Echigo province on the Japan Sea coast, whose domain bordered Shinano to the north.

Kenshin's father, a local warrior and vice-constable of Echigo, had taken the first step to becoming a Sengoku daimyo in 1507 when, in another sensational act of *gekokujō*, he murdered his lord, the Echigo constable. The father was succeeded as family head in 1536 by his oldest son, who, in 1548, was pushed aside in still another act of *gekokujō* by his younger brother, Kenshin. Assuming the title of Echigo constable and emerging as a Sengoku daimyo, Kenshin, a brilliant military commander, became a major player in the politics and warfare that swirled through the provinces of east-central and eastern Honshu in the mid-sixteenth century.

Before discussing the battles fought by Uesugi Kenshin and Takeda Shingen, let me comment on Sengoku warrior politics, much of which was conducted through marriage relations. The Sengoku daimyos used sisters, daughters, and other female kin as marriage pawns in ways that often created bewildering webs of inter-family relationships. Thus in 1554 Takeda Shingen entered into a farrago of nuptial bonds with two neighboring daimyos, Imagawa Yoshimoto to the south and Hōjō Ujiyasu to the east, as part of a Three-Domain Pact (*Sankoku Dōmei*). Sengoku pacts such as this were seldom intended as more than short-term arrangements, and were fragile even during their lifetimes. All three of the daimyos who joined this pact – Shingen, Yoshimoto, and Ujiyasu – had intruded militarily into each other's domains at one time or another in the past. Nevertheless, in 1554 it served their mutual purposes to establish an alliance: Imagawa Yoshimoto wanted the alliance in order to be free to expand territorially into Tōtōmi and Mikawa provinces to his west; Hōjō Ujiyasu desired it so he could concentrate on consolidating his hold over the extensive Hōjō domain (four to five provinces) in the Kantō; and Takeda Shingen wished to use the alliance to protect his eastern and western flanks as he continued his northward aggression in Shinano. Specifically, Shingen hoped to neutralize two neighboring daimyos, Yoshimoto and Ujiyasu, in order to be able to direct his attention fully on to what was developing as a major clash with Uesugi Kenshin.

The marriage ties upon which the Three-Domain Pact was based were: Ujiyasu's daughter married Yoshimoto's son; Yoshimoto's daughter married Shingen's son; Shingen's daughter married Ujiyasu's son. In addition, Shingen adopted another son of Ujiyasu.

Unfortunately, the main sources of information we have about the campaigns between Takeda Shingen and Uesugi Kenshin in the 1550s and 1560s are early-seventeenth-century writings that are not fully reliable as history. One of these sources, for example, claims that Shingen and Kenshin fought no less than 12 times at or near Kawanakajima in northern Shinano.[19] Modern historians have agreed that there were, in fact, only five Kawanakajima battles – in 1553, 1555, 1557, 1561, and 1564 – and that only two of them, the 1555 and 1561 battles (especially the latter), were major encounters.[20] Nevertheless, the fact that two Sengoku daimyos took the field against each other so persistently over such a long period of time and at the same place was itself unusual. It was much more common for two Sengoku daimyos, if they found themselves fighting battles to a draw, to conclude a peace. Each would then direct his aggression elsewhere.[21] In any case, even during the years when Shingen and Kenshin were transforming the previously obscure place name of Kawanakajima into a synonym for relentless warfare, both daimyos, but especially Kenshin, also campaigned repeatedly in the Kantō. Kenshin's principal target in the Kantō was Hōjō Ujiyasu, one of Shingen's allies in the Three-Domain Pact, and Shingen's purpose there was to thwart Kenshin.

Both Shingen and Kenshin claimed victory after each of the Kawanakajima battles, and, from their differing perspectives, both were probably correct. Kenshin achieved what appears to have been his primary aim of preventing Shingen from invading Echigo; and Shingen was never deterred by the battles from continuing to pursue his longstanding goal of incorporating all of Shinano into his domain. Yet, from the larger perspective of events transpiring in Japan in the middle sixteenth century both Shingen and Kenshin were also losers at Kawanakajima. A competition was brewing among the leading Sengoku daimyos to undertake the task of unifying the country and, while Shingen and Kenshin, both of whom avidly aspired to become the unifier, repeatedly butted their heads together at Kawanakajima, another daimyo, Oda Nobunaga of Owari province, seized the initiative, and, beginning in 1560, took the first great steps toward unification.

Nobunaga's advance to national power occurred during a technological revolution in Japanese warfare in the second half of the sixteenth century that was sparked by the introduction of guns from Europe in 1543 (1542, according to European records). But before commenting on guns and their adoption for use by Nobunaga and other Sengoku daimyos, let me discuss in more detail the methods and techniques of Sengoku-period warfare.

We have observed that most battles during Sengoku (that is, before the rise of Nobunaga in the 1560s) were for limited objectives. Typically, one daimyo entered the domain of another on a campaign to seize land. Such a campaign usually lasted, at most, about a month or so, since, as already mentioned, the daimyo had to be careful not to allow his campaigning to interfere with the seasonal planting and harvesting. His foot soldiers were peasants and might break ranks and return home if they were needed there for essential agricultural work.[22] Thus, Uesugi Kenshin, in a series of annual forays into the Kantō beginning in 1560, always set out from Echigo in late autumn and returned before spring. Wintering in the Kantō, he had to plan his battles for times when there was no snow.

Most Sengoku battles were brief, lasting less than a day, and by and large the daimyos avoided pitched battles, preferring to skirmish. The main reason for avoiding pitched battles was the daimyos' wish to keep their own losses to a minimum. There were always future battles to be fought and campaigns to be conducted, and the daimyos' resources in men and supplies were limited.[23] If two daimyos fought a desperate and bloody battle, both might find their armies so weakened that they became easy targets for other daimyos in search of prey. Uesugi Kenshin, however, appears to have been an exception in this regard since he repeatedly sought head-to-head showdowns with Takeda Shingen at Kawanakajima. The fourth battle, in 1561, nearly became such a showdown. But for the most part Shingen was able to avoid major clashes and to limit the Kawanakajima battles to light skirmishing.

Forts were ubiquitous in the Sengoku age (it has been estimated that some 40,000 forts and castles were built in pre-modern Japan, most of them during this age), and much of the game of war involved the taking and losing of forts. The principal forts in early and mid-Sengoku were mountain-top fortifications (*yamajiro*). In the beginning daimyos and other chieftains lived at the base of the mountain and only entered the fort for purposes of defence against attack. Later, the mountain-top forts were enlarged to include also residential quarters, and were often built on levelled-off steps of land leading down from the mountain's summit. Among the defensive installations of these forts were moats (*hori*, usually dry moats), packed dirt ramparts (*dorui*), wooden palisades (*saku*), and watchtowers (*yagura*) from which archers and, later, gunners could shoot.

In addition to their main forts (*honjō*), daimyos and other chieftains often had branch forts (*shijō*). The daimyo family of Hōjō in the Kantō, for example, had a vast network of branch forts and even sub-branch forts (*mata-shijō*), separated one from another by, on average, about five kilometres.[24] Most of these branch and sub-branch forts were not as substantially constructed or as well-situated topographically (for purposes of defence) as the main, mountain-top forts. Nonetheless, they served various important purposes: some were intended as impediments to enemy travel; others served as communication centres or observation posts; some stood guard at borders; others were used primarily for garrisoning troops. In preparing to attack a strong fort, a commander might, on occasion, build still another kind of fort, a "facing fort" (*mukai-jō*), which he used as a base from which to launch his attack.

Forts appeared and disappeared with frequency. Takeda Nobutora, for example, is reported to have destroyed 36 enemy forts in a single day while campaigning in Shinano in 1540.[25] And when a daimyo such as Nobutora or his son Shingen took land in an enemy domain, he typically erected new forts, some in just a day or two.

As noted, sieges were not common during most of the Sengoku age. Attackers wished to avoid sieges for some of the same reasons they sought to avoid pitched battles and long campaigns: they wanted to keep their own losses in men and materiel to a minimum, and they feared that long sieges might result in desertions from their armies.[26] Sometimes attacking chieftains allowed all the defenders of a fort to evacuate to freedom if they surrendered without fighting. In other cases all were allowed to leave except the fort commander, who was obliged to commit suicide. If the fort commander, on the other hand, persisted in prolonging a defence that seemed hopeless, his soldiers might rebel, seize him, and present him, alive or dead, to the besieging commander in the hope that they might be allowed to go free.

Arson was a tool commonly used in attacks on forts. Sometimes attackers simply burned forts down, often with flaming arrows, although defending commanders tried to minimize the effectiveness of such arrows by smearing the walls of their forts with mud. Attackers frequently – one might almost say, regularly – burned the villages and fields surrounding forts. One reason for doing this was psychological intimidation of the forts' defenders, another (in the case of field burning), to hurt the enemy economically, and a third, to destroy the homes of local soldiers who were among the defenders.

A factor that often governed the strategic decision-making of Sengoku commanders in battles, including attacks on forts, was treachery. We are told that Nobunaga, on the eve of one of his greatest battles (and greatest victories),[27] refused to discuss strategy with his leading commanders when the commanders met in what they supposed was a war council. Instead, Nobunaga donned resplendent robes and danced a classical dance on a *nō* stage that he had had built in his main fort. On the way back to their quarters the commanders agreed that Nobunaga was a fool.[28] But Nobunaga feared that, through the treachery of one or more of the commanders, word might be transmitted to the enemy about his battle plans.

Nobunaga himself was a master at persuading the vassals of enemy daimyos and other chieftains to turn coat and join him. It was his policy, when he secured a turncoat, to act immediately in order to use the betrayal to maximum advantage in battle. Thus, for example, in planning an attack on an enemy main fort, Nobunaga might secretly try to lure the commander of a supporting fort to betray the main one. If successful, Nobunaga promptly attacked, both to avoid giving the turncoat time to reconsider and to take full advantage, if possible, of the shock and disarray likely to be caused within the main fort when its occupants learned of the betrayal.[29]

The frequency of treachery and betrayal indicates the unstable nature of many relationships in warrior society during the Sengoku age. As mentioned earlier, vassals frequently abandoned or rebelled against their lords. Foot soldiers also often absconded and sometimes betrayed their commanders. When, for example, the defenders of a fort were allowed to evacuate to freedom as a condition to surrendering the fort, it was not unusual for some or even all of the evacuating soldiers to join the ranks of the attacking army.

On occasion a fort's commander, in offering to surrender, requested that he himself be accepted as a vassal of the attacking commander. A number of besieged commanders, for example, made this request of Nobunaga during his years of campaigning. In some cases Nobunaga refused the request and either ordered the besieged commander to commit suicide or left him with no alternative. In other cases Nobunaga granted the request, but demanded that, as a token of loyalty, the new vassal present him with hostages, such as his mother and one or more sons. It was understood by both parties that if, at a later time, the new vassal turned against him, Nobunaga would not hesitate to execute the hostages and might do so in a humiliating and cruel manner.

Spies were everywhere in the Sengoku age. For fear of espionage, the daimyos in their domainial laws prohibited most forms of intercourse and communication with the inhabitants of other domains, warning those living on the domainial borders to be especially circumspect in their behaviour. We have noted that Nobunaga, on the eve of a battle, suspected that at least one of his commanders might be a spy. Women kin of daimyos who were married into other daimyo families were often suspected of spying. For this reason, an article in the domainial code of the Takeda cautioned warriors with wives obtained through political marriages to keep their swords handy at all times, even when sleeping at night.[30]

The Japanese were exposed to the use of gunpowder during the Mongol invasions in 1274 and 1281, when the Mongol forces of China, landing in northern Kyushu, launched exploding balls at them from catapults.[31] It is also recorded that a type of Chinese gun, which was probably more like a firing tube than a real gun, was introduced to Japan during the Ōnin War. Otherwise, as far as we can tell, the Japanese had no experience with, or knowledge of, gunpowder or guns until, in the eighth month of 1543, some Portuguese traders, probably sailing in a Chinese junk that was blown off course during a storm while headed for Macao, touched shore at the small island of Tanegashima off the southeastern coast of Kyushu. They were the first Europeans to set foot on Japanese soil.

Among their goods the Portuguese traders had two guns – muzzle-loading, matchlock arquebuses – that they either gave or sold to the daimyo of

Tanegashima. Fascinated with these devices, the daimyo immediately set about having guns made in his domain.[32] Subsequently, the knowledge of gunmaking that was painfully acquired by the first gunmakers of Tanegashima was transmitted to the central provinces, where several gun foundries were established. Within a few years, perhaps as early as 1549, guns were used in battle by Japanese warriors. By the late 1550s and early 1560s, most of the leading daimyos had troops equipped with guns. It is recorded, for example, that Takeda Shingen had 300 guns at the battle of Kawanakajima in 1555.[33]

But guns and ammunition were not easy to obtain in quantity. One problem was that sodium nitrate (saltpetre), an essential ingredient of gunpowder, was not available in Japan and had to be imported. Nevertheless, gun units soon became the central features of Sengoku daimyo armies. The formation of gunners into separate units and their training to function cohesively led simultaneously to the creation and training of units of spearmen and archers. The major problem in using the muzzle-loading guns was, of course, the time needed to reload.[34] Gunners standing still to reload their weapons were easy targets for the enemy. Hence, gunners had to be supported by spearmen and archers to keep the fighting going during the pauses in gunfire.

Nobunaga demonstrated the importance he attached to guns when, as he began the unification of the country, he quickly asserted control over the port city of Sakai at the eastern end of the Inland Sea (near today's Osaka), which possessed probably the largest gun foundry in Japan, and over Kunitomo town in Ōmi province, site of another important foundry.

Nobunaga vaulted to prominence and set out on the road to unification with a decisive victory over Imagawa Yoshimoto in 1560. In the fifth month of that year Yoshimoto, then the master of three provinces (Suruga, Tōtōmi, and Mikawa), invaded Nobunaga's domain in Owari, across the border from Mikawa. It has long been thought that Yoshimoto, who led an army of about 40,000, intended to push through Owari and proceed to Kyoto as a first step to unifying the country. But scholars today are inclined to believe that Yoshimoto's purpose was much more limited. With his rear protected by the Three-Domain Pact, he apparently sought merely to seize part of eastern Owari, where he already had forts and landholdings.[35]

It has also been thought that Nobunaga, who had a much smaller army than Yoshimoto, perhaps numbering only 5,000, carefully planned and executed a surprise attack that caught the Imagawa completely off guard while they were bivouacking. And indeed Okehazama has come down in the military annals of Japan as not only a brilliant victory but also as a model of strategic excellence by means of which a small force might defeat a larger one. Thus, for example, in the days leading to Pearl Harbor in 1941, Admiral Yamamoto Isoroku and other Japanese military leaders, writing in their diaries, frequently likened their planned attack on Pearl Harbor to Okehazama.[36] To them, an Okehazama-type surprise attack was sound strategy for a poor country like Japan when fighting a rich one like the United States. To the Americans, on the other hand, the Pearl Harbor attack was an act of heinousness and "infamy" perhaps unparalleled in the history of warfare.

Okehazama was certainly a brilliant victory, helped immeasurably by a sudden downpour that blanketed the Imagawa camp and its environs right before Nobunaga's attack at about 2 pm. When the rain stopped as quickly as it had started, Nobunaga and his attackers instantly fell upon the totally bewildered Imagawa army. The army was routed and its daimyo leader, Yoshimoto, killed.[37] The question is, however, whether Okehazama was a strategically-planned attack. In fact, it appears not to have been. Nobunaga, who received good intelligence reports and was always aware of the enemy's position and actions, was feeling his way toward Yoshimoto, brushing aside the Imagawa advance forces and presumably hoping to pressurize the main Imagawa army into withdrawing from Owari. But, as he approached the main army, Nobunaga was presented with a golden opportunity to launch a full-scale surprise attack by the fortuitous rain shower, and did so. Although he could not have known it at the time, Nobunaga caught the Imagawa completely off guard, not only because of the rain shower, but also because the Imagawa scouts and advance forces had failed to provide Yoshimoto with any significant intelligence about Nobunaga's whereabouts or movements. Thus, the rain shower and the failure of Imagawa intelligence contributed as much as anything to Nobunaga's victory at Okehazama.

Famous in history as the master of the surprise attack because of Okehazama, Nobunaga in fact never again used this strategy in any of his major battles.[38] On the contrary, he achieved some of his finest victories – for example, at Anegawa in 1570 and at Nagashino in 1575 – by establishing strong defensive positions and repelling attacks. But, if we shift our gaze from Nobunaga's great battles to the countless lesser fights, skirmishes, and sieges that he engaged in over the years, we see that, by and large, he fought in the manner of the typical Sengoku daimyo. He usually avoided all-out clashes, sought to minimize his losses in men and materiel, and constantly played what might be called the game of "fort monopoly", by which the players (the daimyos and other warrior chieftains) spent much of their time building, destroying, attacking, defending, seizing and losing forts. Like the other Sengoku daimyos, indeed probably to a greater extent than any of them, Nobunaga also used politics and diplomacy, to paraphrase Clausewitz, as "warfare by other means".[39] He and the other daimyos readily entered into alliances and, just as readily, voided or violated them when it served their purpose. On occasion these hardbitten commanders even sacrificed hostages, including women kin bestowed upon rivals in marriage, by unilaterally violating alliances and virtually inviting their rivals to execute the hostages.

Nobunaga formed one alliance, however, that was enduring and that contributed immensely to his success as a unifier. After the battle of Okehazama, Tokugawa Ieyasu of Mikawa province, who had provided a unit for Imagawa Yoshimoto's army, became Nobunaga's follower (actually, his lesser ally); and from then until Nobunaga's death in 1582, Ieyasu fought frequently with Nobunaga, sharing with him a few defeats but also several of his greatest victories.

Nobunaga entered Kyoto in 1568, receiving recognition as the emergent unifier both from the emperor and the Ashikaga shogun, Yoshiaki. Yoshiaki, whom Nobunaga helped assume his office, expected that he would exercise supreme political power, but Nobunaga intended to use him merely as a figurehead. When Yoshiaki persisted in grasping for power and even conspired with Nobunaga's enemies, Nobunaga deposed him and, in effect, dissolved the Ashikaga Shogunate (1573). From that time Nobunaga was the country's *de facto* ruler, although he held no official office.[40]

Nobunaga's entry into Kyoto in 1568 is usually taken to mark the end of the Sengoku age (1467–1568) and the beginning of the age of unification (1568–90). In terms of larger historical divisions, 1568 was the last year of the medieval period (1185–1568) and the first year of the early-modern period (1568–1867). Although I stated above that Nobunaga fought largely in the manner of the typical Sengoku daimyo, from 1568 the force of events that accompanied his rise as an anointed unifier brought changes that steadily led to a grander and more strategic style of warfare in Japan. In the 1570s and early 1580s Nobunaga was the prime mover in the transition to this style, but in 1582 his life was cut short by assassination before it was completed. It fell to his successor, Toyotomi Hideyoshi, who had risen in Nobunaga's service from lowly sandal-bearer to leading general, to perfect the new style of warfare. Expanding strategic planning to the national level and leading vastly larger armies than Nobunaga, Hideyoshi conducted a series of great campaigns to distant regions to bring the entire country under his hegemonic control, by 1590.

To summarize the major developments and changes to warfare in the age of unification:

1. The continuing technological revolution, reflected in the ever greater use of guns. While, for example, Takeda Shingen is said to have had three hundred gunners in his army at the 1555 battle of Kawanakajima, the records mention several occasions during the 1570s when either Nobunaga or his enemies brought "three thousand" guns into action in battle. Moreover, Nobunaga himself is credited with developing a method of salvo fire – gunners, formed into

ranks, shooting in sequence – that greatly increased the overall striking force of his army.[41]

2. The construction of castles and their use in withstanding sieges. The age of unification was also the great age of castle-building in Japan. Unlike the forts of Sengoku times, the most impressive of which could hardly be called "mighty" and which often relied on mountain-top locations to enhance their defensibility, the unification-age castles, built first on the flat summits of low-lying mountains or hills (*hirayamajiro*) and, later, on open plains (*hirajiro*), were mighty fortresses indeed. Built with massive stone walls, circled by broad moats, and centred on soaring donjons that reached up to seven stories skyward, these castles were, in some cases, virtually impregnable strongholds. Moreover, in addition to meeting the defensive needs of their masters during a time that witnessed a rapid evolution in and expansion of siege warfare, the castles became ostentatious symbols of the power and grandeur of the unifiers and daimyos as well as hubs in the development by them of castle towns (*jōkamachi*), a number of which subsequently grew into imposing cities.[42] Nobunaga, a leader in the technological revolution in warfare through the adoption of guns, took the lead also in castle-building, constructing in 1576 the grandest castle of his day at Azuchi on the shore of Lake Biwa, not far from Kyoto.

3. Larger, more permanently maintained armies. We noted that, for the most part, the Sengoku daimyos were obliged to limit the durations of their campaigns – indeed, to conduct primarily seasonal campaigns – because they could not keep their farmer-soldiers away from home during planting and harvesting. Even the warrior-officers of the daimyos' armies often needed to return home during those times in order to direct the agricultural work. In the age of unification, the process of separation of farmers and warriors (*heinō bunri*) was greatly accelerated; and as armies grew enormously in size – from perhaps a maximum of 30,000–60,000 during Sengoku to Hideyoshi's massive forces of 100,000 and even 250,000 – they comprised ever greater numbers of full-time, professional fighters. The upper echelons of the warrior class, in particular, were increasingly drawn into residence in their lords' castle towns, where they were kept on permanent call for military service.

Although from 1568 Nobunaga was the presumptive unifier, recognized by both emperor and shogun, he was by no means without rivals. Takeda Shingen, for one, still aspired to destroy Nobunaga and assume the mantle of unifier, as did Shingen's longtime foe, Uesugi Kenshin. But more challenging for Nobunaga than any single daimyo rival was the formation, from about 1570, of an anti-Nobunaga league. Membership of this league changed over the decade of the 1570s, in part because Nobunaga was able to destroy, one at a time, some of its leading participants, such as the Asai and Rokkaku of Ōmi province, the Asakura of Echizen, and, finally, the Takeda of Kai. One diehard member of the league was Ashikaga Yoshiaki, who conspired with it both before and after he was deposed as shogun in 1573 by Nobunaga. But, collectively, the most formidable participants in the anti-Nobunaga league over the years were those followers of the True Sect of Pure Land Buddhism who were organized into confederacies (*ikkō ikki*)[43] in provinces throughout the central and east-central regions, including Kii, Ōmi, Echizen, and Kaga.

All of these confederacies had repeatedly challenged and, at times, disrupted the rule of the daimyos of their respective provinces; one, the Kaga confederacy, had even administered its province without a daimyo from the late fifteenth century. Individually, each confederacy was a force to be reckoned with by Nobunaga as he sought to impose his hegemony over the land, radiating outward from the central region. But the problem of dealing with the confederacies was greatly complicated by the fact that all were subordinate to and took orders from the central temple of the True Sect of Pure Land Buddhism, the Ishiyama Honganji of Osaka at the eastern end of the Inland Sea. Honganji was a heavily armed and fortified establishment, whose location at the edge of the Inland Sea prevented encirclement by an army and provided access by water as well as land. For an entire decade, 1570–80, Nobunaga fought a sporadic war with Honganji and its provincial confederacies, which involved periodic sieges. On several occasions he suffered sharp defeats, especially in attacks he launched against Honganji itself. Not until 1580, after defeating and destroying one provincial confederacy after another and constructing a navy of what may have been the world's first ironclad ships to blockade Honganji from the sea,[44] was Nobunaga finally able to force the temple to surrender and open its gates.

Nobunaga is generally regarded, with good reason, as the most brutal commander of a brutal age, and he committed some of his most ghastly atrocities in warfare against those temples and religious confederacies that opposed him militarily. When fighting daimyos and other warrior chiefs, Nobunaga's aim, in most cases, was to defeat and destroy the leaders. Once victory was achieved, he did not usually seek to inflict further suffering on the enemy's rank-and-file soldiers. Indeed, as noted earlier, he sometimes sought to absorb defeated enemy soldiers into his own army. In battling with the armies of temples and religious confederacies, on the other hand, Nobunaga often pursued a strategy of extermination, evidently reasoning that his enemies were sectarian zealots who, if not exterminated, would only continue to fight on and on against him. Thus, for example, in one of his most notorious campaigns of extermination, Nobunaga in 1574 laid siege to and totally destroyed several forts occupied by members of the Pure Land confederacy of Nagashima in Ise province, with whom he had fought periodically for several years. When the occupants of one of the Nagashima forts, their food exhausted, pleaded for mercy, Nobunaga refused and said he intended to see them starve to death (many already had starved to death).[45] Meanwhile, he burned another of the forts to the ground, incinerating everyone within. The forts contained people of both sexes and all ages. In total, Nobunaga is said to have slaughtered as many as twenty thousand members of the Nagashima confederacy at this time.[46]

A leading member of the anti-Nobunaga league in the early 1570s, as noted, was the redoubtable Takeda Shingen, who at long last found himself in a promising position to try to supplant Nobunaga as the unifier. In 1572 Shingen invaded Tōtōmi province, the territory of Tokugawa Ieyasu, and defeated a combined force of Nobunaga and Ieyasu (battle of Mikatagahara). Poised to move next into the central provinces, Shingen died suddenly in 1573. He was succeeded as Takeda head by his son Katsuyori, who was a ferocious warrior but lacked his father's political sagacity and strategic skills.

Determined, if possible, to outdo his father in aggressiveness, Katsuyori continued the fighting against Tokugawa Ieyasu in Tōtōmi, even capturing a key fort that Shingen had failed to take. And in the fifth month of 1575 Katsuyori entered neighbouring Mikawa province, where he laid siege to another Tokugawa fort, held by one of Ieyasu's vassals, at Nagashino. Ieyasu sent a desperate plea for aid to Nobunaga, who rushed with an army to the scene. Nobunaga, however, chose not to fight the Takeda at the place of the siege; rather, with Ieyasu and his main army, he established a defensive position a short distance to the west. The stage was set for one of the most celebrated battles in Japanese history.

Called the battle of Nagashino, even though it was not actually fought at Nagashino but nearby, this encounter is famous in part because it marked the beginning of the end for the mighty Takeda house. But its greater fame lies in the fact that it is believed to have proved, once and for all, the decisive superiority of guns over horses. Nobunaga is said to have had 3,000 gunners positioned in ranks both in front of and behind a long row of wooden palisades (*saku*). Takeda Katsuyori, leading a 15,000-man army spearheaded by the most renowned cavalry in the land, attacked the combined Oda–Tokugawa host (perhaps 38,000) again and again, and each time his warriors were mowed down by the enemy gunners, firing in salvoes.

In the late 1570s Nobunaga launched a major campaign aimed at expanding his control into western Honshu, much of which lay within the broad domain of the Mōri family, whose castle town was at Yamaguchi in Nagato province at Honshu's westernmost end. The principal commanders in charge of this campaign were Akechi Mitsuhide and Toyotomi Hideyoshi. It was during this time that Hideyoshi, who had risen from a peasant background in Nobunaga's home province of Owari, distinguished himself as a brilliant strategist and field commander, especially in the siege warfare that flourished along with the construction of great castles in the age of unification.

One of Hideyoshi's most celebrated sieges was that of Tottori castle, a fortification near the shore of the Japan Sea in Inaba province. Tottori castle was, in fact, probably more of a Sengoku-type fort than a unification-period castle since it was located atop a mountain (*yamajiro*). In any case, Hideyoshi, judging that the castle would be very difficult to take by frontal assault because of its elevated location, commenced a siege of it beginning in the seventh month of 1581. The occupants of the castle numbered some 4,000, approximately half of whom were non-combatants, including women and children. Hideyoshi launched his siege with a clamour of firepower aimed at intimidating those in the castle, even burning torches at night to keep the area ablaze with light while his warriors continued firing their weapons, which included cannon. Severing the castle's contacts with its branch forts, Hideyoshi created an airtight circle of containment around it that included wooden palisades, earthen works, "facing forts" (*mukai-jiro*), and ships deployed as a blockade in the mouth of the river that flowed below the castle into the Japan Sea. Once the circle was completed, Hideyoshi was able to prevent all attempts by the Mōri and others to send men and supplies to the castle by land or by sea.[47]

The effectiveness of Hideyoshi's siege of Tottori castle lay not only in the meticulous care and thoroughness with which he conducted it, but also in his imaginative preparation beforehand. Several months prior to launching the siege, Hideyoshi arranged to have outside merchants enter Inaba and buy up, at highly inflated prices, all the rice available on the province's markets. So tempting were the inflated prices that soldiers garrisoned at Tottori even sold some of the castle's supply of rice. The result was that, once the siege began, the castle had a very limited amount of food. As the siege dragged on, starvation swept through the castle, creating a condition that contemporary sources described as a "living hell". Finally, after four months, the castle's commander sued for peace, and Hideyoshi agreed to spare the lives of the others still alive in the castle in return for the commander's suicide.[48]

Nobunaga was assassinated early in the sixth month of 1582. He had travelled with a small retinue from Azuchi castle to Kyoto, where he lodged at a Buddhist temple. In the early hours of the following morning Akechi Mitsuhide, who was supposed to be campaigning in the west, attacked the temple. Nobunaga and his aides tried to fight back, but were hopelessly outnumbered. The temple was set afire, perhaps by Nobunaga himself, who vanished in the flames.

The distinguished British historian Sir George Sansom says this about Nobunaga: "If his virtues are open to doubt, his vices are unquestionable. He never showed a sign of compassion. His vindictive ruthlessness is apparent from the beginning of his career, when he killed his brother, to his last years, which were filled with wanton slaughter. He became master of twenty provinces at a terrible cost. He was a cruel and callous brute".[49]

Nearly all of the other Oda generals were off campaigning in distant regions when Akechi Mitsuhide attacked and killed Nobunaga in Kyoto. Mitsuhide sought to secure allies to support a claim to become Nobunaga's successor, but had little success. Meanwhile, only one of the other generals acted decisively: Hideyoshi. Quickly settling a siege he was conducting against Takamatsu castle in Bitchū province, Hideyoshi marched with great speed back to the capital, attacked and destroyed Mitsuhide.

Hideyoshi certainly had no better claim to succeed Nobunaga than had at least several of the other Oda generals. In terms of legitimacy, he had no claim at all compared to Nobunaga's surviving sons (the oldest son and heir apparent was killed, along with his father, by Mitsuhide's treachery). Nevertheless, playing on the merit he had achieved as Nobunaga's avenger and utilizing his own considerable political and military skills, Hideyoshi gradually emerged as the successor. His most serious challenge came from Shibata Katsuie, a hereditary vassal of Nobunaga who had been enfeoffed in Echizen province. Hideyoshi's victory over Katsuie at the battle of Shizugatake in Ōmi province in 1583 convinced all who may still have doubted that he was the man to deal with in regard to the future of unification.

At the time of his death Nobunaga controlled perhaps a third of Japan. Admittedly, it was a very important third, since it contained the advanced central provinces. But territorial consolidation had been evolving apace in other parts of the country during this first half of the age of unification; and if he had lived Nobunaga would have faced some very formidable adversaries in those daimyo possessors of multiple-province domains, including the Hōjō in the east, the Mōri in the west, and the Chōsokabe, occupiers of nearly all of the island of Shikoku. One may ask: How successful would Nobunaga have been, with his style of warfare, against adversaries such as these?

Nobunaga was a warrior of conquest. He fought his enemies to the end. Those who lost to him in battle could expect no mercy. He may have occasionally pardoned lesser chieftains, such as the commanders of certain defeated forts, but rival daimyos who failed against him were invariably annihilated. More than that, Nobunaga habitually rounded up and killed the daimyos' wives, children, and even servants. In many cases, he subjected the daimyos themselves to humiliation and debasement in death. At a New Year's Day celebration for his elite personal guard in 1575, for example, Nobunaga brought forth as a visual "hors d'oeuvre" (*sakana*) to be savoured with the drinking of *sake* two lacquered boxes containing the pickled heads of Asai Nagamasa and Asakura Toshikage, whom, after many years of conflict, he had finally driven to their deaths.[50] Nagamasa was in fact Nobunaga's own brother-in-law and, in what appears to have been an unusual act of gallantry before his death by suicide, returned to Nobunaga's care his wife (Nobunaga's sister Ōichi) and their three children.

Hideyoshi was just as capable as Nobunaga of inflicting terrible punishment upon his adversaries. We can observe this in, for example, his siege of Kōzuki castle in western Harima in 1577. After seven days of siege, the castle's soldiers killed their commander, opened the gates of the castle, and presented the commander's head to Hideyoshi. Hideyoshi, however, refused to accept the surrender. Instead, he seized the soldiers and beheaded them. Not stopping there, he took some 200 women and children who were also in the castle and, as an example to others who might consider opposing him, killed them too, skewering the children with spears and crucifying the women.[51]

But, overall, Hideyoshi conducted his battles and dealt with his enemies in a very different manner from Nobunaga. Whereas Nobunaga was a relentless conqueror, Hideyoshi was a negotiator and conciliator. Rather than continue the fighting against the Mōri initiated by Nobunaga, for example, Hideyoshi made peace with them, and subsequently enlisted them as allies in some of his major campaigns of unification. After victory in battle Hideyoshi was often magnanimous, typically allowing defeated commanders (daimyos) and their families to retain parts of their domains in return for swearing allegiance to him.[52] The two most conspicuous recipients of such treatment were the Chōsokabe and Shimazu, whom Hideyoshi vanquished in 1585 and 1587.

Chōsokabe Motochika had been hostile to Hideyoshi since the death of Nobunaga in 1582, and had even schemed with his enemies. Taking advantage of Hideyoshi's preoccupation with other matters, Motochika expanded his control over the entire island of Shikoku. When Hideyoshi in 1585 demanded that he return some of the lands he had taken, Motochika refused. Thereupon Hideyoshi assembled a force, numbering approximately 100,000, that in size exceeded by far anything seen before in Japanese history, and dispatched it to invade Shikoku from three directions. Among the commanders of the force were the Mōri and other chieftains from western Honshu who had fought against Hideyoshi when he campaigned in the west for Nobunaga. The war was no contest. Within weeks Motochika surrendered unconditionally. Hideyoshi divested him of three of the four provinces of Shikoku, but allowed him to keep Tosa, a very substantial domain in itself.

Kyushu Island had a long history of independence. Neither the Kamakura nor Muromachi Shogunates had truly controlled it. During the Sengoku age, the island was the scene of constant conflict as rival daimyos contended for power, first one gaining the upper hand, and then another. By the late 1580s the most powerful daimyo in Kyushu was Shimazu Yoshihisa, leader of a family of ancient roots who was steadily expanding northward from his base in the southernmost province of Satsuma, threatening eventually to consume the entire island. Hideyoshi, in an attempt to end the fighting in Kyushu, demanded that the Shimazu accept the establishment of fixed domainial boundaries, but

Yoshihisa refused. Recruiting soldiers from some 37 provinces, Hideyoshi assembled an expeditionary force of colossal size – perhaps as large as 250,000 – to chastise the Shimazu. Among the commanders of this force were the Mōri and other chieftains of western Honshu and Chōsokabe Motochika of Shikoku. Hideyoshi departed Osaka, where he had his headquarters at the newly-built (and mammoth) Osaka castle, in the first month of 1587, starting out on what became an almost leisurely journey of three months before reaching Kyushu.

Hideyoshi invaded Kyushu along two lines of advance down the eastern and western sides of the island. The Shimazu were able to mount little resistance against such a vast foe. Many Shimazu forts surrendered without being attacked, and a number of Shimazu adherents defected and joined Hideyoshi. Early in the fifth month Shimazu Yoshihisa shaved his head, took Buddhist vows, and surrendered. Hideyoshi accepted the surrender and allowed the Shimazu to keep two provinces and part of a third, thus enabling them to remain one of the richest daimyo families in the country.

Hideyoshi completed unification in 1590 with another massive campaign, this time against the Hōjō of the Kantō. The Hōjō were among the most advanced, socially and institutionally, of all the daimyo families, and had for nearly a century presided over one of the most extensive domains in the land. However, as events were to prove, they were not advanced in their thinking about politics and war. Most tragically for them, the Hōjō did not comprehend that Hideyoshi, in eight years, had completely altered the rules for conducting both politics and war.[53]

Hideyoshi called upon the Hōjō daimyo, Ujinao, to accept his overlordship by the symbolic act of journeying to Kyoto. Ujinao refused to make the journey himself but sent an uncle instead. The uncle informed Hideyoshi that, if he settled a certain land dispute in Kōzuke province in favor of the Hōjō, either Ujinao or his father, Ujimasa, the former daimyo, would come to Kyoto. Hideyoshi gave the Hōjō two-thirds of the land they wanted, and this seemed to settle the matter. But Ujinao, acting unilaterally in the deceptive, predatory manner of a Sengoku daimyo, also took the other third of the land in question. Hideyoshi was enraged, and immediately set about organizing an expeditionary force to chastise the Hōjō.

Hideyoshi's expeditionary force, which numbered more than 200,000 and was recruited from daimyos throughout the country except the east and north, descended upon Odawara castle, the seat of the Hōjō in Sagami province, by land and sea in the third month of 1590. After a dispute over whether to meet the attacking force in open field battle or establish a defensive position by remaining in their castle and numerous branch forts, the Hōjō decided on the latter strategy. Since the Hōjō had only recruited a quarter of the force that Hideyoshi had – about 56,000 – it is hard to see how they could have prevailed in open field battle. Nevertheless, the decision to submit to a siege, urged primarily by Hōjō Ujimasa, was a throwback to Sengoku thinking. Ujimasa recalled how the Hōjō had successfully – and in his mind, gloriously – withstood sieges of Odawara castle by both Uesugi Kenshin and Takeda Shingen. But that was during an age when, for reasons already discussed, commanders did not conduct lengthy sieges. Such recollections as Ujimasa's meant nothing in 1590 when the Hōjō were confronted with attack and siege by the all-conquering Hideyoshi.[54]

Hideyoshi's attackers systematically defeated the Hōjō branch forts. Some capitulated readily; others held out tenaciously, even up to three months. Hideyoshi left no doubt about his intentions toward Odawara castle. His armies would lay siege to it for as long as necessary to force its capitulation. To make that absolutely clear, he invited wives and concubines, entertainers, merchants, and others to the camp at Odawara, enabling his warriors to lead a life of considerable leisure and diversion as they awaited the inevitable outcome of their siege.

Odawara castle capitulated after three months. Ujinao offered to commit suicide in order to save the other occupants of the castle, but Hideyoshi rejected the offer. Instead, he ordered Ujimasa and three others to kill themselves and allowed everyone else to go home. The great Hōjō domain was confiscated, and Ujinao died the following year, 1591. But even on this occasion Hideyoshi displayed a measure of magnanimity to a defeated enemy by allowing Ujinao's successors to become the daimyo family of a minor domain in Kawachi province.

Hideyoshi's last years, from 1590 until his death in 1598, were undoubtedly a time of great fulfillment, as he basked in the extraordinary achievement of unification. Like Nobunaga, he did not take the title of shogun, traditionally the designation of the national military hegemon. He did, however, have himself adopted into the court family of Fujiwara, which enabled him to become imperial regent (*kanpaku*). In ancient times the Fujiwara had used this office to govern the country in the name of the emperor. Now Hideyoshi, as both leading courtier and *de facto* military hegemon, ruled Japan from a status of higher eminence than anyone before, other than the emperor himself.

But Hideyoshi's last eight years also had their dark side. Having conquered Japan, he was led to embark on overseas conquest, launching two disastrously unsuccessful invasions of Korea in 1592–93 and 1597–98. In addition Hideyoshi failed, finally, to provide for a smooth succession to power.

Nobunaga had expressed the desire to undertake conquest on the Asian mainland once he completed the unification of Japan; and Hideyoshi, from at least 1585, began writing in letters to vassals and others of his intention to invade the continent at some time in the future.[55] He started making concrete plans for invasion when he became master of all Japan after the destruction of the Hōjō in the Kantō in 1590. Calling for troop and labour levies from daimyos throughout the country, Hideyoshi assembled a huge expeditionary force of more than 158,000, backed by many thousands more in reserve in Japan.[56]

The scope of Hideyoshi's overseas ambitions was breathtaking. His first target was China, which he planned to conquer by a route leading through Korea. Once China was taken, he would move the Japanese emperor to a new seat in Beijing, and would establish his own continental headquarters in the southern Chinese city of Ningpo. Ningpo, he believed, would be a suitable base for launching an attack against his final target of conquest: India. Meanwhile, Hideyoshi expected the Ryukyus, Taiwan, and the Philippines to submit to Japan.[57] In the event, Hideyoshi was not even able to conquer Korea.

Along with the desire to satisfy his megalomania, Hideyoshi was inspired to invade the continent to keep the military momentum of his unification of Japan going. He saw continental warfare as a means to assert even firmer control over Japan's warrior class, and also to provide new lands to meet the still strong demands of the daimyos for territorial acquisition.[58] The Europeans in Japan at this time had provided much new information to the Japanese about world geography and the known world in general, including East, Southeast, and South Asia. Hence Hideyoshi should have been fairly well informed at least about the geographical risks he faced in invading the continent. But, as one scholar has observed: ". . . ignorance moved [Hideyoshi's] entire enterprise [of continental invasion]".[59] This ignorance can be seen, for example, in the fact that Hideyoshi apparently did not even know that Korea was an independent country, but believed it was subordinate to the Japanese daimyo family of Sō, which ruled the island of Tsushima in the Korea Strait and had traditionally handled Japanese trade with Korea.[60]

When the Koreans refused a request to allow their peninsula to serve as a Japanese corridor for attack on China, Hideyoshi's expeditionary force began invading Korea (landing in Pusan) in the fourth month of 1592.[61] Meeting little resistance from the Koreans, who were woefully unprepared despite foreknowledge of Hideyoshi's plans, the Japanese pushed rapidly northward, capturing Seoul in central Korea within weeks and P'yongyang (the capital of present-day North Korea) shortly thereafter. One branch of the Japanese army drove as far as the northeastern corner of Korea, and even crossed over briefly into Manchuria. During the summer, a Chinese contingent crossed the Yalu River and attacked the Japanese at P'yongyang, but was speedily defeated. Early the following year (1593), however, the Chinese returned in force to drive the Japanese out of P'yongyang and back to Seoul, where Japanese troops wantonly slaughtered Koreans they suspected of colluding with the Chinese and burned much of the city.

As the Japanese found themselves locked in fierce struggle with the Chinese, they also came under increasing harassment everywhere by Korean guerrillas. Although the Japanese had tried to assert administration over the lands they captured in Korea, even contriving a system of taxation, they now found that very little of the land was actually theirs. Guerrilla activities reduced their holdings to little more than the territories around the forts and camps they occupied.

But perhaps most devastating to Japan's cause in Korea was its defeat on water at the hands of the Korean navy under the inspired leadership of Commander Yi Sun-sin. Employing "turtle ships" – vessels with convex decks that carried up to fourteen cannon – Yi Sun-sin denied the Japanese navy access to the Yellow Sea and thus the capacity to supply their troops by water. Instead, the Japanese were forced to try to maintain lengthy supply lines on land, lines that were constantly attacked by Korean guerrillas.

Overall, the Japanese fought well on land in Korea, usually defeating the Korean regular forces easily and winning a number of major battles against the Chinese. By mid-1593, however, the Japanese and Chinese (but not the Koreans), acknowledging that a military stalemate had developed, opened negotiations for peace. These negotiations dragged on for nearly four years, and can only be regarded as one of the more farcical exercises in world diplomatic history. The two sides made almost totally irreconcilable demands, but were deceived into thinking they were working toward agreement by the deceptive dealings of their subordinates. The Chinese expected that the Japanese would withdraw entirely from Korea (a Japanese contingent had remained in forts at the southern tip of the peninsula) in return for which China, the great Middle Kingdom, would deign to appoint Hideyoshi "king" of Japan, thus giving him a title routinely bestowed on the leaders of those countries that accepted an inferior, tributary relationship to China. On the other hand, Hideyoshi, apparently oblivious to the fact that his grandiose invasion had gone awry, expected the Chinese to accept a list of demands, including the cession to Japan of Korea's four southernmost provinces. Not until the very day and hour of the ceremony in 1597 when Chinese envoys to Japan sought to invest Hideyoshi as "king" did Hideyoshi, upon hearing an edict from the Chinese read aloud, finally understand what was happening. Flying into a rage, he verbally abused the Chinese envoys, even threatening them with death, and then peremptorily dismissed them.[62]

Hideyoshi invaded Korea for a second time with a force nearly as great as the one he had dispatched five years earlier in the first invasion. Fierce fighting ensued on land and sea against the Koreans and Chinese. By the next year, 1598, it became clear that the Japanese could not penetrate far up the peninsula. Indeed, their range of action was restricted largely to the territory of the forts they had constructed on Korea's southern coast. There was mounting desire in

Japan to terminate the Korean adventure and, when Hideyoshi died toward the end of the year, a truce was arranged and troop withdrawals begun. Despite the truce, the last Japanese troops got out of Korea only with great difficulty.

For the Japanese, the Korean invasions were utter fiascos. For the Chinese, they were a huge drain on the strength of a dynasty, the Ming, that was already in decline and would fall a half-century later (1644). For the Koreans, the invasions were incalculably devastating, both of life and property. Untold thousands of Koreans were killed, injured, or maimed, many in battle but also many from atrocities committed not only by the Japanese but also by the Koreans' supposed allies, the Chinese. A number of Korea's greatest cities were in ashes, and much of the Korean countryside was laid waste. Years would be required before Korea recovered from these convulsions. Deep-seated animosity toward Japan would continue much longer.

When Hideyoshi died in 1598, he left a son of five, Hideyori, as his appointed successor. He had pleaded with the five greatest daimyos of the land to serve as joint regents (*go-tairō*) for Hideyori until he reached his majority. But almost immediately after Hideyoshi's death one of these daimyos, Tokugawa Ieyasu, began conducting himself as the country's new hegemon.

Ieyasu, it will be recalled, became an adherent of Oda Nobunaga after the battle of Okehazama in 1560, and fought with Nobunaga on many occasions thereafter. When Nobunaga was assassinated in 1582, Ieyasu might have succeeded him as unifier. But Ieyasu happened to be vacationing in the city of Sakai, near Osaka, and by the time he struggled back to the seat of his domain in the east-central region, Hideyoshi had destroyed the assassin, Akechi Mitsuhide, and taken the first steps to become the new unifier. During the next few years Hideyoshi and Ieyasu eyed each other warily, and in 1584 they took the field in battle when Ieyasu, for his own purposes, espoused the cause of one of Nobunaga's sons against Hideyoshi. Ieyasu in fact won this battle (the battle of Komaki-Nagakute in Owari province), but defeat proved only a momentary setback for Hideyoshi. Five years later nobody, including Ieyasu, could oppose him.

After the destruction of the Hōjō at the siege of Odawara castle in 1590, Hideyoshi ordered Ieyasu to move from his domain, which comprised Mikawa, Tōtōmi, Suruga, and Kai provinces and parts of Shinano, to the domain just confiscated from the Hōjō in the Kantō. Both Nobunaga and Hideyoshi frequently shifted daimyos from one domain to another, so the order to Ieyasu was not unusual. Presumably Hideyoshi wished to place the Tokugawa chieftain at an even greater remove from the heartland of his own power in the central provinces. Yet, in the light of later history, Hideyoshi's order was a serious mistake. It gave Ieyasu the largest of all daimyo domains, one that was richer in agriculture than Hideyoshi's own and later served as an ideal territorial base from which to assert Tokugawa hegemony over the country.

Ieyasu became the unchallenged national hegemon after his victory in 1600 at the battle of Sekigahara, the most decisive military encounter in pre-modern Japanese history. But what we call the battle of Sekigahara was far more than simply a clash of arms between two armies that occurred on the fifteenth day of the ninth month of 1600 and lasted some six hours. "Sekigahara", in the larger sense, refers to several months of strategic planning, scheming, and posturing by – and occasional fighting between – Ieyasu and his adversaries that reached its climax on the Sekigahara battlefield.

Hideyoshi had practiced the art of warfare by coalition with unprecedented success, raising armies that were agglomerations of the forces of many daimyos and that dwarfed in size all previous armies. The fact that unification-age commanders like Hideyoshi, and later Ieyasu, could gather such great, disparate groups of daimyos under their banners for particular campaigns reveals, in part, the shifting character of commitments and loyalties among the military leaders of the age. A concomitant to this "shiftiness" was the danger that a daimyo who joined a coalition might not be trustworthy. The Sengoku legacy of treachery was alive and well. As we will soon see, Ieyasu won the battle of Sekigahara because he was able secretly to persuade key members of the coalition army opposing him to change sides during the fighting.

The man who organized the coalition to oppose Tokugawa Ieyasu's rise to national power was Ishida Mitsunari, a daimyo from Ōmi province who was one of the five leading administrators (*go-bugyō*, "five magistrates") of Hideyoshi's government. Mitsunari charged that Ieyasu had violated his pledge to be a protector of the youthful Toyotomi Hideyori, and in the middle months of 1600 he began forming a "Toyotomi coalition" of daimyos to challenge the Tokugawa chieftain. Ieyasu, for his part, already had a number of daimyos committed to him, and was soon successful in recruiting others, including some who had up till then been thought to be staunch Toyotomi supporters. The fighting forces that finally emerged from these coalitions and eventually met on the Sekigahara battlefield were called the western army (of Ishida Mitsunari) and the eastern army (of Tokugawa Ieyasu). Roughly speaking, Mitsunari drew his strength from daimyos of the central and western provinces and Ieyasu from those of the east-central and eastern provinces. But both commanders also had important allies from other parts of the country (in Ieyasu's case, from as far away as Kyushu).

Space does not permit discussion of all the countrywide manoeuvring of Mitsunari and Ieyasu in the months before the Sekigahara clash. In the eighth month of 1600 Mitsunari gathered most of his coalition at Ōgaki castle in Mino province, situated at a main juncture on the route Ieyasu would have to take if he marched westward from his seat in the Kantō. Shortly afterwards part of Ieyasu's coalition occupied a fortification near Ōgaki. On the fourteenth day of the ninth month Ieyasu himself arrived from the east with his personal following and held a war council at which it was decided to bypass Ōgaki castle, move into neighbouring Ōmi province to seize Mitsunari's home castle, and then drive on to Osaka castle, where Hideyori was in residence.[63]

When Mitsunari learned on the evening of the fourteenth that the eastern army intended to bypass his position, he began moving most of his troops out of Ōgaki castle for the 16-kilometer (10-mile) march westward to Sekigahara, a rather narrow basin of land surrounded by mountains. The march was conducted in heavy rainfall. By about 1 am on the fifteenth, Mitsunari had the various elements of his army in place on the western and southwestern sides of the Sekigahara basin and in various positions on the surrounding mountains. Ieyasu received a report of the western army's movement about 2 am. He immediately ordered his army on to the road to Sekigahara.[64]

When a member of the staff of the Prussian Chief-of-Staff, Helmuth von Moltke, visited the Sekigahara battlefield in the late nineteenth century and was informed of the positions and troop strengths of the opposing forces at the commencement of battle, he observed that the victory must surely have gone to the western army.[65] The western army outnumbered the eastern by about 82,000 to 75,000.[66] Moreover, the eastern army, which entered the narrow pass to Sekigahara between 5 and 6 am, formed a battle line on the northeastern side of the basin from which it had little room to manoeuvre on its right flank and was exposed to attack from both its left flank and rear.

Because of dense fog hostilities did not commence until about 8 am. As the battle raged from eight until noon, the western army could surely have won if its forces on the mountain to the rear of the eastern army had attacked. But because of previous, secret agreements with Ieyasu, key commanders on the mountain refused to budge and, as a result, none of the units positioned there saw action that day. It is estimated, in fact, that only about 30,000 troops of the western army – slightly more than one-third of its total of 82,000 – actually participated in the battle of Sekigahara. Even so, the outcome of the fighting was still in doubt at noon when the main act of treachery was committed. Kobayakawa Hideaki of the western army, perched with his following on a mountain on the eastern army's left flank, suddenly attacked the right flank of his own army's battle line. Hideaki was joined in his defection by other western commanders nearby, and their combined assault caused the entire western battle line to crumble. By 2 pm all fighting had ceased. The western army had suffered a catastrophic defeat.[67]

Ieyasu won the battle of Sekigahara in large part because of his skill in coalition formation and the encouragement of treachery among the enemy. In the months before the battle he sent nearly 200 letters to daimyos throughout the country seeking to persuade them to join him outright or co-operate with him, covertly or otherwise, in his plans for the pending clash with Ishida Mitsunari. Mitsunari, on the other hand, sent very few letters during the same time.[68] Ieyasu was a cautious commander. He would not have assumed the battle position that Moltke's staff member, centuries later, judged to be exceedingly poor unless he was confident that the promised defections in the western ranks would occur (although, in fact, Kobayakawa waited far longer than Ieyasu wanted him to wait before showing his true colours).

Victorious at Sekigahara, Ieyasu established a government – the Tokugawa Shogunate – that endured for more than two and a half centuries, until the Meiji Restoration of 1868. It was an age of uninterrupted peace, except for two sieges: the siege of Osaka castle, conducted in two stages in the winter of 1614 and the spring of 1615, where Ieyasu destroyed Hideyori and the remnants of the Toyotomi family and their supporters; and the siege of Shimabara, the quelling of a Christian rebellion in northern Kyushu in 1637–38, which became the last tragic act in the Tokugawa Shogunate's policy of persecution and eradication of Christianity. The transition from Sengoku chaos to Tokugawa tranquillity had occurred with comparative rapidity, testifying to the extraordinary achievement of the three great unifiers – Nobunaga, Hideyoshi, and Ieyasu – in bringing under lasting control a country that had never really been controlled as a totality before.

Notes

1. Sengoku, pronounced Ch'an-kuo in Chinese, was the name originally given to the period 403–221 BC in China that is usually known in English as the period of the "Warring States".
2. Studies of the Ōnin War in English can be found in H. P. Varley, The Ōnin war (New York, Columbia University Press, 1967); and M. E. Berry, The culture of civil war in Kyoto (Berkeley, University of California Press, 1994).
3. Berry, The culture of civil war in Kyoto, p. xv.
4. Two recently published books in English have significantly revised and expanded our knowledge of warriors and warfare in Japan from earliest times through the thirteenth century: W. W. Farris, Heavenly warriors: The evolution of Japan's military, 500–1300 (Cambridge, Harvard University Press, 1992); and K. F. Friday, Hired swords: the rise of private warrior power in early Japan (Stanford, Stanford University Press, 1992).
5. The most thorough discussion of Japanese feudalism is to be found in J. W. Hall, Feudalism in Japan: a reassessment in Hall and M. B. Jansen (eds), Studies in the institutional history of early modern Japan (Princeton, Princeton University Press, 1968).

6. For a study of the war tales, see H. P. Varley, *Warriors of Japan, as portrayed in the war tales* (Honolulu, University of Hawaii Press, 1994).

7. Ishii Susumu contends that if these grooms on foot did participate in the fighting it was only on rare occasions. I. Susumu *Kamakura bakufu* (Tokyo, Chūō Kōron Sha, 1965), pp. 133–4.

8. On the founding of the Kamakura Shogunate: M. Shinoda, *The founding of the Kamakura shogunate, 1180–1185* (New York: Columbia University Press, 1960); and J. P. Mass, The Kamakura bakufu in K. Yamamura (ed.), *The Cambridge history of Japan*, Vol. 3 (Cambridge, Cambridge University Press, 1990).

9. Kawai Yasushi, *Genpei kassen no kyozō o hagu* (Tokyo, Kōdansha, 1996), pp. 64–5.

10. *ibid.*, pp. 87–8.

11. The *akutō* are the subject of L. F. Harrington's Social control and the significance of the *akutō* in J. P. Mass (ed.), *Court and bakufu in Japan* (New Haven, Yale University Press, 1982).

12. For descriptions of the castles by European missionaries, see M. Cooper (ed.), *They came to Japan* (Berkeley, University of California Press, 1965), pp. 131–41.

13. Imatani Akira, *Nihon kokuō to domin* (Tokyo, Shūeisha, 1992), p. 265.

14. *ibid.*

15. *ibid.*, p. 256.

16. *ibid.*, p. 266.

17. A discussion of the various origins of the Sengoku daimyos can be found in Owada Tetsuo. *Sengoku daimyō* (Tokyo, Kyōikusha, 1978), pp. 36–8.

18. Sun-tzu, *The art of warfare*, tr. R. T. Ames (New York, Ballantine Books, 1993). Ames's translation is: ". . . advancing at a pace, such an army is like the wind; slow and majestic, it is like a forest; invading and plundering, it is like fire; sedentary, it is like a mountain". p. 130.

19. The source is *Kōyō gunkan*.

20. Watanabe Yosuke first presented the five-battle theory in 1928.

21. Owada Tetsuo, *Sengoku jū-dai-kassen no nazo* (Tokyo, PHP, 1995), pp. 59–60.

22. Owada, *Sengoku daimyō*, pp. 60–1.

23. Fujimoto Masayuki, *Nobunaga no sengoku gunji-gaku* (Tokyo, JICC, 1993), p. 136.

24. See Naramoto Tatsuya (ed.), *Sengoku jidai, monoshiri jiten* (Tokyo, Shufu to Seikatsu Sha, 1988), pp. 80–1.

25. Sugiyama Hiroshi, *Sengoku daimyō* (Tokyo, Chūō Kōron Sha, 1965), p. 101.

26. Fujimoto, *Nobunaga*, pp. 137–8.

27. The battle of Okehazama in 1560.

28. Ōta Gyūichi, *Shinchō kōki*, ed. Kuwata Tadachika (Tokyo, Jinbutsu Ōrai Sha, 1965), Vol. 1, pp. 53–4.

29. Fujimoto, *Nobunaga*, p. 139.

30. Yoshida Tōyō (ed.), *Buke no kakun* (Tokyo, Tokuma Shoten, 1972), p. 241.

31. These exploding balls can be seen in the famous Mongol Scroll, the painting of which was commissioned by a Japanese warrior participant in both of the defences against the Mongols.

32. The story of the arrival of these first Europeans in Japan and the acquisition of their guns by the daimyo of Tanegashima can be found in *Teppō ki* [The chronicle of the arquebus] in *The east*, **XVI**, n 11, 12. *Teppō Ki* was written by a Zen priest in the early seventeenth century.

33. The extent of the influence of guns on the process of the unification of Japan in the late sixteenth century is still a subject of debate among scholars. One of the first Western scholars to inquire into this subject was Delmer Brown in The impact of firearms on Japanese warfare, 1543–98 in *Far eastern quarterly*, 7 (1948).

34. There were also other problems. One was the difficulty of lighting a matchlock in wet

weather. Another was accuracy. Some scholars believe that people firing guns of this sort had great difficulty hitting their targets. Finally, there was the danger to the operator of such a gun that it might malfunction and injure, if not kill, him.

35. E.g., Fujimoto, *Nobunaga*, p. 79.

36. *ibid.*, pp. 72–3.

37. It was unusual for a Sengoku daimyo to be killed in battle. See *ibid.*, p. 95.

38. Owada, *Sengoku jū-dai-kassen*, p. 35.

39. Fujimoto Masayuki observes that Nobunaga used military force to pursue an aggressive policy of diplomacy, *Nobunaga*, p. 116.

40. Nobunaga briefly held the high court position of Minister of the Right, but did not use this as an office from which to rule.

41. G. Parker states that Nobunaga used this method of salvo fire at least two decades before it was first used in Europe. *The military revolution* (Cambridge, Cambridge University Press, 1988), p. 140.

42. On the subject of the growth of *jōkamachi*, see J. W. Hall, The castle town and Japan's modern urbanization in Hall and Jansen (eds), *Studies in the institutional history of early modern Japan*.

43. *Ikkō ikki* means "single-minded confederacy". The word single-minded was used by the confederacy's opponents to describe what they regarded as the religious fanaticism of the confederacy's members.

44. Stephen Turnbull. *Samurai warfare* (London, Arms and Armour Press, 1996), pp. 102–3. A contemporary diary refers to Nobunaga's vessels as "iron ships". The guess is that their superstructures had iron plating as protection against cannon and fire arrows.

45. Ōta, *Shinchō kōki*, pp. 159–61.

46. *ibid.*, p. 163.

47. Hayashiya Tatsusaburō, *Tenka ittō* (Tokyo, Chūō Kōron Sha, 1966), pp. 248–51.

48. *ibid.*, pp. 251–2.

49. G. B. Sansom, *A history of Japan, 1334–1615* (Stanford, Stanford University Press, 1961), p. 310.

50. Ōta, *Shinchō kōki*, p. 153.

51. *ibid.*, pp. 214–15.

52. See M. E. Berry's discussion of Hideyoshi as a conciliator and as a commander who was magnanimous to those he defeated in battle in *Hideyoshi* (Cambridge, Harvard University Press, 1982), pp. 66–71.

53. Owada, *Sengoku jū-dai-kassen*, p. 162.

54. *ibid.*, p. 164.

55. Atsuta Kō, *Tenka ittō* (Tokyo, Shūeisha, 1992), pp. 325–6.

56. See Sansom, *A history of Japan, 1334–1615*, p. 353, for a detailed listing of the forces mobilized by Hideyoshi for the first invasion of Korea. Sansom says that, including all reserves, the total mobilization figure was about 225,000.

57. Around this time Hideyoshi sent letters to the Philippines and Taiwan calling upon them to submit to him. Atsuta, *Tenka ittō*, p. 329.

58. *ibid.*, p. 327.

59. J. Elisonas, The inseparable trinity: Japan's relations with China and Korea in J. W. Hall (ed.), *The Cambridge history of Japan. Vol. 4, Early modern Japan* (Cambridge, Cambridge University Press, 1991), p. 271.

60. Atsuta, *Tenka ittō*, p. 326.

61. Hideyoshi himself never went to Korea, but remained at the elaborate headquarters he built in northern Kyushu specifically for the conduct of the invasion.

62. Elisonas, The inseparable trinity, p. 285.

63. Kitajima Masamoto, *Edo bakufu* (Tokyo, Shōgakukan, 1975), p. 198.

64. *ibid.*, pp. 198–9.

65. *Senryaku senjutsu heiki jiten* (Tokyo, Gakken, 1994), p. 168.

66. Kitajima, *Edo bakufu*, p. 199.

67. *ibid.*, p. 201.

68. Owada, *Sengoku jū-dai-kassen*, pp. 187–8.

Further reading

The following readings will provide the reader with general coverage of the period and its military affairs and, in the case of the Turnbull book, some detailed information about the great battles.

M. E. Berry, *The culture of civil war in Kyoto* (Berkeley, University of California Press, 1992).

M. E. Berry, *Hideyoshi* (Cambridge, Mass., Harvard University Press, 1982).

N. McMullin, *Buddhism and the State in Sixteenth-Century Japan* (Princeton, Princeton University Press, 1984).

G. B. Sansom, *A History of Japan 1334–1615* (Stanford, Stanford University Press, 1961).

S. Turnbull, *Battles of the Samurai* (London, Arms and Armour Press, 1987).

Chapter Four

War and warfare in China 1450–1815

Peter Lorge

The rise and fall of Chinese dynasties has traditionally been understood as a life-cycle with a dynamic youth, a mature middle, and a corrupt end. The year 1450 marked the beginning of maturity for the Ming dynasty (1368–1644), while 1815 was very near the end of maturity for the Qing dynasty (1644–1911). Even though the dynastic cycle has been discarded by most historians, there is a lingering tendency to look for the roots of a dynasty's eventual collapse somewhere in its middle years. Somehow events or trends begun more than a century before lead to an "inevitable" failure. It has been particularly easy to assume this attitude because Chinese history has not been constructed around great battles or other compact events. If, however, we discard the inevitability of the falls of the Ming and Qing dynasties, we must examine events much closer to their respective ends to understand them. That is not to say that long-term trends are unimportant, but only that many things can change in the course of a century.

The end of the Ming dynasty has been blamed on the incompetence of its emperors, the corruption of the eunuchs at court, the inflexible and short-sighted moralizing of the officials, and even the effects of a worldwide crisis in the seventeenth century. All of these except the last may be true, but the actual destruction of the dynasty was played out over many years on the battlefield. In military terms there were two general shifts during the Ming. The first was the loss of strategic initiative, or active diplomatic engagement, with the steppes to the north after the Ming defeat at the Battle of Tumu in 1449. After this the Ming began to build walls and adopted a generally defensive attitude toward the Mongols and other steppe peoples. The second shift was the loss of tactical initiative, or pre-emptive battlefield engagement, with the steppes after the disastrous Liaodong campaign in 1619. It should be clear that the first change was of much less immediate impact than the second, occurring as it did some two centuries before the dynasty's fall.

Technology was significant, but not decisive, in Ming–Mongol and Ming–Manchu warfare. One of the more dire consequences of the Liaodong campaign for the Ming had been the transfer of firearms and skilled artillerymen to the rising Manchu state. The Ming regained, but soon lost, their technological advantage with the introduction of Portuguese cannon. With equal technology the contest between the Ming and the Manchus was decided by leadership, military acumen, and determination. It was a long, difficult struggle for power.

The Manchus, founders of the Qing dynasty, were a people literally invented for war. A succession of extremely competent leaders transformed a loose confederation of Jurchen tribes into a highly disciplined military state. That military state overthrew the Ming dynasty and established itself as the Qing. In order to overthrow the Ming, the Manchus first had to learn Ming military and administrative methods. The Manchus were superior cavalrymen, but they lacked siege and firearm skills. Once they had acquired them, however, they were able to breach Ming defences. As successful as they were in defeating the Ming, it was not until the third Qing emperor, Kangxi, that the Manchu military machine reached maturity.

The Battle of Tumu to the death of Hideyoshi

On 20 September 1450 Zhu Qizhen,[1] sixth emperor of the Ming dynasty, returned to Beijing after a year in captivity. His capture at the Battle of Tumu on 1 September 1449 by the Mongol leader Esen marked a turning-point in Ming China's relationship with the steppe peoples. Minister of War Yu Qian's resolute leadership had stabilized the court during the crisis, but the damage done to the Ming's military prestige could not be recovered, nor could the army destroyed at Tumu, perhaps half a million strong, be replaced quickly. After Tumu the Ming lost control of the steppe border region and began to build walls to defend its territory from Mongol raids. By the late sixteenth century wall-building had become the only Ming response to the steppe threat, leaving behind what we now call the Great Wall as a monument to desperation and indecision.[2]

Wall-building was augmented by increasing the number of firearms defending strategic positions. Firearms were extremely effective in defending cities against Mongol armies and raiding parties. But the Mongols did not respond to the increase in Ming firearm use by acquiring or developing their own siege train. Mongol armies were first and foremost mobile cavalry forces. All of their advantages in raiding, retreating and rapid concentration were predicated on all-cavalry forces unencumbered by supply trains. Perhaps more important, the various Mongol leaders who directed attacks against Ming China during the fifteenth, sixteenth and seventeenth centuries were not intent upon destroying the Ming state.

Steppe life and empire-building both required the resources of a settled society. Apart from basic needs like food and metal, Mongol leaders required luxury goods in order to make alliances, assure loyalty and demonstrate their ability as leaders. If they could obtain those goods by trade and even tribute relations with China, that was acceptable. But the Ming court took an increasingly hard line with the Mongols, denying them trade because they did not want to look weak, as well as from simple xenophobia.[3] The Mongols turned to raiding to acquire what they needed. The raids further hardened the Ming court's policies and the cycle continued.

The capture of the emperor in 1449 forced the Ming court to confront the deterioration in its military system. Not only had army manpower fallen, but the quality of the remaining troops had also declined. Troops on the northern border were generally in better shape than the rest of the Ming army.[4] The Mongol threat had been nearly constant throughout the Ming dynasty. In 1550 the Mongol leader Altan led a raid up to the walls of Beijing itself. But, while the Mongols were the worst threat to the dynasty, they were not the only military problem facing the Ming. The sporadic pirate raids in the 1520s and 1530s coalesced into a much more serious problem in the 1540s.[5] Then, there were the Three Major Campaigns of the emperor Wanli. Though the campaigns were only connected in the minds of historians and writers, they were nevertheless the last Ming military actions that did not lead to complete disaster.[6] The first campaign was against the rebel Yang Yinglong in the southwest. The second against a mutiny of Chinese and Mongolian troops in the critical Ordos region. The third was the campaign against the Japanese in Korea.

In the light of the emperor's capture and clear signs of decay in the army, Ming policy became increasingly defensive. Offensive campaigns against the Mongols were risky, expensive and yielded only short-term benefits. Building walls and abandoning forward positions was a cheaper, more reliable, long-term solution. Ironically, the first opportunity to try the wall-building policy came as a result of a successful offensive strike against a Mongol force by Wang Yue in 1473. Wang attacked the camp of the Mongol raiders, killing several hundred, probably including women and children, burning tents and leading away their herds. He then ambushed the raiders when they hurried back to save their camp. With Mongol pressure temporarily relieved, wall-building could begin.[7]

Ming wall-building was complemented by cannon and other firearms. Firearms thus became a mostly defensive weapon. There were no Mongol fortifications to overcome and no positions that the Mongols had to defend. Chinese armies had no offensive targets for their cannon. Their field tactics evolved accordingly. Chinese armies usually adopted defensive formations supported with firearms. Ming defensive-mindedness on the strategic and operational level translated down to defensive tactics in the field. With the exception of a few generals like Wang Yue, Ming commanders did not adopt Mongol tactics. At the same time, the Ming court refused to trade with the Mongols, despite the advice of its military commanders. After 1449 the Ming never regained the initiative against the Mongols.

In 1541 drought in North China and Mongolia prompted the Mongol Prince Altan to send a mission to the Chinese border seeking trade. He was turned down, forcing him to raid for food and supplies. Conditions were similar the following year and Altan sent a second mission to the Chinese border. This time his messenger was executed. Altan raided again, in retaliation as well as for supplies. The Ming army lost every encounter and the Mongols returned to the steppes unmolested. Both the drought and Mongol raiding continued through 1545. Altan sent a third mission to the Chinese border. Once again his messenger was murdered. The Jiajing emperor rejected any attempts to placate Altan. He was tired of purely defensive measures.[8]

In January 1547 Ceng Xian proposed building further fortifications and attacking the Mongols in the Ordos in the late spring for three years. The Mongols were weakest in the spring because their horses had had little to eat during the winter. Although the emperor was enthusiastic, few of his officials, particularly in the affected areas, wanted anything to do with it. Ceng had some success that year, but politics at court turned against the campaign. The emperor withdrew his support in 1548.[9]

Altan maintained his pressure against the Ming border, raiding in 1548 and 1549. Although the Mongols suffered some losses in their raids, they warned that they would raid Beijing itself in 1550 if trade did not resume. Despite attempts to further strengthen border defences, Altan broke through and besieged Beijing on 1 October 1550. The Beijing garrison was unwilling to take the field against the Mongols. At the same time, the Mongols could not breach the city's walls or maintain a long siege. Altan looted the suburbs and withdrew several days later. The Mongols raided annually through 1566, but increased wall-building around Beijing kept the capital safe. The Mongol problem was never solved, only contained.[10]

While the Mongols were raiding the northern border and threatening the capital, pirates raided the southern coast. Piracy in the south was intimately connected with overseas trade, and it was not really possible to make a clear separation between the merchants and the pirates. Bans on trade only drove merchants to illegal trade and piracy. Chinese merchants continued to trade with Japanese and Portuguese fleets on nearby islands. In the late 1540s the Ming court took decisive steps to end piracy and overseas trading. The extreme measures backfired, forcing the merchants into even more organized trading or raiding fleets. In the 1550s the pirates, comprised of Chinese, Japanese and other foreign sailors, began more sustained and systematic campaigns against the southern coast. The pirates set up bases and raided inland, capturing garrisons and besieging county seats. It took until 1567 for Ming forces to destroy the largest pirate fleets. Fortunately, just as the military efforts succeeded, the death of the Jiajing emperor allowed a resumption in overseas trade.[11]

The Jiajing emperor was succeeded by his son, the Longqing emperor (1567–72), whose brief reign was peaceful. Longqing's son, the Wanli emperor (1573–1620), ruled an increasingly turbulent empire threatened by the rising power of the Manchus as well as internal rebellions. Altan had been pacified in 1571, but his successors were unable to control all of the separate tribes. The Mongols began to raid again, but in smaller numbers and mostly in the far west. But Wanli's reign is best known for his "Three Campaigns", the rebellion of Yang Yinglong, the rebellion of Pübei, and the war in Korea against the Japanese.

The causes of Yang Yinglong's rebellion in 1587 are uncertain. Yang himself was the overlord of several aboriginal groups in southwest China. His family had managed to hold its territory as a semi-autonomous state since the ninth century, through several dynasties. The "rebellion" was a rather desultory affair which continued until 1600. Yang alternated between raiding and surrendering for more than a decade. His luck ran out when the war in Korea ended. Li Hualong launched his campaign in the spring of 1600. Over 104 days Li's army of 200,000 men, equipped with firearms, killed 22,687 rebels and captured 1,124. Yang Yinglong committed suicide.[12]

Pübei's Sino-Mongolian rebellion in the Ordos was equally as minor as Yang Yinglong's, but of far greater immediate concern to the court. Pübei was a Mongolian officer in Chinese service based at the strategic city of Ningxia. He retired in 1592, passing his title to his son. The same year a Chinese officer revolted over pay arrears, and involved Pübei's son in the uprising. Even though the court was distracted by the Korean campaign, Ningxia's importance on the northern border and the possibility of Mongolian support for Pübei forced a swift Ming response. Several months after the initial uprising, a Ming army besieged Ningxia. When the city had not fallen after two months, a dike was constructed to flood the city. Ningxia fell on 20 October. Pübei's son was captured and later executed. Pübei burned himself alive.[13]

Wanli's Korean campaign was really the only military action of his reign that deserves the description "great". A Japanese army of 158,700 men invaded Korea in 1592.[14] It quickly captured Seoul and P'yongyang, reaching the Yalu river by the fall of that year. Although the Japanese army did not advance into Chinese territory, Wanli mobilized an expeditionary force of 42,000 men including a 3,000-man firearms unit. A further mobilization of 100,000 men was planned in support of the first army. The expeditionary army defeated a Japanese force and recovered P'yongyang in January 1593, but its vanguard was itself defeated twenty days later near Seoul. Peace negotiations were begun, and the Japanese force withdrew south to Pusan. Korean Admiral Yi's turtle ships had wreaked havoc on the Japanese navy, cutting the invasion force's supply lines, and Korean irregulars had begun to take their toll on the occupying soldiers.

The Japanese retained their foothold in southern Korea while peace negotiations continued. Meanwhile most of the Ming army was withdrawn and Admiral Yi was exiled from the Korean court. Negotiations continued until 1596, when an agreement was supposed to have been reached between the Ming court and Toyotomi Hideyoshi, the ruling warlord of Japan. Hideyoshi repudiated the agreement at the last moment and prepared to launch another campaign in 1597. This time the Chinese and Koreans mobilized in advance, holding the Japanese to the southern tip of Korea. The Korean navy did poorly at first, but Admiral Yi was recalled and quickly put it back in shape. The bloody fighting continued into 1598 when Hideyoshi died. The invasion force was quickly recalled.[15]

The rise of Nurhaci and the Liaodong campaign

The campaigns against the Japanese coincided with the rise of the Manchu nation under Nurhaci. At the same time that the Manchu threat was increasing in the north, internal rebellions broke out all over China. The Ming court was caught between two threats and could not decide which one to deal with first. Any compromise with the Manchus was opposed by extremist Confucian officials as capitulation to barbarians. Meanwhile, efforts to put down the rebels foundered on the reluctance to divert troops from the border and the increasing costs of maintaining field armies. Every increase in taxes to pay for the suppression campaigns alienated more peasants and increased rebel support.

Nurhaci, founder of what would become the Qing dynasty, rose to power in the area now known as Manchuria. His tribe was descended from the Jurchens, who ruled north China from 1127 to 1234 as the Jin dynasty. As his power grew in the 1580s, he wisely accepted Ming titles, while consolidating his control over the other Jurchen tribes. He extended his influence over the Mongol tribes living in Manchuria in 1593 while the Ming was occupied with the Japanese in Korea. Nurhaci's nominal submission to the Ming did not hide his growing threat. But the Ming court was nearly paralyzed by factional politics.

What truly distinguished Nurhaci from the earlier Mongol threat was his organization. He was not just trying to achieve overlordship over disparate steppe tribes, but was building a state and creating a people. A Manchu alphabet was introduced in 1599 to replace the Mongolian one. Nurhaci's key reform, however, was the banner system, begun in 1601. The banner system would last until the fall of the Qing dynasty in 1911. Every household was assigned to a banner (red, yellow, blue, white). Approximately 300 households made up a company, and 25 companies made up a banner. Banners were both administrative and military units. A further four banners (bordered red, yellow, blue and white) were added in 1615.[16]

In 1618 Nurhaci was finally ready to challenge the Ming directly. In May he attacked Fushun, a town in Liaodong, before announcing his grievances against the Ming. His peace terms were designed to provoke a hostile response. The Ming court responded as he expected and launched an invasion of his territory in the spring of 1619. The total Chinese force, including a Korean contingent, numbered about 100,000 men. Nurhaci had perhaps 50,000 or 60,000 men.[17] The plan drawn up by Yang Hao, Supreme Commander of the expedition, is still extant. The Ming army was divided into four columns jumping off from a line running roughly north–south. Their objective was Nurhaci's capital, Heta Ala. Although the two northernmost columns, under Ma Lin and Du Song, were fairly close to each other, none of the columns could support each other. Although outnumbered overall, Nurhaci was able to achieve battlefield superiority, fully exploiting the mobility of his all-cavalry army, and to destroy the Chinese columns individually. Tactically, the speed and discipline of the Manchu cavalry was able to overcome the slow-firing Ming firearms.

A variety of criticisms have been made of Yang Hao's plan, mostly of a tactical nature. Much of the criticism is warranted, but the plan's most significant failing was strategic. Heta Ala was not vital to Nurhaci, and the first thing he did when the Ming invaded was to abandon it. He knew, as the Ming court apparently did not, that it was his army in the field that was the most important. As the Chinese columns advanced, the Manchu cavalry concentrated first against Du Song and then Ma Lin. When the northernmost columns were destroyed, Nurhaci fell upon Liu Ting's southern column, Li Rubo having already retreated.[18]

The Ming army never regained the initiative after the failure of the Liaodong campaign. Nurhaci's defence had been desperate, but overwhelmingly successful. In a single campaign, which he had provoked, Nurhaci elevated his nascent state and humbled the Ming. In the wake of the campaign people in Beijing panicked, expecting an invasion. But Nurhaci was too deliberate to overreach himself. He knew that, despite all its problems, conquering the Ming state was still beyond his capabilities. He concentrated his efforts on securing Liaodong. Later that year on 26 July Nurhaci's forces captured Kaiyuan, followed by Tieling on 3 September. By the summer of 1621, Manchu armies had overrun both Shenyang and Liaoyang, completing the conquest of Liaodong. Many Ming soldiers surrendered to Nurhaci with their firearms. These soldiers added a crucial capability to the Manchu war machine – expertise in siege warfare. The Liaodong campaign and its aftermath was a crucial step in the Qing conquest of China.

The Qing conquest

The Qing conquest of Ming China was a long and complex process. Even narrowing our focus almost exclusively to the military aspects of the change in dynasties leaves us with hundreds of major battles, spread over several decades, taking place in widely different circumstances across thousands of miles of Chinese territory. While no single battle was absolutely decisive, certain events did significantly alter or advance the progress of the conquest. By 1621 the Manchu state had closed the technology gap with Ming China by acquiring Chinese firearms and artillerymen. The Ming briefly regained the technological advantage by introducing Portuguese cannon, but they could not keep them out of Manchu hands for long. Portuguese cannon were soon being cast for the Manchus by Portuguese-trained Chinese artillerymen. Dalinghe was captured in 1631 after a long siege, and a large and bloody battle fought almost exclusively with cannon and firearms on both sides.

Nurhaci's successor, his son Hung Taiji,[19] was ambivalent about conquering Ming China. Like his father, Hung Taiji was unsure that his nascent state was strong enough to overcome and control a vast Chinese empire. Ruling a sedentary state was a very different and much greater task than defeating Ming armies in the field. Practical considerations aside, there was still a very large conceptual jump to make from ruling a steppe empire to attacking an established agrarian state in order to conquer it. Why should the Manchus attack the Ming? Nurhaci had really been *primus inter pares* rather than absolute ruler of a Manchu state. The banners were controlled by powerful leaders who saw war as a way to acquire loot and pasture lands for their followers. They were not particularly interested in elevating Hung Taiji to emperor of a Chinese-style state.

There was one group in particular that pressed Hung Taiji to attack the Ming and establish himself as emperor of China – his Chinese advisors. At first glance this seems rather strange. Why should educated Chinese people try to convince a barbarian ruler to overthrow a Chinese dynasty? The answer was quite simple: if Hung Taiji and his Manchus succeeded in taking over China, those same Chinese advisors would be vindicated in the eyes of history. They would become officials of a legitimate dynasty, wise early adherents of the new possessor of the Mandate of Heaven, rather than failed men forced to work for barbarians. Still,

Hung Taiji *was* interested in becoming emperor, if not necessarily of China. But his desire to become emperor of the Manchus began to coincide functionally with conquering the Ming. The Manchu state would have to become Sinified, with a real emperor, in order to govern the Chinese empire. Thus, if Hung Taiji wanted to become emperor of the Manchus, he would have to become emperor of the Chinese as well.

Perhaps the best illustration of the tension between Hung Taiji's imperial goals and the other Manchu leaders' understanding of the purpose of war against the Ming took place in 1629. Hung Taiji led a major raid into Ming territory, up to the walls of Beijing, leaving his brother Amin behind in Shenyang. The Manchu army captured four cities inside the Great Wall, treating the inhabitants well and accepting the surrender of Ming officials.[20] Hung Taiji returned north in 1630 and Amin took control of the captured territory. A Ming counter-attack recaptured one of the cities. Amin decided to abandon the remaining cities after looting them and massacring the Chinese populations. Hung Taiji used the incident to have Amin jailed. Amin's banner, the Bordered Blue, was given to Jirgalang, a younger brother who supported Hung Taiji.[21] And while the massacre was put to good political use, it later proved extremely damaging in the campaign to conquer China. Any city or army considering surrender always had to wonder if they too would be slaughtered after submitting.

Another important result of Hung Taiji's 1629 raid was the capture of Chinese artillerymen at Yongping who were able to cast Portuguese cannon. By February 1631 40 European pieces had been cast. All the Chinese troops were then placed under a separate command whose primary purpose was artillery and siege warfare. Hung Taiji soon turned his new siege capability against the fortress complex at Dalinghe. Dalinghe's impressive defences could only be reached by narrow passes defended by over a hundred fortified towns. Further complicating the attack, just before Hung Taiji arrived with his 20,000 Manchu, Mongol and Han troops on 1 September, Ming General, Zu Dashou, had reached Dalinghe on an inspection tour with an army of 14,000 veterans. The Manchu army settled in for a siege, surrounding Dalinghe with a ditch and palisade. Manchu units contained any sorties from the city, while the Chinese artillery units began bombardment with the new Portuguese-style cannon.

The siege was well under way, several outlying fortresses surrendered and a few closer ones were overwhelmed, when Ming relief forces began to arrive. On 11 September a Ming force of 2,000 men was defeated by 300 bannermen. A second Ming force of about 6,000 troops was defeated soon after by a similarly outnumbered Manchu unit. One of the captured officers was brought before Dalinghe's walls to demoralize its defenders. But word reached Hung Taiji on 7 October that a Ming army of 40,000 troops under General Zu's brother-in-law, General Wu Xiang, was approaching. The Ming army's vanguard was already nearby, across the Xiaoling River. Hung Taiji immediately detached a force to delay the vanguard's advance, following four days later himself with a second force. While most of the Manchu troops waited, Hung Taiji scouted the Ming vanguard with 200 of his guardsmen. When he saw the 7,000 Ming soldiers across the Xiaoling River, Hung Taiji led an impetuous charge across the river which scattered the Ming troops. A second battle was fought a few hours later when the rest of the Manchu force came up, defeating the regrouped Ming vanguard.

Hung Taiji's victory at Xiaoling River was impressive, but it had not stopped the main Ming army. The main relief force under Zhang Chun crossed the Xiaoling River on 31 October and made camp, strongly entrenched with earth ramparts and cannon. The Manchu army remained at Dalinghe and waited for the Ming army to move from its position. Zhang Chun broke camp at 1 am on 22 October and advanced on Dalinghe. The Ming movement was detected about five miles from Dalinghe. Hung Taiji quickly led his entire force of 20,000 men against Zhang Chun's 40,000, now formed into a square protected by cannon and muskets. The Manchu army attacked head-on in two wings. Only the right wing was able to penetrate the Ming lines in the face of intense cannon and musket fire. The left wing wheeled around and charged through the gap made by the right wing. But then the Manchu army stalled in indecision and the Ming army regrouped. Before the Ming firearms could turn the tide, the Manchu artillery opened up from the east. In response the Ming soldiers set fire to the grass, expecting the wind, which was then at their backs, to carry the flames into the Manchu position. The wind reversed direction, blowing the fire back into the Ming lines. Hung Taiji regained the initiative and ordered a second frontal assault. This time, despite still more casualties, the Manchu charge was successful.

General Zu still refused to surrender Dalinghe. Conditions inside the city were desperate but the Manchu army was also running low on supplies. Hung Taiji sent a contingent of his Chinese artillerymen with six Portuguese-style cannon and 54 other cannon against Yuzizhang fort, the largest of the outlying fortified positions around Dalinghe. A three-day bombardment pounded the fort into submission. After Yuzizhang fell, other forts either surrendered or were abandoned. While the Manchu army was now resupplied from the forts' storehouses, the army in Dalinghe had resorted to cannibalism. General Zu began to waver, and Hung Taiji exploited the divisions among Zu's subordinates to bring matters to a head. Finally, after tense negotiations (Amin's massacre was still fresh in the Ming officers' minds) Zu surrendered Dalinghe on 21 November. The siege had lasted 82 days and reduced the city's population from 30,000 to 11,682.[22]

General Zu later betrayed his oath to Hung Taiji and escaped back to Ming territory, but the Manchu cause was strengthened by the addition of Zu's sons, nephew, and former subordinates. These men had been some of the Ming's most experienced officers and they made significant contributions to the Manchu conquest of China. As Hung Taiji brought more and more Chinese troops under his control (they were organized into their own banners in 1639) he found that the war machine he had built was taking on a life of its own. Unlike his Manchu and Mongol troops the Chinese troops could not disperse at the end of the campaign season and live off their banner lands. The Chinese troops were a professional standing army that had to be maintained at great expense by the Manchu state. At the same time, Hung Taiji's administration was also becoming increasingly Sinified. Just as Hung Taiji changed the name of his burgeoning empire to "Qing" and adopted the name "Manchu" for his people in 1636, he was beginning to fear a loss of steppe values and over-Sinification.[23] Thus the Manchus were not seduced by Chinese culture until after the Qing conquest. In order to overcome the Ming army and its fortifications, the Manchus needed firearms and men who knew how to use them. The easiest solution was to acquire Chinese troops with the requisite weapons and expertise. Those troops, and the sieges that were now possible because of them, demanded an administrative structure capable of maintaining them. The conveniences of Chinese administrative methods became a necessity.

Hung Taiji raided China again in December of 1638, before turning and conquering Korea in only two months. As Qing armies continued to probe Ming defences, rebellions throughout China grew in intensity. The Ming court was caught between defending the northern border against the Manchus and suppressing the bandits. Competent Ming commanders were able to defeat rebels like Li Zicheng or Qing attacks on cities like Jinzhou. But they could not do both simultaneously. Hung Taiji continued his practice of offering attractive terms of surrender to Ming commanders while campaigning against them. As the military tide turned in favor of the Qing, changing sides became increasingly attractive. Factionalism at the Ming court exacerbated the situation, paralyzing decision-making and eroding confidence in the regime.

By 1644 Qing armies had penetrated but not fully broken down Ming border defences. Hung Taiji had died the year before on 21 September 1643, and was succeeded by his third son, the six-year-old Fulin (the Shunzhi Emperor). While the Manchus were held up on the border, the bandit Li Zicheng emerged from northwestern China and advanced on Beijing. The court could not decide if it should recall General Wu Sangui and his army from the border to defend the capital. A proposal for the emperor to flee to the south fell to political infighting. The Chongzhen emperor finally recalled Wu Sangui on 10 April 1644, but it was too late. Li Zicheng's army entered Beijing on the night of 24 April. The Chongzhen emperor hung himself on Coal Hill the following day. Wu Sangui was now caught between the Manchus and Li Zicheng. He chose to serve the Qing.

The Qing army under the Shunzhi emperor's regent, Prince Dorgon, ordered Wu Sangui to spearhead the drive on Beijing. Li Zicheng was soon driven out and the body of the Chongzhen emperor given proper burial. The Ming dynasty limped on for a few more years, setting up successive, and sometimes conflicting, regimes in southern China. The last remnants of Ming rule were not wiped out until 1683. Even in defeat the Ming court could not decide whether to fight the bandits or the Manchus. Some officials even hoped the Manchus would defeat the bandits and then negotiate a peace. The Qing court did not hesitate: it crushed both the bandits and the Ming.

The Qing conquest had been aided by a large number of turncoat Ming generals. Three of those generals, Wu Sangui, Shang Kexi and Geng Jimao were rewarded by enfeoffment as princes in the south and southwest of China, the areas they had conquered for the Qing. Wu rebelled in 1673, followed soon after by Geng's son Jingzhong (Geng had died 1671) in 1674 and Shang's son Zhixin, who imprisoned his father, in 1676. The rebellion of the "Three Feudatories" was finally put down in 1681. But the rebellion was only the beginning of the Kangxi emperor's wars. Admiral Shi Lang captured the Pescadores Islands and Taiwan in 1683, eliminating the last remnants of the late Ming loyalist/pirate Coxinga's forces. In 1685 a Qing army captured Albazin, a Russian outpost on the Amur River, abandoned it, and then recaptured it the following year. The Russians sued for peace, leading to the Treaty of Nerchinsk in 1689. With the Russians diplomatically neutralized, Kangxi turned to western China where the Zunghar leader Galdan was gaining power. Kangxi took the field himself, defeating Galdan at Jao Modo in 1696. He later intervened in Tibet, sending troops to install a Dalai Lama loyal to the Qing in 1720.

The Kangxi emperor (1662–1722) was still not firmly in power when the Rebellion of the Three Feudatories broke out. He was undeniably the emperor, but he still had to balance competing factions against each other in order to run the government. The crisis was precipitated by Shang Kexi's request in 1673 to retire and leave his satrapy in Guangdong to his son, Zhixin. Shang was permitted to retire, but Kangxi refused to allow him to pass on his position to Zhixin. Later that year Wu Sangui and Geng Jingzhong also asked to retire. Wu's request was assumed to be a gesture, and the court split over whether or not to accept it. Financially the Qing state was ready for a war and Wu's eldest son was a hostage in Beijing: so, on the advice of his grandmother, Kangxi accepted Wu's resignation.[24] Wu broke openly with the Qing court in December of 1673, followed the next year by Geng Jingzhong and, three years later, by Shang Zhixin.

Wu Sangui and the other rebels won many battles in the early stages of the campaign, and it seemed to many that the Manchus would be driven back to the steppes. But the Qing state was much stronger than Wu had anticipated. Once it became clear that most of China remained loyal to the Qing, it was mostly a question of time before the rebels were defeated. The Qing army was put back in fighting condition with the help of Father Verbiest, a Jesuit missionary reluctantly drafted into casting new cannon. Kangxi was able to turn the superior material resources of China against the rebels, both in armaments and food. The Qing state emerged from the Rebellion of the Three Feudatories firmly in control of China and ready to expand even further.

While Kangxi's reign saw several other successful military actions after the Rebellion of the Three Feudatories, the campaign against the Zunghar leader Galdan was particularly remarkable. The emperor took the field personally, leading a column across the Gobi desert. Galdan was defeated at Jao Modo in the spring of 1696, but managed to escape. Kangxi campaigned again against Galdan in the autumn of 1696 and the spring of 1697. The Zunghar leader committed suicide in 1697, abandoned by his followers after years of relentless Qing campaigns. The Qing military machine had proven itself capable of supplying tens of thousands of men and horses, marching and fighting across deserts and steppes for months at a time. Kangxi's campaign against Galdan demonstrated the maturity of the Qing army. The Manchu army of steppe cavalry aided by Chinese turncoats had become an integrated force of cavalry and infantry, well supplied with firearms and supported by a sophisticated logistical system.

Yongzheng and Qianlong's reigns

In 1723 Kangxi was succeeded by his fourth son, the Yongzheng emperor. Just as his father had done, he secured his northern border with the Russians with the Treaty of Kiakhta in 1728, before dealing with the Zunghars in the west. The campaign went badly, and it was not until 1759, during the reign of Yongzheng's son, the Qianlong emperor, that the Zunghars were finally destroyed. Qianlong's elimination of the Zunghars was part of a larger expansion of Chinese territory to the west. His later military record was more ambivalent. Qing forces failed in Burma in the 1760s and in Vietnam in 1788–89, but succeeded in driving a Gurkha invasion back from Tibet in 1792.

By Qianlong's reign Manchu culture and the martial values that went with it had become seriously eroded. Most of the Manchus living in China had been there for over a century and few had actually seen the steppes, much less learned to live a pastoral lifestyle. Even the Manchu language was falling out of use. Yet

Qianlong was committed to what he perceived to be the martial heritage of the Manchus. At the same time he was also concerned with improvements in European artillery. But Qianlong's interest in preserving Manchu culture and obtaining European technical assistance was not shared by all his officials. Both issues became entangled in Manchu–Chinese politics at court.

The political uses of war, culture, and technology were nothing new. Kangxi had faced similar problems (see above), but they have taken on added historical significance in the light of the nineteenth-century military failure of the Qing against the European powers. Matters were further complicated by European criticism of missionaries providing the Chinese with military assistance. Jesuit missionaries were supposed to use the enticement of science to proselytize. Instead, the Qing used the enticement of proselytizing to obtain western science. It seemed that the Jesuits were doing an awful lot of science and very little preaching. That was to be expected considering that, whatever value the Qing placed on western science, they were wary of the western values that went along with it.[25] Of course, the Qing government was unaware that by the late eighteenth century the military technology that Jesuit missionaries could supply was no longer up to date. Despite all these problems Manchu vigour, Chinese organization, and technical assistance by Jesuits were sufficient to expand the Qing empire under Qianlong to its greatest extent ever.

Conclusion

Perhaps because of its later problems, we frequently forget the power and size of the Qing empire in 1815. Even by that time no nation on earth could truly match its grandeur. While the later humiliation of the nineteenth century tainted the very real military achievements of the Qing in the preceding two centuries, it is only in retrospect that the eighteenth century can be seen as the beginning of the end or the high point of an inevitable decline. If, as Joanna Waley-Cohen has so convincingly argued, the Chinese did not reject Western technology, we cannot accuse them of turning away from the fruits of the European military revolution. The Qing state would have been quite happy to enhance its military power. It was really European culture, in particular Christianity, which the Chinese rejected. As it became increasingly clear that China was not going to transform itself into a Christian nation and adopt Western values, many Europeans began to have second thoughts about giving the Chinese the most advanced military technology. Military technology had also advanced beyond the casual reach of missionaries. Of course these were all issues whose true impact would be felt in the nineteenth century. Still, this suggests that

Chinese weakness in comparison to the West was *only* a nineteenth-century problem with fewer roots in the eighteenth century than a Eurocentric world-view might comfortably accommodate.

It is difficult to consider war and warfare in China from the fifteenth to the nineteenth century without discussing how the end of the Qing dynasty has coloured our views. Military technology plays a far larger role in the interpretation of eighteenth-, nineteenth- and twentieth-century Chinese history than in any other period. Firearms became the symbol of Chinese failure and Western superiority. The fall of the Qing and all of Chinese culture was explained by a simple comparison of Western versus Chinese cannon. This seems like a crude simplification, but it is basically true. If only the Qing had been able to defend itself against the encroaching West, there would have been little cause to question the value of Chinese culture or Qing rule. If only the Qing government had been willing to accept Western technology, it would have been able to defend itself against the West. Inferior military technology was partly responsible for Qing failures, but it was actually out-of-date, Western technology.

The superiority of nineteenth-century Western technology was only significant in clashes between China and European powers. It was far less significant for internal Chinese problems. War within China was fought with more or less equal weapons to challenge or reinforce central government rule. Chinese governments also fought wars to expand the empire, an enterprise which the Qing government had carried out very successfully. War with the West was another kind of fight, one most akin to the raids of the Mongols in the fifteenth and sixteenth centuries. Fending off the West distracted the Qing government from more useful internal applications of force, while offering no chance for gain. European attacks on China weakened the Qing government and helped bring about its downfall. What is perhaps more interesting is that when the European powers withdrew and Japan was defeated in the twentieth century, the Chinese empire was very quickly reconstituted through war and the Qing borders restored.

Just as no one could have predicted in 1450 when or how the Ming dynasty would fall, so too in 1815 the fall of the Qing dynasty could not really be foreseen. This is not surprising considering it still had nearly a century of rule ahead of it. When all the social and cultural factors are examined, it is still war that determined who ruled the Chinese empire and for how long. Warfare in China changed slowly from 1450 to 1815, and did not progress very far. Also changes in warfare were not linked to changes in government or society. This was not because Chinese and Manchu governments rejected new technology, but because both the army and government were already quite sophisticated in 1450. Better firearms did not, therefore, force a re-evaluation of military or administrative methods, because firearms were already an important part of

Ming armies. The Qing government simply incorporated a pre-existing system into its armies. Chinese warfare in 1815 was, minus a few refinements, much the same as it had been in 1450.

Notes

1. Zhu Qizhen was the emperor's personal name. During the Ming dynasty emperors were referred to by their reign period. Earlier emperors had multiple reign periods and did not follow this practice. In Zhu Qizhen's case, since his rule was interrupted by his capture and replacement for seven years by his younger brother, he had two reign periods, Zhengtong and Tianshun.
2. P. De Heer, *The care-taker Emperor* (Leiden, E. J. Brill, 1986); A. Waldron, *The Great Wall of China* (Cambridge, Cambridge University Press, 1990); F. Mote, The T'u-mu incident of 1449, in F. Kiernan and J. Fairbank (eds), *Chinese ways in warfare* (Cambridge, Mass., Harvard University Press, 1974), pp. 243–72; D. Twitchett and T. Grimm, The Cheng-t'ung, Ching-t'ai, and T'ien-shun reigns, 1436–1464, in F. Mote and D. Twitchett (eds) The *Cambridge History of China*, vol. 7, part 1 (Cambridge, Cambridge University Press, 1988), pp. 205–42.
3. J. Geiss, The Chia-ching reign, 1522–1566, in *Cambridge History*, p. 471.
4. E. Dreyer, Military origins of Ming China, in *Cambridge History*, p. 104; D. Twitchett and T. Grimm, *Cambridge History*, p. 320.
5. For a full account of this period see R. L. Higgins, *Piracy and coastal defense in the Ming period, government response to coastal disturbances, 1523–1549* (Ann Arbor, University Microfilms International, 1981) and K. W. So, *Japanese Piracy in Ming China During the 16th Century* (Michigan State University Press, 1975).
6. R. Huang, The Lung-ch'ing and Wan-li reigns, 1567–1620, in *Cambridge History*, p. 563.
7. A. Waldron, *Great Wall*, pp. 103–5.
8. J. Geiss, *Cambridge History*, pp. 471–4.
9. *ibid.*, pp. 474–5; A. Waldron, *Great Wall*, pp. 126–39.
10. *ibid.*, pp. 476–9.
11. *ibid.*, pp. 490–505.
12. R. Huang, *Cambridge History*, pp. 564–5.
13. *ibid.*, pp. 566–7.
14. The figure of 158,700 men does not include the approximately 9,000 sailors in the navy. Hideyoshi's total mobilization was approximately 225,000 men.
15. R. Huang, *Cambridge History*, pp. 567–74; G. Sansom, *A History of Japan 1334–1615* (Stanford, Stanford University Press, 1961), pp. 252–9.
16. *ibid.*, pp. 574–6.
17. R. Huang, "The Liao-tung Campaign of 1619," *Oriens Extremus*, 28, 1981, pp. 30–3.
18. *ibid.*, pp. 33–50.
19. Also known as Abahai, the second Qing emperor's name has not been consistently romanized. I follow Wakeman, see below. Other variations include Hong Taiji, Huang Taiji, and Hung T'ai-chi.
20. The four cities were Luanzhou, Qian'an, Zunhua, and Yongping.
21. F. Wakeman, *The Great Enterprise: The Manchu reconstruction of imperial order in seventeenth-*

century China (Berkeley and Los Angeles, University of California Press, 1985), pp. 164–6. The massacre is usually called the "Yongping Massacre."

22. *ibid.*, pp. 170–90.

23. *ibid.*, p. 206.

24. *ibid.*, pp. 1099–1101.

25. For a more detailed discussion of these issues see J. Waley-Cohen, China and Western technology in the late eighteenth century, *American Historical Review*, **98**/5, 1993, pp. 1525–44.

Further Reading

T. J. Barfield, *The perilous frontier: nomadic empires and China*, Oxford, 1989

A. Chan, *The glory and the fall of the Ming Dynasty*, Norman, 1982

S. Jagchild and V. J. Symons, *Peace, war and trade along the Great Wall*, Bloomington, 1989

J. Needham, *Military technology: the gunpowder epic*, Cambridge, 1987

L. A. Struve, *The Southern Ming, 1644–1662*, New Haven, 1984

F. Wakeman, *The great enterprise. The Manchu reconstruction of imperial order in seventeenth-century China*, Berkeley, 1985

A. Waldron, *The Great Wall of China: from history to myth*, Cambridge, 1990

A. Waldron, 'Chinese strategy from the fourteenth to the seventeenth centuries', in W. Murray, M. Knox and A. Bernstein (eds.) *The making of strategy. Rulers, states, and war*, Cambridge, 1994

Chapter Five

Warhorse and gunpowder in India[1] *c.1000–1850*

Jos Gommans

Introduction

Since Michael Roberts launched his thesis on the military revolution it has been vehemently debated among the military historians of the West. His revolution occurred in western Europe during the century after 1560. Basically, it came down to the replacement of relatively small, undisciplined, cavalry troops by huge, well-disciplined and well-drilled, gunpowder infantry armies.[2] More recently, Geoffrey Parker has complemented Roberts' thesis by stressing the radical development of European fortification as a response to the increased challenge of artillery. Parker's main contribution, however, was his successful attempt to extend the Roberts' debate to Asia. Hence, it was Roberts' infantry, the *tercio* – or rather its ever more linear adaptations – and Parker's bastion, the *trace italienne*, which came to represent the European military *sonderweg* that would ultimately pave the way for the rise of the West. According to Parker's subtle formulation, the native peoples of America, Siberia, Black Africa and Southeast Asia lost their independence to the Europeans because they seemed unable to *adopt* Western military technology, whereas those of the Muslim world apparently succumbed because they could not successfully *adapt* it to their military system.[3]

The impact of gunpowder technology in Asia had been discussed before. The Chicago historians Marshal Hodgson and William McNeill applied the term gunpowder empire to the large sixteenth- and seventeenth-century Muslim states of the Ottomans in the Middle East, the Safavids in Iran and the Mughals in India. These empires were supposed to owe their long-term stamina to their effective and exclusive use of firepower, employed by both infantry and artillery. Hence, as is often claimed for the European case as well, the coming of gunpowder in Muslim Asia blew up the old feudal order of forts and heavy cavalry.[4] This idea was also implicitly present in David Ayalon's pioneering work on Mamluk Egypt in which he claimed that the traditional, cavalry-oriented Mamluks were defeated by the more innovative Ottomans, who made effective use of infantry equipped with modern matchlocks. Here again, modern gunpowder, in this case employed by a disciplined infantry of Janissaries, stood at the basis of rapid imperial expansion.[5]

Combining the debates on the military revolution and the gunpowder thesis raises the paradox that, although a stagnant Muslim east was believed to have failed to adapt gunpowder, it was nevertheless able to exploit it for impressive imperial expansion. Of course, it may be argued that their gunpowder weaponry was good enough for their Asian rivals but failed to impress their Western ones, although this argument has never been made explicitly. Interestingly, a similar contradiction appears in the discussion on military fiscalism, where historians have stressed the enormous fiscal pressures exerted by the state's urge to adopt modern gunpowder armies. In Europe this is claimed to have stimulated the emergence of highly centralized states, whereas in Muslim Asia the results appear to have been more ambiguous. For example, in the case of the sixteenth-century Ottoman empire, military expansion and state-wide decentralization went hand in hand. According to Halil Inalcik, the spread of modern firearms and the resulting increase in financial burdens provided the local elites and peasantry with the military and financial means to withstand the central authorities.[6] A similar dual tendency was noticed by Burton Stein in the case of fifteenth- and sixteenth-century south India. Although Stein stressed the prominent role of modern gunpowder in the making of the Vijayanagar empire, he also rightly observed a fundamental contradiction between, on the one hand, military fiscalism leading to centralization, and on the other, the ongoing existence of vigorous regional chieftaincies.[7]

This essay sets out to examine this apparent contradiction in the process of state-formation by focusing on the foremost military developments in medieval and early-modern India. After stressing the *longue durée* of India's geographical context and military culture, it will specifically address revolutionary changes in the use of the warhorse and gunpowder. It is only in the conclusion that I will briefly discuss the way these military developments may have brought about, simultaneously, both state-formation and deformation.

The inner frontier

Warfare in pre-modern India was not a matter of sovereign states. Indeed, from a European perspective Indian wars were often described as permanent "civil" wars waged by inveterate rebels and traitors. All this is not very surprising since India lacked the idea of a closed, sovereign state, favoured with well-demarcated borders in which the king enjoyed a monopoly on the use of legitimate violence. As early as the eleventh century the Latin West started to live up to this ideal and came very near to achieving it in the eighteenth century. By contrast, Indian kingdoms remained open-ended entities without fixed external borders, but with numerous inner frontiers. These open marches marked the divide between a highly productive sedentary society mainly inhabited by peasants, and the still extensive space of arid lands and humid jungle, traversed by highly mobile pastoralists, traders and all sorts of warrior bands. In other words, these transitional zones gave access to mobile resources such as cattle, cash and military recruits, all crucially needed for the exploitation of the sedentary, agrarian economy. Thus, to wield power the Indian king had to have his stakes on both sides of the divide.[8] One way to achieve this was through warfare, or rather, through campaigning along the inner frontiers of empire. Any Indian king with imperial ambitions had to be constantly on the move, as may be seen in the case of the more successful Indian rulers such as Akbar (r.1556–1605), Shivaji (1627–80) and Aurangzeb (r.1658–1707). Indeed, as in the case of Iran and the Middle East, warfare and state-formation often eccentrically gravitated towards the frontier.[9]

Apart from being focused on the peripheral zones, Indian campaigns danced to the tune of the monsoon. Any military expedition, or *mulkgiri*, had to wait for October, when the monsoon rains withered away, the roads became dry and the rivers fordable. As such, it was also nicely attuned to the grazing season and the *kharif* or autumn harvest, both of which facilitated the supply of food and fodder to the army. Before the start of the hot Indian summer, in about March or April, or in any case before the busy time of harvesting the winter crops and sowing the summer ones, the war season came to an end and most warriors returned to their urban quarters or to their villages. For many Indian rulers this seasonal campaigning was part and parcel of the annual administrative routine. In the case of the Mughals these campaigns should not be considered as exclusive military affairs: their expeditions not only involved the movement of the army but of the entire royal court with all its entourage of thousands of officials, merchants, ladies, musicians, dancers, artists and other non-military personnel. Far from being swiftly moving forays, imperial campaigns often came down to dignified, slow-moving processions, with a usual speed of about five km a day, taking breath every one or two days. What was viewed was not an army but a moving *darbar* with all the proper offerings of homage and wealth to the emperor, the latter distributing numerous robes of honour, ranks and other gifts in return. Of course, in all this, the emperor was theatrically presented as the glorious and conquering warrior, the possessor of vast riches, all lavishly displayed to both his following and his enemies.[10] Even though, from the purely military point of

107

view, these pompous and noisy campaigns may have been tactical disasters, for the Mughals they proved to be the *sine qua non* of empire.

Fitna

While gazing at these carnavalesque parades, we are faced with another structural feature of pre-modern Indian warfare: before, during and after a battle or siege, the enemy's loyalty was nearly always for sale. Military alliances were as easily forged as broken, taking no account of so-called ascribed affiliations of caste, religion or ethnicity. On the contrary, warriors usually affiliated along open, pragmatic loyalties, which could change as rapidly as their identities.[11] Although this kind of political arithmetic was not in accordance with the prescriptions of Indian *dharma*, it was in full agreement with the traditional Indian "science of politics" of *arthashastra*, which also recommended a policy of conciliation, gift-giving and sowing dissension. In the Islamic sources this permanent tendency of sedition is often referred to as *fitna*, literally meaning "rebellion", but realistically implying the manipulation of ever-crumbling alliances.[12] In this context the unembarrassing exhibition of riches by the Mughal army merely served to entice potential allies into the imperial camp. After an often pre-arranged desertion or defeat, the former rebels were usually left unharmed and were symbolically incorporated into the imperial *mansabdari* system, a system which conveniently translated each warrior's honour in more quantifiable terms of rank and salary. Obviously this ostentatious ritual of incorporation depended critically on the bold expenditure of enormous treasures. Hence, the imperial army was always accompanied by a huge military bazaar. Its merchants and bankers not only facilitated the transfer of cash and commodities back and forth to the imperial camp, but also demonstrated the ongoing creditworthiness of the army's commanders.[13]

In order to keep his ground under such volatile conditions, every Indian ruler was eager to create an elite corps of trusted warriors who were personally attached to the royal house. For this, the early Turkish rulers of India turned to the traditional Islamic expedient of purchasing military slaves or *mamluks*. At a later stage, the Afghan sultans of Delhi attempted to establish elite loyalties on the basis of shared ethnic identities. The Mughals forged bonds of loyalty through marital relations with the Rajput gentry of northern India. In addition, relying on religious models of sufism and *bhakti*, they created an esoteric circle of personal disciples who served both in the army and the bureaucracy.[14] In the end, though, even these *mamluks*, relatives, disciples and other "sons" of the royal house could not withstand the huge incentives offered through *fitna*.

What does all this mean for the military historian? Does it imply that Indian rulers were not interested in effective instruments of war, and that they were not sensitive to technological innovations? Partly, the answer is yes. One example is the curious Maratha behaviour during the early eighteenth century, after their defeat of the Mughal army. Despite the fact that they had clearly demonstrated the superior logistics of their light cavalry against the slow-moving, heavy armies of the Mughals, they decided to adopt the pompous ways of their former overlords. They probably realized that these moving *darbars-cum-bazaars*, accompanied with all the superpower panoply of unwieldy artillery and elephants, still played a significant role in preventing violent and costly battles and sieges. Besides, considerations of purely military effectiveness gave way to their prime need to demonstrate their rise to political eminence and to administer their newly conquered territories. Hence, they established a full imperial court with all proper pomp and circumstance, geared to collect the revenue and to control the flow of trade. At the same time, however, the rise of the Marathas proves the point that military power did make a difference. Like the early Turkish and Mughal invaders, their conquests were launched from the arid and semi-arid zones of the subcontinent. Their early campaigns were swift-moving operations with relatively small but disciplined armies which could produce staggering victories on the battlefield. Their initial successes were not achieved through ritual or monetary means, the blessings of the settled powers, but mainly through their military might.[15] Even in India, military power and technology could still achieve tremendous fortune and, only slightly less, fame. In the political game of *fitna*, military superiority always remained an important trump card. In order not to waste its costly use, once or twice it had to be majestically demonstrated. But, after the initial show of force, the typical pattern of *fitna* usually reasserted itself: conquerors gradually compromised their early ways of violent raiding and turned to the more usual ways of peaceful accommodation and incorporation in which violence was only used in the last resort.[16] In the case of the Mughal army, it also explains the shift from Babur's small but effective warrior band to Aurangzeb's large and pompous court retinue.[17] Nevertheless, both were equally effective, and both made extensive use of the military instrument *par excellence* in India: the warhorse.

The horse-warrior revolution (1000–1200)

During the eleventh and twelfth centuries India experienced a sudden rise of formerly peripheral but highly mobile warrior tribes. While the north witnessed the well-known inroads of Muslim horse-warriors from Central Asia, the south saw the ascendancy of new dynasties, such as the Yadavas, Kakatiyas and Hoysalas, who issued from the drier uplands of the Deccan and the Carnatic.[18] It appears that all these developments are more or less related to a more effective use of the warhorse. The south experienced some major technological innovations regarding the horse's harness. The saddle, for example, was turned into a large hollow seat giving more support to the rider. In addition, a breastplate was attached to the saddle, which improved its steadiness. The introduction of the martingale permitted a better control of the horse, while the old, complicated headstall was superseded by a simpler one. Hence, except for the curb bit, the south-Indian rider could dispose of all the pieces constituting the modern harness. Together with the diffusion of nailed horseshoes and the stirrup, the latter having already been introduced one or two centuries earlier, these improvements must have considerably enhanced the manoeuvrability and shock-power of the twelfth-century cavalry trooper in south India.[19]

Conspicuously absent at this stage in south India was the mounted archer, who had become the prominent military figure in the northern plains of Hindustan. Although mounted archery was not entirely new to the subcontinent, with the coming of the Turks it experienced a marked revival during the eleventh and twelfth centuries.[20] Mounted archery became particularly effective in the hands of nomadic warriors who could build on the rich Central Asian legacy of equine technology and mobile tactics. In terms of technology, it appears that the combined use of the stirrup and the composite bow gave the Turkish warrior a decisive edge against their Indian counterparts: the first relatively recent, the latter a relatively rare phenomenon in India. Although both were earlier inventions, it was only after the eleventh century that their full impact was felt throughout the Indian subcontinent. Apart from the well-known fact that the improved stability of the stirrup stimulated the rise of heavy cavalry, it also enhanced considerably the firing power of the mounted archer. Much older than the stirrup, the composite bow had already been the longtime weapon of the Central Asian horse-warrior. It had evolved in a Central Asian arms race against the ever-improving quality of mail and plated body armour.[21] As a result, it had an effective range of over 250 yards, within which the arrow retained much of its excellent penetrating qualities. However, its construction, in particular under humid Indian conditions, required specific skills, since it was glued together from a number of materials, mostly containing horn, wood and sinew.[22] Although India was already familiar with the composite bow, at the time of the Turkish invasions many Indian warriors appear to have stuck to the simpler, single-curved bow made of a single piece of wood, mostly of bamboo. Most probably, these served perfectly well against warriors barely covered by body armour, but made no impression at all against the mail and plated protection of Central Asian heavy cavalry.[23]

In terms of tactics, mounted archery came only fully into its own when employed on a massive scale. While wheeling around at a safe distance, large contingents of archers would launch a relentless rain of arrows on the enemy. Then, after wearing out the enemy in a series of skirmishes and feigned retreats, the charge of the heavy cavalry often struck the final blow. Hence, next to mounted archery, the deployment of heavy armoured cavalry remained an important feature of Turkish battle tactics. Even more so, as late as the seventeenth century, heavy cavalry once more came to represent Mughal invincibility on the battlefield, whereas the sultanates of the Deccan and Central Asia continued to rely more on mounted archery.[24]

Apart from technology and tactics, mounted warfare, naturally, required special training and strong warhorses. Both were major assets in the hands of the nomadic pastoralists of Central Asia. As a result, mounted archery became the prized speciality of the Turks, whether it was as nomads or as professional *mamluks* with a nomadic background. At the same time, the Turks were particularly well placed for drawing horses from Asia's best breeding grounds. However, there was no Turkish monopoly on the breeding of good warhorses. As long as Indian breeders were regularly supplied with new foreign stock, they were perfectly capable of producing excellent warhorses of their own. In fact, the location of the best Indian horse-breeding grounds often coincided with the inner marches along the drier zones of the subcontinent.[25] These extensive breeding zones not only brought forth excellent warhorses but also the most important beasts of burden in India: dromedaries and bullocks. Any major military campaign was unthinkable without the help of an extensive service network of professional camel and bullock transporters. It generally appears that during the eleventh and twelfth centuries, these animals began to be employed on a wider scale than before. In any case, while the rapid developments in equine technology and tactics made the warhorse far more effective on the battlefield, the simultaneous spread of dromedaries and bullocks further extended its radius of action.[26] It was this horse-warrior revolution which gave rise to new state-formation and, at the same time, uprooted the more settled parts of Indian society and made these more open to outside influences.

Despite these equine developments, medieval Indian armies continued to deploy India's most traditional war-animal, the elephant. Comparable to heavy cavalry, elephants were mostly used as massive breaking rams. They were, however, far less manageable than horses, and great care had to be taken to avoid them trampling their own troops. At the same time, when well targeted, the elephant's frenzy could be extremely effective in raising panic in the enemy's ranks. The coming of the more mobile and evasive mounted archers made these tactics less effective but, as late as the eighteenth century, elephants continued to serve as an eye-catching element in Indian armies, albeit because they fitted so well into the grand style of Indian warfare.[27] Nevertheless, by about 1200 the warhorse had definitely replaced the elephant as the queen of Indian battles.

Sieges and forts (1200–1400)

The uprooting effects of the horse-warrior revolution during the eleventh and twelfth centuries began to be experienced even more thoroughly during the following two centuries, mainly as a result of a sudden advance in siege technology. This was also the first time that gunpowder came to play a more prominent role in oriental warfare: rising portions of saltpetre had turned it from a mere incendiary into a far more powerful explosive device. These gunpowder bombs and grenades proved particularly effective in sieges, both by having them thrown by traditional mangonels (manjaniqs) into the besieged fort, or by having them dug under the rampart. In the latter case, sappers needed to operate directly under the fort's walls, for which an underground tunnel (naqb) had to be dug, or, if the subsoil was too hard, a covered passage (sabat) had to be built. Under the rampart a widened hole would be filled with gunpowder and other explosive and combustible material, after which the whole construction would be set ablaze. Although there was always a danger that the explosion would fall on the onrushing attackers themselves, as a result of gunpowder, mining became increasingly effective in breaching a wall or, merely by its threat, in driving the besieged to an early surrender. Although the rising potency of early gunpowder has mainly been studied for the Middle East and China, it generally appears that Indian armies speedily adopted this new technology. Apart from mines, this involved related devices such as explosive and fire-throwing bamboo tubes, most of which had come from China, reaching India through Mongol channels.[28]

As important as early gunpowder was the simultaneous introduction, from the Middle East, of the so-called "counterweight" mangonel or the trebuchet (manjaniq maghribi, lit. western mangonel). The trebuchet was a great technological advance on earlier ballistic machines that were operated by crews of men pulling down on the arm. More specifically, the trebuchet could launch heavier missiles – from 130 by the mangonel to 560 pounds by the trebuchet – and, from a greater distance – from 133 by the mangonel to 300 yards by the trebuchet. Clearly, these maghribis – as they are called in the Indo-Persian sources – posed an increased threat to most of the existing walls of the time. In contrast with later artillery, trebuchets did not hinder the army's mobility, since they were mostly fabricated from the wood available near the beleaguered strongpoint. Not surprisingly, for a long time after the introduction of cannon the trebuchet remained an important siege weapon.[29] Although more research is certainly needed in this subject, it is highly plausible that early gunpowder and trebuchets provided a significant advantage to the besiegers vis-à-vis the besieged. It would explain, for example, the fact that during the early fourteenth century virtually every city and fort of importance in central and southern India succumbed to the Muslim raids of Malik Kafur. More generally, one may conclude that, together with the earlier horse-warrior developments, improved siege technology clearly marked the heyday of offensive warfare in India. As mentioned already, it was also the time of new conquering elites who staged their careers starting from the fringes of settled society. By ruling from the saddle and by destroying ramparts, these new dynasties were perfectly situated to bridge India's inner frontiers and to bring about a renewed fusion between the mobile world of the horse and the sedentary world of the fort.[30]

Improved siege technology immediately raises the question of military architecture. How did gunpowder and trebuchets affect the building of forts in India?[31] From the Middle East we know that the more sophisticated siege techniques of the thirteenth century caused major adjustments in fortification. For example, to counter an easy approach of sappers and mangonels, walls were provided with towers which could give flanking fire, while more loopholes and machicolations were used to throw down naphtha and other anti-siege incendiaries.[32] Taking account of the scattered information on various Indian forts, it is very possible that India went through a similar process. For example, the appearance of round towers may have been directed against sappers who would have found easy cover at the tower's corners. At some places, earlier massive walls were provided with inner vaulted chambers and depots which improved the ability to provide counter-fire against attackers along the walls. To compensate for the building of these inner chambers and gangways, walls became much thicker and more solidly built. At some places, such as at Tughluqabad in Delhi, the increased threat of mining and trebuchets may also have led to the building of projecting bastions, often provided with a base of scraped rock and sloping bolster plinths. Besides these improvements, more and more forts were built on steep, rocky hills and in the middle of dense, thorny forests, making them harder to approach by sappers or other siege engineers. Hence, it appears that thirteenth- and fourteenth-century siege technology did indeed give fresh impetus to the building and rebuilding of Indian forts. By the sixteenth century most Indian forts were better equipped than ever to sustain sieges, even if the besiegers employed the newest gunpowder device of the day: cannon.

The false dawn of gunpowder (1400–1750)

As mentioned already, the gunpowder thesis is mostly related to the sixteenth century, when new armies equipped with cannon and matchlock firearms paved the way for the ascendancy of more centralized states. Before touching briefly upon the latter supposition in my conclusion, this section will first broadly examine the thesis's relevance from a purely military perspective and will, accordingly, focus primarily on "true" guns, i.e. guns in which a gunpowder charge exerted a propellant effect on a projectile launched from a metal barrel. Although a much earlier invention, it appears that it was mainly during the fifteenth century that cannon was diffused more widely in India, most prominently in the Muslim sultanates of the Deccan. During the second half of the century their use spread towards the north, while light firearms (*banduq, tufang, toredar*), equipped with matchlock-trigger mechanisms, also became more widespread. Subsequently, both cannon and portable firearms figure prominently in the Mughal chronicles. In due course gunpowder, cannon and firearms were manufactured in considerable numbers all over the Indian subcontinent. It remains to be seen, however, to what extent these new weapons were really effective on the actual battlefield or in sieges.

To begin with the latter – even for the new gunpowder armies, investing a fort remained a protracted and complicated affair. Usually the main problem was to find a proper staging ground from which the, often extremely heavy, siege guns could be employed effectively. Actually, from the fourteenth to the late eighteenth century, there are only rare instances of artillery being successfully employed against forts. From time to time walls were adjusted to accommodate artillery, but this principally involved the levelling of towers and walls to make room for the installation of heavy guns – in other words, for defensive purposes. It appears that cannon became at least as important to the besieged as to the besiegers. The numerous failures of artillery to take forts suggests that the thirteenth- and fourteenth-century adjustments of fortification, together with the particular geographical conditions of the Indian subcontinent – remember its steep hills and inaccessible forests–made a later development following Parker's *trace italienne* rather superfluous.

As a consequence, there was nothing like the widespread decastellization – or as Joseph Needham would say, Sinification – witnessed in Europe.[33] On the contrary, forts re-emerged as the strongholds of a new martial elite – in the north often referred to as Rajputs, in the Deccan as Marathas, and in the south as Nayakas. This was a self-conscious gentry comprising armed settlers of mostly marginal areas, who had gained certain protection rights in return for military services to the conquering dynasties of the previous centuries. As these warriors became settled, their forts became the new centres of an expanding agrarian economy. However, these agrarian estates should not be equated with the more primitive, closed, feudal fiefs of Europe, since they were highly monetized economies that remained as open as ever to the outside influences of interregional trade and politics. This implied that the gentry could never fully settle down in their flourishing estates. As mentioned already, they were in fact permanently subjected to the uprooting forces of *fitna*. Although they could withstand the siege technology of the day, they could not reasonably be expected to reject endless offerings of cash and employment. Except for new conquerors who wanted to set an early example, taking a fort became less about shelling and more about bribing the besieged. Or to use the words of Douglas Streusand, even the strongest of Indian forts became ideal "units of political bargaining power".[34]

The crucial importance of *fitna* in taking forts reveals itself most explicitly in the numerous sieges of Aurangzeb in which his commanders outstripped each other in offering the highest bribes to the besieged Marathas. After every submission the latter were allowed to leave the fort unharmed and with all their personal belongings. Not surprisingly, only a few months after the Mughal train had taken up another siege, the fort was easily recaptured by their former occupiers. Characteristically, all these sieges took place in a hostile environment in which the Mughals were mostly besieged themselves, forcing them to spend considerable time and effort in building and digging extensive lines of defence. But this was nothing compared with the efforts they had to put into the maintenance of the numerous supply lines to the north. In this respect, their fate hinged once more on the mobile horse-warrior who foraged the countryside for food and supplies and protected the caravans, bringing fresh supplies along the trade routes.[35]

Not greatly different from sieges, the tactical deployment of cannon on the battlefield proved extremely troublesome. Characteristically, the firing of guns, always stationed at the front rank, served as a solemn announcement of the start of battle, after which the guns lay inactive on the ground to make room for the cavalry. Usually the heaviness of most Indian guns made rapid manoeuvring in the field impossible. Although Indian armies disposed of various brass and bronze specimens, most of their guns were bound together from wrought-iron bars, which made them not only heavy but also unreliable and extremely inaccurate. While aiming such a heavy Indian bombard was already a major problem in itself, the lack of standardization of both barrels and shot – the latter had often to be hammered in order to fit into the barrel – made it extremely difficult to co-ordinate the firing of guns in number. Apart from these drawbacks with the gun itself, it also appears that Indian gunpowder was less powerful through not being granulated.[36] Besides, mobility was hampered by very primitive gun carriages. Indeed, there is a general consensus among military observers that most Indian armies failed to introduce a light field artillery that could be employed in combination with cavalry. To repeat the argument of Geoffrey Parker, they adopted cannon but failed to adapt it to their cavalry.[37]

To alleviate the problem of mobility, guns were at times produced at the very spot where they were needed. Attempts were also made to affix guns to elephants (*gajnal* or *hathnal*, both lit. elephant barrel) and dromedaries (*shutarnal*, *zamburak*, *shahin*, camel barrel, little wasp, falcon, respectively). During the eighteenth century light camel-guns were successfully employed by the Durrani Afghans, but even these rapidly moving units had only a limited range of action and could only serve in the drier parts of the Indian subcontinent.[38]

Coming now to the use of firearms, the prime focus should be on the effectiveness of Indian infantry. We should keep in mind that, according to received opinion, it was new infantry tactics based on rigid squares or *tercios* comprising drilled, military professionals, equipped with standardized, hand-held matchlocks and pikes, that during the sixteenth century announced a new gunpowder age in western Europe. At the same time, the rise of infantry also signalled the decline of heavy cavalry. Turning to sixteenth- and seventeenth-century India, the presence of infantry is certainly eye-catching. As argued by Dirk Kolff, there appears to have been an almost limitless availability of armed peasants who presented themselves continually to an extensive military labour market.[39] For most of these armed peasants, military employment was only a part-time business, complemented by other activities such as sowing, harvesting and weaving. As mentioned already, military employment neatly followed the agrarian calendar. Especially in the semi-arid zones of India, such as in Rajasthan, Maharashtra and the Carnatic, which often depended on only one uncertain crop, military services could become a crucial part of the population's survival strategy.[40] Despite the sheer masses of Indian foot soldiers, their role appears as only marginal on the actual battlefield. Although the Indo-Persian chronicles give relatively high figures for infantry, the latter figures barely in the battle accounts, which remain dedicated to the horse-warrior. The same goes for the many pictorial representations in miniatures. Although this may have been the result of a cultural bias on the part of the horse-loving artist, the minor role of infantry in battles is confirmed by the disparaging comments of European contemporaries and modern military scholars alike.[41] Most of all, following the almost endless availability of superior cavalry, India lacked the inducement to develop disciplined and drilled infantry which could operate in the open field or keep up permanent fire. As in the case of artillery, their firearms and shot lacked standardization. It further appears that the bulk of Indian infantry served off the battlefield, as local militia or as various attendants (*ahsham*) of court and cavalry. From a purely technological point of view, the foot soldier remained at a clear disadvantage *vis-à-vis* the horse-warrior. For the most part they lacked any body armour and were only equipped with primitive bows and spears. Even when the foot soldier could dispose of a matchlock arquebus, he was still at a loss against the mounted archer. For example, the firing rate of the matchlock could not compete with the composite bow. A trained archer could get off six aimed shots per minute without difficulty. According to the French observer Bernier this was, in any case, three times as often as a musketeer could shoot his matchlock. Besides, at long range the bow retained more of its penetrating power and was definitely more accurate. Nevertheless, both matchlockmen and archers had great difficulty in penetrating the horseman's body-armour, which could only be achieved from within 100 yards:[42] Hence the ongoing popularity of heavy Mughal armour, consisting of helmet, vambraces, mail shirt and trousers, and, in particular during the seventeenth and eighteenth century, the *chahar ayina* (lit. four mirrors), a plated cuirass in four sections.[43]

We should bear in mind that, notwithstanding the many defects of the matchlock gun, its use required considerably less training and less expense than cavalry warfare. As such it was naturally the weapon *par excellence* of the peasant who preferred to employ it on an individual basis. In fact, there were only a few relatively well-trained, regular infantry units consisting mostly of peasants and petty landlords such as the Baksariyas and Bundelas. Other infantry troops were recruited from so-called savage tribesmen from the fringe of sedentary society, such as Kanarese Berads, who, apart from being notorious dacoits and cattle-lifters, had a reputation for being the best matchlockmen of the Deccan. These infantry units hired their services to the highest bidder, and they were certainly an asset for any military commander. They failed, however, to revolutionize Indian warfare. Indian matchlockmen, usually operating their guns behind trenches or some other cover, should certainly not be confused with the Swiss *tercios* of Europe. But even if they had been organized in drilled formations, the slow-firing matchlockmen, whether or not assisted by pikemen, would still have been at a loss against the massive deployment of the highly professional, well-armoured, and still much more mobile cavalry troops. *Tercios* could only be deployed successfully in western Europe, where cavalry lacked both numbers and sophistication. Or, to formulate it from the Indian perspective, the almost cornucopian availability of professional horse-warriors and, at the same time, the lack of rapidly-firing gunpowder arms, was responsible for the ongoing supremacy of cavalry in India. The latest Turks in India, the Mughals, could only follow in the path of their predecessors. Even the Mughal's best-known gunpowder victory at the battle of Panipat (1526) was not the work of heavy artillery but of traditional Central Asian tactics of combining mounted archery with the so-called *tabur* or "wagenburg". This consisted of a number of wagons chained together to form an effective barrier against cavalry charges and to give cover to matchlockmen and a few light guns. At the start of the sixteenth century the wagenburg made an initial impact, but it certainly failed to herald a new gunpowder era in which artillery and infantry were to dominate Indian warfare.[44] Illustratively, almost 250 years later, on the same battlefield, the heavy artillery of the Marathas was again defenceless against the more mobile cavalry forces of the Afghans.[45]

The gunpowder revolution (1750–1850)

It is my contention that it was only during the second half of the eighteenth century that gunpowder really came to revolutionize Indian warfare. Improved casting and boring techniques made artillery a more effective instrument of war, not only in Europe but also in India. Employed by European specialists, it proved more effective, both in sieges and – being lighter and, hence, more mobile – in the field. Next to artillery, the effectiveness of infantry also radically improved. First of all, the introduction of the flintlock mechanism considerably enhanced the firing power of European infantry units.[46] The new flintlock musket had many advantages against the older matchlock arquebus. Basically, it was lighter, less unreliable, easier to fire and blessed with more hitting power. Thanks to the spread of prepackaged paper cartridges, the fire rate was almost doubled. Equipped with the new socket bayonet, the defensive and offensive capacities of infantry against cavalry were increased. Moreover, it simplified the very complicated drill of the *tercio*, since the new system could dispense with the pikemen. Although flintlocks had been in use in both Europe and Asia before, it was only during the early eighteenth century that flintlocks were generally adopted in Europe. India rapidly followed suit. Obviously, this did not mean that the traditional horse-warrior could be pensioned off immediately, but it certainly marked a general shift from cavalry to infantry, or rather, to well-drilled sepoy regiments equipped with flintlock muskets and socket bayonets.[47] Although Indian armies lacked experience with drilling infantry regiments, they could easily hire European officers who adjusted the training of Indian foot soldiers to the simplified European tactics.[48] Thanks to the flintlock, the period from 1750 to 1820 was to be the heyday of the European military adventurer who gradually replaced the traditional Turkish and Afghan mercenary dealing primarily in cavalry and warhorses. It remained difficult, however, to integrate the infantry units fully into the larger Indian armies which were still emotionally attached to the horse. Now the dialectics of progress began to work to the advantage of Europe. For example, the new armies of the East India Company effectively combined the new infantry with a highly mobile field artillery. In terms of technology, the Company's army in no way lagged behind their European counterparts. In fact, the so-called India Pattern musket of the Company became the standard British infantry weapon throughout the Napoleonic wars.[49]

Not surprisingly, the new flintlock mechanism also had a considerable effect upon cavalry tactics. First of all, Indian cavalry began to follow the Turkish and Afghan example of using short blunderbusses (sherbashas, lit. lion's whelps), preferably equipped with flintlock trigger mechanisms. The way they used these muskets was similar to the Central Asian tactics of the archer, wheeling around and wearing out the enemy by relentless fire.[50] Both in comparison with composite bows and matchlocks, flintlocks simplified the deployment of such tactics and opened up their feasibility to the non-specialist. There was also a gradual shift from heavy to light cavalry.[51] In India this was certainly the result of the improved firing and hitting power of infantry, but, as in Europe, it also marked a revival of nomadic tactics practised by tribal cavalry, Skinner's and other Indian light horse finding their counterparts in the hussar and cossack regiments of Europe. Away from the battlefield, light cavalry still served well as a part of various guerilla tactics and, more important, in maintaining supply lines over long distances. Besides, the Indian nobility often stuck to their horses, since these offered superior opportunities for raiding and plundering. This is heard, for example, in the numerous complaints of European foot soldiers who were always too late to claim the war booty, since all of it had long since been carried off by their mounted Indian allies who had awaited the outcome of the battle from a safe distance. Hence, it would still take a century and a Mutiny before the proud mounted warrior of India finally succumbed to the more pliable sepoy. In the end, however, the combined use of more advanced field artillery and drilled infantry broke the longstanding paramountcy of the Indian horse-warrior.

Conclusion

From about 1000 to 1850 India experienced two military breakthroughs. The first occurred from about 1000 to 1200 and involved the ascendancy of the horse-warrior in general, and the mounted archer in particular. In the following two centuries this horse-warrior revolution gained its full weight following the marked improvement in siege technology. For about 700 years the effects of the revolution were perpetuated in varying degrees all over the Indian subcontinent. The second breakthrough took place from about 1750 to 1850 and involved improved gunpowder technology in the hands both of artillery and infantry, and should genuinely be called a gunpowder revolution. From the Indian perspective both revolutions were introduced by outside "barbarians", infiltrating the sub-continent along the long inner-frontier and littoral zones that connected India with the Central Asian steppes and the Indian Ocean. Both started their Indian political career as relatively small, armed units that proved their military superiority on the battlefield against their outmoded Indian counterparts. Both successfully crossed India's inner frontier and brought about a renewed fusion of a settled society with the more mobile world of pastoralism or trade. However, in the case of the Turks, this fusion could only be achieved through invigorating the disordering forces of the frontier. Hence, their rule remained wedded to the culture of the camp, the horse and the bow. This also explains the apparent contradiction, mentioned in the introduction, between military expansion on the one hand, and disintegration on the other. Here the military superiority of horse-warrior could never achieve fully-centralized states. To put it differently, horse-warriors could never fully control a densely-fortified countryside without losing the very base of their supremacy. Hence, their political organization stood somewhere midway between a sedentary and nomadic empire. Once again, military chiefs broke away, built their own forts and started a princedom for themselves. Obviously, the traditional Indian politics of *fitna* served these vola-tile circumstances very well. Its working was further stimulated by a highly monetized military labour market in which the military entrepreneur had always played a prominent part. Perhaps one may even say that the easy availability of both horses and money precluded the rise of centralized medieval states in India. Of course, military superiority could bring rapid conquests but its consolidation required the extremely malleable and uprooting politics of *fitna*. In other words, the continued vigour of the inner frontier, *fitna* and the warhorse conditioned both the rise and, almost simultaneously, the fragmentation of empire.[52]

In contrast to the Turkish and Afghan horse-warriors, the Indo-European armies of infantry and artillery succeeded in eliminating India's inner frontiers and, after more than a century, imposed a full monopoly on the use of legitimate violence. For the colonial government the heroic frontiersmen became "criminal tribes", whereas *fitna* was equated with corruption and treason. India at large was sealed off from the outside world, and after about 1850 came very near to being a modern centralized state. Clearly, all of this would have been unthinkable without the help of gunpowder.

Notes

1. Since India lacks a general analytical survey of the major military developments during the medieval period, the following cannot be a trustworthy account of the received wisdom on the

subject but merely an attempt to formulate a first hypothesis. The first version of this essay was presented at the conference on the new military history of South Asia, Cambridge, 15–17 July 1997. I wish to thank Jan Heesterman, Douglas Streusand, John Richards and René Barendse for comments or helpful reflections.

2. M. Roberts, *The military revolution 1560–1660* (Belfast, 1956). See also J. Black, *A military revolution? Military change and European society* (London, 1991).

3. G. Parker, *The military revolution: military innovation and the rise of the West 1500–1800* (Cambridge, 1988), p. 136. Parker made an exception for the Far East.

4. M. G. S. Hodgson, *The gunpowder empires and modern times*, vol. 3 of *The venture of Islam* (Chicago, 1974); W. H. McNeill, *The pursuit of power: technology, armed forces and society since AD 1000* (Chicago, 1982); Interview with William H. McNeill, *The Historian*, 53, 1990, pp. 1–16.

5. D. Ayalon, *Gunpowder and firearms in the Mamluk kingdom: a challenge to medieval society* (London, 1956).

6. H. Inalcik, Military and fiscal transformation in the Ottoman empire, 1600–1700, *Archivum Ottomanicum*, 6, 1980, pp. 283–337.

7. B. Stein, State formation and economy reconsidered, *Modern Asian Studies*, 19, 1985, pp. 387–413. Apart from gunpowder Stein also mentions the state's need to purchase warhorses.

8. The idea of such an Indian inner frontier derives from Jan Heesterman, see e.g., his The Hindu frontier, *Itinerario*, 13(1), 1989, pp. 1–17 and, more recently, Warrior, peasant and Brahmin, *Modern Asian Studies*, 29(3), 1995, pp. 637–54. For further elaborations on the theme, see A. Wink, *The slave kings and the Islamic conquest 11th–13th centuries*, vol. 2 of *Al-Hind: the making of the Indo-Islamic world* (Leiden, 1997) and my forthcoming, The silent frontier of South Asia, *c.* 1100–1800 AD, *Journal of World History*, 1998.

9. Hence the eccentric location of imperial capitals such as Delhi, Vijayanagar, Bijapur in India; Tabriz, Qazwin and Teheran in Iran; and perhaps even Vienna and Berlin in Europe.

10. There are numerous descriptions of the pomp and circumstance of royal Indian armies. For an early seventh-century example, see E. B. Cowell and F. W. Thomas (tr.), *The harsacarita of Bana* (London, 1897), pp. 199–211. For the Mughal camp, see e.g., M. A. Ansari, The encampment of the Great Mughals, *Islamic Culture*, 37, 1963, pp. 14–24. For an eighteenth-century example, see the account of Maistre de la Tour of the so-called "grand safari" of Haider Ali of Mysore in *Les indes florissantes: anthologie des voyageurs français*, G. Deleury (ed.) (1750–1820), pp. 568–72.

11. Unfortunately, a great deal of energy has been wasted by stressing the political inhibitions of the Indian caste-system. It is most prominent in the "divided we fell" (against the united Muslim and British forces) thesis. Political alliances were not about rigid caste loyalties but about the ever-shifting loyalties of *fitna*.

12. For the role of *fitna* in Indian politics and warfare, see A. Wink, *Land and sovereignty in India: agrarian society and politics under the eighteenth-century Maratha svarajya* (Cambridge, 1986), pp. 9–51. See also D. H. A. Kolff, The end of an ancien régime: colonial war in India, 1798–1818, in J. A. de Moor and H. L. Wesseling (eds) *Imperialism and war: essays on colonial wars in Asia and Africa* (Leiden, 1989), pp. 22–49 and my Indian warfare and Afghan innovation during the eighteenth century, *Studies in History*, 11(2), 1995, pp. 261–80. For southern India, see P. Price, *Kingship and political practice in colonial India* (Cambridge, 1996).

13. In general, its almost permanent "trade deficit" appears to have facilitated the drawing of cash (and thus revenue) to the royal court by bills of exchange. For the logistics of bills of exchange in India, see S. Subrahmanyam's introduction to S. Subrahmanyam (ed.) *Money and the market in India 1100–1700* (Delhi, 1994), p. 33.

14. For this, see the excellent studies of J. F. Richards, The formulation of imperial authority under Akbar and Jahangir, in J. F. Richards (ed.) *Kingship and authority in South Asia* (Madison, 1978) and Norms of comportment among imperial Mughal officers, in B. D. Metcalf (ed.) *Moral conduct and authority: the place of adab in South Asian Islam* (Berkeley, 1984), pp. 255–90.

15. For Maratha warfare, see S. Sen, *Military system of the Marathas* (Calcutta, 1928).

16. In the case of the Delhi sultanate, the continued threat of a Mongol onslaught from the northwest served as an important brake on this development and kept alive the nomadic traditions of mobile warfare.

17. I am fully aware that this argument comes very near to that of the fourteenth-century Arabian historian Ibn Khaldun. See his *The muqaddimah*, tr. F. Rosenthal (London, 1967).

18. It is very well possible that India, like the Middle East, witnessed a growing interest in technical treatises on statecraft (*nitishastra*) and warfare (*danurveda*) at about this time. This remains speculative, however, since the dating of these works remains extremely troublesome.

19. Interestingly, the Turkish harnesses were provided with a curb bit which thus may have given the Turkish rider a more severe control of his horse. On the development of horse-equipment in southern India, see the pioneering studies of Jean Deloche, *Military technology in Hoysala sculpture (twelfth and thirteenth century)* (New Delhi, 1989) and *Horses and riding equipment in India art* (Pondicherry, 1990).

20. There is a great deal of literature on the horse-archer. Latest is A. Wink who takes issue with S. Digby on the issue whether or not the horse-archer signalled the decline of the elephant on the Indian battlefield (*Slave kings*, pp. 79–110). According to Digby the elephant remained of prime importance to the Delhi sultanate (S. Digby, *War-horse and elephant in the Delhi sultanate* (Oxford, 1971).

21. C. Uray-Kühalmi, La périodisation de l'histoire des armements des nomades des steppes, *Études Mongoles*, 5, 1974, pp. 145–55.

22. For the composite bow, see the studies of J. D. Latham and W. F. Paterson, *Saracen archery* (London, 1970) and Archery in the lands of Eastern Islam, in R. Elgood (ed.) *Islamic arms and armour* (London, 1979), pp. 78–88; J. D. Latham, Some technical aspects of archery in the Islamic miniature, *The Islamic Quarterly*, 12(4), 1968, pp. 225–34; J. D. Latham, The archers of the Middle East: The Turco-Iranian background, *Iran*, 8, (1970), pp. 97–103; W. F. Paterson, The archers of islam, *Journal of the Economic and Social History of the Orient*, 9 (1966), pp. 69–87 and A. Boudot-Lamotte, *Contribution à l'étude de l'archerie musulmane* (Damascus, 1968). For the composite bow in India, see the studies of W. F. Paterson, Archery in Moghul India, *The Islamic Quarterly*, 16(1–2), 1972, pp. 81–95 and Edward McEwan, Persian archery texts: chapter eleven of fakhr-i mudabbir's adab al-harb (early thirteenth century), *The Islamic Quarterly*, 18(3–4), 1974, pp. 76–99; The chahar-kham of "four-curved" bow of India, in *Islamic arms and armour*, pp. 90–6.

23. For the use of the simple bow in India, see Deloche, *Military technology*, p. 12; G. N. Pant, *Indian archery* (Delhi, 1978), pp. 264–301 and K. S. Lal, The striking power of the army of the sultanate, *Journal of Indian History*, 55(3), 1977, pp. 98–9.

24. This follows from the military exploits of Aurangzeb in both Central Asia and the Deccan. See the detailed accounts in the 4-volume study of Jadunath Sarkar, *History of Aurangzeb* (Calcutta, 1925–30).

25. J. Gommans, *The rise of the Indo-Afghan empire, c. 1710–1780* (Leiden, 1995), pp. 68–104. For example, between Lahore and Delhi there were long-time horse-breeding tracts which sustained the tenth-century Hindu Shahi state based at Bhatinda as well as the later Muslim

states centred round Lahore and Delhi. For the Hindu Shahis, see B. K. Majumdar, *The military system in ancient India* (Calcutta, 1960), p. 108.

26. See my forthcoming, The silent frontier.

27. For the role of elephants in medieval Indian warfare, see the studies of J. Sarkar, *Military history of India* (Delhi, 1970), pp. 163–8; Digby, *Warhorse*, pp. 50–83; Lal, *Power*, p. 97; J. Larus, *Political-military behaviour: the Hindus in pre-modern India* (Calcutta, 1979); S. K. Bhakari, *Indian warfare: an appraisal of strategy and tactics of war in early-medieval period* (Delhi, 1981), pp. 61–85; Gommans, Indian warfare, pp. 266–7 and Wink, *Slave kings*, pp. 79–111.

28. For the use of early gunpowder in China, see J. Needham *et al.*, *Military technology: the gunpowder epic*, part 7 of *Chemistry and chemical technology*, vol. 5 of *Science and civilization in China* (Cambridge, 1986), pp. 1–18, 161–92. For the Middle East, see A. Y. al-Hassan and D. R. Hill, *Islamic technology: An illustrative history* (Cambridge, 1986), pp. 106–120; for India, see Iqtidar Alam Khan, Coming of gunpowder to the islamic world and north India: spotlight on the role of the Mongols, *Journal of Asian History*, 30(1), 1996, pp. 27–45.

29. For the trebuchet in China, see J. Needham and R. D. S. Yates, *Military technology: missiles and sieges*, part 4 of *Chemistry and chemical technology*, vol. 5 of *Science and civilisation in China* (Cambridge, 1994), pp. 203–40. For the Middle East, see D. R. Hill, Trebuchets, *Viator*, 4, 1973, p. 115 and under the heading "hisar", in *Encyclopaedia of Islam*, new edition (Leiden, 1954–). For India, see several references in M. Habib, *The campaigns of 'Ala'u'd-din Khilji being the Khaza'inul futuh (Treasures of victory) of Hazrat Amir Khusrau of Delhi* (Madras, 1931).

30. cf. Wink, *Slave kings*, p. 3.

31. Information on Indian forts has been gathered from various studies on specific forts. Of a more general nature are: J. Burton-Page, A study of fortification in the Indian subcontinent from the thirteenth to the eighteenth century AD, *Bulletin of the School of Oriental and African Studies*, 23(3), 1960, pp. 508–22; P. V. Begde, *Forts and palaces of India* (New Delhi, 1982). Again paving the way is Jean Deloche in his Études sur les fortifications de l'Inde, I: les fortifications de l'Inde ancienne, *Bulletin de l'École française d'Extrême-Orient*, 81, 1994, pp. 89–131 and "Études sur les fortifications de l'Inde, II: les monts fortifiés du Maisur méridional (1re partie)", *Bulletin de l'École française d'Extrême-Orient*, 82, 1995, pp. 219–66.

32. See, e.g. H. Kennedy, *Crusader castles* (Cambridge, 1994), pp. 180–5.

33. Needham and Yates, *Military technology: missiles and sieges*, p. 240.

34. D. E. Streusand, *The formation of the Mughal empire* (Delhi, 1989), p. 65.

35. For a detailed account of these sieges, see J. Sarkar, *Southern India, 1645–1689*, vol. 4 of *History of Aurangzeb* (Calcutta, 1930).

36. See the accounts of Cossigny and Modave in G. Deleury, *Les indes florissantes*, pp. 471–3.

37. See, e.g. Sarkar, *The art of war in medieval India* (New York, 1984), pp. 324–5 and B. Lenman, The weapons of war in 18th-century India, *Journal of the Society for Army Historical Research*, 46 (1968), pp. 33–6.

38. See my, Indian warfare, pp. 275–7.

39. D. H. A. Kolff, *Naukar, Rajput and sepoy: the ethnohistory of the military labour market in Hindustan, 1450–1850* (Cambridge, 1990), pp. 1–31.

40. cf. S. Gordon, Zones of military entrepreneurship in India, 1500–1800, in his *Marathas, marauders and state formation in eighteenth-century India* (Delhi, 1994), pp. 182–208. It was only during the nineteenth century that new crops began to change the existing agrarian calendar and to reduce the peasant's off-season. It is no coincidence that it was just at this time that the British authorities finally managed to disarm the Indian gentry and to impose a near monopoly on the use of violence.

41. See, e.g. G. L. Coeurdoux, *Moeurs et coutumes des Indiens* (1777) (Paris, 1987), p. 180; Sarkar,

Art of war, pp. 320–1; and the still classical account of W. Irvine, *The army of the Indian Mughals* (London, 1903), p. 161ff.

42. For this information on the bow and the matchlock, see R. Elgood, *Firearms of the Islamic world in the Tareq Rajab Museum, Kuwait* (London, 1995), p. 16. It also contains the best general survey on Oriental and Indian firearms to date.

43. See, e.g. D. Nicolle and A. McBride, *Mughul India 1504–1761*, vol. 263 of *Men-at-arms series* (London, 1993), pp. 40, 43; and H. Russell Robinson, *Oriental armour* (London, 1967), p. 107.

44. The same argument could be made for Central Asia and Iran. Even Ayalon's claims that Ottoman victories against the horse-loving Mamluks and Safavids were based on their superior command of gunpowder may be questioned. See e.g., the comments on the battle of Caldiran by D. Morgan, *Medieval Persia 1040–1797* (London, 1988), p. 117, and J. R. Walsh in "Caldiran", in *Encyclopaedia of Islam*, new edition (Leiden, 1954). For the Mamluks, see the review by Robert Irwin of Shai Har-El, *Struggle for domination in the Middle East: the Ottoman-Mamluk war 1485–91* (Leiden, 1995), *Journal of the Royal Asiatic Society*, 7(1), 1996, p. 136.

45. There are numerous descriptions on both battles: e.g., for Panipat 1526, see Streusand, *Formation*, p. 52; and for Panipat 1761, see T. S. Shejwalkar, *Panipat 1761* (Poona, 1946).

46. J. Black, *European warfare 1660–1815* (London, 1994), pp. 38–9. Black emphatically shifts the European military revolution to the period 1660–1760.

47. See, e.g. Lenman, Weapons, pp. 37–9; Elgood, *Firearms*, pp. 144ff and P. K. Datta, Guns in Mughal India, *Bulletin of the Victoria Memorial Hall*, 2 (1968), pp. 30–8.

48. For the effectiveness of the late-eighteenth and early-nineteenth century Maratha infantry – only lacking bayonets – and artillery, see, e.g. J. Pemble, Resources and techniques in the second Maratha war, *The Historical Journal*, 19(2), 1976, pp. 375–404.

49. D. W. Bailey and D. Harding, From India to Waterloo: The "India Pattern" musket, in A. J. Guy (ed.) *The Road to Waterloo* (London, 1990), pp. 48–57.

50. See my Indian warfare, 270–8. It remains unclear, however, whether the Afghans approached the enemy slowly, like the European *caracole*, or rapidly like the traditional archers (personal communication by J. P. Puype, Delft Army Museum).

51. Interestingly, very heavily armoured cavalry came back into fashion in eighteenth-century Hyderabad which suggests that body-armour was still bulletproof (Nicolle and McBride, *Mughul India*, p. 43).

52. In the case of *fitna* a similar argument has been made already by A. Wink in his *Land and sovereignty*, p. 34.

Further reading

For information on various aspects of Indo-Islamic warfare, see *Encyclopaedia of Islam*, new edn (Leiden, 1954–) under the following headings: *asb, arrada, barud, burdj, djaysh, fil, harb, hisar, hisn, kaws, lashkar, mandjanik, naft, sur.*

General

✝ S. K. Bhakari, *Indian warfare: an appraisal of strategy and tactics in the early-medieval period* (New Delhi, 1981).

W. Egerton, *Illustrated handbook of Indian arms* (London, 1880).

P. K. Gode, *Studies in Indian cultural history IV* (Poona, 1960).

P. Horn, *Das Heer- und Kriegswesen des Großmoghuls* (Leiden, 1894).

W. Irvine, *The army of the Indian Moghuls* (London, 1903).

K. S. Lal, The striking power of the army of the Sultanate, *Journal of Indian History*, 55(3), 1977.

D. Nicolle and A. McBride, *Mughul India 1504–1761*, vol. 263 of *Men-at-arms series* (London, 1993).

G. N. Pant, *Indian arms and armour* [3 vols] (New Delhi, 1978–).

S. P. Rosen, *Societies and military power: India and its armies in comparative perspective* (Ithaca/London, 1996).

J. Sarkar, *Military history of India* (Delhi, 1970).

J. N. Sarkar, *The art of war in medieval India* (New Delhi, 1984).

D. E. Streusand, *The formation of the Mughal empire* (Delhi, 1989).

Elephants and horses

R. A. Alavi, New light on Mughal cavalry, In *Medieval India: A Miscellany*, 2, 1972.

J. Deloche, *Horses and riding equipment in Indian art* (Pondicherry, 1990).

J. Deloche, *Military technology in Hoysala sculpture (twelfth and thirteenth century)* (New Delhi, 1989).

S. Digby, *War-horse and elephant in the Delhi sultanate* (Karachi, 1971).

E. McEwan, The chahar-kham or "four-curved" bow of India, in R. Elgood (ed.) *Islamic arms and armour* (London, 1979).

W. F. Paterson, Archery in Moghul India, *The Islamic Quarterly*, 16(1–2), 1972.

H. Russell Robinson, *Oriental armour* (London, 1967).

K. K. Trivedi, The share of mansabdars in state revenue resources: a study of the maintenance of animals, *The Indian Economic and Social History Review*, 24(4), 1987.

A. Wink, Kings, slaves and elephants, in his *The slave kings and the Islamic conquest: 11th–13th centuries*, vol. 2 of *Al Hind: the making of the Indo-Islamic world* (Leiden, 1997).

N. Ziegler, Evolution of the Rathor state of Marvar: horses, structural change and warfare, in K. Schomer *et al.* (eds) *Institutions*, vol. 2 of *The idea of Rajastan: explorations in regional identity*, (New Delhi, 1994).

Gunpowder

P. K. Datta, Use of rockets in warfare in Mughal India, *Bulletin of the Victoria Memorial*, 1, 1967.

P. K. Datta, Guns in Mughal India, *Bulletin of the Victoria Memorial*, 2, 1968.

P. K. Datta, Cannon in India during the Mughal days, *Bulletin of the Victoria Memorial*, 3–4, 1969–70.

R. Elgood, *Firearms of the Islamic world in the Tareq Rajab Museum, Kuwait* (London, 1995).

Alam Iqtidar Khan, Origin and development of gunpowder technology in India: AD 1250–1500, *The Indian Historical Review*, 4(1), 1977.

Alam Iqtidar Khan, Early use of cannon and musket in India: AD 1442–1526, *Journal of the Economic and Social History of the Orient*, 24(2), 1981.

Alam Iqtidar Khan, The coming of gunpowder to the Islamic world and north India: spotlight on the role of the Mongols. *Journal of Asian History* 30(1), 1996.

B. P. Lenman, The weapons of war in eighteenth-century India, *Journal of the Society for Army Historical Research*, 46, 1968.

Muhammad Yar Khan, The use of artillery during the Sultanate period, *Islamic Culture*, 35, 1961.

M. K. Zaman, The use of artillery in Mughal warfare, *Islamic Culture*, 57(4), 1983.

Z. Zygulsky, Oriental and Levantine firearms, in C. Blair (ed.) *Pollards History of Firearms* (London, 1983).

Fortification and sieges

P. V. Begde, *Forts and palaces of India* (New Delhi, 1982).

J. Burton-Page, A study of fortification in the Indian subcontinent from the thirteenth to the eighteenth century AD, *Bulletin of the School of Oriental and African Studies*, 23(3), 1960.

J. Deloche, Études sur les fortifications de l'Inde, I: les fortifications de l'Inde ancienne, *Bulletin de l'École française d'Extrême-Orient*, 81, 1994.

J. Deloche, Études sur les fortifications de l'Inde, II: les monts fortifiés du Maisur méridional (1re partie), *Bulletin de l'École française d'Extrême-Orient*, 82, 1995.

J. Sarkar, Aurangzib's siege of Satara (as described in contemporary records), *Proceedings of the Indian Historical Record Commission*, 4, 1922.

S. Toy, *The strongholds of India* (London, 1957).

S. Toy, *The fortified cities of India* (London, 1965).

The military labour market

S. Alavi, *Sepoys and the company: tradition and transition in northern India 1770–1830* (Delhi, 1995).

S. Gordon, Zones of military entrepreneurship in India, 1500–1800, in his *Marathas, marauders and state formation in eighteenth-century India* (Delhi, 1994).

D. H. A. Kolff, *Naukar, Rajput and sepoy: the ethnohistory of the military labour market in Hindustan 1450–1850* (Cambridge, 1990).

S. I. A. Zaidi, Structure and organization of the European mercenary armed forces in the second half of eighteenth-century India, *Islamic Culture*, 63(1–2), 1989.

Regional developments

F. Bajwa Singh, *Military system of the Sikhs* (Patna, 1964).

J. Gommans, Indian warfare and Afghan innovation during the eighteenth century, *Studies in History*, 11(2), 1995.

R. K. Saxena, *The army of the Rajputs* (Udaipur, 1989).

S. Sen, *Military system of the Marathas* (Calcutta, 1928).

R. K. Sharma, The military system of the Jodhpur state, *c.* 1212 to 1947 AD, *Asiatische Studien*, 45, 1991.

B. Stein, State formation and economy reconsidered, *Modern Asian Studies*, 19(3), 1985.

S. Subrahmanyam, Warfare and state finance in Wodeyar Mysore 1724–25: a missionary perspective, *The Indian Economic and Social History Review*, 26(2), 1989.

V. N., Rao D. Shulman, and S. Subrahmanyam, The art of war under the Nayakas, in their *Symbols of substance: court and state in Nayaka period Tamilnadu* (Delhi, 1992).

East India Company

G. Bryant, Pacification in the early British raj, 1755–1785, *Journal of Imperial and Commonwealth History*, 14 (1985–6).

G. Bryant, The military imperative in early British expansion in India, 1750–1785, *Indo-British Review* (1996).

R. G. S. Cooper, Wellington and the Marathas in 1803, *The International History Review*, 5(11), 1989.

T. A. Heathcote, *The military in British India* (Manchester/New York, 1995).

D. H. A. Kolff, The end of an ancien régime: colonial war in India, 1798–1818, in J. A. de Moor and H. L. Wesseling (eds) *Imperialism and war: essay on colonial wars in Asia and Africa* (Leiden, 1989).

J. P. Lawford, *Britain's army in India: from its origins to the conquest of Bengal* (London, 1978).

B. P. Lenman, The transition to European military ascendancy in India 1600–1800, in J. A. Lynn (ed.), *Instruments, ideas and institutions of warfare, 1445–1871* (Champaign, 1989).

P. Mason, *A matter of honour: an account of the Indian army, its officers and men* (London, 1974).

D. M. Peers, *Between Mars and Mammon: colonial armies and the garrison state in India 1819–35* (London, 1995).

J. Pemble, Resources and techniques in the second Maratha war. *The Historical Journal*, 19, 1976.

Chapter Six

Warfare, slave trading and European influence: Atlantic Africa 1450–1800

John Thornton

"According to the news that many Negroes in the West Indies have given me of their fate, I see that most of them were captured in open warfare." Thus wrote the Moravian missionary Georg Oldendorp, who interviewed dozens of slaves in the Danish West Indies to collect linguistic information in 1767–68.[1] Oldendorp was not unique in reporting this fact: other missionaries and travellers in the Americas noted the same thing.

When one considers that perhaps as many as 15 million Africans crossed the Atlantic to the Americas between 1500 and 1850, this would make African wars of the period one of the most important elements of human history. African wars laid the foundation for the largest transoceanic migration in history up to that time, dwarfing the European immigration to America before the post-industrial migrations of the second half of the nineteenth century. Yet, surprisingly, African wars have been relatively little studied in this period,[2] although political histories of African countries of the sixteenth to nineteenth century have, of course, noted wars and battles. African wars have sometimes been imagined as simply slave raids, supported by European armaments and encouraged by slave traders, or as inexplicable "tribal wars" – the result of irrational and incomprehensible hatreds that somehow well up into violence among the unsophisticated and backwards people of the earth, and that require no special explanation.

Of course, African wars were far more complicated than that – no human society can wage something as complex as war, especially on the scale that we know it was waged in Africa, involving tens of thousands of combatants, moving considerable distances and campaigning over months, on a whim or without substantial organization. Like wars elsewhere, African wars need to be studied on their own terms, whatever their ultimate motivations, in order to understand the possibilities and limitations of war's role in shaping the modern world in Africa.

Not all wars in Africa were the same, no more than all armies were the same – hardly surprising to note when one considers that Atlantic Africa had something in the order of 25 million inhabitants in the seventeenth century and was divided into well over 100 independent, sovereign political bodies of radically different sizes and complexities.[3] In addition, the portion of Africa that bordered on the Atlantic contained many different environments, ranging from desert areas in the north and south to dense tropical forest in the central region, bounded by savannas of varying degrees of woodedness and humidity.

Considering these factors, we can still divide Africa into two broad zones – the areas from the Sahara south to the borders of the west and central African rainforest where horses could survive in spite of a generally hostile disease environment, and the rest of Africa where ecology or disease made horses or any form of cavalry impossible. The rainforest was clearly inimical to cavalry operations, but even in the great central African savannas, where open country seemed ripe for cavalry warfare, disease kept cavalry out. Portuguese commanders, seeing the unhorsed people of Angola in the late sixteenth century living in open savannas, imagined that they could sweep from coast to coast on cavalry, rivalling the unstoppable march of their horse-riding Iberian cousins in America.[4] But they were soon disappointed, for disease wiped out horses, and cavalry were reduced to ceremonial roles throughout the Portuguese "conquest" of Angola.

In addition to this basic ecological division, the history of war in Africa also has an important chronological division occasioned by the advent of European weapons in the region. While European visitors and, especially, their ships bore guns from the start of Afro-European contact in the sixteenth century, it was not until the flintlock replaced the matchlock around 1680 that African armies in some places switched to European-manufactured muskets as their primary missile weapons.

The spatial and temporal intersections of these two fighting components, horses and guns, have created Jack Goody's fascinating argument that one could trace decentralized, aristocratic societies of the West African savannas back to their reliance on cavalries, whose expensive mounts gave power to the wealthy who could sustain them; while the bow, a democratic weapon, promoted another form of decentralization in the forests. Guns, he continued, made it possible for the rulers of forest kingdoms to concentrate power by obtaining a monopoly of the "means of destruction" as opposed to the means of production, thus standing Marx's maxim on its head.[5] Goody's work, intriguing and controversial as it is, has not been sustained in detail, but has led scholars to consider the impact of military technology on state forms and social structures as well as warfare.

130

Scholars of the slave trade have studied these ecological and political approaches to devise a variety of "cycles" that explain how Europeans, and before them Arabs, were able to entice African rulers to fight wars and deliver thousands of slaves. A "horse-slave cycle" argued that the only way rulers of the savanna could afford to pay for expensive, and often short-lived, imported mounts was to buy them with slaves, while at the same time possessing horses made it supremely easy to gather slaves for payment. A parallel and more widely known "gun-slave cycle" argued that unscrupulous European merchants could do more or less the same thing with guns. By selling guns to one society, they could demand payment in slaves, and the rulers would then attack their neighbours with the guns. The threatened neighbours would be prepared to offer slaves to obtain guns to defend themselves and in this way both groups would be forced to participate in the slave trade, even if it were against their will or best interests.[6] As with Goody's "means of destruction"-centred explanation of state structure, the cycles work better in theory than in documented detail, but they too have driven research and shaped historical questions.[7]

Closer examination of African wars waged in the sixteenth to nineteenth centuries reveals military officials and leaders grappling with the kinds of question that puzzled their colleagues elsewhere in the world. Examining the earliest testimony about African wars, we can judge the impact of European technology and the demands of the slave trade on the conduct of war in Africa.

The geographical background

Africa's military geography is characterized by three zones, depending on the dominant military arm: cavalry, infantry, or marines. The southern Sahara desert and Western Sudan – the savannas north of the coastal tropical rain forest – was the land of the horse and dominated by cavalry, even though the disease environment made it difficult to maintain the horses in much of the region. South of the horse zone, often in the tropical rainforest that blanketed the south coast of west Africa, was the land of the foot soldier where only infantry could operate, although all along the edge of the two ecological zones were places where the two different military cultures met with varying results. In one zone, filled today by Benin and formerly largely by the Kingdom of Dahomey, cavalry could operate so far south that infantry and cavalry cultures met intensely almost in sight of the coast.

In the Atlantic portions of central Africa, what we will term Angola, horses could not survive and infantry predominated. Although much of the area was open savanna, the disease environment did not permit the effective breeding of horses or maintenance of cavalry, despite Portuguese attempts to do so from the late sixteenth century.

The third zone, that dominated by what we are terming "marines", was defined by the complex coastal waterways that prevail along much of the Atlantic coast of west Africa from Senegambia around to Cameroon, although in differing degrees in different areas, but especially in the region of modern Senegambia, Guinea-Conakry, Guinea-Bissau and Sierra Leone on the west, and the coast of modern Ghana, Togo, Benin, and Nigeria on the east.

African ecology also correlates to some degree with political structures, so that the Western Sudan was often dominated by states of fairly large size and population. On the west these might be the mighty empires of Mali, Great Jolof, or Songhay; in the east the large but lesser states of Kebbi, the Hausa kingdoms, and Oyo. In 1500, most of the coast was dominated by a host of small states, the only exception being the Kingdom of Benin, which controlled much of the western end of the Niger Delta area and the coastal lagoons, largely through naval dominance of the marine zone.

In sixteenth-century Angola much of the area was dominated by large states like Kongo and its southern neighbour Ndongo, while the mountainous region between them fell to smaller polities who defended their freedom in the rugged terrain. Northwards the Kingdom of Loango held sway, at least after about 1550, and inland from there was another region of splintered sovereignty.

Europeans came into this military environment bringing with them new trading opportunities, and especially a demand for war captives as slaves, and new or sometimes improved weapons. Much of African military history revolves around debate on the issue of this impact.

The art of war in sixteenth century Africa

In the Sahara desert, armed forces were purely cavalry. In the fifteenth century they rode on simple saddles without stirrups, although these were added later,[8] and carried only a tough, hide-covered shield as a defensive arm. For offensive weapons they had a lance, sword, and a handful of javelins.[9] The savanna armies were primarily infantry with cavalry being less numerous, although their cavalry was armed and equipped similarly to that of the desert – with lance, javelins and sword, as well as with bows. Early sixteenth-century accounts gave the strength of armies as improbably large but, if the ratios of infantry to cavalry are correct, at that point there were ten foot soldiers to every rider.[10] The best sources lead us to believe that larger states like the Jolof Kingdom could muster several thousand cavalry for a major engagement[11] – while Songhay, the most powerful state in the region, brought, by its own estimate, 18,000 cavalry to the battle of Tondibi in 1591, a major showdown with an invading force from Morocco.[12]

The tactics of all the cavalry forces were also quite similar, in that the attacking cavalry employed primarily missile tactics, showering enemies with their javelins (or, less commonly, arrows) and only riding home with lance and sabre if the enemy was broken.[13] Observers often praised the skill and horsemanship of the cavalry, which were typically horsed on small breeds used more for mobility than for shock, given the problems of breeding and maintaining horses in the region.[14] The primary task of breaking enemy ranks might be done by inflicting heavy casualties with missiles, or using other techniques – at the battle of Tondibi the generals of the empire of Songhay sought to break their Moroccan attackers by driving cattle into their ranks.[15]

Cavalry were even more important in the eastern part of this zone. The Empire of Oyo, which from the late seventeenth century onwards conducted periodic military operations in the area of the ecological gap that allowed horses to live almost as far south as the coast, employed armies composed entirely of cavalry. Like the horsemen of the west, Oyo riders were equipped with bows, javelins, and "cutting swords".[16] Apparently, they also used their missile weapons to break up their enemies, and then followed up with sword-charges against disorganized enemies.

In Senegambia, African infantries had to co-exist with cavalries on the battlefield, a fact which obviously affected both organization and tactics. The states of the Benin region, on the other hand, seem to have little contact with the cavalries of the northern zones until the late seventeenth century, despite the fact that their ecology made invasions of northern cavalry possible. Infantry in Senegambia relied heavily on bows for their missile weapons, and the arrows were poisoned. Even though local remedies to the poison were known, any wound was likely to incapacitate its victim, who either took the time to apply the remedy or sickened. As would be expected in warfare involving cavalry, infantry developed fairly disciplined formations to prevent horses from penetrating their ranks, and suffered worst when they were broken. Jolof formations of the sixteenth century drew up with archers in the middle and shield-bearers on the front ranks and flanks to protect the formation.[17]

In the purely infantry regions, one can note two regional styles of fighting. In the most common, employed in both Angola and the open country of Benin, free from cavalry until the late seventeenth century, warfare focused on a heavily-armed, often professional soldier, who fought in an open order that gave soldiers the opportunity to support each other, but allowed them enough space to exercise their individual fighting skills. In the Benin region armies opened engagements with a short missile phase in which the opponents were first showered with arrows. Then, as the troops closed in, there was a brief exchange

133

with javelins and a locally-favoured, heavy, wooden throwing club that could deliver tremendous blunt force trauma if thrown correctly by a skilled fighter. This phase was followed by a rapid closing of the two forces in a loosely-organized melee, where soldiers in open order fought with lances and swords while protected by shields. This open order of fighting made European observers both exaggerate the size of armies and underestimate their effectiveness.[18]

As in the Benin region, sixteenth-century armies in Kongo and Ndongo fought in open order with skilled soldiers. Typically, archers opened engagements with limited arrow strikes, rapidly followed by skilled infantry, in Kongo protected by shields and carrying lances, swords, or battle axes, but in Ndongo relying on personal skill rather than shields for protection, but using the same mixture of weapons. This general melee often lasted a short time, when one side broke and fled the battlefield.[19]

In the Gold Coast, modern Ghana, the heavy forests required large numbers of troops to be restricted to narrow areas along roads and clearings and made the employment of open order more difficult. Although a heavily armed infantry was still the dominant force, tactically a much more tightly closed order was used. Late-sixteenth-century accounts reveal that engagements, opened by skirmishers harassing the enemy with javelins and arrows, were followed by heavily-armed soldiers wearing helmets and some protective armour carrying shields and using lances and swords, who advanced on their enemies in a fairly close formation, while archers, placed in a second row, launched arrow strikes by firing in arcs over their heads. At the end of this complex chain of fighters were lightly armed soldiers with cutting weapons who finished off, or captured, the wounded. The most decisive phase of the fighting was a melee of hand-to-hand fighting that often lasted a short time.[20]

Marines, both in the Upper Guinea (Senegambia to Sierra Leone) and Lower Guinea (Ghana to Cameroon) areas, were forced by their environment to be much more focused on missile tactics than their infantry counterparts. Early visitors to Upper Guinea reported craft that carried up to 50 armed men, and engaged their opponents from a distance with arrows and javelins. Flotillas of several such craft could thus deliver considerable manpower anywhere that could be reached by creeks, estuaries, or rivers, for the watercraft drew little water and could be easily manoeuvred.[21]

In Lower Guinea, Benin developed a marine force that was capable of subjugating the region, and in the early sixteenth century Benin's dominion extended as far west as Lagos and well into the delta. As in Upper Guinea, control in this area was dependent upon marshalling fleets of shallow draft canoes, some of which were of substantial size, and moving troops with them. As Benin's power in the region declined in the late seventeenth century, no other state took over, and throughout the eighteenth century a fairly large number of states, based on

134

offshore islands or directly on the lagoons, with local navies prevented the landward states from dominating them.[22]

Europeans in African war

The European presence in most of Africa was limited by the difficulties which they experienced operating from the sea. The coast of west Africa lacked natural harbours, and the combination of coastal islands with difficult surf, lagoons, and coastal creeks made any sort of naval landing out of the question. European visitors to the African coast from the 1440s onwards encountered African marine infantry, and a number of engagements fought in the early years of the encounter showed the newcomers that they could not win against such opponents in spite of their seagoing craft, gunpowder weapons like cannon, and armour. These battles were of great significance for the history of Atlantic Africa in general, since they ensured that Europeans visited the coast, not only in Senegambia but all along the west African coast, as guests, invited visitors, remaining at the sufferance of local rulers and not as conquerors or colonists.[23]

However, from very early in their relationship, Europeans obtained the right to build fairly substantial military posts in African territory. Senegambia and the Gold Coast exported gold, and some guarantees of security for gold awaiting shipment had to be provided. While the Portuguese began the tradition with the building of the castle of São Jorge da Mina (later known as Elmina) in 1482, the more than half-dozen other European trading companies (from, at various times, the Netherlands, England, France, Sweden, Courland, Brandenburg-Prussia, and Denmark) that worked the coast from the seventeenth century onwards all had their own forts, – often with a sizable garrison of European and African troops – a treaty with the local ruler, and rental payments.[24]

Although Europeans established a series of forts, first in Senegambia (including some French posts on the Senegal River, quite deep in the interior for part of the eighteenth century) and the Gold Coast, and then, in the late seventeenth century, also on the Slave Coast, these establishments did not result in the political domination of any but the small towns that were built directly under the guns of the fort.[25] The European garrisons and closely allied soldiers, sometimes amounting to some hundreds of troops, might participate in the changing politics of the small polities of the region. European troops often served as mercenaries in African armies, and sometimes fought to acquire trading rights against rival Europeans in alliance with African powers. But outside Angola, these garrisons never effected any conquest, and for the most part they were buried in local politics.

In Angola conquest and the exercise of sovereignty over a significant African population was as much from good fortune and local circumstances as from any great military advantage. Portugal began its contact with central African societies by providing mercenaries for African rulers, first in Kongo, where they were particularly helpful as naval support on the Congo River. After founding a base at Luanda in 1575, they entered into a similar alliance with the Kingdom of Ndongo. When the Portuguese were expelled from Ndongo in 1579, however, they were able to use their alliance with Kongo to save their position, and thanks to their ability to use naval power on the Kwanza River from their base at Luanda, the only natural port on the Atlantic coast, they were eventually able to persuade a number of local African rulers to abandon their allegiance to Ndongo and support the colony. By 1589 they were able to use the army raised from these rulers to attack Ndongo, although unsuccessfully.

After 1617 this initial group of military allies was expanded by recruiting large numbers of Imbangala, mercenary bands from south of the Kwanza River, to break their stalemate with Ndongo and go on the offensive again.[26] Most of their seventeenth-century gains came through the adroit use of this largely African army (the "black army" or *guerra preta*), to exploit the dynastic problems of Ndongo in the War of the Ndongo Succession (1624–55).[27]

Even where they were unable to make conquests, however, Europeans did make important indirect contributions to warfare. In the cavalry region they briefly affected events through providing war horses, especially larger European-bred horses, to the leaders of coastal societies, often being paid for them with slaves. Some historians have argued that it tipped the balance of power in favour of those with access to the coast,[28] but the numbers of horses were probably too small to be significant over a long run, and the large-scale horse trade did not last much past the sixteenth century.[29] Eighteenth-century sources do not describe the distribution and numbers of African cavalry as much different from those to be found in the sixteenth century.[30]

It was as suppliers of gunpowder weapons and purchasers of slaves that the Europeans made their largest impact. Of course, guns were available in Africa after the sixteenth century, and during much of the seventeenth century they were incorporated in various armies. In the Gold Coast, guns were quite common by the sixteenth century, but they were integrated into the skirmishing phase of the fighting. Even the Portuguese in Angola used their musketeers in the same way as African armies employed archers, as did their African opponents when guns were available to them. Portuguese soldiers served as a heavy, armoured infantry, roughly the equivalent of the Kongolese shield-bearing infantry that made that country so powerful, but it was their skill as swordsmen that carried them, not their new weapons.[31] It was only after the introduction of the flintlock musket in 1680 that war was genuinely transformed in Africa.

The impact of gunpowder weapons was felt least in the cavalry areas. In eighteenth-century Senegambia armies cavalry began carrying carbines and sabres as their principal weapons. Infantry added firearms, especially the elite and guards units, but many others continued with archery, even in the late eighteenth century.[32] The new weapons replaced archery but tactics were essentially unchanged.

There was, however, a real revolution in the art of war in most of the infantry armies of the forest zone and the region of modern Benin in the early eighteenth century. Muskets completely replaced the bow and javelin as missile weapons in the Gold Coast and Benin and, moreover, the older style of hand-to-hand combat all but disappeared.[33] In the Gold Coast the tightly-closed formations of earlier periods that favoured hand-to-hand fighting gave way to much more dispersed combat that relied on firepower. The Danish observer Rømer noted with some exaggeration that on the Gold Coast in the 1740s, after an hour of fighting, the lines would be just ten paces apart and still firing at each other, burning their opponents with powder, even though their weapons were now too fouled for the musket rounds to come out. For all that there was little hand-to-hand combat.[34]

The Kingdom of Dahomey, a powerful state in the Benin region that came to dominate its politics in the early eighteenth century, equipped virtually all soldiers with muskets, and for close fighting carried swords. Dahomey's King Agaja could boast in a letter to George I in England in 1726 that he had "allmost intirely left of[f] the use of bows and arrows", although he did mention that the older weapons were still widely employed in other armies in the area.[35]

Firearms and European advice helped Dahomey deal with the problems of its cavalry-using northern neighbours. In the late seventeenth century Oyo, a renewed empire dependent on cavalry, began a series of raids to the south, and shortly after Agaja boasted of converting his troops to firearms, Oyo launched the first of a series of extensive invasions of Dahomey.[36] As in Senegambia, Oyo cavalry was largely unaffected by the changes in warfare taking place as a result of the adaptation of gunpowder weapons. Nevertheless, Dahomey had to respond quickly to meet this challenge, and it did so, first by being the only army in the region to adopt a close order of fighting, appropriate for dealing with cavalry-using forces, and in constructing field fortifications that prevented Oyo from using its cavalry to full effect, while maximizing the value of the new firearms.[37] These rapid changes may have been introduced by French advisors, at least one of whom, Sieur de Galot, was charged by his superiors with serving in the Dahomey army and instructing them in the building of fortifications.[38] However, in order to preserve itself, the Dahomey army had to concentrate, leaving the country open to pillage by the more mobile cavalry of Oyo. Ultimately, after several years of unsuccessfully seeking to defeat Oyo and defend its population,

Dahomey surrendered in 1747 and for the rest of the eighteenth century had to pay humiliating tribute and accept Oyo supervision of some of its affairs.[39]

While aggressive cavalry forces were not a factor for most of the Gold Coast, after 1739 Asante, emerging as the most powerful state in the region, sought to extend its power north of the forest into the cavalry-dominated savanna. Its earliest expeditions in the area were hardly successful, and guns proved no match for horses. In one expedition Asante was able to preserve its forces by fortifying themselves, but they had to withdraw without effecting any conquest.[40] Like Dahomey, they found that cavalry forces were too strong for them to defeat. It was only through recruiting their own allies with cavalry that Asante was eventually able to extend its power over the savanna states to its north.

European weapons also transformed marine warfare on the coast of Benin in particular, as the rulers of Dahomey learned to their cost. Although Dahomey's armies were able to defeat the major coastal powers, Allada in 1724 and Whydah in 1727, and to occupy their capitals, the Dahomian forces failed to occupy either country completely. In both cases, the rulers were able to escape to islands in the coastal lagoons and successfully resisted all Dahomey's attempts to dislodge them. With artillery mounted on canoes and the capability of moving quite sizable armies who now carried muskets by water, the kings of Badagry, Little Popo and other lagoon towns, operating in conjunction with military forces from the area of the Gold Coast to the west, defied Dahomey. Although Dahomey sought to counter these forces by hiring naval forces of their own, it never managed to complete its conquest of the region.[41]

Muskets largely replaced archery in those armies in Angola that had contact with the coastal trade in the early eighteenth century, including the Portuguese army, which in most respects was not organized differently from its opponents, except for the maintenance of a largely symbolic cavalry.[42] Likewise in 1781 in Kongo the entire army that fought in the civil war between partisans of Pedro V and José I was equipped with muskets.[43] But archery did survive, since elsewhere in Kongo a mixture of archers and musketeers fought in armies even in the 1790s.[44] One of the units serving in the Portuguese army in its frontier campaigns in 1766 was equipped, one half with archers, and the other half with musketeers.[45]

The art of war changed less when one moved inland to the Kwango Valley where a number of powerful states, Matamba to the north and Kasanje and Muzumbo a Kalunga to the south, dominated the region and faced the advancing forces of the Lunda empire from the east in the middle of the century. Guns were certainly not unknown. Kasanje, which enjoyed good trading and political relations with Portugal, had many, but other armies used far more archers and javelins than those closer to the coast. Most armies continued to rely on heavily-armed infantry, carrying shields and fighting hand-to-hand, often without much of a softening-up phase with missile weapons. The Lunda armies which swept down on the Kwango River valley in the mid-eighteenth century[46] were so enamoured of hand-to-hand fighting, especially with swords, that they were said to hammer guns into swords when they captured them, and eschewed any missile weapons, even arrows, as "destructive of valour". Although the Kwango states managed to stop the Lunda advance to the west, it is difficult to say whether this was due to Lunda's overextension or the effectiveness of their resistance.[47]

War and the slave trade

In Africa, as elsewhere, war was very much an extension of politics. But the availability of new weapons from European sources had an impact on wars, and the possibility of enslaving the conquered for profit played a role in shaping the consequences and sometimes the conduct of war.

The evolution of the course of warfare in Senegambia after 1500 altered as much because of political developments as any great changes in technology or the availability of horses. In the earliest period most of the country was dominated by the great empires, like Songhay along the Niger, the Empire of Jolof in the Wolof-speaking parts of the Senegal Valley, and the Empire of Mali on the Niger and Gambia Rivers and south of there. These states maintained considerable internal order, and most warfare was focused on their borders or in the suppression of rebellion. The nomads of the desert were able to conduct raids, but they do not seem to have been on a large scale or particularly destructive.[48] Even though Jolof fell apart after 1549, and Songhay fell under the attack of Morocco in 1591, the seventeenth century was not much different. The Empire of the Great Fulo, based in the Senegal Valley continued the tradition of large states, its easternmost marches reaching as far as the Niger and its western end covering much of the cavalry country beyond the Atlantic coast.[49]

The late seventeenth and eighteenth century saw quite a different configuration, however, which cannot be principally explained by changes in weapons. The Empire of Great Fulo with its core in Futa Tooro lost its sway over the Senegal Valley and was replaced by smaller states with less centralized constitutions. The result was a period beset with considerable wars between the states, as well as civil wars within them.[50]

This was typified by the states that succeeded the Empire of Jolof in the lower Senegal Valley. For much of the late seventeenth and eighteenth century the Wolof-speaking area was divided between the states of Kajoor and Bawol:

sometimes united under one rule; at others divided into their two constituents; sometimes able to dominate their neighbours of Waalo, Salum, Siine and other areas; at others unable to. In addition, both Kajoor and Bawol underwent sporadic civil wars over succession, so that disputes between brothers over the throne might last a very long time as neighbouring states harboured defeated candidates. In a crisis of 1724, Beetyo Maalixuri was driven from his throne of Kajoor by a rival, who was in turn supported by the king of Futa Tooro. Maalixuri, for his part, called in the nomads to support his claim.[51] Any party or state that felt itself weaker than its rivals might up the stakes by inviting the nomads of the desert to help them, as happened in 1742, for example, when Ndyak Aram faced a rival for the throne of Waalo who called in the nomads to help him.[52] The nomads, with their large cavalry forces, were able to intervene effectively, but more often the long-range result was large-scale pillage of the region. At the same time, as war weakened internal cohesion, the states of the region lost their ability to defend their lands against freebooting nomads, whose raids became larger and less disciplined, as was one on Galam in 1731 in the wake of a civil war among the Bacily families that dominated the region.[53]

This environment of war, civil war, and pillage created the situation that is found in eighteenth-century accounts of war in Senegambia which is often seen as dominated by pillaging of one sort or another. Already in the 1680s the leaders of the Wolof area were seen engaging in warfare against neighbours as well as pillaging the villages within their own territories, making a distinction between two types of war, one being formal and on a large scale, the other composed of small attacks and raids.[54] Eighteenth-century writers often describe pillaging as a sort of business, sometimes conducted to reinforce authority, at others almost a sort of taxation,[55] although in the eighteenth century, as earlier, what appears as pillage often had an ultimately political cause, in civil wars or the aftermath of wars between states, mixed with invasions by the nomads. There was also a thin line between thwarted political ambition and brigandage, as illustrated by the case of Farakaba, a former slave of Kajoor, who rebelled and whose career was furthered by political rivalries with Bawol and within Kajoor in the 1760s and 70s. Operating from a series of fortified locations, Farakaba and some 4,000 troops spread terror and resisted attempts to unseat him.[56]

European traders were prepared to provide assistance to the various parties in these disputes in exchange for commercial favours and the right to buy captives of the wars. Because of this, it is impossible to dismiss wars simply as purely political instruments and the resulting slave trade as incidental to warfare. On some occasions Europeans were able to enlist rulers, pretenders, or nomads in raiding solely for the production of slaves, although they were participants in the larger programme of civil war and intervention, rather than its initiators. Perhaps the most celebrated such interventions was led by the English governor of Gambia, O'Hara, and the French Governor of Senegal, Le Brasseur, who were said to have encouraged the nomads to invade the lands along the Senegal in order to revive an otherwise flagging slave trade, although this was in part made possible because political divisions among the inhabitants of Kajoor presented the opportunity.[57]

Local people also saw a fairly clear link between war and "tyranny" and the export slave trade. Two popular religious movements, the first led by Nasr al-Din in 1673–77 and the second by Abd al-Kadir after 1776, aimed at ending the pillaging of the countryside by rulers, as well as curbing the export slave trade in the name of Islamic reform. Both movements also had deeper political and even dynastic roots, and the former was also unable to prevent pillaging by nomads who allied with it, although each also played on popular discontent about both problems.[58]

The rise of Dahomey might also be linked to the Atlantic trade: indeed, many historians view most of Dahomey's actions as driven by the demands of the slave trade, and especially the need for guns, primarily to fend off Oyo's threat. But Dahomean rulers themselves denied the linkages, and saw their policies as connected to matters of state.[59]

At the end of the seventeenth century, as imported guns altered the art of war, several regional powers emerged in the interior of the Gold Coast, such as Asante, Denkyira, Akwamu, and Akyem. These countries enjoyed some strength and were able to make strategic alliances with smaller but still independent states. Warfare increasingly involved showdowns between alliances of these powers, as well as continuing smaller-scale fighting between the lesser states. Larger battles, such as the Asante–Denkyira war of 1701, or Asante's defeat of Akyem in 1717, Akyem's defeat of Akwamu in 1730 and Asante's final defeat of Akyem in 1741, punctuated smaller engagements, as well as occasionally civil wars within the larger states.[60]

The slave trade played some part in warfare in this period, which had demographic dimensions as mass-recruited armies replaced the smaller professional ones of earlier times. Some of the dynamics of warfare, such as the deliberate pillaging, including the stripping of the countryside, of defeated countries of inhabitants to be sold as slaves, were shaped by the large and growing numbers of willing European purchasers. By reducing the inhabitants of defeated countries through mass deportation, often known locally as "eating the country", generals could insure profits for replenishing weapons as well as weaken enemies who could not be completely conquered. This lessened their ability to continue as a military power. This possibility was well illustrated when Akyem, upon winning a notable victory over Akwamu in 1730, decided against stripping the countryside, believing that they could win the loyalty of the people and, thus, bolster their army for what they feared would be a showdown with Asante (which came, disastrously for Akyem, in 1742). But most observers felt this was a special case and an exception to the general rule that military interests were best served by the demographically destructive practice of deportation.[61]

Eighteenth-century Angolan warfare focused on a long and intermittent civil war in Kongo, ignited after a defeat by Portuguese forces at Mbwila killed king António I and left no capable successor.[62] At times the breakdown of authority in Kongo made it possible for bandits, whose primary goal was to enslave people to sell overseas, to flourish, such as the notorious Mbwa Lau ("Mad Dog"), a nobleman once associated with partisans fighting in the civil war, who created a major scandal in the 1780s by openly raiding and defying royal orders to stop.[63]

Elsewhere war was confined to the frontiers of the Portuguese colony of Angola, south in the central highlands of Angola and east along the Kwango River valley between independent states. In the eighteenth century the Lunda empire began a long expansion westward, perhaps in search of commercial prospects in Angola, and forces under Lunda commanders were fighting along the Kwango River in the 1740s and 1750s.

In central Africa, more than anywhere else in Africa, there was a tradition of direct capture of slaves by European-led forces, although one cannot easily disentangle these campaigns from Portuguese participation in Angolan politics, including the survival of the colony or the War of the Ndongo succession. Portugal left off its aggressive military policies in the late seventeenth century. Beyond that point their role was not different from Europeans elsewhere in Africa. Although the wars of the mid-eighteenth century Kwango and the Lunda advance westward were seen by Portuguese observers as primarily about enslaving people for export,[64] it was the areas that were least inclined to use firearms that were charged with this programme.

It is probably true that European weapons and European trade demands had a shaping influence on African warfare, affecting tactics and decisions about taking and using prisoners. The possibility of selling war captives, while it may have caused few wars by itself, certainly did shape the financing of wars, and made possible the policy of demographic stripping well attested in the Gold Coast and Senegambia, if not elsewhere.

African warfare, therefore, answered to local needs and ambitions as well as to its place in the larger political and economic world shaped by European contact. Africans managed their wars within the limits imposed by the environment, both its diseases and its physical limitations and possibilities, making use of water, marsh, forest and plain. They responded to external demands and to opportunities to change weapons and tactics, while accommodating the demands of their trading partners so as to overcome their military rivals.

142

Notes

Abbreviations:
AHU Arquivo Histórico Ultramarino (Lisbon)
ANF Archives Nationales de France (Paris)
BIFAN B *Bulletin de l'Institute Foundamental de l'Afrique Noire* Series B.
MMA António Brásio (ed.) *Monumenta Missionaria Africana* (1st Series, 15 volumes, Lisbon, 1952–88, 2nd Series, 5 volumes, Lisbon 1958–79)

1. C. G. A. Oldendorp, *Geschichte der Mission der evangelischen Brüder auf den Caraibischen Inseln St Thomas, St Croix und St Jan* (ed. J. J. Bossart), (Barby and Leipzig, 1777) p. 350.

2. An important exception is the pioneering study of R. Smith, *Warfare and Diplomacy in Pre-Colonial West Africa*, 2nd edn (Madison, 1989) (1st edn 1976); and the fundamental detailed work of R. Kea, *Settlements, trade, and polities on the seventeenth century Gold Coast* (Baltimore, 1982).

3. For an overview, see J. Thornton, *Africa and Africans in the making of the Atlantic world, 1400–1800* (2d edn, Cambridge, 1998), pp. xii–xiv, xvii–xxxviii.

4. F. Pigafetta, *Relatione del Reame di Congo et delle circonvince contrade, tratta dalli scirtti e ragionamenti di Odoardo Lopez, Portoghese* (Rome, 1591, mod. edn G. Cardonna, Milan, 1978 with original pagination), p. 23.

5. J. Goody, *Technology, Tradition, and the State in Africa* (Cambridge, 1971).

6. For a good collection of representative literature and introduction, J. E. Inikori (ed.), *Forced migration. The impact of the export slave trade on African societies* (New York, 1982).

7. For a more careful updating, R. Law, Horses, firearms, and political power in pre-colonial West Africa, *Past and Present*, 72, 1976, pp. 112–32.

8. R. Law, *The horse in West African history* (Oxford, 1980), p. 91 for evidence.

9. A. Malafante, Copia cujusdam littere per Antonium Malafante a Tueto scrip[t]e, Janue Johanni Mariono. 1447, in C. de Roncière, *La découverte de l'Afrique au moyen Âge* (3 vols, Cairo, 1925–27), 1: p. 153; A. da Mosto, Mondo Novo in T. G. Leporace (ed.) *Le Navigazioni atlantiche del Veneziano Alvise da Mosto* (Milan, 1966), p. 38.

10. D. P. Pereira, *Esmeraldo de Situ Orbis* (mod. variorum edn A. E. da S. Dias), (Lisbon, 1905)], pp. 81, 89; V. Fernandes, Descrição do Cepta e sua Costa, A. Baião (ed.) *O Manuscrito 'Valentim Fernandes'* (Lisbon, 1940), fols 90v–93, a revised reading *MMA* 2nd ser, 1, pp. 672–739 with original foliation marked.

11. Fernandes, Descrição, fol. 90v; P. Perreira, *Esmeraldo*, pp. 81, 87; G. L. Africano, Descrizione dell'Africa, in Ramusio, *Navigazione e Viaggi* (mod. edn), 1: p. 378; I. al-Mukhtar, *Ta'rikh al-Fettash*, p. 70.

12. I. al-Mukhtar, *Ta'rikh al-Fettash* (c. 1650, mod. edn and tr. O. Houdas and M. Delafosse), (Paris, 1913, reprinted 1964), p. 264 (from "a trustworthy source"), but the Moroccan account gives Songhay only 8,000 horsemen, Relacion de la Jornada que el Rey de Marruecos ha heco a la Conquista del Reyno de Gago . . . in H. de Castries, La conquête du Soudan par el-Mansour (1591), *Hésperis*, 3, 1923, p. 461.

13. I. al-Mukhtar, *Ta'rikh al-Fettash*, pp. 96–7 (description of an action in 1480).

14. G. L. Anania, *L'Universale Fabrica del Mondo* (Naples, 1573, 2nd edn, 1576, 3rd edn, 1582 in Venice) p. 332; variorum edition of D. Lange and S. Berthoud, L'intérieur de l'Afrique Occidentale d'après Giovanni Lorenzo Anania (XVIe siècle), p. 324; A. A. de Almada, Tratado breve dos Rios de Guiné . . . in *MMA* 2nd ser., 3, p. 241–2.

15. Relacion de la Jornada, p. 462; *Ta'rikh al-Fettash*, p. 264.

16. W. Snelgrave, *A new account of some parts of Guinea and the slave trade* (London, 1734, facsimile, London: Cass, 1971), pp. 55–9.

17. De Almada, Tratado, *MMA* ser. 2, 3, pp. 242–3.

18. Principle accounts: W. Bosman, *A new and accurate description of the coast of Guinea* (Dutch original 1704, tr. London, 1705, repr., 1967) pp. 394–6; ANF, Dépôt des archives d'outre mer, MS 104 Relation du Royaume de Judas en Guinéé . . . (*c.* 1712), pp. 82–4; J.-B. Labat, *Voyage du Chevalier des Marchais en Guinée, isles voisines, et a cayenne, fait en 1725, 1726, & 1727* (4 vols, Amsterdam, 1731), 2, pp. 188–96 (a late account, but may use material from as early as 1704).

19. J. Thornton, The art of war in Angola, 1575–1680, *Comparative Studies in Society and History*, 30, 1988, pp. 362–71.

20. R. Kea, *Settlements, trade and polities on the seventeenth century Gold Coast* (Baltimore, 1982), pp. 130–68.

21. Fernandes, Descrição, fol. 102v, 117v.

22. R. Law, Trade and politics behind the Slave Coast: The lagoon traffic and the rise of Lagos, 1500–1800, *Journal of African History*, 24, 1983, pp. 321–48.

23. J. Thornton, *Africa and Africans in the making of the Atlantic world, 1400–1680* (Cambridge, 1992), pp. 36–40.

24. P. E. H. Hair, *The founding of the Castelo de São Jorge da Mina. An analysis of the sources* (Madison, 1994) for the original foundation. For later times, L. Yarak, *Asante and the Dutch, 1744–1873* (Oxford, 1990), pp. 133–70.

25. For an overview, A. van Dantzig, *Les Hollandais sur la côte de Guinée à l'époque de l'essor de l'Ashanti et du Dahomey, 1680–1740* (Paris, 1980).

26. J. C. Miller, *Kings and kinsmen: the Imbangala impact on the Mbundu of Angola* (Oxford, 1977).

27. D. Birmingham, *Trade and conflict in Angola: the Mbundu and the neighbours under the influence of the Portuguese, 1483–1790* (Oxford, 1966), pp. 88–132; B. Heintze, Das Ende des unabhängigen Staates Ndongo (1617–1630), *Paideuma*, 27, 1981, pp. 197–273.

28. B. Barry, Senegambia from the sixteenth to eighteenth century: evolution of the Wolof, Sereer and "Tukulor", *UNESCO General History of Africa* (8 vols, London and Los Angeles, 1981–93), 5, pp. 262–99.

29. I. Elbl, The horse in fifteenth century Senegambia, *International Journal of African Historical Studies*, 24, 1991, pp. 99–103; J. L. A. Webb, *Desert frontier: ecological and economic change along the western Sahel, 1600–1850* (Madison: University of Wisconsin Press, 1995). Webb, The horse and slave trade between the western Sahara and Senegambia, *Journal of African History*, 34, 1993, pp. 221–46 makes it clear that the major horse-slave exchanges came between desert breeders and the sahel area.

30. L. M. de Chambonneau. Traité de l'origine des nègres du Sénégal, coste d'Affrique, de leurs pays, religion, coutoumes et mœurs, in C. I. A. Ritchie, Deux textes sur le Sénégal (1673–77), *BIFAN* B, 30/1, 1968, pp. 324–5.

31. Thornton, Art of War, pp. 371–8; for the later periods, see J. Thornton, African Soldiers in the Haitian Revolution, *Journal of Caribbean History*, 25, 1991, pp. 65–68.

32. Bibliothèque Nationale de Paris, Fonds Français, MS 9557, Mémoire sur les mines de Bambouc, 30 November 1762; M. Jacques Doumet de Siblas, Mémoire historique sur les différentes parties de l'Afrique . . . 1769, (mod. edn C. Becker and V. Martin, Mémoire inédit de Doumet [1769] *BIFAN* B, 36/1, 1974), pp. 38–40.

33. These changes are described in Kea, *Settlements*, pp. 162–8.

34. Ludevig Rømer, *Le Golfe de Guinée 1700–1750. Récit de L. F. Rômer, marchand d'escalves sur la côte ouest-africaine* (Danish original, 1760, tr. M. Dige-Hesse, Paris, 1989), pp. 149–51.

35. [Agaja] Emperor of Pawpaw to George I in *The parliamentary history of England, from the earliest period to the year 1803*, vol. 23 [1789–91] (London, 1816), p. 85 published in facsimile in R. Law, Further light on Bulfinch Lambe and the "Emperor of Pawpaw": King Agaja of Dahomey's letter to King George I of England, 1726, *History in Africa*, 17, 1990, pp. 211–26 original pagination marked.

36. W. Snelgrave, *A new account of some parts of Guinea and the slave trade* (London, 1734, facsimile, London, Cass, 1971), pp. 55–9.

37. Dupetival to Council of Indes, 20 May 1728 in R. Law (ed. and tr.), *Contemporary source material for the history of the old Oyo Empire, 1627–1824* (Ibadan, 1992), pp. 20–2.

38. ANF C6/25 Mémoire. Trahison du Sr. Galot, 8 November 1730.

39. R. Norris, *Memoirs of the reign of Bossa Ahádee, king of Dahomey an inland country of Guiney* (London, 1789, reprint London: Cass, 1968), pp. 12–15.

40. Rømer, *Golfe de Guinée*, pp. 136–7.

41. Norris, *Memoirs*, pp. 26–7, 56–60; Archibald Dalzel, *History of Dahomey an inland kingdom of Africa* (London, 1793, 2nd edn, London: Cass, 1967), pp. 166–70.

42. Described in the 1770s by E. A. da S. Corrêa, *História de Angola* [1798] (mod. edn Manuel Múrias, 2 vols., Lisbon, 1937), 2, pp. 48–61.

43. Academia das Ciências de Lisboa, MS Vermelho 296, Viagem do Congo do Missionario Fr. Raphael de Castello de Vide, hoje Bispo de S. Thomé, [1781], p. 118.

44. AHU, Angola, Caixa 76, documento 73, Manuel de Almeida e Vasconcellos, 7 August 1791, fol. iv.

45. Archives of the Sobado of Caculo Cahenda (Angola), Provision of António Anselmo Duarte de Siqueira to Paulo Sebestião Cheques, Luanda, 25 April 1766, summarized in A. de Almeida, Relações com os Dembos das cartas do Dembado de Kakulu-Kahenda, in *I Congresso da História da Expansão Portuguesa no mundo* (4th section, Lisbon, 1938), doc. 21, p. 36.

46. For an overview of political history, D. Birmingham, *Trade and conquest in Angola: The Mbundu and their neighbours under the influence of the Portuguese, 1483–1790* (Oxford, 1966), pp. 133–61.

47. Relação e breve sumário da viagem que eu, o sargento-mor dos moradores do Dande, fiz às remotas partes de Cassange e Olos, por mandado do Il.mo e Ex.mo Sr Governador e capitão-general dêstes Reinos, D. António Alvares da Cunha (1755–6), in G. S. Dias (ed.), *Uma viagem a Cassange nos meados do seculo XVIII, Boletim da Sociedade de Geografia de Lisboa*, **56**, 1938, pp. 18–22, 25.

48. G. E. de Zurara, Chrónica do descobrimento e conquista de Guiné, ed. Torquato de Sousa Soares (2 vols., Lisbon, 1978), cap. 77 (based on reports of *c.* 1446); da Mosto, Novo Mondo (ed. Milanesi), p. 46 (*c.* 1455).

49. See map of this period in Thornton, *Africa and Africans*, pp. xii and xvii–xxi.

50. For a brief overview of the situation see J. Boulègue and J. Suret-Canale, The Western Atlantic Coast, J. F. Ade Ajayi and M. Crowder (eds), *History of West Africa* (3rd edn, London, 1985), 1, pp. 511–29.

51. ANF, C6/8 Julien Dubellay, 18 December 1724; (for more context see Barry), *Waalo*, p. 187–9; for a different variant on the same theme in 1754, ANF, C6/14, letter of 20 October 1754.

52. ANF, C6/12 Senegal, 1 August 1742.

53. ANF, C6/10, Le Begue, Fort St. Joseph, 7 March 1731.

54. François de Paris, Voyage à la coste d'Affrique dete de Guiné et aux isles de l'Amerique fait ez années 1682 et 1683, fols 32v–33 in G. Thilmans, Le Relation de François de Paris (1682–83), *BIFAN* B, **38**/1, 1976, pp. 1–51 (marks original foliation of text).

55. M. Jacques Doumet de Siblas, Mémoire historique sur les différentes parties de l'Afrique . . ." 1769, (mod. edn C. Becker and V. Martin, Mémoire inédit de Doumet (1769) *BIFAN* B, **36**/

1, 1974, pp. 39–42; Mirabeau to Clarkson, 20 December 1789 in Fr. Thesée, Au Sénégal, en 1789. Traite des nègres et société africaine dans les royaumes de Sallum, de Sin et de Cayor, in S. Daget (ed.) *De la traite à l'esclavage du Ve au XVIIIe siècle* (2 vols., Nantes and Paris, 1988), 1, pp. 226–30 based on testimony of Geoffrey de Villeneuve, resident in area in the mid-1780s.

56. J. A. le Brasseur, Détails historiques et politiques sur la religion, les mœurs et le commerce des peuples qui habitent la côte occidentale d'Afrique . . . [1778] variorium edn from three texts in C. Becker and V. Martin, Détails historiques et politiques, mémoire inédit de J. A. le Brasseur, *BIFAN* B, 39/1, p. 1977, p. 97.

57. ANF, C6/18, Remarques sur l'Etat et aperçu des esclaves, 1783; and D. H. Lamiral, *L'Afrique et le peuple Afriquaine* (Paris, 1789), p. 171 (for the political background). For further documentation and arguments, see Barry, *Waalo*, p. 209 and Searing, *West African slavery*, p. 153.

58. B. and S. Canale, Western Atlantic Coast, pp. 520–9.

59. The linkages are studied in W. Peukert, *Der Atlantische Sklavenhandel von Dahomey, 1740–1797. Wirtschaftanthropologie und Sozialgeschichte* (Wiesbaden, 1978); for the view of Dahomean rulers, see Dalzel, *History of Dahomey*, pp. 217–19.

60. J. K. Fynn, *Asante and its neighbours, 1700–1807* (London and Evanston, 1971).

61. Rømer, *Golfe de Guinée*, p. 120; also see Fynn, *Asante*, p. 72.

62. On the war and its background, J. Thornton, *The Kingdom of Kongo: civil war and transition, 1641–1718* (Madison, 1983), pp. 69–121.

63. Castello de Vide, Viagem, pp. 260–2.

64. Correia Leitão, Relação, pp. 19–20, 25 where the Lunda advance is called "conquest of slaves".

Further reading

J. Goody, *Technology, tradition, and the state in Africa* (Cambridge, 1971).

R. Kea, *Settlements, trade and polities on the seventeenth century Gold Coast* (Baltimore, 1982).

R. Law, Horses, firearms, and political power in pre-colonial West Africa, *Past and Present*, 72, 1976, pp. 112–32.

R. Law, *The horse in West African history* (Oxford, 1980).

J. C. Miller, *Kings and kinsmen: the Imbangala impact on the Mbundu of Angola* (Oxford, 1977).

R. A. Smith, *Warfare and diplomacy in pre-colonial West Africa* (2nd edn, Madison, 1989).

J. Thornton, The art of war in Angola, 1575–1680, *Comparative Studies in Society and History*, 30, 1988, pp. 362–71.

J. Thornton, African soldiers in the Haitian revolution, *Journal of Caribbean History*, 25, 1991, pp. 65–8.

J. Thornton, *Africa and Africans in the making of the Atlantic world, 1400–1800* (2nd edn, Cambridge, 1998).

J. L. A. Webb, *Desert frontier: ecological and economic change along the Western Sahel, 1600–1850* (Madison, 1995)

Chapter Seven

Ottoman war and warfare 1453–1812

Virginia Aksan

Introduction

In 1453, while western Europe finally brought to an end the long series of confrontations and skirmishes which had characterized the Hundred Years' War, the Eastern Roman Empire faced its last and most formidable foe in the Ottomans, whose conquest of Constantinople meant an end to the city which had resonated for a thousand years as the capital of eastern Christendom. Within the Christian world the fall of Constantinople served henceforth as the icon of the destruction of the civilized east by the barbarian Turk, a threat which dated from the eleventh century and formed part of the history and lore of the Crusades. For the Muslim world the fall of Constantinople remained equally iconographic – the triumph of Muslim armies who had attempted the conquest of the city on numerous occasions since the seventh century.

The events of 1453 are equally important in military history as witnessing the inauguration and escalation of new kinds of warfare organized around the use of gunpowder. Without the enormous firepower of the huge cannons which the Ottomans brought to bear on the formidable walls of Constantinople, breaching those walls would have remained an impossibility. Similarly, the Hundred Years' War is often characterized as the last gasp of medieval chivalric warfare, and the beginning of the age of absolutist monarchies in Europe, whose rise to power was dependent on varying success in harnessing the new tools of war.

Such historical comparisons have only recently become part of the apparatus of military historiography in Europe. For centuries the Ottomans straddled east and west on the Dardanelles, but were never fully integrated into the construction of European history, which, for reasons far beyond the scope of this discussion, elaborated two trajectories of development: one, western Europe and the naval empires; the other, eastern Europe and the persistence of agrarian and neo-feudal-style empires. The Balkans, occupied for close to 500 years by the Ottomans, was viewed as the theatrical set on which great power politics and diplomacy were staged. Balkan and Turkish Republican historians, similarly, have simply ignored the Ottoman presence whenever possible, casting back to the pre-Ottoman period for ethnicities and grand narratives to bolster nationalist aims. As a result, there is a paucity of studies on the Ottoman military – surprising in light of the fact that the Janissaries constituted the "Terror of the World" for Europe until the end of the seventeenth century.

The absence of the Ottoman voice has led to many lopsided versions of the east–west confrontation which are based primarily on the accounts of travellers and the chancellery and foreign office documents of various European powers. Little of empirical or archival evidence has been readily available until recently, allowing for the persistence of certain assumptions about a 600-year history which would be ludicrous if applied, say, to Roman, or Byzantine history. One assumption is that the Ottoman military structure and financing did not change after the death of Süleyman the Magnificent in 1566, and the empire only survived until 1918 because it was rescued and bolstered by the European powers after 1800. The Ottoman house is often described as having set up its tents in the city of Constantinople and squatted there in true Central Asian nomadic fashion until brought down in the First World War. Another misconception insists on calling the Ottomans "Turks": this because Europe continued to call them that – a legacy of the crusades, when "Turk" replaced "Saracen" as the enemy of Christendom. No Ottoman sultan after Orhan (1326–62), the second in line, had a Turkish mother: they were Circassian, Georgian, Slavic, Greek, etc., but not "Turk" – a term reserved for the rude and ill-lettered until the end of the nineteenth century. The Ottomans, and anyone who identified with them, were part of a cultural milieu which amalgamated Middle Eastern cultures and languages: Arabic, Persian, Turkish, and a range of ethnicities from Slavic to North African. Conversion to Islam was the prerequisite.

In military histories this translates into a reluctance to give the Ottoman dynasty any agency in organizing or controlling violence. The history of Ottoman warfare has been built around difference, rather than similarity. There are, however, obvious parallels in the Ottoman context with many of the recent concerns of military historiography – for example, the increased use of standing armies to replace militia-style warfare in the late seventeenth and eighteenth century; the role of foreign advisors and technology-transfer in military reform; and, finally, the stalemate imposed by the limitations on warfare in pre-modern societies. As Guilmartin has noted: "the roots of war lie deep within the social fabric".[1]

This discussion of Ottoman warfare will consider the most important campaigns in three chronological periods, following a brief description of the formative period 1300–1453: "the imperial age 1453–1566"; "the limits of empire 1566–1699", and "the compromise 1699–1812". Coverage for each period will also include the major peace treaties, Ottoman approaches to evolving military technology, and an assessment of the impact of war on Ottoman society at large.

The formative period 1300–1453

In the late thirteenth century the territory surrounding Constantinople belonged largely to the Byzantines, who represented Orthodoxy in the eastern Mediterranean. Schisms within the western and eastern churches, as well as external threats from numerous Muslim kingdoms in the south and east, had long since broken the back of a centralized empire, making Anatolia and large parts of the Balkans frontier "march" territory, where petty dynasties played out their endless quarrels, and energetic mercenaries were very much in demand. The main Muslim threat of the period was the Seljuk Turkish dynasty, actually a series of petty kingdoms, the principal one by the thirteenth century centred in Konya in southern Anatolia. The warriors for the Seljuks included Turkish cavalrymen, horsemen who could use a compound bow with ease and devastating accuracy.

It was also a time of disorder in the Balkans, as the breakdown of Byzantine hegemony, schisms between Catholic and Orthodox, and nomadic incursions exacerbated the natural rivalries of the Kingdoms of Bulgaria, Serbia, and Hungary, and increased the vulnerability of lesser lords, such as those in Macedonia and Albania. In that context, just as in eastern Anatolia, effective warriors, regardless of religious affiliation, were in great demand.

Nonetheless, how did it happen that the Ottomans emerged from a number of rivals in Anatolia? The Seljuk dynasty maintained its power through a system of clients, called principalities, whose vassals were allied by military service to the Seljuk figurehead in Konya. In the mid-thirteenth century one of several rival principalities was that of Osman, eponymous founder of the Ottomans, who held the territory nearest Constantinople and the Balkans.

Osman (1280–1326), son of Ertuğrul (d. 1280), assumed the leadership of his loyal bands of *gazis* (warriors for the faith) in the 1290s, making a name for himself by defeating the Byzantines at Bapheon, near Nicea in 1301. Victory over the infidel brought Osman fame and more warriors, creating the basis for the political and cultural development of the empire, which his son and successor, Orhan (1326–62), consolidated in the first capital, Bursa, in 1326. Their expansion was slow, but was aided by having the Byzantines call on them as allies, and by actually marrying into the imperial family. The new Ottoman power was permanently established in Europe by 1354, when the Ottomans crossed the Dardanelles at Gallipoli. Under Murad I (1362–89), *gazi* raids became consolidated offensives, culminating in the famous battle of Kosovo in 1389 against the Serbian aristocracy. The distinguishing feature of this Muslim dynasty was its occupation of both east and west, concentrating on the latter as a result of their early history, but also because of the rich agricultural lands which became the bread basket of the new imperial capital after 1453.

The Ottoman notion of rule, combining central Asian and Muslim elements, was based on the perception of the state as the patrimony of the sultan, with the court organized as a grand household. That patrimony was divided up into those who ruled, called the *askeri*, or military, and those who were ruled, the *reaya*, or flock, the tax-payers, primarily peasants. When the sultan went on campaign, he was accompanied by his household, which was also his army; military headquarters were arranged around the sultanic tent, with proximity determining status. This accounts for the colourful names surrounding the Ottoman palace contingents: *ocak*, the word for a regiment, literally means hearth, for example, and the *Bostancılar*, or Gardeners, were actually the sultan's elite guard. Ottoman military thinking was determined by the household hierarchy, which accorded primary place to the elite infantry, and left and right wings to the cavalry: the order of battle was arranged in a crescent spreading out from the sultanic tent.[2] Between 1389 and 1453 most of the elements which made up the Ottoman military battle formation and strength were forged into a formidable balance of infantry, cavalry and artillery, supported by a well-regulated system of supply, a century before similar institutions were effectively in place in Europe.

The bulk of the fighting force was made up of the Anatolian and Balkan cavalryman (*sipahi*, or *timariots*). They were obligated to outfit themselves and report to the battlefront in return for the distribution of land grants known as *timars*, assignable by the sultan and his deputies, but not generally inheritable. Failure to appear could mean the revocation of the grant; success on the battlefield could mean an increase to the size of the estate. This system was in place until at least the last siege of Vienna in 1683, although alternative methods of recruitment were by then already in existence. There were, additionally, six regiments of palace horsemen, distinguished by unique names, but generally also referred to as *sipahis*. These were the sultan's own standing cavalry, numbering 2,300 at the time of Mehmed II (1451–81).[3] They were generally better paid than the Janissaries.

The Janissaries constituted the standing, salaried infantry of the Ottomans, starting out as the elite troops of the court, an innovation at least partially driven by the need of the dynasty to counter the strength of the provincial *timariots*. At sometime between the years 1380 and 1390 a levy of Christian male children, from 8 to 15 years old, called the *devşirme*, was inaugurated. Approximately every three to five years after the initial conquest the Christian territories of the

Balkans were visited to collect one boy from every 40 families. At its peak, under this system these children were brought to Constantinople, trained in the palace schools, and the majority of them relegated to the fighting troops that came to be known as the New Troops (*Yeni-Çeri*), the Janissaries. A smaller number of the hand-picked, intelligent boys were especially trained for bureaucratic service, and a number of them served as Grand Viziers (Prime Ministers) of the empire, second in command to the sultan.

Two thousand archers were reported as being with the Commander of the Janissaries at the battle of Kosovo against the Serbs in 1389. By the beginning of the reign of Mehmed II the Janissaries numbered 3,000. In addition to a daily salary, the Janissaries were given rations, cloth for uniforms, and weapons. Besides those in the imperial city, garrisons of these troops were stationed at all the major fortresses of the Ottoman borders along the Danube, Black Sea, Dardanelles and eastern frontiers. We know very little about their conditions of employment in the fortresses before the time of Mehmed II, when documentation about military rules and regulations becomes more plentiful. It was Ottoman practice to leave a garrison, representing sultanic law, a judge, representing Islamic law, and Muslim preachers in all newly-conquered territories. Fortress and mosque symbolized the sultan's presence in these early cities, sometimes built within the Christian towns, but equally often built apart. Relocation of populations into Balkan territories and, after 1453, to the new imperial capital was a routine policy of Ottoman settlement.

Firearms were also present at Kosovo in 1389. New research on the transfer of military technology between the east and west has demonstrated that knowledge of firearms, both cannons and arquebuses, was fairly common by the mid-fourteenth century, both in the Balkans and in Mamluk territory (Egypt, Palestine and syria). Italian and Ragusan merchants alike exported arms to the Ottomans. It was, however, Mehmed II who made them a regular part of the Ottoman arsenal, as his interest in military science was well-known in Europe, and attracted the interest of military experts.[4] The widespread adoption of firearms by the Janissaries was a slow process – probably a majority used arquebuses by 1590 – with even more disdain for the clumsy arquebus expressed by the cavalry, although even they wore pistols by the mid-seventeenth century.[5]

Locally-raised infantrymen, and auxiliary corps, called by a bewildering variety of names, but most often *azabs*, were also part of the Ottoman army from an early period. These were troops whose primary duties included guarding roads and passes, digging trenches, serving as local militias or marines in the navy, fighting alongside the Janissaries as infantrymen or cavalrymen, and raiding in front of the army, the latter called *akıncı*. Both *azab* and *akıncı* were at Kosovo. Drawn from the countryside, they were generally supplied by villagers as part of military taxation.

The Tatar Khan, ruler of the descendants of the Golden Horde in the Crimea, would assume the role of the *akıncıs*, once they became vassals to the Ottomans, following the completion of conquest of the Black Sea region in 1475, when the Black Sea is said to have become an "Ottoman lake". Until Catherine II's annexation of the Crimea in 1783, they could and often did contribute up to 100,000 horsemen to Ottoman campaigns, a third wing of the army, capable of inflicting considerable damage. The Tatar Khan, whose legitimacy was often determined by Ottoman recognition, was handsomely rewarded for his efforts by the sultan.

The process of subduing and consolidating an empire was a long-drawn-out one, and the Ottomans made use of a variety of strategies to accommodate new territories, which included: negotiations or strategic campaigns to maintain Balkan loyalties; establishing a buffer zone between Venetian and Ottoman in Ragusa (Dubrovnik); adding Wallachia and Moldavia as vassals; sustaining the Dulkadir and the Karamanid dynasties in Anatolia as allies and marcher territory between Ottoman and Mamluk, until they were in a position to confront the Mamluks and establish the Taurus Mountains as a boundary by 1491.[6] Military strategy had to be augmented with the creation of a navy before the Ottomans could conceivably take control of the Dardanelles, the Bosphorus and the Black Sea. By the 1470s, the Ottoman fleet included 92 galleys.[7]

The story of Mehmed II's conquest of Constantinople has been well-documented.[8] What needs to be re-emphasized is the fact that the city had been reduced to a population of 30,000 by the time of the siege, and contained within itself the seeds of its own destruction in the endless quarrels between Catholic and Orthodox, and also in the foreign merchant quarter of Galata (Pera), where Genoese and Venetian were slow to defend and quick to join the victors to gain commercial advantage. Mehmed II is generally accounted as the true founder of the empire, both because of the conquest and because of the imperial vision he brought to the new Ottoman capital, which reached an estimated population of 100,000 by 1500, rivalling all the cities of Europe in size, and also because of the almost 30 bellicose years following 1453, when much of the core territory which made up the empire until 1918 came under Ottoman hegemony.

The imperial age 1453–1566

The era between the conquest of Constantinople and the death of Süleyman I (1520–66) is generally acknowledged as the golden age of the empire, when a series of extraordinary sultans expanded Ottoman territory to bring into, at least nominal, Ottoman control: North Africa as far as Algeria; Mecca and Medina,

Egypt, Syria and all of Anatolia; the Morea, Bosnia and Albania; Belgrade and large parts of Hungary, the Crimea and the Black Sea. It is an equally important period for the consolidation of Ottoman institutions, court life and ceremonial, including the construction of a new palace, the Topkapı Sarayı, started by Mehmed II on the site of a Byzantine palace. The Ottomans of the sixteenth century had imperial ambitions to match those of Habsburg and Valois or Bourbon, and were a significant factor in European politics and diplomacy of the age. The Spanish Habsburgs and the Ottomans played out their rivalry in the western Mediterranean, while the Austrian branch of the house and Hungary fought one another and the expansion of the Ottoman frontier across the Danube into Europe. In the Muslim world the Ottomans became the supreme power, and the greatest of the Muslim empires, their chief rival for control of eastern Anatolia after 1500, the Shiite Safavids in Iran. Besides the significant dates already mentioned, there are major victories and setbacks in this period that warrant discussion: the eastern campaigns of Selim I (1512–20), especially the 1514 defeat of Shah Ismail (1501–24) at Çaldıran, and the 1517 capture of Cairo; Süleyman's addition of Belgrade, the gateway to Central Europe, to the empire in 1521; his victory at the battle of Mohacs against the Hungarians in 1526; the addition of the Hungarian province of Buda in 1541, but equally Süleyman's failure to capture Vienna in 1529, are indicative both of the successes and of the failures of the Ottoman military machine.

The various military units of the empire, as well as the navy, saw tremendous growth in this period. The continued development of the artillery branches, the *topçular* (artillerymen), the *cebeciler* (the armourers), and the *top arabacılar* (the gun carriage drivers), is one of the striking features of this growth. Mehmed II is credited with building the state cannon foundry (the *Tophane*), probably on the site of a Genoese foundry in Pera. Foreign experts were numerous in the court of Mehmed II, establishing a pattern of borrowing expertise that continued until the nineteenth century, although this may have impeded the development of indigenous expertise. Bronze cannons were cast locally by the mid-fifteenth century, but standardization and quality would never keep up with Europe. Until the late seventeenth century, the Ottomans were self-sufficient in the production of copper, iron and gunpowder, maintaining mines and factories all over the empire.[9] Ottoman gunners were esteemed by the Mughals in India, and gunpowder played a large role in Babur's conquest in 1526.[10] The Ottomans maintained a large fleet of specially-designed ships for use in troop, artillery and munitions transport on the Danube.

Selim I, whose sobriquet in western sources, "the Grim", is apt, spent most of the eight years of his reign on horseback. He had 10,000 Janissary infantry, the majority with firearms, and 348 artillerymen accompanying him on campaign to Çaldıran, where he defeated Shah Ismail and the Safavids, a confrontation that would continue for 200 years, requiring repeated, gruelling campaigns in inhospitable territory. After the victory at Çaldıran, attributable to the impressive firepower of the Ottomans, Selim I turned south and, in a series of confrontations with the Mamluks in 1516–7, completely defeated that Muslim power, again at least partially because the Mamluk military ethos completely rejected the use of the messy firearms.

Two imperatives drove Selim I's campaigns. The contemporary Reformation movement in Europe had its parallel in the East in the religious confrontation between Sunni and Shiite. The hard-won treaty of Amasya in 1555, like the treaty of Augsburg in the same year, attempted to delineate the border between Orthodox Sunni and minority Shiite views of Islam. Capture of Cairo in 1517 would make the Ottomans the supreme Sunni Muslim dynasty, since Cairo was the gateway to the two most sacred Muslim cities: Mecca and Medina. The Ottomans adopted "Guardian of the Two Sacred Cities", as part of their titulature, and profited from the annual tribute, an extremely important source of revenue for the palace.

Equally important was control over the Red Sea and access to the lucrative spice trade of the Far East, routes challenged by the Portuguese when they captured Hormuz in 1511. The capture of Cairo gave the Ottomans the port of Suez, where a fleet was maintained to counter the Portuguese presence in both Red Sea and Indian Ocean, and new considerations about Ottoman strategy suggest that they tried hard, with some success, to reopen the trade routes, which were important to their economy. The last major campaign in the Indian Ocean in 1552, against Hormuz itself, reputedly failed only because of the sinking of a supply ship, leaving the troops short of munitions and food.[11] Mediterranean naval historians have demonstrated that the Ottoman galley, designed for coastal warfare and defence, was useless in open water against the ocean-going ships of the Portuguese.[12] The Ottoman Mediterranean fleet was built around the imperative of protecting fortresses such as Suez, Basra and Aden, as well as the shipping lanes to Istanbul. For the confrontations with the Spanish Habsburgs, the Ottomans relied on famous captains such as Barbarossa, with local fleets and Ottoman supplies, primarily from Algiers, which began as a garrison, then became a vassal to the Ottomans in the 1520s.

By the time of Süleyman I's succession to his father's throne in 1520, the Ottoman threat to Europe proper was real, Martin Luther had dubbed the sultan the Antichrist, and politicians like Machiavelli saw much to admire in the Ottoman system. The core of that system as viewed by Europeans was the Janissary and the slave household of the sultan. Impressions of foreign visitors, like Ogier Ghiselin de Busbecq, Austrian ambassador to Süleyman (1554–62), have strongly influenced our thinking about the military of the Ottoman sixteenth century:

The Turks come together for war as if they had been invited to a wedding; I think there is no prince in the world who has his armies and camps in better order, both as regards the abundance of victuals and other necessities, and as regards the beautiful order and manner they use in encamping without any confusion; The Turks surpass our soldiers for three reasons; they obey their commander promptly; never show the least concern for their lives in battle; they can live a long time without bread or wine, content with barley and water; peace and silence reign in a Turkish camp – such is the result produced by military discipline.[13]

The palace Janissary corps stood at roughly 11,000–12,000 in 1527, rising to *c.* 20,000 in 1567[14] and to 37,000 by the end of the Long War (1593–1606).[15] This number does not include the palace cavalry regiments, whose numbers increased from 5,088 to 11,251 in that same time-period. Nor does it take into account the provincial *timariot* forces, called to war in large numbers (as many as 100,000 throughout the sixteenth and seventeenth centuries), or the local garrison forces, averaging 100–200 at the lowest, while several thousand might be assigned to the major fortresses serving as the Ottoman primary line of defence, especially on the European frontier.[16]

In fact, for the Ottomans to organize and go on campaign was a cumbersome and lengthy process. The call to arms was sent out on the main campaign routes to Anatolia and the Balkans in December of the year before the campaign. Troops raised from the countryside were ordered to join the main army on the march; those in Istanbul mobilized and left the city in early spring. The tremendous distances, and an average day of no more than 10–12 miles, meant that arrival at the actual battlefields in Hungary or in eastern Anatolia might not occur until mid-June. Major confrontations were often confined to August–October, when field conditions and the lack of fodder generally forced the suspension of hostilities, and, traditionally, the Janissaries returned to Constantinople.

Ottoman soldiers were well, if frugally, fed, and sober. Bread and/or biscuit were imperatives, with rice and mutton forming part of the rations, and barley for the horses and pack animals. Camels, water buffalo and oxen were the draught animals of supply wagons and artillery, the largest of the cannon requiring up to twenty oxen. Early on, supporting the numbers described above forced the creation of a system of warehouses and well-stocked way-stations, a responsibility of the towns and villages of the area, who, at least in this period, were paid for the goods they brought to the army, or whose taxes reflected their commitments to military supply. Representatives from all the guilds of Istanbul were required to accompany the army on campaign: millers, bakers, butchers, saddlers, cobblers and the like – again part of the commitment of the population to the military effort, in an age when all expected to be tapped to support the campaigns.

It was with this "wedding party" that Süleyman embarked on the conquest of Hungary, taking the western gate to Europe, Belgrade, in 1521, engaging and routing the forces of young king Lajos (Louis) II of Hungary at Mohacs in 1526, and establishing by the end of his reign the provinces of Buda in 1541, the vassalage of Transylvania, and a second province of Temeşvar (Timişoara) in 1552. His final campaign in 1566 meant the capture of yet more Hungarian territory, especially Szigetvar, before his own death on that campaign. His successor, Selim II (1566–74), signed a treaty with the Habsburgs in 1568 which survived until 1593. Maintaining control over such distant lands was costly, requiring a large system of fortresses along the Drava, Sava and the Danube, as well as the chain of garrisons bordering on the Hungarian Kingdom.[17] Between 1569 and 1590 an average of 10,500 troops were stationed in Buda, of which only 900 roughly were designated as Janissaries.[18] In the 1520s, an estimated 58 per cent of 41,000 registered Ottoman troops were stationed in the Balkan Peninsula; by 1613, perhaps 73 per cent of an estimated 38,000 were stationed in Hungary and Bosnia alone. Such estimates demonstrate the paramount importance of Danubian defence to Ottoman strategy.[19]

Süleyman's campaigns on land and sea were costly, and the imperial endeavours required a court and administration reflective of that power. İnalcık has estimated that the palace personnel (excluding the *Kapıkulu* troops of Janissary and cavalry) grew from 3,742 in 1514 to *c.* 12,971 in 1609.[20] Such a figure excludes the harem organization, an exclusively feminine domain which housed not only the salaried favourites and mothers of sultans and heirs to the throne, but all their servants, closely controlled by the black eunuchs, themselves some of the most politically powerful palace administrators of the post-Süleymanic age. Much of Süleyman's later reign was taken up with the control and manipulation of palace rivalries.

The Janissaries had begun to acquire the reputation for unruliness, rebellion and stubborness that was to become such a feature of later descriptions of the corps. Süleyman's decision to leave Vienna in 1529 was based as much on their restlessness, and also the lateness of the campaign season and insufficiency of supplies, as it was on the threat mounted by Ferdinand and Charles V. The demands of the provincial, fief-based *timariots* were equally pressing, for most wished to return to their assigned lands over the winter. The over-emphasis on the role of the Janissaries has long eclipsed the significance of the mounted troops, who until well into the seventeenth century remained the most dreaded and unpredictable of all the forces at the sultan's command. The Ottomans were attempting to support two military systems: the *timariots*; and the salaried palace army from the centre in Constantinople, in order to cover campaigns east and west.

Internal problems start to make their appearance in the latter days of Süleyman. Inflation in prices due to shortages of gold and silver, driven at least partially by the European expansion from 1500 onwards, led to coin debasement and new exigencies, such as extraordinary taxes and the confiscation of the estates of the empire's wealthy. The eastern frontier remained nomadic and uncontrolled, causing disruption to agrarian systems, and desertion of the land. Demobilized armed soldiery began to influence political and military thinking, as local bands could be manipulated to gain control of the countryside and to counterbalance governmental attempts at centralization. Thus, the "golden age" that lost its lustre with the death of Süleyman in 1566 was equally a harbinger for the problems which faced his successors.

The limits of empire 1566–1699

Between 1566 and 1699, the Treaty of Karlowitz, the Ottoman Empire experienced a critical challenge to its hegemony on the Hungarian frontier, on the Safavid border and in the Mediterranean. To maintain the focus on the military, this discussion of the crisis period will consider two lengthy campaigns which open and close the seventeenth century: the Habsburg–Ottoman War of 1593–1606; and the War of the Holy League of 1683–99. In the middle of the century Murad IV's campaign to Baghdad in 1638, which consolidated that frontier until the end of the empire, is also worth noting, as is the direction of Ottoman naval policy in the Mediterranean after the battle of Lepanto in 1571.

The 200 years following 1566 are commonly described as the era of decline, stagnation, decentralization and decomposition. Much has been made of the feebleness of the sultan, the killing of potential rival brothers and cousins, the confinement of heirs to the palace proper, and the influence of the harem, dubbed the "sultanate of the women". It is equally the period when the Grand Vizierate, exemplified by the extraordinary Köprülü family, assumed control of the administration, acquiring autonomy from the palace in separate quarters in 1657, initiating reforms in both army and finances, and gaining some notable successes in the field against the Safavids and even on the European front. Preference for the sensational and the exotic has prohibited historians from attempting an integrative view which might interpret the changing role of the sultan and his elite groups as a reconfiguration of monarch and aristocracy, and as the emergence of potential rival provincial households, strengthened by the empire's constant need for men and supplies which only they could supply. Crippling expenses, exacerbated by the demands of the Janissary corps for payment of the "accession fee" by the new sultan, diverted revenues and the sultan's private treasury away from military essentials, and forced the conversion of extraordinary into ordinary taxes, increasing the burden on peasant and grandee alike. In this regard the Ottoman sultans were restricted to the limited choices agrarian societies offered for financing, and failed to make the conversion to the kind of mercantilism that enabled their European counterparts to begin to exert some control over the military in this transitional period.

Finkel's masterful account of the 1593–1606 Habsburg–Ottoman struggle in Hungary allows us some glimpse into the state of the Ottoman military of the period, the obduracy of the Janissary corps, and the acceleration of alternative systems for getting the job done. The borderlands described in the previous section remained the scene of cross-border skirmishes, but until the Ottomans closed a long confrontation with the Safavids in 1590, by which they established a tenuous hegemony over Azerbaijan and the Caucasus, they were unable to turn their attention to the Danubian battlefront. According to contemporary historians, the choices then open to the Ottomans were: to renew war with Persia; or to attack Morocco, Spain, Malta, Venice, some part of Italy, Poland, or the Habsburgs and Hungary.[21] Lateness of the annual 30,000-ducat tribute money from Vienna, combined with a Hungarian–Ottoman confrontation at Siska in 1593, gave Murad III (1574–95) and Grand Vizier Sinan an excuse to order the Balkan troops to mobilize in the spring of 1593, the Habsburg emperor having already abrogated the treaty. Ottoman troops were initially successful in 1593 and 1594, saving Estergom from an Austrian attack and capturing the fortress of Györ (Yanık) farther west.

The issue of contention continued to be the vassal territories of Transylvania, Wallachia and Moldavia (the Principalities), who turned to the Habsburgs for protection in this round of confrontations. In 1595 the Austrians regained the advantage, but a thrust of the entire Ottoman force in 1596, with the sultan (Mehmet III 1595–1603) at their head for the first time since 1566, forced a major confrontation and success at Mezokeresztes in October. By the end of 1598, in spite of the successes, disarray in command and in the forces headquartered in Belgrade led the grand vizier to initiate inconclusive peace talks in 1599. Further events, such as the capture of Kanija by the Ottomans, and the realignment of the principalities as vassals (Wallachia in 1599, Moldavia in 1600 and Transylvania in 1605) which left the Ottomans in a position of strength, were offset by the necessity to mount a campaign against the Safavid Shah Abbas (d. 1629) in the east after 1603, and by a very considerable countrywide rebellion in the Celâli Revolts which began in 1599.

The 1606 Treaty of Zsitva-Torok, which conceded Kanija, Eger to the

Ottomans and confirmed their control of Estergom, represented little else for an effort which left both sides exhausted and reflective, although the reacquisition of the loyalties of the Principalities, which remained the bread basket of Istanbul, was also vitally important. By 1699, however, the military balance would no longer be a *status quo*, because the Thirty Years' War would change European warfare forever.

The significance of the 1593–1606 war to Ottoman military history is in the increased recruitment of the peasantry to form regiments of infantrymen and cavalrymen. This is in addition to the Janissary infantry and garrison troops, who continued to be paid on the tri-monthly basis, according to their enrolment in the pay registers. Access to Janissary pay tickets, the *esame*, was the greatest privilege of the corps, coveted by many but leading to abuses such as maintaining long-dead or inactive soldiers on the rolls for the sake of their salaries. The effective fighting force of palace troops in this period was probably somewhere about 50,000 infantry and cavalry, and certainly the palace contingent of some 10,000 made the difference at Mezokeresztes.

The issue of the *timariots* role in this war is still a matter of some controversy. The revenues extracted from their assigned lands no longer supported an individual soldier, and being called to campaign had become an expensive ordeal to be avoided. An alternative force, the countryside landless, was mobilized as armed infantry regiments (*sekban* is the most common name) in this war, leading to a cycle of lawlessness and banditry in the countryside, which was influenced by the cycles of warfare and peace of the later empire, the first being the Celâli Revolts referred to above.[22] The general cause of the revolts has been assumed to be the demobilization of both *timariots* and *sekban* after Mezokeresztes, and the confiscation of the assignments of as many as 20,000–30,000 *timariots*, who had failed to appear, or deserted. The effort to restore some control over the system backfired in violent rebellion, affecting even the capital, and was not brought under control until 1603, continuing sporadically until mid-century. Anyone who has studied European warfare of the period may recognize the general phenomenon, as mercenaries and autonomous regiments came to be replaced by indigenous standing armies of the idle, hungry, potentially lawless, and often willing peasants.

The means of financing such local troops were various: villages could volunteer and finance soldiers from their midst as part of their military effort as in earlier campaigns; or provincial governors, appointed from the palace, could be ordered to bring together 1,000–2,000 troops in additional to their personal retainers and entourage, financed out of their own pockets. The possibility of aggrandizement at the local level should be obvious, and it is one of the most significant provincial trends of the seventeenth century.

The Crimean Tatars (and other smaller contingents from the Principalities), remained the Ottoman mercenaries, an unpredictable and increasingly unreliable force, at least partially so because of increased Ottoman interference with succession quarrels in the khanate, but equally because of mixed loyalties, and the threat of an emerging Russia in the Ukraine, the Black Sea and the Caucasus. In open, mobile warfare, the Tatars excelled at raiding and harassing supply trains and soldiers on the march, but, at the siege warfare which characterized much of Danubian fortress campaigning, they were inept. In the subsequent European and Ottoman diplomacy over Poland and the Ukraine, they continued to be both an irritant and a significant catalyst of events. Countryside manpower continued to staff the auxiliary needs – whether for drovers, trench diggers, the preparation of roads – in a bewilderingly complex systems of compensation and exemptions.

The Ottoman army was often compared with a mobile fortress which dragged around with it everything it required to live and fight. This continued to be the practice, one which would work to the detriment of later campaigns. Nonetheless, supply systems in 1593–1606 were very resilient and relied on two variables: the well-defined series of warehouses at billets and in frontier fortresses, stocked by state commissioners, and the willingness of local peasantry to bring supplies to the troops in return for cash. The period under discussion saw the gradual imposition of new extraordinary taxes (in cash rather than in kind) to replace more voluntary systems, as contingents and their demands grew larger.

To what extent the Ottoman soldier fed off the land or purchased his own supplies is as yet undetermined, but the salaried palace troops expected rations, and the system was constructed to satisfy that demand first and foremost. The single largest item of concern to pre-modern armies was grain: for the Ottomans it was for wheat flour and barley, the latter used primarily for fodder for the horses and other stock. Biscuit, or hardtack, substituted for fresh bread, when battlefront circumstances necessitated it, were the staples of the Ottoman soldier's diet. Any given district (a collectivity of villages, called *avarizhane*) could be required to contribute a portion of their crops at fixed (and generally lower) prices, or to prepare (bake) and ship biscuit to the front. That same district might also find it had to supply firewood, hay and straw, oxen, horses, mules, and carriages, again for fixed rates for leasing or wages for the drovers and wagoneers. Some districts close to billets found their taxation linked to supplying the way-stations, and many may have benefited from being allowed (required – the term *sürsat* remaining a matter of controversy among historians) to sell their goods directly to the soldiers at market rates.

Local, centrally-appointed judges and members of the gentry were responsible for both mobilization and supply. State-appointed commissioners and fortress commissaries were also an integral part of the Ottoman supply system. Each major fortress had its own commissary official and chief accountant (who might be one and the same), and records even for the eighteenth century indicate that the supply levy (*nüzül*) system was still in force. Cash substitution for kind makes its regular appearance by the mid-sixteenth century, contributing to an evolution of countryside indebtedness that created provincial gentry families, many of whom started out as Janissaries.

Records for Murad IV's (1623–40) campaign to Baghdad in 1638 permit a glimpse of Ottoman organization in mid-century. Murad, who, for the first decade of his reign, faced significant military resistance and open revolt in Anatolia, a continuation of the Celâli Revolts, is often credited with restoring order to the anarchy. His predecessor, the hapless young sultan Osman II (1618– 22), had undertaken to curb the excesses of the Janissaries, to attempt to stem the flood of successes of the Safavids (Baghdad eventually fell in 1629) and to fend off the Poles at Hotin (1621) in a pitiful performance by both sides. Although an energetic and idealistic ruler, Osman II's attempts at reform simply hastened his downfall, as the former "terrors of the world" had now become the terrors of Constantinople and the sultan himself.

Murad's solution was to encourage the countryside to eliminate the rebels themselves, after securing the oath of loyalty from the majority of the Janissaries. In effect, his brutality allowed for a systematic review of the *timariot* lands, with many transferred to Janissaries and palace staff, and the further evolvement of the system known as *iltizam*, which substituted a tax-farming system for the fief-based *timariots*. Murad also used the campaign to regain Baghdad in 1638 as an opportunity to do some scouring of the countryside himself, eliminating Shiite resistance, and in the treaty of 1639 generally fixing the Iraq–Iran border much as it stands today. A *devşirme* levy was conducted in 1638, one of two in Murad's reign. Probably 70,000–80,000 provincial troops and levies, all the Janissaries (60,000–80,000), and Turcoman (Kurdish) and Tatars numbering 60,000– 100,000 horsemen were mobilized in the course of the two seasons spent in the east. For an estimated 80-day, 80,000-man march, approximately 5,000,000 kilograms of biscuit were requisitioned, on a proposed ration of 200 grams of biscuit per day. 200 grams of mutton was also the daily ration for the Janissaries.[23]

Murad IV had as advisor, Koçu Bey, a palace official whose brief essay on the ills of the empire has long served as the prime source of information on reform agendas of the seventeenth century. In a tradition of criticism which would continue into the nineteenth century, Koçu Bey described four causes of the anarchy of the period: (1) lack of leadership, i.e. the sultan's withdrawal from military affairs; (2) eclipse of the office of the grand vizier; (3) the rise and dominance of factional politics and (4) widespread corruption. Included in further lists by early reformers were the corruption of the muster rolls of the Janissaries, and the ineffectiveness of the provincial troops. Koçu Bey proposed an idealized version of the age of Süleyman as the model for a revived empire, which became a standard theme of Ottoman political discourse. Its accuracy as representative of the real state of affairs has only recently been questioned.[24]

A moment of crisis in 1656, during the reign of Mehmet IV (1648–87), can be used to illustrate Ottoman politics and negotiations. A major revolt in Constantinople, initiated by the Janissaries who were protesting about the debasement of the coinage used for their salaries, in effect closed down the city. Their chief opposition lay in the provincial *timariots* and the *sekbans*, the local militias who replaced them. Large numbers of these provincial troops were then in the city. This era also saw the dominance of an intolerant Muslim revival movement, the *Kadizadeler*, which was attempting to reimpose a strict orthodoxy upon both the sultan and the city's population, attacking particularly the pervasive Sufi mystical orders. A decade of incompetent grand viziers, generally palace favourites, meant the dominance of factional politics between the Janissary Commander-in-Chief, the harem and the black eunuch. Finally, the Venetians, in May 1656, defeated and destroyed an Ottoman fleet at the Dardenelles, blockading them so thoroughly that scarce food and fear of enemy attack created panic in the populace at large. Comparisons with the house of Bourbon in France are apt in this period, particularly under Louis XIV, where the buying and selling of offices, the extension of government in the *intendant* system, household politics in an inflated palace operation, religious opposition and the suppression of the Huguenots, and constant warfare forced oppressive and unwanted exactions on aristocrat and peasant alike. The extension of the arm of the sultan over proud autonomies and deeply-entrenched privileges led countryside and city to raise its voice.

The normal Ottoman palace response to such revolts was to give in to the demands, sacrifice high officials of the state, up to and including the sultan himself, and distribute largesse. In this case, the 80-year old respected and honest Mehmed Köprülü negotiated sole power as Grand Vizier (1656–61), and proceeded with rare swiftness to restore order to the city by banishing and confiscating the property of his rivals, military and religious, and installing loyal men from his own household into positions of power. Bozcaada (Tenedos) and Limni (Limnos) were recaptured from the Venetians, and the Straits secured by 1657. A significant revolt under Abaza Hasan Pasha was similarly quelled by the harsh measures and political savvy of the first of the Köprülüs, a dynasty continued with his son Fazil Ahmed (1661–76).[25] It was still possible to restore the fortunes of the Ottoman house, and even immediately to rebuild the Ottoman fleet, as had been the case in 1571 after the battle of Lepanto.

There is a certain refusal in Mediterranean historiography to accord the Ottomans a naval policy. Against that might be set Süleyman's capture of Rhodes in 1522, to eliminate the Knights of St. John from within striking distance of the Ottomans; the brief alliance with Francis I of France which saw an Ottoman fleet winter over in Marseilles in 1536, and rewarded the French with the first of the favourable trade agreements known as the "Capitulations"; and, finally, the operations in Yemen against the Portuguese in 1538 and again in 1552. After Kazan and Astrakhan were conquered by Tsar Ivan IV in 1552–6, the Ottomans under the renowned Grand Vizier Sokollu Mehmed Pasha, conceived a project to build a canal between the Don and the Volga to accommodate the fleet, an unrealistic undertaking attempted in 1569. The building of such a canal would not be achieved until the twentieth century. In 1570–1, the conquest of the island of Cyprus required significant mobilization of both army and navy, and one of the consequences of Ottoman aggression was the amassing of an allied fleet, under Don Juan of Austria, which confronted and destroyed the Ottoman fleet at Lepanto, a naval battle involving 438 ships. Of the 230 which the Ottomans brought to the conflict 200 were destroyed, but the Ottomans rebuilt the navy over the winter, and the Venetians were finally forced to accept the surrender of Cyprus in 1573.

The lengthy siege of Crete, by contrast, represented the final struggle of two naval powers, Venice and the Ottomans, for the largest of the islands in the eastern Mediterranean. It would not be completely conquered until 1669, after a long siege. While the Venetians received support from Malta, the Pope, and the French, the Ottomans supported the effort in the Mediterranean at the same time that they were defending the Black Sea littoral against Cossack raids even into the Bosphorus, and extending Ottoman power to its farthest north point, with the temporary gain of Podolia (1671–99). Ottoman naval practice continued to operate on the principle of defence of the ports and the trade corridors, concerned as it always was with the feeding of Constantinople and the mobilization and feeding of troops. Crete remained nominally in Ottoman hands until 1913, an important source of olive oil, wine and grain. Cyprus was occupied by Britain in 1878.[26] By the late eighteenth century, Ottoman naval efforts were rarely rewarded with success. In 1770, the entire fleet was destroyed, when, to the astonishment of Europe, a Russian flotilla (with a number of British captains), appeared in the Aegean and engaged the Ottomans at Çeşme, west of present-day Izmir. The Ottomans did rebuild, but the creation of a modern style navy was a product of the mid-nineteenth century.

The latter half of the seventeenth century saw some success in re-establishing order in the army and treasury, and extending Ottoman control, for example, along the Black Sea littoral, reforms which were checked by the extended war against Habsburg, Pole and Hungarian which broke out in 1683. The Ottoman–Habsburg War of 1683–99 focused Ottoman attention on the Danubian border and the north coast of the Black Sea, the centre of confrontation with Austria and Russia for the next 200 years. The years 1683–99 were those of the struggle for possession of Hungary between Ottoman and the Holy League which by 1697 included Austria, Venice, Poland, the Pope and Russia, but also of considerable upheaval at the centre of power, as four different sultans were enthroned and deposed in the course of the war. Two battles, the siege of Vienna in 1683, and the massive confrontation at Zenta in 1697, demonstrate the strength and weaknesses of the Ottoman military organization. The 1683 siege, late in the campaign season, and lifted by the arrival of a Polish army under Jan Sobieski, was on the brink of success, when the obstinancy of Grand Vizier Kara Mustafa Pasha left the Ottomans unaware of the impending attack of the Poles from the rear, and forced a rout of the entire army, leaving behind enough booty (300 guns, 5,000 tents, provisions and all the banners of the Janissary regiments) to fill the many museums which proudly display their trophies in Vienna today.[27] Buda held out till 1686, but following its surrender, the Ottomans retreated to Belgrade. Grand Vizier Fazıl Mustafa (1689–91) briefly made great strides in reforming the army, but was himself killed in August 1691 at Szlankemen. The Janissaries were still capable of considerable resistance in entrenchments, such as that at Sofia in 1697, but further humiliation followed in September, when the renowned commander Prince Eugene of Savoy destroyed another Ottoman army, under Sultan Mustafa II (1695–1703), at Zenta. Outnumbered two to one, the imperial forces suffered 2,100 casualties by contrast with the 30,000 Ottomans wounded and drowned in the river Tizsa.[28] In spite of that Austrian triumph, lack of money, and the general exhaustion of both main belligerents forced a conclusion of the Karlowitz treaty in January 1699, with the Ottomans ceding Hungary and Transylvania, and recognizing the equality of their fellow European rulers – a first in Ottoman–European diplomatic relations, which now entered a new phase, as bureaucrats rather than military men served as the chief negotiators, and the notion of "fixed" borders and "permanent" peace began to replace the Muslim version of peace with infidels – that is, temporary truce in the perpetual war for the expansion of the world of Islam.

According to Marsigli, soldier, engineer, messenger and diplomat, who was captured by and escaped from the Tatars at the siege of Vienna, the Ottomans fielded no more than 30,000 *kapukulu* (Janissary and other corps) troops and approximately 155,000 provincial troops, the latter being divided into cavalry and infantry, *timariots*, troops raised by the governors of provinces, and the Tatars. Marsigli also noted that the Ottomans made strategic adjustments to their entrenchments and the positioning of their forces as a result of the lesson learned at Vienna in 1683. While he described the variety and quality of armanents, few statistics were included, although he did remark on the presence of Christian-style muskets and fusils, which he attributed to the Ottoman willingness to learn from the infidel.[29] Astute military observers of this and subsequent campaigns claimed as did Maurice de Saxe: "neither valour, nor number, nor wealth was lacking to them – but order, discipline, and 'la manière de combattre'". Others added the following list: incompetence in high command, lack of an efficient artillery, ignorance of tactics and of the art of manoeuvre.[30]

The compromise 1699–1812

Faced with considerable failure on the battlefield, another round of which led to the fall of the reputedly impregnable Belgrade to the Habsburgs in August 1717, and increasingly aware of the threat of Russia on the northern and eastern frontiers, the Ottomans began an imperceptible tilting toward things European, both in diplomacy and in military reform. For the sake of this discussion, the century can be framed by the Russian humiliation and lucky escape at Pruth in 1711, and the Ottoman debacle and diplomatic humiliation at the 1774 treaty of Küçük Kaynarca, ending the 1768–74 Russo-Ottoman war. The chapter ends with the description of another treaty, that of Bucharest of 1812, which capped a series of three debilitating and futile wars with the Russians (1768–74, 1787–92 and 1806–12), ruinous in their effects on the Balkans, especially the Principalities, and inaugurating, in many ways, the Eastern Question of the nineteenth century.

The confrontation between Russian and Ottoman in July 1711, when the Ottomans completely surrounded the Russians on the Pruth, outnumbering them by more than six to one (260,000 to 40,000; casualties 3,000 Ottomans, 7,000 Russians),[31] but failed to press the advantage, has very often been held up as an example of Ottoman stupidity and cupidity in warfare and negotiations. Pruth was probably the last time that the Tatars and Cossacks effectively united against the Russians, one of the significant reasons for the victory, a lesson understood by Catherine and her famous Field Marshal Rumiantisev in the 1768–74 war in the same arena, when Cossack regiments served as auxiliaries of the Russian main army.

Mistrust of mutinous local rulers of the Principalities (Wallachia and Moldavia) by the Ottomans led to a new administrative tactic there – the appointment of overlords from the Phanariote Greek families of Istanbul, a policy which led to the disaffection of the populace at large. The changes reflect the significant difference between Ottoman and Russian frontier strategies: for the Ottomans, the Principalities were always perceived as clients and vassals; for the Russians of the eighteenth century, in spite of much rhetoric about Orthodox brothers, the chief aim was territorial expansion. Catherine's strategy in the Crimea was clearly that: territorial victories were always accompanied by settlement, to the detriment ultimately of the Tatars, exiled after 1783. At Pruth the check on that expansion by the Ottomans was only temporary.

Frederick the Great, whose own experience of Russian might was quite recent, in conversation with Ahmed Resmi Efendi, the first Ottoman Ambassador to Russia in 1763, wondered why the Ottomans had been so lenient with Tsar Peter? Ahmed Resmi in true ambassadorial fashion equivocated, stating that the mobilization had only been to halt the onslaught of the Russians and regain Azov, and that the sultan had been charitable.[32] In fact, the frontier fortresses captured by the Russians, including Azov, were surrendered. Given the general Ottoman fixation with the frontier fortress strategy, that may have been considered sufficient.

The Russian army developed more effective tactics in its conflicts with the European powers, especially during the Seven Years' War (1756–63), a war which helped to perfect the use of mobile, rapid-fire, small calibre cannons, and which relied on the rapid deployment of highly-trained and disciplined infantry. The socket bayonet came back into use, and represented a formidable weapon against the headlong charges of cavalry, all tactics which Rumiantsev put to good use against the Tatars in the 1768–74 war. Siege warfare was gradually being abandoned because of wastefulness and inconclusiveness. Massive confrontations, generally to be avoided, and carefully orchestrated when necessary, grew to be the norm by mid-century. European warfare had reached its apogee of pre-modern warfare, when mobilization of huge numbers of soldiers and the logistics of transportation and supply stretched the limits of even the healthiest state budgets.

For Russia, distance and manpower were a continual preoccupation in the Danubian context, conscription a lifetime sentence of the serf (for 25 years only after 1793). Self-mutilation was a frequent method of avoiding the levy.[33] In the 1680s the Russian standing army was more than 200,000 strong, representing 4.4 per cent of the population.[34] During Peter's reign, there were 53 levies of 300,000 recruits.[35] For the 1768–74 war alone 300,000 troops were levied.[36] The massive Pugachev Rebellion of 1773, started among the Cossacks, can easily be interpreted as evidence of the strain which constant warfare in the south had begun to have on the populace at large.

By contrast, conscription in the Ottoman army did not become a mobilization tactic until the 1790s. One of the striking aspects of this period is the continued volunteerism evident in the campaigns that unfold, though death and desertion were endemic to both Russian and Ottoman, with losses (wounded, dead and from disease) as high as 25 per cent, often higher on the long forced marches. The Ottomans sat out most of the developments evident in the Seven Years War, although not entirely. They remained wedded to siege warfare and the efficacy of the horseman, even as they increased the proportion of infantry in the provincial levies. Consolidation of the Danube frontier with "an unprecedented program of fortress building during the first decades of the century gave perfect architectural expression to a more defensive outlook on the world", a system which ran from Belgrade to Azov.[37] Such a strategy was consistent with that of both Russian and Austrian military thinking, as studies of the military frontiers of both have indicated.[38] The battlefield moved home: Ottoman military headquarters were often south of the Danube, especially after 1768, a fact which made supplying the troops difficult, when the Principalities and their agricultural wealth were cut off. Diplomatic alternatives became the norm. In most of the major campaigns after 1700, the Ottomans sought mediators, preferring truces to sustained warfare.

The 1736–9 Austro-Russian-Ottoman War is illustrative of many of the problems just described. Austrian incompetence in leadership and French brilliance in diplomacy are the usual reasons proffered for the Austrian return of Belgrade to the Ottomans in the 1739 treaty of that name. Little was gained by either side, but in many ways the psychological impact of the recapture of Belgrade blinded Ottoman administrators to the true state of the army. By 1739 the Ottomans had gained the upper hand against Austria, whose commanders decided to settle. French Ambassador Villeneuve's negotiated Belgrade treaty was a true disaster for Austria, which had to surrender the gains of 1718. The Russians were initially victorious in capturing Azov in 1736, when Field Marshal Münnich and 50,000 soldiers marched 300 miles on biscuit to face 4,000 Janissaries and, reputedly, 100,000 Tatars[39] They were crippled in the end by the distance from sources of supply and forced to evacuate the Crimean Peninsula. More successful in the Principalities, they were forced to conclude a separate peace when the Austrians deserted them, even though they had penetrated Moldavia and captured Hotin (August 1739) as part of a plan to join the Austrians at Belgrade. Russian losses were severe, estimated at 100,000.

During Frederick the Great's bid for power in the Austrian War of Succession 1740–8 and the subsequent continental conflict, the Seven Years' War (1756–63), the Ottomans struggled to contain the integrity of their eastern frontier, which was once again disrupted by the collapse of the Safavid dynasty in the 1720s. The eastern frontier always represented a different series of challenges to the Ottomans: "unwalled cities and restless nomads" as one author has recently argued.[40] Artillery and siege warfare were less useful than cold steel and the sturdy little Central Asian horse. The Janissary revolts were frequent in the period because of their reluctance to travel the distances, fight fellow Muslims, and suffer the deprivations involved in eastern warfare. Neither the 1736–9 conflict nor the Iranian Wars have been given the attention they deserve from the Ottoman point of view.

Emerging in this period, and accelerating until the final dissolution of the

Janissary corps in 1826, is a concern among Ottoman statesmen about the need for improvements along western lines, the thinking being that disembodied Western technology would be sufficient to restore Muslim-Ottoman greatness. The earliest efforts in the eighteenth century surrounded the Bombardier (*Humbaracı*) Corps under Ahmed Bonneval Pasha, a renegade who reorganized and began to school the troops in the expertise required for artillery and its uses. The century is dotted with many such men, and the best-selling *Memoirs* (1786) of one of them, Baron de Tott, who claimed to have reformed the Ottoman artillery single-handedly, established a rapid-fire regiment, and rebuilt the defences of the Dardanelles in the 1770s, remains the paradigmatic view of Ottoman obscurantism, religious fanaticism, and decadence, which has only recently been challenged.[41]

The real issues involved in military reform in the late Ottoman context are only now beginning to emerge. One was the intractability of a fictitious Janissary Corps, a supposed standing force of perhaps as many as 400,000 members, of which maybe 20,000–50,000 could be considered "actives". The other was the Ottoman alternative fighting forces which became a reality in the 1768–74 war, necessity requiring the circumvention of the traditional force. The fictional fighting force was based on corrupt muster rolls, and the pay tickets of the Corps started to be sold as stock or bond certificates. This system began as early as in the reign of Mahmud I (1730–54). Such sales generated much needed income, and benefited Ottoman administrators and bureaucrats at large.[42] The functioning army strength remained unknown.

Fighting forces were increasingly drawn from the Asian countryside, as the *devşirme* had been discontinued by 1700, and the few remaining *timariots* were no longer of any use as a military force. While empressment was practised among prisoners (especially for the navy), volunteers could still be counted on to fill the Janissary regiments on the road. Manpower was not the issue: organization and training were. Records from the 1768–74 war refer to the use of provincial levies (*levend*) in very significant numbers: perhaps as many as 100,000 such men were called up during the course of the campaigns. Payment came directly from the centre, with a significant sign-on bonus as part of the incentive, and enlistment periods of six months, with frequent two-month renewals. A very careful formula of rations accompanied the records of troop mobilization, with cash equivalents ascribed. These were both infantry and cavalry troops, commanded most often by local provincial officers, resembling to some degree the milita of earlier periods in Europe, organized out of a central treasury.[43]

The unintended result of such a system was the considerable aggrandizement of a lower level of gentry, at the district (*sancak*) level, reflected in a new series of taxes controlled by them, the *imdad-i seferiye* (campaign tax), which was first assessed in the early decades of the 1700s, specifically tagged for these locals for the purpose of organizing troops. Such governors and tax collectors always maintained a household corps, as well as mustering the *levend* described above, and were expected at the front with both.

The 1768–74 war included the Khan and his horsemen, again estimated at the magical number of 100,000, whose precipitous flight occasioned the general rout at the battle of Kartal (Kagul) in 1770. Sources on troop strength are widely various: 80,000 Ottoman infantry *v.* 40,000 Russian infantry represents the most realistic spread, but both sides made extensive use of irregulars as described. The triumph of the outnumbered, but far better organized and disciplined, Russians under Field Marshal Rumiantsev astonished the rest of Europe, and signalled to all the true state of the Ottoman military. Thousands of Ottoman soldiers drowned attempting to cross the Danube to reach their headquarters at Babadağı.

The major problems of the Ottoman 1768–74 campaigns concerned leadership and systematic discipline, both of which were noticably less visible than in previous wars, a curiosity which cannot be explained away entirely by unruly Janissaries. Supply systems remained unaltered, and in a context where fighting and quartering troops were concentrated on one's own territory, famine and desertion were inevitable. Janissary pay was erratic, but no more or less than in the European context, and the provincial levies were recruited with cash. 50,000,000 lb of biscuit were requisitioned for the 1769 campaign, one of the few aspects of this war which has been examined from the Ottoman side, leaving the field wide open for study and reinterpretation.[44] The opportunities for abuse and self-aggrandizement were legion: the narratives of the period include exemplary, loyal and brave citizens, but just as many corrupt state commissioners, accountants, local judges, and provincial regimental commanders. This war is also notable for the three years of truce and negotiations which followed 1770, testimony to Grand Vizier Muhsinzade Mehmed's clear understanding of the state of his forces, but more often represented as a hiatus until Austria, Poland and Russia had decided on the fate of Poland.

By the time of Selim III (1789–1807), when disastrous defeats in the 1787–92 campaign against Russia led to pressure for serious reform, Ottoman military thinking had grown accustomed to the recruitment of youth from the Anatolian heartland, the advantage being they could be moulded into the type of modern army required to defeat the Europeans. Many of the advisors around Selim III were perfectly aware of the need for a dissolution of the lucrative Janissary pay system, since it represented an excuse for the maintenance of a completely outmoded military organization, but they were incapacitated by the lack of significant leadership from the palace, and by intrigue and collusions among different factions. It must also be stated, unequivocally, that the three decades of futile warfare left the Ottoman state at the brink of bankruptcy.[45] The failure of Selim III's *Nizam-i Cedid* or "new order" troops (some 22,700 and almost 1,600 officers by 1806) to replace the Janissaries, was at least partially due to the state of the economy, but mostly to Selim III's spinelessness when faced with the rebellion of the Janissaries over the parallel army.[46] Selim III's hesitation in employing the new army against the rebels led to his own overthrow in 1807.

The creation of significant numbers of western-style, uniformed troops, an officer corps, systematic training schools, and modern ministries, is a product of the nineteenth-century reforms, begun under Selim III, but truly established by Mahmud II (1807–39), whose careful planning and conciliatory gestures to reactionary forces allowed him finally, in 1826 to eliminate the traditional corps. Interestingly enough, his success in doing so was based on a continuous and careful attention (from the time of Mustafa III (1757–74)) to the maintenance and reform of the artillery corps – a process which accelerated in the time of Baron de Tott, to be sure – but which continued demonstrably as indigenous reform throughout the latter period under discussion, an Ottoman equivalent of similar, but more successsful, reforms in France, which gave centrality of place to the artillery as the basis of the modern army.[47] By 1826 Mahmud I could count on the loyalty of some 15,000 modern artillerymen, who served as an effective counterweight to the Istanbul Janissaries.[48]

Michael Mann has argued that inventiveness in large territorial empires has less to do with technological innovation or change, but rather with "extensive social organization", and the ability to expand and organize a wide variety of multicultural elites, and diverse agrarian environments.[49] Throughout the eighteenth century the Ottomans were negotiating the social and cultural transitions required for them to be able to field an army, and to survive, and allowing, without acknowledging it, the access to power of a series of provincial elites. Such negotiations altered permanently the relation of the household of Osman to its citizenry, a prelude to nineteenth-century absolutism, as part of the adoption, not just of western military technology, but also of the cultural system embedded in the control exerted by the modern nation-state.

The emphasis here has been on indigenous reform, but by 1798 the larger context is, of course, the Great Power conflicts of the Napoleonic Wars, inaugurated in Ottoman territories by Napoleon's invasion of Alexandria in that year. The British armed response, the rise of Muhammad Ali in Egypt, and the 1807 Franco-Russian Tilsit agreement over division of the Ottoman Empire inaugurated a century of imperial ambitions and diplomacy on the part of Britain and France, whose chief aim in the eastern Mediterranean was the blocking of Russian aspirations, and the protection of trade corridors. Clearly the 1812 Treaty of Bucharest, which ended another exhausting round of Danubian confrontations between Russians and Ottomans, each time with the Russians moving closer and closer to Istanbul, was simply a respite in the long process of curing the "sick man of Europe".

Notes

1. J. Guilmartin, Ideology and conflict: the wars of the Ottoman Empire, 1453–1606, *Journal of interdisciplinary history*, 18, 1988, p. 746.
2. S. T. Christensen, The heathen order of battle, in S. T. Christensen (ed.) *Violence and the absolutist state: studies in European and Ottoman history* (Copenhagen, Center for Research in the Humanities, Copenhagen University, 1990), pp. 75–138.
3. G. Káldy-Nagy, The first centuries of the Ottoman military organization, *Acta Orientalia Academiae Scientiarum Hungaricae*, 31, 1977, p. 168.
4. G. Ágoston, Ottoman Artillery and European Military Technology in the Fifteenth and Seventeenth Centuries, *Acta Orientalia Academiae Scientiarum Hungaricae*, 47, 1994, pp. 24–6.
5. V. J. Parry, Bārūd iv. Ottoman Empire, *Encyclopedia of Islam* 2nd edn (Leiden, E. J. Brill, 1960-[unfinished]), pp. 1061–6.
6. Shai Har-El, *Struggle for domination in the Middle East: the Ottoman-Mamluk War, 1485–91* (Leiden, E. J. Brill, 1995).
7. H. İnalcık, *The Ottoman Empire: the classical age, 1300–1600* (London, Weidenfeld & Nicolson, 1973), p. 26.
8. S. Runciman, *The fall of Constantinople* (Oxford, Oxford University Press, 1961) and bibliography.
9. Ágoston, Ottoman artillery, p. 46.
10. Parry, Bārūd, p. 1062.
11. S. Özbaran, Ottoman naval policy in the south, in M. Kunt and C. Woodhead (eds) *Süleyman the Magnificent and his age: the Ottoman Empire in the early modern world* (London, Longman, 1995), p. 64.
12. C. M. Cipolla, *Guns, sails and empires: technological innovation and the early phases of European expansion, 1400–1700* (New York, 1965); also J. F. Guilmartin, *Gunpowder and Galleys, changing technology and Mediterranean warfare at sea in the sixteenth century* (Cambridge, Cambridge University Press, 1974).
13. A. Stiles, *The Ottoman Empire, 1450–1700* (London, Hodder & Stoughton, 1989), p. 72.
14. Káldy-Nagy, p. 167.
15. H. İnalcık, Istanbul, *Encyclopedia of Islam*, 2nd edn (Leiden, E. J. Brill, 1960-[unfinished]), p. 242.
16. Káldy-Nagy, pp. 168–9.
17. K. Hegyi, The Ottoman military force in Hungary, in G. David and P. Fodor (eds) *Hungarian-Ottoman military and diplomatic relations in the age of Süleyman the Magnificent* (Budapest, Loránd Eötvös University, 1994), pp. 133–4.
18. Hegyi, pp. 139–40.
19. Hegyi, pp. 147–8.
20. Inalcık, Istanbul, p. 242.
21. C. Finkel, *The administration of warfare: the Ottoman military campaigns in Hungary, 1593–1606* (Vienna, VWGÖ, 1988) p. 9.

22. K. Barkey, *Bandits and bureaucrats: the Ottoman route to state centralization* (Ithaca, Cornell University Press, 1994); H. İnalcık, Military and fiscal transformation in the Ottoman Empire, 1600–1700, *Archivum Ottomanicum*, 6, 1980, pp. 283–337.

23. R. Murphey, *The functioning of the Ottoman army under Murad IV (1623–1639/1032–1049): key to the understanding of the relationship between center and periphery*, 2 vols (PhD thesis, Department of History, University of Chicago, 1979), especially vol. 1, chaps 2, 4–5. Vol. 1, p. 133 includes one round-up of 19,901 sheep from the period (1633) to give an idea of the quantities required.

24. The issues and texts are discussed in the following articles: D. Howard, Ottoman historiography and the literature of "decline" of the sixteenth and seventeenth centuries, *Journal of Asian History*, 22, 1988, pp. 52–77; V. H. Aksan, Ottoman political writing, 1768–1808, *International Journal of Middle East Studies*, 25, 1993, pp. 53–69; G. Piterberg, Speech acts and written texts: a reading of a seventeenth century Ottoman historiographical episode, *Poetics Today*, 14, (1993), pp. 387–418, concentrates on the "orality" of the narratives.

25. İnalcık, *The Ottoman Empire* p. 48: timariots numbered about 8,000 in this period. See also S. J. Shaw, *History of the Ottoman Empire and modern Turkey* (Cambridge, Cambridge University Press, 1976), vol. 1, pp. 208–12.

26. R. C. Jennings, *Christians and Muslims in Ottoman Cyprus and the Mediterranean world, 1571–1640* (New York, New York University Press, 1993), offers a revised look at this period from Ottoman sources.

27. G. Goodwin, *The Janissaries* (London, Saqi Books, 1994), p. 176.

28. D. Chandler, *The art of warfare in the age of Marlborough* (London, B. T. Batsford, 1976), p. 302, lists 60,000 Ottoman infantry, 40,000 cavalry and 200 guns.

29. J. Stoye, *Marsigli's Europe, 1680–1730: life and times of Luigi Ferdinando Marsigli, soldier and virtuoso* (New Haven, Yale University Press, 1994), p. 93; L. F. Marsigli, *Stato militare dell'Imperio ottomanno, L'État militaire de l'empire ottoman* (La Haye, Amsterdam, 1732), pp. 20–8.

30. V. J. Parry, Harb iv. Ottoman Empire, *Encyclopedia of Islam*, 2nd edn, p. 193.

31. Chandler, p. 305.

32. V. H. Aksan, *An Ottoman statesman in war and peace: Ahmed Resmi Efendi 1700–1783* (Leiden, E. J. Brill, 1995), pp. 89–90.

33. J. L. H. Keep, *Soldiers of the Tsar: army and society in Russia 1462–1874* (Oxford, Clarendon Press, 1985), p. 155.

34. Keep, p. 88.

35. Keep, p. 107.

36. R. Ungermann, *Der russisch-türkische Krieg 1768–1774* (Vienna, 1906), p. 232.

37. H. İnalcık and D. Quataert (eds) *Economic and social history of the Ottoman Empire* (Cambridge, Cambridge University Press, 1994), p. 639.

38. G. E. Rothenberg, *The military border in Croatia 1740–1881: a study of an imperial institution* (Chicago, University of Chicago Press, 1966); C. B. Stevens, *Soldiers on the steppes: army reform and social change in early modern Russia* (DeKalb, University of Illinois Press, 1995).

39. L. Cassels, *The struggle for the Ottoman Empire 1717–1740* (London, John Murray, 1966), p. 103.

40. R. Mathee, Unwalled cities and restless nomads: firearms and artillery in Safavid Iran, in C. Melville (ed.) *Safavid Persia, the history and politics of an Islamic society* (London, I. B. Tauris, 1996), p. 404.

41. Baron de Tott, *Memoirs of Baron de Tott*, 2 vols. (London, J. Robinson, 1785).

42. *Economic and social history*, p. 716.

43. V. H. Aksan, Whatever happened to the Janissaries? *War in History*. In press.
44. V. H. Aksan, Feeding the Ottoman troops on the Danube, 1768–1774, *War and Society*, **13**, 1995, pp. 1–14.
45. *Economic and social history*, pp. 966–70.
46. S. Shaw, *Between old and new: the Ottoman Empire under Sultan Selim III, 1789–1807* (Cambridge, Mass, Harvard University Press, 1971), pp. 130–2.
47. W. McNeill, *Pursuit of power: technology, armed force and society since AD 1000* (Chicago, University of Chicago Press, 1982).
48. Shaw, *History*, vol. 2, p. 6.
49. M. Mann, *The sources of social power* (Cambridge, Cambridge University Press, 1986), vol. 1, p. 285.

Further reading

General

G. Goodwin, *The Janissaries* (London, Saqi Books, 1994).

H. İnalcık, *The Ottoman Empire: the classical age, 1300–1600* (London, Weidenfeld & Nicolson, 1973).

H. İnalcık, and D. Quataert (eds), *Economic and social history of the Ottoman Empire 1300–1914* (Cambridge, Cambridge University Press, 1994).

C. Kafadar, The Ottomans and Europe, in Thomas Brady *et al.* (eds) *Handbook of European History*, 2 vols (Leiden, E. J. Brill, 1994–5).

J. L. H. Keep, *Soldiers of the Tsar: army and society in Russia, 1462–1874* (Oxford, Clarendon Press, 1985).

M. Mann, *The Sources of social power*, 2 vols (Cambridge, Cambridge University Press, 1986–93).

J. McCarthy, *The Ottoman Turks: an introductory history to 1923* (London, Longman, 1997).

W. McNeill, *Pursuit of power: technology, armed force, and society since AD 1000* (Chicago, University of Chicago Press, 1982).

V. J. Parry, Bārūd, iv. The Ottoman Empire, *Encyclopedia of Islam*, 2nd edn, pp. 1061–6.

V. J. Parry, and M. E. Yapp (eds), *War, technology and society in the Middle East* (London, Oxford University Press, 1975).

D. P. Ralston, *Importing the European army: the introduction of European military techniques and institutions into the extra-European world, 1600–1914* (Chicago, University of Chicago Press, 1990).

S. Runciman, *The fall of Constantinople* (Oxford, Oxford University Press, 1961).

S. J. Shaw, *History of the Ottoman Empire and modern Turkey*, 2 vols (Cambridge, Cambridge University Press, 1976–7).

A. Stiles, *The Ottoman Empire 1450–1700* (London, Hodder & Stoughton, 1989).

1300–1453: the formative period

C. Imber, *The Ottoman Empire 1300–1481* (Istanbul, Isis, 1990).

H. İnalcık, Ottoman methods of conquest, *Studia islamica*, **2**, 1954, pp. 104–29.

C. Kafadar, *Between two worlds: the construction of the Ottoman state* (Berkeley, Calif, University of California Press, 1995).

R. P. Lindner, *Nomads and Ottomans in medieval Anatolia* (Bloomington, Indiana University Press, 1983).

1453–1566: the imperial age

G. Ágoston, Ottoman artillery and European military technology in the fifteenth and seventeenth centuries, *Acta Orientalia Academiae Scientiarum Hungaricae*, 47, 1994, pp. 75–96.

K. Barkey, *Bandits and bureaucrats: the Ottoman route to state centralization* (Ithaca, Cornell University Press, 1994).

C. W. Bracewell, *The Uskoks of Senj: piracy, banditry and holy war in the sixteenth century Adriatic* (Ithaca, Syracuse University Press, 1992).

P. Brummet, Foreign policy, naval strategy and the defence of the Ottoman Empire in the early sixteenth century, *International history review*, 11, 1989, pp. 613–27.

S. T. Christensen, The heathen order of battle, in S. T. Christensen (ed.) *Violence and the absolutist state: studies in European and Ottoman history* (Copenhagen, Center for Research in the Humanities, Copenhagen University, 1990).

C. M. Cipolla, *Guns, sails and empires: technological innovation and the early phases of European expansion*, 1400–1700 (New York, 1965).

A. Clot, *Suleiman the magnificent: the man, his life, his epoch* (London, Saqi Books, 1992).

G. Dávid, and P. Fodor (eds), *Hungarian–Ottoman military and diplomatic relations in the age of Süleyman the Magnificent* (Budapest, Loránd Eötvös University, 1994).

J. F. Guilmartin, *Gunpowder and galleys, changing technology and Mediterranean warfare at sea in the sixteenth century* (Cambridge, Cambridge University Press, 1974).

S. Har-El, *Struggle for domination in the Middle East: the Ottoman-Mamluk War, 1485–91* (Leiden, E. J. Brill, 1995).

A. Hess, *The forgotten frontier: a history of the sixteenth-century Ibero-African frontier* (Chicago, University of Chicago Press, 1978).

G. Káldy-Nagy, The first centuries of the Ottoman military organization, *Acta Orientalia Academiae Scientiarum Hungaricae*, 31, 1977, pp. 147–83.

M. Kunt, and C. Woodhead (eds) *Süleyman the Magnificent and his age: the Ottoman Empire in the early modern world* (London, Longman, 1995).

J. M. Rogers, and R. M. Ward, *Süleyman the Magnificent* (London, British Mueum Publications, 1988).

1566–1699: the limits of empire

G. Ágoston, Gunpowder for the sultan's army: new sources on the supply of gunpowder to the Ottoman army in the Hungarian campaigns of the sixteenth and seventeenth centuries, *Turcica*, 25, 1993, pp. 15–48.

L. Darling, *Revenue-raising and legitimacy: tax collection and finance administration in the Ottoman Empire 1560–1660* (Leiden, E. J. Brill, 1996).

C. Finkel, *The administration of warfare: the Ottoman military campaigns in Hungary, 1593–1606* (Vienna, VWGÖ, 1988).

C. H. Fleischer, *Bureaucrat and intellectual in the Ottoman Empire: the historian Mustafa Âli (1541–1600)* (Princeton, Princeton University Press, 1986).

D. Howard, Ottoman historiography and the literature of "decline" of the sixteenth and seventeenth centuries, *Journal of Asian History*, 22, 1988, pp. 52–77.

H. İnalcık, Military and fiscal transformation in the Ottoman Empire, 1600–1700, *Archivum Ottomanicum*, 6, 1980, pp. 283–337.

L. F. Marsigli, *Stato militare dell'Imperio Ottomanno. L'Etat militaire de l'empire ottoman* (The Hague, 1732).

R. Mathee, Unwalled cities and restless nomads: firearms and artillery in Safavid Iran, in C. Melville (ed.) *Safavid Persia, the history and politics of an Islamic society* (London, I. B. Tauris, 1996), pp. 389–416.

R. Murphey, *The functioning of the Ottoman army under Murad IV (1623–1639/1032–1049): key to understanding of the relationship between center and periphery*, 2 vols (PhD thesis, Department of History, University of Chicago, 1979).

J. Stoye, *Marsigli's Europe, 1680–1730: life and times of Luigi Ferdinando Marsigli, soldier and virtuoso* (New Haven, Yale University Press, 1994)

J. Stoye, *The siege of Vienna* (New York, 1964).

1699–1812: the compromise

V. Aksan, *An Ottoman statesman in war and peace: Ahmed Resmi Efendi 1700–1783* (Leiden, E. J. Brill, 1995).

L. Cassels, *The struggle for the Ottoman Empire 1717–1740* (London, John Murray, 1966).

I. M. D'Ohsson, *Tableau général de l'Empire othoman*, 7 vols (Paris, 1788–1824).

H. Grenville, *Observations sur l'état actuel de l'Empire Ottoman* (Ann Arbor, University of Michigan Press, 1965).

J. Hathaway, *The politics of households in Ottoman Egypt: the rise of the Qazdağlıs* (Cambridge, Cambridge University Press, 1997).

J. Porter, *Observations on the religion, law, government and manners of the Turks* (London, 1768).

S. J. Shaw, *Between old and new: the Ottoman Empire under Sultan Selim III, 1789–1807* (Cambridge, Mass., Harvard University Press, 1971).

Chapter Eight

European warfare 1450–1815

Peter Wilson

European warfare underwent a series of major transformations in the three and a half centuries following 1450, contributing to the political reorganization of the continent into sovereign states of unequal size and the concomitant projection of their powers across the globe. Political coalescence within distinct geographical areas was driven by the accumulation of the means to make war by those who held power. Organized violence, or warfare, became an exclusive prerogative of these states which disarmed their subject populations whilst devising ever more sophisticated methods of harnessing their productive capacity to sustain larger armed forces. Changes in the conduct of war, including those at the tactical or battlefield level, have to be understood within this wider context.

Any discussion of these events must confront the idea of a "military revolution", since this had dominated the debate on the relationship of war to wider changes since its first exposition by Michael Roberts in 1956[1]. The original idea maintained that changes in the conduct of war between 1560 and 1660 were so profound as to warrant the term "revolutionary". The limited effectiveness of new weaponry based on gunpowder technology had made war less decisive since the late Middle Ages. The full potential of these earlier changes was only realized with the introduction of new forms of training, first by the Dutch rebels fighting a war of independence against Spain (1568–1648), and later by the Swedish King Gustavus Adolphus (ruled 1611–32). Tactics were transformed, making warfare allegedly more decisive in the sense that it was possible to achieve a significant political advantage on the battlefield. Increased military effectiveness encouraged an expansion in the general scale of warfare, fuelling the growth of the state as it adapted to cope with the new demands placed upon its infrastructure.

These arguments stimulated renewed interest amongst historians in an area which, in the English-speaking world at least, had come to be regarded as the preserve of those concerned only with the arcane minutiae of drums and trumpets. Of the many subsequent contributions, that of Geoffrey Parker has been perhaps the most influential as he modified elements of the original concept while retaining its essentials. In contrast to Roberts, Parker emphasizes technology as the driving force of change, and moves the start date back to 1500 to take greater account of innovations made by the Spanish forces. Not only did the introduction of firearms and other hand-held weapons change battlefield tactics from this earlier date, but the introduction of new styles of fortification based on defence in depth fuelled the growth in the scale of warfare. Larger armies were required to defend and besiege the improved and extended fortifications, in turn fuelling, as Roberts had argued, the general growth of the state. Parker has drawn greater attention to the global significance of these changes, in addition to the Eurocentric consequences. The new weaponry, particularly firearms and the use of cavalry in areas where horses were previously unknown, gave Europeans a decisive advantage in their violent encounters with other peoples, enabling, for instance, the conquest of the vast Aztec and Inca empires by a handful of Spaniards in 1519–1536.

As with any historical concept there have been numerous dissenting voices, not least because in Parker's revision the timespan has been stretched to 1800 to encompass the global consequences of European development. Criticism had been levelled at points of detail as well as the central belief that war was the motor of wider change. Just as the idea is being favourably received by political scientists and social theorists, some historians have begun to argue that it has lost its intellectual vitality.

Any attempt at periodization must accept that it imposes a framework on the past, and that the price of clarity for the bigger picture is some fuzziness when it comes to the details. History cannot be bent to fit analytical models, but no more does it make sense to discuss it as a seamless flow of unique events. Warfare and the means to wage it were undeniably different in 1815 as compared to 1450, and we need some way of explaining this. The concept of a military revolution begins to make sense when we cease trying to apply it to a single period of innovation as, in order to encompass everything deemed to be of significance, we are compelled to extend the term to such an extent that it becomes meaningless.

If the criterion for a military revolution is for it to be a time when, not only was warfare transformed, but this transformation was also related to wider historical change, then three periods qualify between 1450 and 1815. The first, 1450–1530, was influenced by the widespread use of gunpowder technology and transformed both tactics and the composition of armies. The second followed in 1660–1720, largely as a result of the political consequences of the first, and witnessed the first sustained expansion of permanent armies. The final stage came after 1789 when the upheavals associated with the French Revolution enabled states to increase the scale of warfare through greater direct exploitation of their military potential. The driving forces behind these changes varied, with weapons technology playing a significant role only in the first period. The nature and intensity of their impact was also far from uniform throughout Europe, and the intervening periods were by no means devoid of significant change. Warfare in medieval Europe had been far from static, and displayed many features more commonly associated with the later periods, including the use of professional mercenaries which was a major factor from at least the twelfth century. Finally, as with any periodization, the dates used here do not signify major turning-points in themselves, but serve as approximate markers of more gradual under-lying trends.

Before proceeding, it is helpful to conceive of war's relationship to wider change as taking place within four overlapping spheres. The first is the domestic context provided by the state, in the sense of the recognized political authority encompassing a defined area and its inhabitants. As we shall see, this domestic context underwent a profound transformation, since much of European warfare was directed at establishing and delineating the nature and geographical extent of state authority. Inter-state relations provides the second, or international context, as wars determined which states would exist within Europe. The nature of warfare itself constitutes a third aspect, comprising the duration, scope and intensity of conflict and the variation in the means to conduct it. What prompted change in each of these areas provides us with our fourth, and probably most intractable, issue for consideration.

1450–1530

The military origins of the early modern European state lie in the period immediately preceding the dates commonly associated with a military revolution. All the technological developments credited with transforming warfare after 1530 were already well under way before that date. The pre-eminent innovation was the spread of gunpowder technology since all other changes in weaponry were related to this.

Gunpowder had been used in European warfare since the 1330s, but required specialized knowledge to make both it and the weapons required to use it. In some respects these weapons were less effective than existing methods of firing projectiles such as the bow and arrow, but, although handguns had a slower rate of fire, they did have greater penetrative power, while cannon could demolish the high, but generally fairly thin, stone walls that constituted the main form of permanent fortification. The new weapons could not alone transform war. Early forms of handguns were ill-suited for use on horseback at a time when cavalry still formed the mainstay of most armies. Even when used by foot soldiers, they were generally only accurate up to 100 metres, while their slow rate of fire deprived them of defensive capability against swift-moving attackers. Regardless of size all guns suffered problems in inclement weather, and all required a supply of powder and shot that was difficult to procure.

Effective use of the new technology depended on two prerequisites. The first was political and involved the development of an authority with sufficient coercive power to extract the resources necessary to produce and maintain the expensive weaponry on a scale sufficient to make a difference. The second was provided by military change, with the emergence of a disciplined infantry capable of maximizing the use of the new technology. At this stage development was less concerned with the deployment of large numbers of handgunners in tight formations than with the appearance of soldiers capable of supporting them against cavalry attack. Such troops were those armed with another relatively new weapon, the pike, which was also only effective when used *en masse* by a disciplined formation. The Swiss were the first to develop tactics suited to large bodies of pikemen, although they were also used in other parts of Europe by 1450. Their infantry were drawn up in a few large, fairly deep formations that were capable both of static defence against cavalry attack and forward movement against enemy foot. In a significant innovation, the Swiss deployed their blocks *en echelon* so that all provided mutual support, while simultaneously bringing the full force to bear on the enemy. Handgunners could shelter on the front, crouched under the pikes, or on the flanks or within the pike block when faced by cavalry, moving outwards to fire when it was safe to do so.

The significance of these developments was felt first in the domestic sphere, where they tipped the balance in favour of the centralizing princes in the elimination contests which characterized late medieval politics. States in the modern sense did not yet exist in Europe, where political power was diffused through interlocking, overlapping networks of patronage and feudal obligations. These networks stretched vertically between prince and vassal as well as horizontally at various levels in the hierarchy. The relationships were reciprocal but asymmetrical, allowing those higher up the scale to extract material resources from local networks of trade and production, and to mobilize manpower at regional or national level in return for supplying protection and rewards to their clients. Full state sovereignty did not exist, since even the comparatively centralized areas of the western European monarchies were not entirely free from external influence. The Catholic Church maintained its own international network, claiming temporal as well as spiritual jurisdiction in many areas, and was capable of commanding economic resources independent of secular political authority. Religion remained a vital factor in politics at all levels, since it lent legitimacy to the existing social order.

Key areas associated with modern states were not yet monopolized by a single political authority. There was no single monopoly of violence or war-making, nor even one of taxation, since both areas remained partially decentralized. The emergent state also lacked a monopoly of justice, since it was often possible for subjects of one ruler to appeal to another for redress, especially in border areas. All forms of rule within Catholic Europe remained largely indirect, mediated though a variety of intermediary bodies between ruler and subjects. These corporate groups, such as the English Parliament, the French provincial estates or the Spanish Cortes, were connected by the personal ties of individual members to the ruler and his dependent administration, while simultaneously retaining an autonomous identity entrenched in ancient charters, custom and tradition. The areas of Orthodox Europe that were to become the Russian empire lacked a tradition of representative institutions and were already showing signs of the development of autocratic rule, although the actual power of the ruler in Moscow was often tentative at best.

Major political questions remained unresolved. It was often far from clear whether an individual ruler could monopolize power within a given area and exclude external influence. The extent to which this monopoly would be a personal one or one shared with wider elites remained in dispute, as did the size of the territory over which its authority was deemed legitimate. In short, the outcome of the European state-building process remained to be determined.

Those who were able to benefit from the new military technology enjoyed distinct advantages over potential rivals during this struggle of monopoly formation. Within the domestic context it was almost invariably the dynasty which already enjoyed a pre-eminence as prince or king that emerged victorious, since their position lent greater legitimacy to their extraction of material resources. This in turn was only possible through wider changes largely beyond the influence of individuals. The gradual shift to a money economy enabled a transition to extraction in cash rather than kind, which permitted the accumulation of capital that could be deployed to maintain men not committed to a productive role.

The first to take advantage of this were not princes but the Italian city states where from the early fifteenth century a more commercialized economy furthered the concentration of capital necessary to sustain modest permanent forces. By 1500 recognizable fiscal–military monopolies began to emerge elsewhere following the outcome of the major late medieval wars. The Valois Kings in France, particularly Charles VII (1422–61), finally excluded English influence in their domains in the latter stages of the Hundred Years' War. The parallel absorption of the key frontier provinces of Normandy, Provence, Brittany and parts of

Burgundy during 1450–91 helped define the extent of Valois authority more precisely. A similar process took place in Spain with the completion of the *Reconquista*, or wars of reconquest, in 1492 expelling Moorish influence from the southern part of the peninsula. In England the Wars of the Roses ended in 1485 with the Tudor defeat of rivals for control of what was, by European standards, already a highly centralized kingdom.

The new military technology played little part in these conflicts, which were largely decided by conventional medieval armies based on a core of heavily armoured cavalry, raised partly through feudal obligations and partly from mercenaries. Moreover, much of the political consolidation and expansion proceeded without violence as in 1469 dynastic marriages secured unification of the two main Spanish kingdoms, Castille and Aragon, and led later to their absorption into the greater Habsburg territorial complex. The latter was itself acquired primarily by strategic marriages with the ruling families of Bohemia, Hungary and Burgundy, as well as the election in 1519 of Charles V as Holy Roman Emperor, the pre-eminent secular European title and nominal overlord of Christendom. Nonetheless, it became obvious that the defence of power against internal and external opponents was impossible without control over the new military technology and the means to acquire and sustain it. All victors in the late medieval contests tried to prohibit ownership of artillery or the construction of artillery-proof fortifications by private individuals, while also enforcing obligations to contribute taxes towards the maintenance of forces under their exclusive control. Domestic politics shifted from armed struggles to control all or part of the territory to quarrels over the means to sustain a monopoly of violence. Opposition to royal authority lay less in the military capacity of corporate groups within society than in their ability to entrench their influence in formally constituted assemblies with a say in taxation.

However, it was still far from clear by 1530 that the new monopolies would survive, since it was questionable whether rulers could develop the infrastructural power necessary to extract the resources required for permanence. Potential opponents were not yet completely disarmed, not least because most monarchs still relied on their assistance in foreign wars. Further uncertainty was introduced by the crisis of legitimacy associated with the Reformation after 1517, as the new interpretations of Christianity became intermeshed with competing political ideas. No confession was exclusively related to a particular attitude, although the varieties of Protestantism were more generally associated with attempts to territorialize the European state by excluding external influence, particularly papal jurisdiction, and to mark out distinct frontiers. Given the continued importance of theology for political legitimacy, centralization was generally accompanied by a process of confessionalization, whereby, through an alliance of throne and altar, attempts were made to impose religious uniformity within the territory.

The problems were most pronounced in central and eastern Europe, where the lack of hereditary monarchy in Poland and the Holy Roman Empire inhibited attempts to monopolize violence and taxation over a wide area. The Habsburg monopoly was restricted to the area of their hereditary lands around Austria within the Holy Roman Empire. The religious divide was especially pronounced in the Empire which had seen the start of the Reformation, and the process of confessionalization reinforced the existing territorial fragmentation inhibiting the growth of a single, national, fiscal–military monopoly. The semi-autonomous German princes and city-states entrenched their position at the expense of centralized power at national level, creating separate territorial monopolies. The Polish magnates also monopolized military power, but the rough political balance between them and their king, together with the underdeveloped commercial sector of the economy, prevented the formation of regional or national infrastructures capable of sustaining large permanent forces.

The religious controversy did not extend to Orthodox Europe, where political development took a different course after the conclusion of the civil war in Moscow in 1453. Although they adopted the new gunpowder technology, often directly with Western expertise, the Russian grand princes expanded their territory by devolving military organization to a new service class, which provided the backbone of what was still a cavalry army in return for direct control over landed income. Russian society was transformed, leading to the gradual enserfment of the rural population between the 1580s and 1649, as both state and landlords depended on controlling peasant labour. This sharpened the contrast with developments elsewhere on the continent, since the parallel enserfment of German peasants east of the river Elbe and those in Poland were driven by the restructuring of the agrarian economy in the wake of the Black Death, and the rise of commercialized production for western European markets.[2]

Before 1530 the incomplete nature of European states affected the international context of war. The distinction between civil, or internal, and international, or external, wars remained ill-defined, while the spread of confessional strife created new links between domestic and foreign conflicts. Nonetheless, the Reformation did further the division of Europe into distinct political units by shattering the traditional concept of a universal Christendom and elevating feuds between individual princes, aristocrats and cities to inter-state wars.

Attitudes to war were also changing. Traditional Christian teaching divided wars into just and unjust, depending on whether they could be reconciled with the Commandments prohibiting murder and hostility to neighbours. To qualify as just, a conflict had to conform to certain criteria, the first of which was that it had to be waged by a recognized, legally-constituted authority. There also had to be a "just cause", or sufficient reason to take up arms, such as self-defence or upholding legal rights. Finally, a war had to serve the "right intention" of promoting good and combating evil, while the actual conduct of the war should adhere to certain rules forbidding what would now be termed a "dirty war", which included the ill-treatment of prisoners and non-combatants and the poisoning of wells.[3]

Conflicts against non-Christians could generally be justified under these terms, particularly if they, like the Muslims, were held to have heard the word of God but to have wilfully rejected it. Matters became more problematic when the enemy was also a Christian people with the question of what constituted a proper authority forming the crucial political issue. Princes sought to consolidate their hold on power by fostering the belief that only *they* had the right to wage war. Armed resistance to their authority was deemed illegitimate, while attempts were made to eliminate all internal conflict by deflecting disputes through courts controlled by the crown. Civil society was further demilitarized by curbs on extra-territorial violence to prevent subjects waging war elsewhere as mercenaries or pirates.

The Reformation complicated this process by establishing competing Christian confessions to supplement the political rivalry within Europe. Christians had of course fought each other throughout the middle ages and with considerable brutality, but the new religious divide surpassed all previous schisms in western and central Europe, because it became irreversible, especially after the Council of Trent (1545–62) failed to reconcile the theologians. It now became possible to wage an ostensibly just holy war against other Christians, both within a territory and outside it, simply on the grounds they were adherents of an opposing confession.

These international and domestic developments helped transform the nature of warfare. Wars remained protracted and intermittent with short bursts of fighting interrupted by long periods of relative inactivity or uneasy peace. However, there was a perceptible increase in the scale and intensity of conflict along with greater opportunities to achieve a genuinely decisive victory on the battlefield. The former set the period after 1450 apart from that which preceded it, while the latter distinguished it from warfare after the 1530s.

Estimates of army size are notoriously problematic, especially for the period before the mid-seventeenth century. Nonetheless, it seems that by the early sixteenth century, France, England, Spain and the Austrian Habsburgs were all capable of putting upwards of 30,000 men into the field, while Italian states like Venice, Florence and the Papacy could each muster about a third of that strength. Such armies were not unknown before 1450, but they were rarely maintained for more than a few months at a time, whereas the major western

European monarchs could return to the field with these numbers for several years in a row. Moreover, their forces now consisted entirely of trained fighting men who could be supplemented by additional levies or militia, rather than relying on such inexperienced troops for primary strength.

Although it changed the way battles were fought, technology had little to do with this increase in scale. Pikes and handguns were weapons of large, disciplined formations, while the new-style fortifications did require greater numbers to garrison and attack them, although not as great as some have made out. However, none of these changes necessitated an increase in overall strength, and the Italian states absorbed the new technology before 1494 without significantly raising the numbers they deployed or, indeed, altering their tactical reliance on manoeuvre and skirmishing. The primary reason was the political centralization which concentrated war-making potential in the hands of individual monarchs, whose ambitions tended to grow with the size of their territories and the power of their immediate enemies. However, the explanation is not wholly top-down, since political centralization only provided the means to unlock the increased human and material resources provided by demographic recovery following the Black Death and a general growth in the European economy. It has been estimated that the population of France may have doubled between 1450 and 1560, while Spain gained access to American gold and silver from the 1520s precisely when most of Europe's mines were being exhausted. The continued influx of bullion did fuel inflation in the later sixteenth century, but it is significant that Spain was the only major European power with sustained military growth after 1530.

The new decisiveness was not due to greater numbers but to a temporary imbalance in the organization, tactics and equipment of the contending forces, thanks to an uneven diffusion of the new technology and the political infrastructure needed to sustain war under the new conditions. The considerable regional variations resulted in the clash of often very dissimilar forces, enabling some spectacular victories until the inferior side could adapt. The regional variations were partly a consequence of differing socio-economic structures, and are best illustrated by the proportion of cavalry found in the European armies. Cavalry were especially numerous in France at the beginning of the period where they formed up to two-thirds of field strength, reflecting the importance of the mounted armoured knight in late medieval warfare. The Spanish had fewer cavalry, often only one-fifth of their armies being mounted. The proportion declined in both countries after 1450 as the importance of disciplined infantry became more apparent, until by the mid-sixteenth century cavalry formed only one-quarter of French and one-twelfth of Spanish field forces. The fact that the proportion remained higher in France was partly due to the greater availability of suitable horses, and to the traditional association of the French nobility with

185

mounted service. Similarly, even as late as the eighteenth century, the north German territories had a greater proportion of cavalry than most south German armies due to their proximity to the horse-breeding area of Lower Saxony. East European armies had an even greater proportion, especially of light cavalry mounted on swifter, less stocky animals, which the Poles and Austrian Habsburgs used for skirmishing and raiding parties. Such tactics were also better suited to the terrain which included vast, under-populated regions like the Hungarian Great Plain. Not surprisingly, mountainous Switzerland, which lacked a large indigenous nobility, was not a great cavalry country and the contingent hired by France in 1480 comprised only 400 horse soldiers to 6,000 foot.

By 1500 such factors reinforced the association of certain parts of Europe with particular types of soldier. By 1475 Switzerland, for example, was most famous for the disciplined tactics capable of maximizing the effectiveness of the pike to break even skilled conventional armies like the Burgundian. The Swiss became sought after by other rulers, thus fuelling the proliferation of foreign mercenaries serving the major crowns. The use of outsiders lessened a monarch's dependence on the native nobles and towns which often opposed his attempts at centralization, but the principal reason for preferring mercenaries was simple expediency. Mercenaries were combat-ready professionals who could be deployed wherever and whenever a ruler desired, provided he could pay them. Charles VII of France had already forged an alliance with the Swiss in 1453, and ties grew through mutual opposition to Burgundian expansionism. From 1481 there were 5,000–10,000 more-or-less permanently in royal service despite periodic Franco-Swiss hostility, while the "Perpetual Alliance" of 26 November 1516 gave the French crown nominal first call on Swiss support, although many cantons continued to recruit for other powers.

The southern Netherlands and German territories developed a similar disciplined infantry commonly known as the *Landsknechte*. Attempts by the Habsburgs to establish exclusive control over them foundered on the growth of separate monopolies of violence in the larger German territories and on the inability of the emperor to control extra-territorial violence. Bans on entering foreign service proved difficult to enforce in such a fragmented region as the Holy Roman Empire, and the *Landsknechte* fought for other monarchs, including the King of France who had about 5,000 between 1512 and 1528. German mercenaries served both sides during the later French Wars of Religion 1562–94, while others were employed by Henry VIII in England in the 1540s.[4]

Northern Germany produced mercenary cavalry known by the generic name of *Reiter* who carried pistols in an attempt to combine the mobility of mounted troops with the firepower of infantry. Such efforts continued with the development of mounted infantry called dragoons, who were armed with muskets, and by the mid-seventeenth century most cavalry had pistols as well as swords. eastern Europe continued to provide genuine light cavalry more suited to scouting and harassing enemy positions. The best-known were the *Stradiots* who originally came from Albania and were to be found in French and Italian service by the early sixteenth century. Other important regional variations included the Spanish use of infantry armed with swords and small shields to attack the flanks of pike columns, and the English preference for the longbow over firearms even in the late sixteenth century.

Victories could be achieved by forces whose composition gave them an edge over their opponents. The classic example is the French invasion of the Italian peninsula in 1494 with a force of 16,000–20,000 men, the core of which was similar to any late medieval army but also contained 4,800 Swiss infantry and a strong train of heavy artillery. The Italian states had adapted their fortifications to take account of gunpowder technology, but not on the scale deployed by the French, who soon captured several major installations. Similarly, Italian field forces, although more numerous, were unable to break the disciplined Swiss and were defeated at Fornovo in 1495. Subsequent competition for prestige and territory in Italy lasted until 1559, and sucked into conflict in the Peninsula all the major European monarchs, thus exposing their forces to the innovations of their opponents. Increasingly, victory went to the side which managed to combine the best of the new methods in an optimal balance, rather than to forces relying heavily on one principal weapon or tactic. The Swiss infantry army suffered a crushing blow at Marignano 1515 at the hands of a French force of cavalry, artillery and infantry, including the *Landsknechte* who used a greater proportion of firearms.

Such engagements were extremely costly in human life, since they were fought in a restricted area at relatively close quarters, imposed by the limited range of the weapons and the continued reliance on tactics which necessitated closing with the enemy. Sixteen thousand corpses are said to have been buried after Marignano, representing perhaps half the Swiss army and a quarter of their opponents, while at Ravenna in 1512 the victorious French lost one-fifth of their strength to two-thirds of the Spanish–Papal force.[5] The strategic implications were to restrict the number of field armies and to limit the number of major engagements which they had to fight. Even the great monarchies rarely deployed more than one field army, preferring to concentrate their efforts on a single front and leave the defence of other areas to garrison troops and militia. Defeat of the main force could thus spell political disaster, particularly if it involved the capture of the ruler, as at Pavia in 1525 when the French King Francis I was taken by the imperialists. However, as the examples of Ravenna and Marignano indicate, victory was also expensive, and this helps explain the still intermittent and protracted nature of warfare in this period. Few victors could exploit their advantage to the fullest extent, as their own losses and the usual near bankruptcy of their finances prevented their delivering the necessary final blow.

Attempts to solve these problems concentrated on various combinations of foreign mercenaries with large numbers of native subjects trained in the current tactics. Existing obligations to serve for home defence were gradually reworked by the expanding monarchies to provide the basis of new militias capable of serving in offensive operations. Most of these attempts, such as the establishment of provincial "Legions" in France after 1507, were fairly ineffective, but selected militiamen increasingly formed a significant proportion of the infantry. Native mercenaries maintained by the royal exchequer were more successful and France already had permanent cavalry companies from 1445, followed after 1481 by infantry modelled on the Swiss. Russia participated in these developments, chiefly in response to technological changes rather than shortage of manpower, developing semi-permanent infantry companies recruited from native mercenaries after 1510. Unlike western and central European infantry, these *streltsy* were exclusively musketeers and carried portable log walls rather than pikes for protection against cavalry.

A basic pattern was emerging by the 1530s – the mixing of old and new forms of recruitment, and combining experienced professionals (native and foreign) with militia trained to varying competency to handle modern weapons and tactics. A good example is the force assembled by Landgrave Philip of Hessen to restore his friend Ulrich to the duchy of Württemberg in 1534. Traditional feudal obligations produced 1,500 heavy cavalry supplemented by 2,500 professional mercenaries hired throughout northern Germany. A remodelled militia structure raised 6,000 Hessian peasants to reinforce 16,350 *Landsknechte*, while Philip's own nascent fiscal–military monopoly helped provide the artillery. However, the actual events revealed that a ceiling had been reached in the state's capacity for war. Operations lasted only three months, and Philip made peace after his victory over the Habsburgs at Lauffen, disbanding his army to avoid bankruptcy immediately afterwards.[6] Although his political objective had been achieved, warfare in general was becoming less decisive thanks to the growing uniformity in composition and tactics of most belligerents. The key area of change shifted to the political arena, in particular to the relative ability of rulers to master the problems of sustained resource mobilization.

1530–1660

This seemed doubtful at first as several of the emergent fiscal monopolies collapsed under the strain of prolonged conflict, opening the way to a resurgence of those groups which had lost ground to royal centralization. The situation was most extreme in France, where confessional strife coincided with a royal minority and led to a prolonged struggle for influence between the crown and rival factions of the traditional elites. Although royal authority was preserved, its military monopoly was undermined by concessions to the dissenting Huguenot minority in 1594, which granted them considerable political autonomy with the right to maintain their own garrisons. The crown clawed back these rights with considerable violence during 1621–9, but its position remained far from uncontested as it faced further opposition from elite groups, as well as mounting popular protest at its fiscal–military exactions, until the resumption of relative calm after the demonstrative shift to direct personal rule by Louis XIV in 1661.

The Habsburgs also suffered considerable problems, as it proved impossible to sustain the vast empire assembled by Charles V who partitioned his domains in 1556, creating the separate branches of Spain and Austria. The Spanish fiscal–military monopoly survived in the core area of Spain itself, but broke down in peripheral regions, notably the Netherlands where, as in France, religious discontent became associated with elite opposition to political centralization, resulting in a protracted struggle for Dutch independence after 1568. The Austrian monopoly broke up even in the core area of the hereditary lands owing to a coincidence of dynastic weakness with similar religious and political discontent after 1612. Attempts to reassert and extend control at the expense of traditional provincial autonomy sparked the Bohemian revolt which merged with wider German and European tension as the Thirty Years' War 1618–48. England experienced a similar internecine conflict in 1642–51, caused primarily by the crown's inability to fund its military and political ambitions without provoking opposition from the interests entrenched in Parliament. Finally, Russia also collapsed in a period of internal chaos known as the Time of Troubles 1598–1618 as foreign invasion and social unrest coincided with dynastic weakness and attempts by the traditional boyar nobility to reassert their autonomy.

Direct control over all aspects of raising and maintaining military power was clearly beyond most rulers' capacity, forcing them to extend a process of decentralization already apparent before 1530. Professional military contractors or entrepreneurs took over responsibility for recruiting, organizing, equipping and leading troops in return for cash or other rewards. These men often came from groups excluded from established networks of wealth and power, such as the free imperial knights in the Holy Roman Empire whose limited and fragmented estates were too small to sustain a viable existence in the face of encroachments by the princely territories. Many others came from Scotland, England and Ireland, especially after the persecution of Catholics there became better established, but it should be stressed that, though often foreign, most contractors were not the rootless adventurers of popular mythology. Most came from within or close to the territory of their warlord and paymaster, and were bound to him by ties other than the contract they signed. The system was also different from that in Switzerland where the cantonal authorities collaborated with local patricians and nobles to raise units for foreign powers.

Notable early contractors included Georg von Frundsberg (1473–1528) and Sebastian Schertlin von Burtenbach (1496–1577), while the most famous of all is undoubtedly the Bohemian noble Albrecht von Wallenstein (1583–1634) who raised forces for the Emperor Ferdinand II in the Thirty Years' War. Such individuals had existed before as the *condottieri* who raised small companies of professionals for the Italian states, but they were now far more numerous and significant: 1,500 were active in Germany alone during the Thirty Years' War. Moreover, the contract system was now directly related to the new forms of military organization. Since the early sixteenth century it had become common for a prince to hire one or two renowned, well-connected entrepreneurs who undertook to raise large units by subcontracting elements to others. The contractual pyramid mirrored the emergent military hierarchy with the main military entrepreneur serving as colonel of what was increasingly called a "regiment" of roughly standard size, while his subcontractors captained the individual companies. In rare cases, such as Wallenstein or Duke Bernhard of Weimar (1604–39), the supreme contractor became general of an entire army.

This system enabled the early modern state to dispense with a large, permanent bureaucracy which, in any case, it could neither afford nor organize. Entrepreneurs not only provided the expertise that the state's existing officials generally lacked, but they were not normally integrated into established patronage networks tied to elite groups opposing centralization. Their use also eased the acute cash-flow problems that beset all early modern war-making, since contractors often had access to capital or credit denied the state and at the beginning bore the start-up costs in the hope of later rewards which only a ruler could provide. However, the concomitant decentralization retarded monopoly formation by inhibiting direct control in a key area of state activity. Like most early modern civil officials, the military enterprizers were officeholders rather than state servants, since they were the owners of their positions and means of employment, even though their paymaster had greater liberty to terminate their contracts than he had in the case of appointments of the magnates and aristocrats to the great civil positions. Colonels enjoyed considerable autonomy over the appointment of their subordinates, and acted as proprietors of their regiments. Captains tended to own the weapons and equipment of their companies, in a significant shift from the early sixteenth century when soldiers had often been expected to appear fully armed themselves. Officers viewed their service as a personal investment upon which they wanted a good return both in material wealth and personal prestige. Although few fortunes were made, the great riches accruing to the favoured and distinguished continued to encourage the others.

The relative autonomy of the officers undermined royal executive control over the armed forces, especially in times of crisis. Emperor Ferdinand II was compelled to enfief Wallenstein with the captured duchy of Mecklenburg in lieu of the money he owed him, and later, in 1634, had him murdered when it was feared he might defect to the Swedes. Wallenstein's case was exceptional, and most contractors remained loyal despite broken promises and mounting arrears. The rank and file were less willing, however, since their meagre personal resources made it imperative that they secure regular income and sustenance. Mutinies and pay strikes were common, especially as political ambition drove army size beyond what the state could actually afford.

In consequence strategy became as much directed at the control of war-making resources as at the defeat of the enemy. This took two forms. The first, what has been called "offensive logistics" involving the deliberate invasion of unplundered zones which were exploited, either by direct occupation, or an indirect form of extortion known as "contributions", whereby an army threatened to destroy life and property unless certain sums were paid and supplies delivered. Contributions became highly sophisticated during the Thirty Years' War, as armies tapped into existing fiscal structures to divert regular flow of funds away from public treasuries and into their own coffers. The second form was the "tax of violence" used by countries like France which were compelled to make war on their own territory. Here, the state bypassed its own inefficient, civil-tax-collection system as well as potential opposition from entrenched interest groups by billeting its soldiers directly on the inhabitants, who were obliged to feed, pay and often clothe them subject to nominal regulations and central supervision. In practice the rules were frequently ignored and there was little to distinguish billeting from an enemy occupation.[7] Both expedients were detrimental to military efficiency and the achievement of political objectives. The need to detach garrisons to hold ground and ensure the continued flow of contributions inhibited the concentration of force against the enemy. Contributions antagonized neutral and friendly territory, while the tax of violence undermined state legitimacy, which rested in a large part on its guarantee of domestic tranquillity.

These factors promoted the search for alternative ways to organize war. One solution favoured by small or impoverished states such as those in the German Rhineland was to revive and modify existing militia systems to provide a cheap home defence force that could be mustered at short notice to confront an external threat. Introduced from the 1580s, these "trained militias" were never considered as substitutes for the professional mercenaries who still had to be hired for major offensive operations. Sweden went further by adapting its militia structure as a recruitment pool for its professional army in 1617–18, when each region was made responsible for providing conscripts for specific regiments. Revisions in 1642 replaced militia selection as the basis for conscription with a method of maintaining individual soldiers, whereby groups of farms were responsible for supporting a soldier who served for life. Further modifications were introduced in 1682 to harmonize military needs with those of agriculture. Soldiers were now granted land to support themselves until they were called up, whereupon their civilian neighbours tended their plots and supported their families. The new system provided the core of the Swedish army into the early twentieth century, but did not entirely replace reliance on supplementary mercenary units or emergency drafts by direct conscription to replace heavy casualties.[8] Recruitment through a militia system continued to be favoured by the German territories after 1648, either drawing men directly into the regular regiments for the duration of a conflict, or embodying militia formations as temporary field units. The chief advantage was economic, since it reduced the cost of recruiting and maintaining at least part of the army which could afterwards be discharged into civil society, unlike mercenaries who generally had no stable environment to which to return.

The Dutch model provided a second alternative based on access to commercial wealth to finance a large army of paid professionals. The Dutch achieved this seemingly impossible goal through a low-cost loans system that did not mortgage inflexible tax revenues years in advance of their collection, or necessitate the alienation of valuable territory or sources of income as security to foreign creditors. Their success was based on a combination of political legitimacy with an expanding commercialized economy that continued to grow despite the long war of independence against Spain (1568–1648). The rebels retained the traditional representative institutions in a republican system, balancing provincial autonomy with a degree of central co-ordination through a central assembly (the States General), and a separate network of provincial military commanders (the Stadholders), generally held in combination by a prince from the House of Orange. This apparently cumbersome constitution worked because of the relatively close ties between the people dominating the political institutions and those engaged in commercial activity, and because the higher degree of urbanization placed those in power closer to wider sections of the population. This limited but real degree of representation fostered a consensus amongst those who held political, social and economic power, thus providing a basis for legitimacy and encouraging the bourgeoisie to invest in the growing public debt. Underwritten by an expanding economy, the Dutch fiscal–military state sustained a large, permanent professional army, composed mostly of native mercenaries and supplemented by Swiss, Germans, English and Scots, that ultimately secured victory against Spain.[9]

England followed a modified verson of the Dutch model after Parliament's victory in the Civil War, already having established a professional "New Model Army" in 1645 which, despite the anti-military political rhetoric, was never entirely disbanded. Parliament retained great influence over the fiscal apparatus even after the Restoration of the monarchy in 1660, but the major change came with the Glorious Revolution of 1688, when the entrenched interest groups which had expelled the Stuart King, James II, were compelled to co-operate with their own candidate William III against a potential Jacobite attack. Parliament strengthened its budgeting control, establishing accountability and legitimacy in the eyes of the broad social elite with access to political power. As in the Dutch case this was underwritten by an expanding commercialized economy facilitating relatively inexpensive war finance through the central clearing house of the Bank of England, established in 1694.

The circumstances that encouraged these systems were not found elsewhere, and this led to a third method of organizing war-making which can be termed the "absolutist" model. This relied on creating an infrastructure capable of extracting resources from what were still generally fairly inflexible, agriculturally-based economies, legitimized not by limited formal representation through assemblies but by reworked ideologies of kingship which stressed the advantage of benevolent, authoritarian rule in an age of civil and religious strife. This was supplemented by an informal bargaining process, focused on the magnificent and elaborate royal courts. Taxation was predominantly direct rather than indirect as in England and the Dutch Republic, and the money went via bureaucracies of varying efficiency to sustain the great land armies created by monarchs like Louis XIV of France.[10]

All three methods utilized new intellectual trends as well as technological advances. The philosophy of Neostoicism, associated with the Dutch thinker Justus Lipsius, was particularly important, and influenced much of continental military organization through its use in the Swedish, Dutch and German reforms from the 1590s. Neostoicism was itself part of a wider movement advocating the application of the best of classical learning to contemporary problems. Lipsius' reading of ancient Roman history led him to a new concept of discipline, of great political and military significance. Exercise or drill was transformed from simple training in weapons-handling to a means of instilling discipline and obedience. The soldier's individual identity was now to be subsumed within that of his unit, while the contractual character of mercenary service was revised to emphasize a hierarchical command structure held together as much by self-discipline as by overt coercion. Officers and men were integrated into the same structure, motivated by punishment and reward, and bound by a common subordination to the greater authority of the state. Lipsius' ideas provided the ideological framework for the transformation of the independent contractor into the salaried professional officer, and for the general subjugation of military personnel to direct state authority.[11]

Technological advances provided the means to put this into practice. Unlike the period before 1530 these had little to do with developments in weaponry, which remained evolutionary rather than revolutionary.[12] The significant changes were now in the technology of rule, particularly in the exploitation of relatively recent ideas for the first time on a massive scale. The spread of a written culture to all levels of administration represented a considerable expansion in the surveillance capacity of the state, and was assisted by greater use of printing and the adoption of new accounting procedures based on Arabic rather than Roman numerals. Such coded information, along with improved mechanisms for its storage and retrieval by a small but growing number of specialized officials, enabled the state to extend its supervisory reach deeper into society, monitoring and curbing the activities of previously autonomous groups. The military contractors were a particular target for special commissars who gradually evolved from liaison officers to agents of direct state control.

The long-term success of these methods helped consolidate monopoly formation in western and central Europe, making it by 1660 effectively irreversible without the destruction of the state itself. It is especially significant that the defeat of monarchical centralization in England and the Netherlands did not end the concentration of coercive power, but merely ensured that it took a different form from the more absolutist structures of Spain, France and Austria.

These processes affected the international dimension of conflict by furthering the fragmentation of Europe into distinct states. The confessional divide remained, and all attempts to return to a pre-Reformation state system were defeated. The concept of a single "universal monarchy" remained on the political agenda till the mid-seventeenth century, but continued to mean only the preeminence of one monarch within a system of fragmented and overlapping sovereignty rather than direct rule over an European super-state. Only the Habsburgs stood any chance of achieving this, but their prospects were diminished by Charles V's decision to partition his empire. Defeat of all efforts at Christian unity, either by compromise or military conquest, provided a further setback, while the religious outcome of the various internal wars reinforced the distinct identity of individual states by stamping relative confessional uniformity. These trends were confirmed by the Westphalian Settlement of 1648, which not only ended the Thirty Years' War in Germany, but also secured international recognition for Switzerland and the Dutch Republic as separate states.

Consolidation of state sovereignty reinforced the distinction between civil and international conflict. Despite the various forms it took, monopoly formation identified a single sovereign power within each state as the sole possessor of legitimate armed force. Violent domestic opposition, which had existed before as justified resistance to tyranny, was gradually delegitimized as rebellion, while private recourse to arms, once recognized in the institution of the feud as a legal means to settle a dispute, was criminalized as a breach of the peace. Rhetorical justifications for international conflict were secularized, emphasizing the necessity and public utility of war as a means of advancing the common good, often defined in dynastic, absolutist terms.[13]

In practice, however, war was far from the orderly and controlled application of force advocated by theorists, remaining protracted, costly and generally inconclusive. Individual battles could be politically decisive, but it was rare that they effected more than localized change. The Habsburg victory at White Mountain 1620 broke Bohemian resistance to political centralization but did not end the Kingdom's relative autonomy within the wider Austrian monarchy. France remained at war with Spain for another 16 years despite its triumph at Rocroi in 1643. Moreover, the size of the contending forces in individual engagements remained roughly similar to those present at major battles prior to 1530. What had changed was the ability of substantial monarchies like France and Spain to campaign with more than one battleworthy army simultaneously, transforming warfare into operations on several fronts. Nonetheless, with the partial exception of France and Spain, the overall growth in size was not sustained, but continued to fluctuate dramatically in line with the expansion and contraction of the resource-mobilization by individual states.

Logistical problems continued to inhibit the prolonged assembly of more than 30,000 men in a single field army even in relatively fertile regions and, together with the continued growth in the geographical scope of political ambitions, this encouraged the dispersal of forces over a relatively wide area.[14] The incidence of battles and sieges had less to do with strategic preference than with the human geography of the war zone. Fighting in urbanized areas like the Low Countries or northern Italy tended to be dominated by the latter, while the former was more common in central Europe where only major cities had extensive artillery-proof fortifications. Raiding and skirmishing predominated further east, where low population density and an underdeveloped commercial sector made heavy troop concentration difficult to sustain.

Tactics were dominated by the continued evolution of innovations made before 1530. Despite their preference for massive blocks of infantry, early-sixteenth-century armies already displayed considerable tactical flexibility and were perfectly capable of subdividing large formations for specific tasks. Such subdivisions were now standardized and integrated into the new system of hierarchical control. The gradual reduction in company size from an average of about 400 men in the early sixteenth century to under 200 by the mid-seventeenth century also reinforced this trend, by increasing the ratio of officers to men. The proportion of firearms continued to rise to the point where, by the 1660s, some infantry regiments were entirely composed of musketeers. Tactics were modified in accordance with this change with the development of larger, shallower formations to maximize firepower. Although armies like those of the Swedes and Dutch achieved notable successes by adopting such practices ahead of their opponents, any advantage was soon neutralized by the diffusion of their ideas. Moreover, victory did not always go to the most technically advanced side, as is indicated by the Swedish defeat at the hands of a more conventional Spanish army at Nördlingen in 1634.

1660–1720

Change only became apparent with the consolidation of the domestic state monopolies from the mid-seventeenth century onwards, which permitted sustained growth in army size for the first time throughout most of western and central Europe. States still reduced their forces upon termination of hostilities, but they rarely retained fewer soldiers than they had done before the war started, forcing overall size inexorably upwards to peak in most areas by the early eighteenth century.

The largest single army was that of France, which rose from about 50,000 in the 1660s, equivalent to the maximum effective strength of the previous century, to number 279,600 by 1678, greater than any force seen in Europe since the Roman Empire. Thereafter, it hit a maximum effective strength of 340,000 during the Nine Years' War (1688–97), a figure not exceeded until after the French Revolution. French strength was sometimes surpassed by the collective total of the various components of the Holy Roman Empire, including Habsburg Austria and Brandenburg-Prussia. The Habsburgs maintained the largest with about 25,000 field troops in 1650, rising to an average of 60,000–70,000 in the 1660s and 1670s, then climbing steeply from the 1690s to peak at a paper strength of 162,700 by 1718. The larger, secular electorates along with the militarized ecclesiastical territories of Münster and Würzburg all maintained significant forces from the mid-1650s, with the average rising from about 5,000 to three or four times that figure by the early eighteenth century. Considered in terms of the ratio of soldiers to civilians, these levels of militarization were rarely exceeded until the introduction of truly universal conscription in the 1890s. This growth was not matched by the major military powers of the earlier seventeenth century and, although Spain and Sweden continued to maintain considerable forces, their wartime totals did not surpass previous levels. The Dutch could put about 75,000 of their own men into the field, equivalent to their maximum strength in their war of independence, but they could now add nearly as many more by hiring German and Scandinavian auxiliaries.[15] The English adopted a similar practice after 1688, and generally fought their continental wars with large contingents of foreign troops subsidized by their increasingly sophisticated methods of war finance.

The domestic dimension of warfare no longer centred on attempts to destroy or dismantle the fiscal–military infrastructure, but on struggles to control it and to distribute the burdens and benefits it entailed. Apart from in the British Isles, these struggles were no longer violent, but were subsumed within the bargaining process that lay at the heart of most state-elite relations. Defeat of the Stuarts' attempts to move British politics along absolutist lines involved heavy fighting in Scotland and Ireland in 1689–91, followed by the repulse of several attempts at armed restoration. Violence in the core area of England itself was replaced after 1688 by a struggle within the formal constitutional framework provided by Parliament. On the continent these battles for influence took place within the largely informal patronage networks linking political life at the centre with that in the localities. The general result was to strengthen the state regardless of which particular form it took. The exceptions were Poland, where foreign interference furthered political decentralization and prevented firm central control over taxation and violence, and the Holy Roman Empire, where monopoly formation continued at territorial level at the expense of the old national institutions associated with the imperial title.

As the internal threats to the state structure and the elites controlling it declined, so too did the domestic use of armed force. The army remained the primary bulwark of the state, and continued to be deployed to protect the vital lifeblood of tax collection against attempts to reduce the burden. Increasingly, however, internal opposition was deflected by a variety of more peaceful strategies, including greater sensitivity to popular grievances and judicial redress as the state responded to pressure from below as well as seeking to impose order from above. One result was to anchor the legitimacy of the state more securely in a broader consensus amongst the population, achieved to best effect in England but also in Sweden, Denmark and most of the German territories. The absence of such a consensus, coupled with the inability to affect infrastructional reforms, contributed to the collapse of the French monarchy after 1787.

A second result was to accelerate the demilitarization of civil society as the state now not only monopolized organized coercion within its territory, but increasingly directed its armed forces exclusively against external threats. This was reflected in the normal peacetime deployment of western and most central European armies, which were now stationed predominantly in the peripheral areas of troublesome or threatened border provinces. The bulk of England's small standing army was deployed in the subject kingdoms of Scotland and Ireland as well as the colonies, while French forces were concentrated in the fortress ring along the frontier.

A third consequence of domestic consolidation was to enforce the distinction between internal and external affairs; something which also reflected the primary driving force behind the military expansion of this period. The principal threats now came from outside, as European warfare centred on deciding the pecking order within a single hierarchy of independent sovereign states. Although those situated on the Atlantic seaboard as well as those around the Baltic continued to struggle for economic predominance and the control of lucrative trade routes, inter-state conflict was generally expressed in dynastic terms, since the prestige associated with lands and titles was a major currency in the new international order. Religion remained important in mobilizing international support, as is indicated by the use of a "Protestant cause" in the wars against Louis XIV's Catholic France. However, the imposition of religious beliefs on opponents no longer formed a major objective and was even disappearing from the great struggles against the Ottoman Turks in the Balkans. Although France sponsored Jacobite rebellions after 1688 as well as encouraging Hungarian rebellions against Habsburg rule, civil and international conflict was no longer so closely interwoven, while the emergence of new forms of diplomatic protocol helped enforce a sharper distinction between war and peace.

The organization and composition of the forces engaged in these conflicts reflected the permanence of the fiscal–military monopolies. Armies were broken into subunits which had a continuous existence, facilitating the development of a professional career structure within the officer corps, regulated by a recognized hierarchy of ranks and greater state control over appointments, salaries and, now, even pensions. Officers' social origins also changed, as native aristocrats displaced the commoners and foreign nobles who had formed a significant proportion in most armies before the mid-seventeenth century. Organization also displayed greater specialization, as each army maintained specific units for particular tactical functions. Infantry now formed the mainstay of all armies, except that of the Poles who continued to rely heavily on cavalry. The more effective flintlock replaced the earlier matchlock musket, while the gradual introduction of iron rather than wooden ramrods improved the speed and reliability of reloading and so increased the rate of fire. The only true innovation was the introduction of the bayonet which improved the defensive capacity of infantry against cavalry, thereby removing the need for pikemen. Western and central European armies adopted it first, with its use becoming widespread amongst the larger German territories by the 1690s, slightly ahead of its universal introduction in France. The Swedes were a little slower, while the Turks first used bayonets in action in 1739. The main consequence was a further increase in firepower, since all foot soldiers now carried muskets, encouraging deployment in longer, thinner lines to maximize the effect. The relative advantage of firepower over the shock tactics of attacking with bayonets continued to be debated throughout the eighteenth century with neither proving universally decisive on the battlefield.

Infantry training tended to emphasize standardization, whereas that of the cavalry reflected their more varied role. Heavy cavalry, mounted on larger horses and often still wearing an armoured cuirass and a metal skullcap under their hats, was employed for battle-winning charges to exploit tactical opportunities. Dragoons, originally trained as mounted infantry, were increasingly used as heavy cavalry, and were replaced in reconnaissance and skirmishing roles by varieties of light cavalry, often modelled on the east European hussars. Specialization was probably most pronounced in the supporting arms which were now organized as part of the regular army. Foremost amongst these was the artillery, often divided into various sections, depending on the type of weapon they served, while other functions were performed by special detachments of engineers, miners and sappers for siege work, and pontooneers for the mobile bridging train. Habsburg forces also included sizeable naval units operating the Danube flotilla in support of operations against the Turks.[16]

Militias and irregulars remained important in central and eastern Europe, especially as a means of mobilizing large numbers in wartime with limited resources at the state's disposal. The Habsburgs placed their so-called Military Frontier on a more regular footing after the reconquest of Hungary from the Turks in 1699. This institution had developed after the early sixteenth century to protect the eastern border against Ottoman attack. Local families and settlers were given religious and economic freedoms in return for serving as frontier guards, but from the 1740s growing numbers were also made to serve as light infantry in the monarchy's conflicts against western opponents.[17]

Elsewhere, militia systems continued to be exploited to provide cheap recruits for the regular formations in emergencies. Apart from Austria, most German territories developed a supplementary system of extended leave within the permanent regiments, to reduce costs. Introduced as these territories began to maintain substantial peacetime forces from the 1670s, this practice involved releasing soldiers into the civilian economy for up to ten months a year once they had completed a period of basic training. Even the men nominally with the colours often only did duty once every three to four days, spending much of the remaining time in menial civil employment to supplement their meagre pay. This combination of a militia and professional force was most pronounced in the famous Prussian canton system introduced by 1733 and mirrored by roughly similar structures in some other German territories. Most of the professional core of the army, recruited from local volunteers and other German territories, was permitted to find what work it could within certain sectors of the civilian economy during off-duty hours. The rest of the force was recruited from revived militia lists drawn up in each district or "canton" assigned to an individual regiment, which could take men to maintain its official strength. After basic training, cantonists were released into the civilian economy for most of the year to save on their maintenance.[18] While both Denmark and Sweden used roughly comparable systems, the separation of regulars and militia was retained in France, England, Spain and the Italian states, all of which tended to use militiamen as a secondary, supplementary force to hold rear areas or garrison fortresses in wartime.

Russia continued to move along a different path, replacing its combination of paid musketeers and cavalry provided by the landlords with the so-called new formation regiments recruited and officered largely by foreigners in the mid-seventeenth century. These proved too expensive to maintain in large numbers, and gave way to a mass army raised by Peter the Great after 1700 from serf conscripts who served for life. Militia formations, inasmuch as they existed at all, were relegated to the defence of peripheral frontier regions.[19]

1720–89

These structures were firmly in place by the end of the War of the Spanish Succession (1701–14) and remained unchanged in their essentials until the French Revolutionary Wars after 1792. The period after the great wars of the late seventeenth century and early eighteenth century was mainly one of consolidation, characterized by increasing standardization throughout most of Europe. While important differences remained, armies became more alike in terms of tactical doctrine, drill, organization and even outward appearance than they had ever been before. Tactical change was more one of the refinement of existing techniques than of true innovation. Nevertheless, there were important indications of future developments during the War of the Austrian Succession (1740–8) and especially the Seven Years' War (1756–63). The French began to make greater use of formations between the single mass of an entire army and its individual component regiments. These intermediate units, variously called brigades or divisions, depending on their size, were used to move troops as tactical task forces across wider areas, concentrating on a specific battlefield to engage the enemy. Although their use of brigades was less clearly defined, the Austrians also used converging columns to concentrate their forces, most notably in their defeat of the Prussians at Hochkirch 1758. Both they and the Prussians made greater tactical use of heavy artillery to prepare an attack by battering the enemy positions with a sustained barrage. Unlike engagements before 1720, the heavy guns now accompanied the advance in several batteries to give prolonged support rather than just a preliminary bombardment. The Prussians developed this further by providing lighter pieces towed by horse teams that could keep pace with the cavalry, and both they and, especially, the Austrians developed the use of light troops to harass the more solid formation of the line infantry. None of these changes was developed to the point where it transformed the way of fighting but, taken as a whole, they formed the basis of revolutionary and Napoleonic warfare.

The most significant change was the continued growth of the powers on the western and eastern fringes of Europe. The increases in Britain's land forces were relatively modest, but its military reach now extended around the globe thanks to the continued expansion of naval and financial power. The great east-central and eastern European monarchies remained primarily land powers, but the size of their forces grew dramatically. Russia's position as a truly European military power was confirmed by the intervention of its forces in northern Germany and Denmark in 1711–16 during the later phases of the Great Northern War (1700–21), and by their appearance in south Germany in 1735 and 1748 to assist the Austrians. Logistical problems continued to inhibit effective intervention much beyond Poland but, with its large conscript army, Russia was clearly the dominant power in eastern Europe and the Balkans by the 1790s. The considerable territorial gains in northern Italy and Hungary made by the Habsburgs since the 1680s made a separate Austrian existence possible by the 1720s, clearly marking it out as a major power in its own right, and no longer merely dependent on the dynasty's influence within the Holy Roman Empire. Austria's new international standing rested on a force which had grown to 314,800 men by 1789, excluding the semi-regular frontier militia. The newest major power was Prussia, whose survival against a hostile coalition during the Seven Years' War confirmed its place as a state of more than regional significance. The growth of Prussia's forces was dramatic, rising from 40,000 in the early eighteenth century to reach 195,300 by the eve of the French Revolution but, compared to other powers, the country was under-resourced and could not survive a prolonged conflict without external assistance.[20]

Infrastructural growth associated with the enlightened or reform absolutism of all three monarchies only partly explains their military power. All experienced significant territorial expansion, not least at Poland's expense, as this state, larger than France, was partitioned between them in three stages 1772–95. Demographic growth, which began to take off in parts of western and central Europe by the mid-eighteenth century, suggested that this increase in scale might extend elsewhere on the continent if other states could develop the means to tap expanding resources.

This potential was realized in the wake of the French Revolution of 1789 which signalled a new period of profound change. As in the past, this had less to do with how wars were fought than how they were sustained. The internal structure of European states was being transformed, as the struggle for political influence pushed the still largely private control of the fiscal–military monopoly into the wider public sphere. The state became an entity transcending the lives of individual rulers and officials, while its social base broadened as further sections of the population gained access to political power. The transformation was most dramatic and extensive in France where the inability of the existing structure to cope with the burden of eighteenth-century wars precipitated the fiscal crisis behind the monarchy's collapse in 1787. The revolutionaries' subsequent abolition of feudalism, along with provincial and local privileges, destroyed many of the barriers which had hindered resource mobilization in the past. Indirect rule, mediated by patronage and protective of particularism, was being replaced by greater direct rule from the centre, extending the reach of the state into what had long been largely autonomous, private spheres of social and economic life. The new ideologies associated both with the revolution and with enlightened philosophy legitimized this transformation, enabling the state to extend the political consensus upon which it rested, while simultaneously intervening more directly in everyday life. Resistance was considerable, particularly in France where the new governments faced a variety of popular revolts against its centralizing and anti-clerical policies 1792–1801. Elsewhere, domestic violence was less pronounced, partly because the authorities refrained from such radical change, and partly because earlier reforms often rendered the state more advanced than that of pre-revolutionary France.

The impact of the domestic political transformation was most pronounced in the wars unleashed by revolutionary France through genuine ideological conviction and as a desperate attempt to solve its deepening internal crisis. The initial French attack on the Austrian Netherlands in April 1792 collapsed before it met serious resistance and, though the subsequent Austro-Prussian invasion was repulsed, it was clear that the war could not be won by relying on volunteers to fill out the army. Between 1793 and 1798 the new regime moved over to conscription, justified by revolutionary universalism and the new ideology of nationalism. In its final form, annual drafts of the 20–21 age groups kept the army up to strength, finally destroying the division between militia-type recruitment and the professional army which had persisted in all *ancien régime* systems.[21]

The success of this army against those of the old regime has led to much comment about the inherent superiority of the motivated French citizens-in-arms against the supposedly disinterested mercenaries who opposed them. Like the widespread belief that the French Republic already had a million under arms by 1794, the contrast is an exaggeration. French forces were larger than those of their opponents, individually though not collectively, and they generally won those engagements where they had local superiority, losing many of those where they were evenly matched or outnumbered. Desertion in France remained a drain on resources, particularly as it was compounded by growing draft avoidance, and was as significant as that suffered by the opposing forces. French tactics were more flexible, but their main advantage came from their more ruthless war management.

The highly political nature of the new French high command drove its generals to accept higher losses, while implementation of conscription and systematic plundering of occupied territory enabled the home government to sustain greater casualties. States in the anti-French coalition meanwhile adhered to the earlier style of war, one which can genuinely be called limited only in its reluctance to break the accepted norms of political and social behaviour. In the face of the seemingly boundless ambition of the French state, personified after 1804 by Napoleon, the others clung to a concept of war still governed by the acquisition of pieces of territory and adjustments to a continental balance of power. Significantly, Napoleon suffered his first major defeat in 1812 at the hands of Russia, the one power that made war with similar ruthlessness, having arguably done so long before 1789. Napoleon's major opponents also modified their methods, partly in direct response to defeats by France and partly in continuation of existing efforts to mobilize greater resources. That all did so without destroying the basically monarchical character of their political structures is testimony to the relative strength of their prewar, fiscal–military monopolies.

The emergence of these monopolies since the mid-fifteenth century had transformed Europe and European warfare, resulting in the division of the continent into separate sovereign states. Each had a distinct domestic and external sphere characterized by the demilitarization of internal politics and the concentration of armed force in the hands of a single, largely depersonified agency constituting the state. All maintained land forces primarily to defend and advance interests that were articulated in language that transcended the individual and spoke to some real or imagined greater whole. Although they continued to fluctuate in size, these forces were now permanent, sustained by a fairly sophisticated state infrastructure staffed by men who, like the soldiers themselves, were expert professionals. Conscription, which produced the mass armies of the revolutionary and Napoleonic period, remained, but was reduced after 1815 in line with political concerns about the reliability of such large forces. Technology, which had helped in the initial transformation of warfare 1450–

1530, played only a modest role thereafter, with human ambition and the power structure through which it made itself felt continuing to be the single most important factor promoting change. This was not to remain the case, since the technological changes associated with emergent industrialization were set to transfom war once again later in the nineteenth century.

Notes

1. The key contributions are reprinted in C. J. Rogers (ed.), *The military revolution debate. Readings on the military transformation of early modern Europe* (Boulder, 1995).

2. D. Moon, Reassessing Russian serfdom, *European History Quarterly*, 26, 1996, pp. 483–526; R. Hellie, *Enserfment and military change in Muscovy* (Chicago, 1971); S. Ogilvie and B. Scribner, *Germany. A new social and economic history* (2 vols, London, 1996).

3. K. Repgen, Kriegslegitimationen in Alteuropa. Entwurf einer historischen Typologie, *Historische Zeitschrift*, 241, 1985, pp. 27–49; J. T. Johnson, *Ideology, reason, and the limitation of war. Religious and secular concepts, 1200–1740* (Princeton, 1975).

4. D. Potter, The international mercenary market in the sixteenth century. Anglo-French competition in Germany 1543–50, *English Historical Review*, III, 1996, pp. 24–58.

5. H. Harkensee, *Die Schlacht bei Marignano* (Göttingen, 1909); F. L. Taylor, *The art of war in Italy 1494–1529* (reprint, Westport, 1973).

6. A. Keller, *Die Wiedereinsetzung des Herzogs Ulrich von Württemberg durch den Landgrafen Philipp von Hessen, 1533/4* (Marburg, 1912); L. F. Heyd, *Die Schlacht bei Lauffen den 12. und 13. Mai 1534* (Stuttgart, 1834).

7. F. Redlich, Contributions in the Thirty Years War, *Economic History Review*, second series, 12, 1959/60, pp. 247–54; J. A. Lynn, How war fed war: The tax of violence and contributions during the *Grand Siècle*, *Journal of Modern History*, 65, 1993, pp. 286–310.

8. H. Ehlert, "Ursprünge des modernen Militärwesens. Die nassau-oranischen Heeresreformen", *Militärgeschichtliche Mitteilungen*, 38, 1985, pp. 27–56; J. Lindegren, The Swedish "military state", 1560–1720, *Scandinavian Journal of History*, 10, 1985, pp. 305–36; both with extensive references.

9. Detailed coverage of organization and finance in F. G. J. Ten Raa *et al.*, *Het staatsche Leger 1568–1795* (8 vols. in 11 parts, The Hague, 1911–59).

10. P. T. Hoffman and K. Norberg (eds), *Fiscal crises, liberty and representative government* (Stamford, 1994); R. Bonney (ed.), *Economic systems and state finance* (Oxford, 1995).

11. G. Oestreich, *Neostoicism and the early modern state* (Cambridge, 1982).

12. For examples see J. A. Lynn, Tactical evolution in the French army 1560–1660, *French Historical Studies*, 14, 1985, pp. 176–91.

13. M. Behnen, "Der gerechte und der notwendige Krieg. 'Necessitas' und 'utilitas reipublicae' in der Kriegstheorie des 16. und 17. Jahrhunderts", in J. Kunisch (ed.), *Staatsverfassung und Heeresverfassung in der europäischen Geschichte der frühen Neuzeit* (Berlin, 1986), pp. 42–106.

14. For logistics throughout this period see the collection *Die Bedeutung der Logistik für die militärische Führung von der Antike bis in die neueste Zeit* (Vorträge zur Militärgeschichte vol. VII, Hereford, 1986) and the somewhat controversial work of M. van Creveld, *Supplying war. Logistics from Wallenstein to Patton* (Cambridge, 1977) which is best read in conjunction with

the critique in J. A. Lynn (ed.), *Feeding Mars. Logistics in western warfare from the middle ages to the present* (Boulder, 1993).

15. On this practice see P. H. Wilson, The German "soldier trade" of the seventeenth and eighteenth centuries: A reassessment, *International History Review*, 18, 1996, pp. 757–92.

16. For the latter see W. Aichelberg, *Krieggschifte auf der Donau* (2nd edn, Vienna, 1982).

17. G. E. Rothenberg, *The Austrian Military Border in Croatia 1522–1747* (Urbana, 1960) and his *The Military Border in Croatia 1740–1881* (Chicago, 1966).

18. O. Büsch, *Military system and social life in old regime Prussia 1713–1807* (Eng. tr. Atlantic Highlands, 1997).

19. D. B. Ralston, *Importing the European army. The introduction of European military techniques into the extra-European world, 1600–1914* (Chicago, 1990), pp. 13–42.

20. For Russia see C. Duffy, *Russia's military way to the west. Origins and nature of Russian military power 1700–1800* (London, 1981). For Austria see J. Zimmermann, *Militärverwaltung und Heeresaufbringung in Österreich bis 1806* (Munich, 1983). For Prussia see C.v. Jany, *Geschichte der Preußischen Armee von 15. Jahrhundert bis 1914* (4 vols, Osnabrück, 1967).

21. J.-P. Bertaud, *The army of the French Revolution. From citizen soldier to instrument of power* (Princeton, 1988); A. Forrest, *Soldiers of the French Revolution* (Durham, 1990).

Further reading

R. G. Asch, *The Thirty Years War: The Holy Roman Empire and Europe 1618–1648* (London, 1997).

R. Baumann, *Landsknechte. Ihre Geschichte und Kultur vom späten Mittelalter bis zum Dreißigjährigen Krieg* (Munich, 1994).

J. Black, *European warfare 1660–1815* (London, 1994).

T. C. W. Blanning, *The French Revolutionary Wars 1787–1802* (London, 1996).

J. Brewer, *The sinews of power. War, money and the English state, 1688–1783* (New York, 1989).

P. Contamine, *War in the middle ages* (tr. M. Jones, Oxford, 1986).

A. Corvisier (ed.), *Histoire militaire de La France* (2 vols, Paris, 1992).

M. van Creveld, *Technology and war from 2000 BC to the present* (New York, 1989).

B. M. Downing, *The military revolution and political change. Origins of democracy and autocracy in early modern Europe* (Princeton, 1992).

C. Duffy, *Fire and stone. The science of siege warfare 1660–1860* (London, 1975).

N. Elias, *The civilizing process* (Oxford, 1994).

C. J. Esdaile, *The wars of Napoleon* (London, 1995).

A. Forrest, *Soldiers of the French Revolution* (Durham, 1994).

A. Giddens, *The nation state and violence* (Berkeley, 1985).

D. Kaiser, *Politics and war. European conflict from Philipp II to Hitler* (London, 1990).

J. L. Keep, *Soldiers of the Tsar. Army and society in Russia 1462–1874* (Oxford, 1985).

F. Lot, *Recherches sur les effectifs des armées françaises des guerres d'Italie aux Guerres de Religion 1492–1562* (Paris, 1962).

E. Luard, *The balance of power. The system of international relations 1648–1815* (London, 1992).

M. Mallett, *Mercenaries and their masters. Warfare in Renaissance Italy* (Totowa, NJ, 1974).

M. Mann, *The sources of social power* (2 vols, Cambridge, 1986–93).

B. Nosworthy, *The anatomy of victory. Battle tactics 1689–1763* (New York, 1992).

G. Parker, *The military revolution. Military innovation and the rise of the west 1500–1800* (Cambridge, 1988).

B. D. Porter, *War and the rise of the state. The military foundations of modern politics* (New York, 1994).

F. Redlich, *The German military enterprizer and his workforce* (2 vols., *Vierteljahreshefte für Sozial- und Wirtschafts-geschichte, Beihefte*, 47 & 48, Wiesbaden, 1964–5).

C. J. Rogers (ed.), *The military revolution debate. Readings on the military transformation of early modern Europe* (Boulder, 1995).

W. Schaufelberger, *Der alte Schweizer und sein Krieg* (3rd edn, Frauenfeld, 1987).

H. Schwarz, *Gefechtsformen der Infanterie in Europa durch 800 Jahren* (Munich, 1977).

D. E. Showalter, *The wars of Frederick the Great* (London, 1996).

F. Tallet, *War and society in early modern Europe 1495–1715* (London, 1992).

M. C. t'Hart, *The making of a bourgeois state. War, politics and finance during the Dutch revolt* (Manchester, 1993).

C. Tilly, *Coercion, capital and European states* AD *990–1992* (Oxford, 1992).

J. E. Thompson, *Mercenaries, pirates and sovereigns. State-building and extraterritorial violence in early modern Europe* (Princeton, 1994).

Chapter Nine

War, politics and the conquest of Mexico

Ross Hassig

As the fifteenth century ended and the sixteenth began, the Spaniards emerged as a major military power, pushing out or subjugating the remaining Moors on the Iberian peninsula, and controlling other kingdoms, such as Austria, the Low Countries, and much of Italy. Spain also expanded overseas into the West Indies, Panama, and Florida, though with mixed success, since the groups they encountered were relatively unsophisticated and could not easily be controlled through their own political structures; nor were many tied to their lands, so that they simply fled in the face of Spanish predation.

Cortés and the conquest of Mexico[1]

Traders and explorers sailed throughout the West Indies in the early sixteenth century, doubtless landing in areas such as Mesoamerica, but left few or no records. Unquestionably, shipwreck survivors reached the mainland. Yet Mesoamerica is not generally considered to have been discovered until years later, with the landing of Francisco Hernández de Córdoba in Yucatán in 1517.[2]

Córdoba met a hostile reception, lost more than half of his 110 men, and died shortly after returning to Cuba.[3] But the expedition reported sophisticated civilizations, great cities, and gold and other wealth. Governor Velásquez dispatched four ships and 200 men under Juan de Grijalva. They reached Yucatán on 3 May, 1518, but Grijalva proved a timid explorer and, after clashing with the native inhabitants,[4] he sailed as far north as the central Veracruz coast before retracing his route and returning to Cuba.[5] Even before Grijalva's return, however, Governor Velásquez began preparing a third expedition to be led by

Hernán Cortés. Before long, however, Velásquez grew wary of Cortés and tried to relieve him, but, forewarned, Cortés had already sailed, though the ships were not fully provisioned or staffed.[6] Cortés landed at other Cuban ports for more men and equipment, before sailing for Yucatán on 10 February 1519 with eleven ships and as many as 450 men.[7]

Following the same route as the first two expeditions, Cortés landed in Yucatán, where he found a shipwrecked Spaniard, Gerónimo de Aguilar, who lived among the Maya and spoke their language.[8] He then sailed eastward along the coast of Yucatán, where he also clashed with the natives, defeating the Maya at the city of Potonchan in present-day Tabasco, though with an ultimate loss of 35 of his men.[9] He then sailed on until he reached Grijalva's stopping-place on the central Veracruz coast.

Central Veracruz was home to the Totonac people, but was under Aztec control, and Cortés was greeted by an Aztec official and 4,000 men bearing food and gifts.[10] When the Spaniards proved difficult in the following days, the Aztecs stopped supplying them with food, and departed.[11] This turned out to be a bad decision, as the Aztec departure freed the Totonacs to visit the Spaniards, and Cortés first learned that the Aztecs had enemies.[12]

Many of Cortés's men, especially those chosen by Velásquez, wanted to return to Cuba since they had now achieved their authorized objectives, but, in a clever bit of legal manipulation, Cortés founded the town of Villa Rica de la Vera Cruz and appointed a city council that claimed authority directly from King Charles V of Spain. The town council then declared Cortés's mandate fulfilled, claiming that Velásquez's authority had now lapsed, and elected Cortés as captain directly under the king's authority, thus freeing him from any constraints imposed by Velásquez and allowing him to act as he saw fit.[13] Cortés sought an alliance with the Totonacs against the Aztecs and, at his urging, they seized the Aztec tribute collectors in an open act of rebellion.[14]

To secure the royal backing that his venture would need if he were to avoid prison, or worse, Cortés sent a ship to Spain with all the gold they had gathered thus far as a gift to the king. Faced with internal dissension, however, Cortés sank the ten remaining ships, leaving his men little option but to follow him.[15] With 60 to 150 men remaining in the fort at Vera Cruz, Cortés began his trek inland with 300 Spanish soldiers, 40 to 50 Totonac soldiers, and 200 porters.[16]

Unmolested by the Aztecs, Cortés's force marched toward Tenochtitlan by way of Tlaxcallan, which was hostile to the Aztecs.[17] Nearing that province, the Spaniards saw a small party of armed Indians and advanced to capture them, but the Indians fought back, then fled, drawing the Spaniards forward into an ambush in which they lost four wounded and one dead.[18] The Spaniards were saved only by their superior weapons, which were more lethal than those of the Indians, and could penetrate native armour with ease.

The Spaniards were attacked repeatedly in the days to follow, but managed to fend off the Tlaxcaltecs, though with more Spanish losses.[19] With supplies running low, many wounded, and facing large hostile forces, Cortés sent peace overtures to the Tlaxcaltecs.[20] He took care to hide the number of his dead and wounded from the Tlaxcaltecs and, finally, the Tlaxcaltecs agreed to peace. Cortés then travelled to the city of Tlaxcallan, which he entered on 23 September 1519, and accepted the Tlaxcaltecs as vassals.[21]

Cortés stayed in Tlaxcallan for 17 days and then marched to Cholollan, overriding Tlaxcaltec objections, in order to gather supplies for the rest of the journey.[22] The Spaniards were welcomed by the Chololtec nobles and entered Cholollan the next day, where they were housed and fed for two days before the food inexplicably stopped arriving.[23] When Cortés learned that the Chololtecs were planning to attack him with the aid of a hidden Aztec army, he had them assemble in the main courtyard, guarding every entrance, and massacred them all, including the king.[24] Cortés then placed another noble on the throne and two weeks later marched into the Valley of Mexico, avoiding one road in which the Aztecs had set up an ambush, before reaching Amaquemecan.[25]

From there, the Spaniards marched to Tenochtitlan and arrived on 8 November, escorted by the many kings and nobles who met them en route, and entered the Aztec capital to be greeted by Moteuczoma.[26] Moteuczoma presented the Spaniards with gifts, fed them, housed them in the palace of Axayacatl, and publicly befriended Cortés.[27]

Tenochtitlan was a formidable city: its population was enormous and it was located on an island connected to the mainland by only three major causeways that could easily be severed.[28] Word soon reached Cortés that the Aztecs had attacked the Totonacs for refusing to pay tribute, and when the Spaniards at Vera Cruz tried to intervene, seven were killed before the rest fled.[29] Cortés seized Moteuczoma, held him captive and effectively ruled the city through him for the next eight months.[30] Under pressure from Cortés, Moteuczoma ordered the seizure of the leader of the Aztec army which had attacked the Totonacs and had him brought to Tenochtitlan. Once there, he denied that Moteuczoma had ordered the attack and, at Cortés's insistence, the king had him burned to death.[31]

This act shocked the Aztecs and led the kings and nobles of the allied cities to conspire against the Spaniards. Moteuczoma, however, learned of the plot and told Cortés, who insisted that he seize the plotters.[32] Internal dissension was quelled, but another threat was growing in Cuba.

Intent on capturing and punishing Cortés, Governor Velásquez assembled a fleet of 19 ships and at least 800 soldiers under the command of Pánfilo de Narváez.[33] But when Cortés learned of their arrival at Vera Cruz, he marched to the coast with 266 men, reached Narváez's camp at Cempohuallan about 27

May, and launched a surprise night attack, resulting in the capture of Narváez and the surrender of his men.[34]

Meanwhile, Pedro de Alvarado was in charge in Tenochtitlan, with a force of 80 soldiers. During Cortés's absence Alvarado learned of a plan to attack the Spaniards, and pre-emptively attacked the Aztecs in the courtyard before the Great Temple while they celebrated the monthly festival.[35] Unarmed and trapped within the walls, an estimated 8,000–10,000 Aztec nobles were killed. When word of the massacre spread throughout the city, the people turned on the Spaniards, killing seven, wounding many, and driving the rest back to their quarters.[36] When word of the uprising reached Cortés, he quickly began the return march. His force, now including Narváez's men, numbered over 1,300, to which he added 2,000 Tlaxcaltecs *en route*, and the entire party reached Tenochtitlan on 24 June 1520, entering the city unopposed.[37]

Once the Spaniards were inside, however, the causeway bridges were raised to prevent a retreat, and they were besieged for 23 days, all of Cortés's forays being repulsed.[38] With their food and water cut off, and unable to negotiate a withdrawal, Cortés brought Moteuczoma on to the roof to order his people to stop the attack, but the king was struck down by stones thrown from the Indian throng.[39]

With escape imperative, Cortés had a portable wooden span built to bridge the gaps in the causeways. Just before midnight on 30 June the Spaniards began their escape under cover of darkness and a heavy rainstorm. Soon the alarm was raised and the Spaniards were attacked, only a third reaching Tlacopan on the western shore.[40] From there they marched north around the lakes, under constant assault,[41] and finally managed to reach Tlaxcallan territory, with the loss of over 860 Spanish soldiers, five Spanish women who had arrived with Narváez, and more than 1,000 Tlaxcaltecs.[42]

On reaching Tlaxcallan, Cortés and his men were well received and the alliance was recemented. Since all the surviving 440 Spaniards were wounded, they rested there for three weeks.[43] Once they had recuperated, Cortés sought Tlaxcaltec assistance to conquer the towns of Tepeyacac, Quecholac, and Tecamachalco.[44]

About 1 August, Cortés marched against Tepeyacac with 420 Spaniards, routing its army.[45] The lords of Tepeyacac pledged fealty to the Spaniards, and Cortés subdued the rest of the region in a matter of weeks.[46] To secure the area, he founded the fortified town of La Villa de Segura de la Frontera at Tepeyacac, which also controlled the main route to Vera Cruz.[47] The Aztecs struck back by sending troops to Cuauhquecholan and Itzyocan, but Cortés defeated them with a force of Spanish and Tlaxcaltec soldiers.[48]

By the autumn, smallpox brought by Narváez's men had swept through central Mexico, killing vast numbers of Indians, including Cuitlahua, who had succeeded the slain Moteuczoma as king. In the midst of this plague and the political upheaval caused by the death of two successive Aztec kings, Cortés planned his return to Tenochtitlan.[49] First, however, he ordered the construction of 13 brigantines in Tlaxcallan, using the rigging salvaged from the ships he sank at Vera Cruz.[50]

Supplemented by new arrivals from the coast, Cortés had 40 horsemen and 550 Spanish soldiers by 28 December 1520. Accompanied by 10,000 Tlaxcaltec soldiers, Cortés began his return march to the Valley of Mexico.[51] When he reached Coatepec, near Tetzcoco, nobles approached the Spaniards and invited them into the city in peace.[52] Tetzcoco was politically divided and, when the Spaniards arrived, the king, Coanacoch, and his followers fled to Tenochtitlan.[53]

The Tetzcocan crown eventually fell to Ixtlilxochitl,[54] who allied himself with Cortés, and the kings of adjacent towns soon pledged their loyalty as well, giving the Spaniards a secure base of operations in the eastern Valley of Mexico.[55] Cortés then marched south to the Chalca cities, which had long been hostile to their Aztec lords, and secured their allegiance. He also marched against Ixtlapalapan, but was forced back when the Aztecs broke the dikes and flooded the city.[56]

Following more minor battles, Cortés sent a demand for surrender, but this was rejected by Cuauhtemoc, who had succeeded Cuitlahua as king.[57] Since Tenochtitlan was supplied by canoe, and Aztec naval forces were free to attack the Spaniards anywhere along the shoreline, Cortés had to control the lake if he was to succeed. So he sent for the timbers being cut for the ships, and a large contingent of Tlaxcaltecs carried them to Tetzcoco, arriving around 1 February, and began assembling the brigantines.[58]

Next, Cortés began the first of two major campaigns to encircle and isolate the Aztecs. Marching north, he conquered Xaltocan,[59] continuing anticlockwise around the lakes. The inhabitants of Cuauhtitlan, Tenanyocan, and Azcapotzalco fled to Tlacopan, where the Spaniards were met by a large army.[60] Despite fierce resistance, they broke through and entered, sacking and burning the city, before Aztec reinforcements forced them to withdraw and return to Tetzcoco.[61]

On 5 April 1521 Cortés began his second major campaign, sweeping clockwise south of the Valley of Mexico, to conquer Cuauhnahuac.[62] He then marched back into the Valley of Mexico, to Xochimilco, only for his forces to be badly mauled and repulsed.[63] He retreated, but under constant attack continued marching clockwise around the lakes to Tlacopan, then passed through the deserted cities of Azcapotzalco, Tenanyocan, and Cuauhtitlan, retracing his earlier route until he reached Tetzcoco on 22 April.[64]

On 28 April, Cortés began his campaign to control the lakes by launching the 13 brigantines that had been assembled near Tetzcoco. Twelve of the ships were 12.8 m (42 ft) long and 2.4–2.7 m (8–9 ft) abeam, with the flagship slightly larger at 14.6 m (48 ft).[65]

The Spaniards now numbered 86 horsemen, 118 crossbowmen and harquebusiers, and 700 foot soldiers.[66] From these each ship drew 12 oarsmen (six to a side), 12 crossbowmen and harquebusiers, and a captain, making a total of 25 men per ship plus artillerymen, since each ship had a cannon mounted in the bow.[67]

The remaining forces were divided into three armies. Pedro de Alvarado commanded 30 horsemen, 18 crossbowmen and harquebusiers, 150 Spanish foot soldiers, and a force of 25,000 Tlaxcaltecs and marched to Tlacopan. Cristóbal de Olid commanded 20 crossbowmen and harquebusiers, 175 Spanish foot soldiers, and a force of 20,000 Indian allies and marched to Coyohuacan. Gonzalo de Sandoval commanded 24 horsemen, 14 harquebusiers, 13 crossbowmen, 150 Spanish foot soldiers, and a force of more than 30,000 Indian allies and marched to Ixtlapalapan.[68]

These armies left Tetzcoco on 22 May 1521, each bound for a city anchoring a major causeway to the Aztec capital. The Spaniards severed the aqueduct that brought freshwater into Tenochtitlan and then began fighting their way across the causeways toward the capital. With the attack funnelled along these relatively narrow conduits, the Spaniards could concentrate their firepower, but the Aztecs countered by building barricades.[69] Moreover, Aztec canoes assaulted the Spaniards on the sides, where they could not answer effectively.[70]

Cortés responded by breaking through the causeways, sailing his ships among the canoes, and keeping them at bay with superior speed and firepower.[71] The Aztecs responded in turn to this new threat by placing sharpened stakes in the lake floor to impale the Spanish ships and hinder their movements.[72]

The Spaniards soon learned to avoid such traps and used their ships to interdict the flow of food and water to Tenochtitlan. Famine soon gripped the city.[73] The Aztecs were also being pushed back along the causeways, though they did enjoy some success, as when the over-eager Spaniards were trapped between two Aztec forces and 68 were captured alive.[74] Ten of these Spanish captives were immediately sacrificed at the Great Temple and their severed heads were thrown back to the Spaniards at the battlefront. The others were sacrificed at the Great Temple that night, which could be seen from the Spanish camps. The sacrificed Spaniards were flayed and their faces — with beards attached — were tanned and sent to allied towns, both to solicit assistance and to warn against betraying the alliance.[75]

Despite such setbacks, the Spanish forces continued their assault on Tenochtitlan.[76] On two separate occasions armies from Matlatzinco and Malinalco marched toward Tenochtitlan, but Cortés dispatched Spanish and Indian troops to turn them away.[77]

When the Spaniards finally reached Tenochtitlan itself, they began razing all the buildings, so that the Aztecs would not use them for ambush.[78] Fighting

212

became hand-to-hand, and on 13 August, the Spaniards broke through the last Aztec defences[79] and, after a final assault, the Aztecs surrendered.[80] Once the city was lost, Cuauhtemoc fled with a fleet of 50 canoes. But Sandoval ordered the brigantines to pursue and, when García Holguin's ship overtook Cuauhtemoc, the king surrendered.[81] After the three-month siege, Tenochtitlan lay in ruins.[82] Despite the surrender, the Spaniards' Indian allies continued to attack the Aztecs for four days, killing thousands and taking booty. The city was filled with the dead, mostly the victims of starvation rather than combat; the survivors marched out of the city for the next three days, and Cortés ordered the aqueduct repaired and the dead removed and buried. Of the Spaniards, 900 survived.[83]

Explaining the conquest

The foregoing is a Spanish version of events, based primarily on the five, major, first-hand accounts,[84] which form the bedrock of most interpretations of the conquest. But, despite numerous discrepancies among these accounts, most histories of the conquest largely take the Spanish records at face value.[85] Once these are accepted, the conquest becomes a truly miraculous event in which a band of Spaniards numbering only hundreds managed to conquer an empire controlling millions of people in just two years.

Given the near-miraculous nature of this feat, how, then, can one explain the conquest? Because normal explanations do not seem adequate, a number of extraordinary ones have been offered: (a) The Aztecs believed that the Spaniards were returning gods or vassals of gods and therefore they could not prevail against them.[86] (b) The Aztecs only fought ritual wars and were therefore incapable of engaging the Spaniards in a real war of conquest like those fought in Europe.[87] (c) The confrontation with the Spaniards led to the psychological or ideological collapse of the Aztecs, leaving them incapable of sustaining any resistance.[88] (d) Cortés and the Spaniards possessed personal qualities of an extraordinary nature that enabled them to prevail over the Aztecs.[89] (e) The Spaniards were culturally, religiously, or psychologically superior to the Aztecs, and thus were able to dominate them.[90] (f) The Spaniards possessed superior military weapons and tactics that enabled them to defeat the Aztecs.[91] (g) The Aztec political system was fatally flawed, so that their empire could not stand up to the Spanish onslaught.[92] (h) The impact of smallpox, a disease hitherto unknown in the New World, was so devastating that the Aztecs were fatally weakened by the epidemic.[93] (i) Being literate, the Spaniards possessed a superior grasp of the symbolic system to the Aztecs, and this superior intellectual capability allowed them to triumph.[94]

213

Many of these explanations are far-fetched, but they have, nevertheless, been proposed because, otherwise, the seemingly astonishing defeat of the Aztecs cannot be explained, *if one accepts the Spanish version of events*. If the conquest is examined from an Indian point of view, however, things look decidedly different. Once events are presented with an understanding of indigenous history, politics, and military affairs, the Spaniards' role can no longer be seen as the impressive and pivotal event that their own chroniclers suggest it was. On the contrary, other factors become more significant, and the campaign's outcome becomes more ordinary and more understandable in the light of them.

Many of the factors suggested as pivotal to the conquest were not, in fact, as important as they are often made out to be. For instance, the various forms of psychological and ideological explanation offered by modern authors do not accord well with actual events. The Aztecs of Tenochtitlan did not surrender, did not relinquish their beliefs, and were not paralyzed, but rather fought to the end – bitterly, effectively, and valiantly – with no sign of the various forms of ideological or psychological collapse to which their defeat is often attributed.

In fact, the Spanish accounts cannot be taken at face value because they were not written to be dispassionate accounts of what happened. Rather, they were petitions for royal patronage in which the authors invariably overstated their case, placing their own actions in the best possible light. All the compilers stood to gain politically and financially if their own roles were sufficiently important, and they wrote their accounts accordingly. Moreover, events were recounted in ways that made sense to the Spaniards, though they knew little of Mesoamerican practices that even long acquaintance did little to clarify.

Accepting a Spanish-centred interpretation requires one to assume that Cortés fully understood native politics and manipulated them unerringly, which is highly unlikely. In fact, virtually everything that had to be "manipulated" was firmly in Indian control, and it was *they* who understood their political system and the personalities involved. It is much likelier that the Indians understood how the Spaniards could be exploited than that Cortés saw how he could use the Indians in a political system he clearly did not understand.

If a Spanish-centred interpretation is, for these reasons, unreliable, how would an Indian-centred one recast the conquest? Such an analysis would not support the notion that the Aztecs were defeated by a series of fortunate, though highly improbable, events from which the Spaniards benefited. Rather, it makes the actions understandable in terms of both Spanish and Indian political interests, without recourse to chance as an explanation.

Regrettably, the native accounts were all written after the conquest, and often by people who were not participants in the events they described.[95] Nor are they always dispassionate accounts. But they do include matters and perspectives absent from Spanish accounts, and adding them to the Spanish record not only serves as a corrective but offers a fuller version of the conquest, suggesting that other factors might be of importance.

Reinterpreting the conquest

Many of the things Cortés chronicled actually happened, and this re-examination need not address every detail. Moreover, the basic chronological outline found in the Spanish accounts can be employed. Reinterpreting the Conquest does, however, require a reassessment of certain key events.

While it is possible (though uncertain) that the Aztecs heard of Córdoba's arrival in Yucatán, they did meet Grijalva when he reached Veracruz in mid-June, 1518.[96] In fact, when he landed, Aztec nobles greeted Grijalva, dressed him in fine attire, and gave him gifts from Moteuczoma.[97] This first Aztec meeting with the Spaniards resulted in considerable debate among the king and his advisors. Little was resolved, but Moteuczoma did order that the coast should be watched for the return of these strangers.[98]

Although the Aztecs had not determined who these white-skinned strangers were, this meeting undermines the widely-accepted interpretation that the Aztecs thought Cortés was the returning god, Quetzalcoatl. Cortés landed in 1519, the Aztec Year 1 Reed, which was also the birth year of Quetzalcoatl and thus, presumably, the year in which he might return. But Grijalva's arrival in the Year 13 Rabbit makes this interpretation less plausible.[99] Moreover, there was little the Aztecs could have done about Cortés's arrival, no matter who he was, since he reached central Veracruz in late April, which was the end of the war season, when most of the men had to return to their fields for the summer rains that determined the agricultural season.

Cortés did ally with the disaffected Totonacs, but it is just as likely that the Totonacs initiated the relationship as to assume that the Spaniards did so. Nevertheless, securing some local alliance was crucial to Cortés's position. He faced opposition within his own camp, and only local allies could provide the necessary supplies, porters, guides, and intelligence about the lands beyond.

With Cortés's assurances, the Totonac rulers seized and imprisoned five Aztec tribute collectors. He may have seen this act as signalling a definite break with the Aztecs, but Cortés had a poor understanding of Mesoamerican political structures.

Rather than being a structurally-linked and hierarchically-controlled entity, the Aztec empire was a hegemonic polity that relied on conquest or intimidation to subdue opponents.[100] Once these were vassals, however, the Aztecs left the local rulers and armies in place and exercised their control through power – the perception that they could enforce their will should it be challenged. Consequently, no imperial offices or officeholders held the system together. Compliance ultimately depended on the tributaries' belief that the Aztecs were willing and able to enforce their will. But, the emergence of another contender would shift the local power balance, and could quickly and easily alter allegiances. Hence, the Spanish arrival changed the Totonacs' political universe, and they seized the opportunity to secure a potentially more beneficial alliance, leading Cortés to overestimate his own significance.

At Tlaxcallan, Cortés tried to capture a small party of armed Indians and was drawn into an ambush. Only his superior firepower saved him, though days of intermittent battles with a well-trained and numerically superior foe left the Spaniards in a precarious position. With their food and weapons almost exhausted, many dead, virtually everyone wounded, and his men near mutiny, Cortés was, at most, days away from total defeat. But then the two sides forged an alliance. But it was neither a Tlaxcaltec surrender to the Spaniards nor a Spanish initiative. The Tlaxcaltecs knew they could defeat the Spaniards, but they decided to form an alliance with them for their own purposes.

The decision to ally with Cortés took into account Tlaxcallan's military situation. They had been engaged in a series of wars with the Aztecs for decades and their situation was worsening. Many of their allies had been conquered or had defected to the Aztecs, and the Tlaxcaltecs were now completely encircled and cut off from external trade. Without a profound alteration of the political situation, Tlaxcallan's defeat by the Aztecs was only a matter of time.

What made an alliance with this handful of Spanish soldiers so desirable was not their numbers, but the magnifying effect they promised Tlaxcaltec forces.[101] A standard goal of Mesoamerican warfare was to breach the opposing lines, pour through, and turn their enemies' flanks, which was extremely difficult with evenly-matched armies, weapons, and tactics. Spanish cannons, harquebuses, crossbows, and horsemen could disrupt enemy lines in a way Indian arms could not match. The Spaniards were too few to follow through and exploit the advantages which their weapons offered, but the Tlaxcaltecs could use them as shock troops to breach the lines, and then allow their own vastly larger forces to pour through. Alone, the Spaniards could only hope to fend off attackers, but this alliance multiplied the effectiveness of the Tlaxcaltec army. Both sides recognized the Spaniards' technological advantages, and both may even have recognized the benefits of an alliance, but the decision to seek one lay not with the Spaniards, who were being battered, but with the Tlaxcaltecs, since only they could halt the attack and start negotiations. The Tlaxcaltecs could have defeated the Spaniards or simply withdrawn: their decision to seek an alliance was a deliberate choice and it was theirs alone. Cortés's claim to have accepted the Tlaxcaltecs as vassals is disingenuous.[102]

Cortés next marched to Cholollan for the stated purpose of gathering supplies for the march to Tenochtitlan, but Cholollan was no closer to Tenochtitlan than was Tlaxcallan, where supplies were already available, so a logistical purpose for the trip is unlikely. And Huexotzinco, which was an ally, was a full day's march closer to Tenochtitlan.[103]

The notable event in Cholollan was the massacre, which unquestionably occurred. But the Spaniards' explanations for why it occurred are, again, disingenuous. Cortés claimed that it was a pre-emptive strike against the Chololtecs who, with the aid of an Aztec army, were planning to kill the Spaniards. But it has long been noted that, despite the invoking of an Aztec army before the Cholollan massacre, there is no mention of it in Spanish accounts thereafter,[104] which throws its existence into considerable doubt. Moreover, it is unlikely that Moteuczoma even had 20,000 soldiers available to send to Cholollan as reported, since this was still the agricultural season. And even if he had, only three days had elapsed between Cortés's arrival in Cholollan and the alleged reports of that army,[105] yet Tlaxcallan lay three days' journey from Tenochtitlan each way, which would not leave enough time for a messenger – even running – to reach Tenochtitlan, and for an army to be raised, armed, supplied, and then march for three days to Cholollan.

There were, nevertheless, good reasons to remove Cholollan as a threat – not for Cortés, but for the Tlaxcaltecs. A Spanish attack on Cholollan would test their loyalty to the Tlaxcaltecs and force them into opposition to the Aztecs. But these goals could be accomplished against any Aztec tributary along the Spaniards' line of march, so why march out of their way to attack Cholollan? The answer lies in the internal politics of Mesoamerica.

The Chololtecs had been one of Tlaxcallan's strongest allies until shortly before Cortés's arrival, when they switched their allegiance to the Aztecs. But massacring their leadership was more than simple revenge for the Tlaxcaltecs.

Kings in Mesoamerica were drawn from the upper nobility. Although not usually chosen by strict hereditary succession, the king's successor did often come from among his sons. But choosing one successor also meant not selecting any of the other potential contenders and divisions fuelled by the disgruntled unchosen often ran through Mesoamerican polities. However geopolitically sound Cholollan's shift in alliance from Tlaxcallan to Tenochtitlan may have been, so dramatic a political move would have been dangerous. Whether the switch occurred during the time of a reigning king or, more likely, when a new king was about to come to power, such a move would have alienated many of the other nobles who were contenders for the kingship, especially those with ties to Tlaxcallan, since their political importance would now be diminished, along with their prospects.

Shifting allegiance from Tlaxcallan to Tenochtitlan would not only have

distressed the Tlaxcaltecs but would also have alienated their strongest supporters among the Chololtec nobility. Hence, the killing of the Chololtec rulers, the
selection of a new noble to be king, and Cholollan's realliance with Tlaxcallan,
all point to the Tlaxcaltecs being the masterminds behind the massacre. After
all, Cortés would have been unfamiliar with the way in which the institution of
kingship operated in Mesoamerica, or who among the Chololtecs fell into which
factions. But the Tlaxcaltecs were not, and killing the king and his noble
supporters left the field clear for a successor with pro-Tlaxcallan sympathies and
political support. This was not a revolution, but a *coup*, and, though a Spanish
hand was on the sword, it was guided by Indian minds.

The next peculiarity in the Spaniards' account was their selection of a route to
Tenochtitlan. Of the two feasible routes, one led toward Tetzcoco and the other
toward Chalco. Cortés claims he chose the Chalco option because the Aztecs had
set up an ambush in the other route.[106] But the one he chose was narrower, and
thus could more easily conceal an ambush, and both were equidistant from
Tenochtitlan. The choice was motivated, not by what lay along the route, but
rather by the exit point: Tetzcoco was governed by a strongly pro-Aztec king,
but Chalco bore a simmering resentment toward the Aztecs over their subjugation. Yet Cortés would have known little of this – either the routes or the
political history of the Valley of Mexico – so this decision too was probably made
by the Tlaxcaltecs.

But why would Moteuczoma have permitted Cortés to enter Tenochtitlan at
all? Perhaps he was still uncertain of Spanish intentions. But more important,
when Cortés entered on 8 November 1519, it was still the harvest season and
Moteuczoma could not muster his entire army. Moreover, the nobles of
Tenochtitlan were politically divided, and opposing Cortés might well have
emboldened his opponents. Besides, once inside Tenochtitlan, Cortés would be
within Moteuczoma's grasp where he could be seized and killed at any time.
While these considerations may help to explain Moteuczoma's willingness to
allow the Spaniards into Tenochtitlan, why would Cortés enter this city, with its
population of over 200,000? He did so because he was not free to choose. If he
failed to enter, he would lose the support of his Indian allies, leaving him
friendless and surrounded in a hostile land.

But it was Moteuczoma who was seized, and his failure to resist was clearly a
mistake, although he surely realized that his men could free him virtually at will,
and that the Spaniards could go nowhere without his acquiescence. Besides, he
may well not have regarded this with the seriousness that subsequent events
suggest he should have. But this aside, the next inadequately explained event of
the Conquest was not Cortés's victory over the vastly larger forces of Narváez –
judicious bribery of Narváez's men, surprise, and duplicity account for that – but
the Toxcatl massacre.

Pedro de Alvarado claimed he learned of an Aztec plot to attack them while Cortés was absent from the city, so in yet another pre-emptive move, he massacred the assembled nobles in the courtyard of the Great Temple. This version of events is almost certainly false. Alvarado did carry out a massacre, but the Aztecs were completely unsuspecting. Was this simply an error on Alvarado's part? No. In fact, it is likely that Cortés himself ordered the massacre. A similar massacre of the nobles in Cholollan had worked out well, and he no longer trusted Moteuczoma, who he believed was plotting with Narváez.

In other cases in which Spaniards had violated Cortés's orders, punishment was swift and harsh.[107] Yet, despite the fact that this massacre led to the worst losses the Spaniards were to suffer, Alvarado not only weathered it, but emerged in an even higher position in Cortés's army.[108] This is not on the face of it the reward meted out to someone who violated orders, but to someone who followed them: the events and their consequences suggest that Cortés ordered the massacre, but wanted it to take place while he was absent. If he failed against Narváez, whatever happened in Tenochtitlan would not matter to him, but if he succeeded, his forces would be greatly increased, and the elimination of the cream of the Aztec nobility would have strengthened his position – or so he thought. In any event, the responsibility for this lies with Cortés, though the consequences were not those he expected.

Once Cortés returned to Tenochtitlan, he found himself besieged along with Alvarado, and sought the assistance of Moteuczoma, whom he took on to the roof to order his people to stop the attack, but to no avail. The Spanish accounts say that Moteuczoma was struck by a stone thrown from below by his own people, and that he subsequently died from the blow. Aztec accounts, however, claim that Moteuczoma was killed by the Spaniards and that, after they fled the city, his body was found, bearing Spanish knife wounds.[109] These accounts have a truer ring. Depending, as it did, on maintaining the outward appearance of power in order to hold his office, Moteuczoma's position had steadily eroded since he was seized. And the Toxcatl massacre was the final straw: a successor was named and Moteuczoma could no longer aid the Spaniards. Moteuczoma as a prisoner was now a liability rather than an asset – he could not command his people, yet his continued captivity might still inspire Aztec attacks. Released, he would at best, be ignored, but might still unite his people against the Spaniards, so that they had little to gain by keeping him alive, but more to gain if he died.[110]

When Cortés fled Tenochtitlan, he was welcomed in Tlaxcallan, where his fate was again decided by the Tlaxcaltecs rather than by the Spaniards. Cortés had proved a disappointment and could not carry out a conquest by himself. He was still valuable to the Tlaxcaltecs, however, since they could exploit his shock power to increase the effectiveness of their own troops. So, after considerable deliberation, the Tlaxcaltecs decided to continue their alliance with him.[111]

Cortés had one other ally in his subsequent efforts to conquer Mexico: small-pox. A member of Narváez's expedition was infected and touched off an epi-demic that killed some 40 per cent of the population of central Mexico in a year, including Moteuczoma's successor, King Cuitlahua, who ruled for only 80 days.[112] While this plague unquestionably affected the course of the conquest, the epidemic spread and devastated both Aztecs and their opponents, with the net effect that both sides were reduced. Thus, the devastation wrought by the smallpox cannot account for the conquest of itself, but the loss of Cuitlahua did mean the Aztecs had three successive kings in less than six months, with all the political disruption that that entailed.

By his own account, Cortés next turned to the conquest of towns near Tlaxcallan.[113] But many of these and later "conquests" were little more than defections, resulting from internal factional politics, since Aztec succession problems prevented them from making a strong showing to support their tributaries.[114] Each city-state's king also had potential rivals among his own nobles, and the arrival of the Tlaxcaltecs buttressed by Spaniards offered a major opportunity for a power shift. Kings loyal to the Aztecs often had rivals who approached the Spaniards with intelligence, expecting to seize the throne in the event of a Spanish victory. And kings who sought a new ally were threatened by rivals who would then try to maintain their Aztec ties and seize the throne in that way. But even when kings resisted and were defeated, shifting loyalty was both simple and logical, given the hegemonic imperial system. In short, the Spaniards altered the extant political equation, but the choices and possibilities were all inherent in the Mesoamerican political system, and it was the Indians, not the Spaniards, who recognized and seized these opportunities.[115]

A large question is why the Aztecs failed to follow up their rout of Cortés. Tenochtitlan was in turmoil as a result of the death of Moteuczoma, and the period between the Spaniards' flight and the death of Cuitlahua was still the agricultural season when raising a large army would be economically devas-tating. Moreover, there were sound reasons for adopting a defensive posture in Tenochtitlan rather than taking the offensive against the Spaniards in Tlaxcallan. First, remaining in and around Tenochtitlan minimized Aztec logistical difficulties and allowed them to assemble the largest possible army, leaving the enemy with the problem of mounting and supplying a force far from home. Secondly, it allowed them to bring food into the city by canoe far more easily and cheaply than their enemies could supply themselves by land. Thirdly, it gave the Aztecs much greater mobility because their canoes enjoyed shorter interior lines of communication through the valley, while their enemies would be forced to march around the valley along the shore. Fourthly, the Aztecs could mobilize, concentrate, and support troops by canoe at any point around the valley, depriving their enemies of a secure rear and forcing them to defend everywhere at once. Fifthly, with their great canoe fleets, the Aztecs would not be hemmed in by land assaults and could reinforce their own land forces, greatly complicating any enemy attack. Sixthly, horses would be of little use against the island city of Tenochtitlan as an attack would have to move along the causeways where they had little room to manoeuvre and could more easily be hemmed in and defeated. Seventhly, the Spaniards' ability to disrupt Aztec formations would be limited because of the depth of their lines on the causeways and the Aztecs could adopt effective countermeasures. Finally, channelling the offensive along the causeways also minimized the number of enemies that could fight at any one time, greatly reducing any numerical advantage. In sum, withdrawing to Tenochtitlan would minimize their enemies' main advantages and force them onto the offensive that would require greater risks and higher losses.

Accepting the logic of this position, Cortés and his allies did not wage the same battle they fought the first time. Then, Cortés had been trapped inside the city, cut off from outside support, and assailed from all sides. When his supplies ran out, he was forced to flee. The goal now was to reverse that situation, cut the Aztecs off from outside support, besiege their capital, and force them to fight under conditions of Cortés's choosing.

But what helped the Spaniards most was the internal politics of Tetzcoco. The Aztec support for Cacama to succeed King Nezahualpilli, who died in 1515, had alienated other contenders. Notable among these was Ixtlilxochitl, who fled, raised an army, and conquered the area north of Tetzcoco, which he then ruled in an uneasy accommodation with Tenochtitlan.[116]

When Cortés reached Tetzcoco, the reigning king fled, and Ixtlilxochitl eventually assumed the throne,[117] giving the Spaniards an ideal base for their attack and enormously simplifying the logistical difficulties of bringing additional troops from Tlaxcallan. Other cities hostile to the Aztecs followed suit, freeing Cortés to pursue his twin treks around the Valley with the aim of cutting Tenochtitlan off from external support.

The Aztecs were, nevertheless, able to strike throughout the Valley by canoe, making Cortés seek to control the lakes with his brigantines. But just as tens of thousands of Indian allies joined the 500 Spanish soldiers who comprised less than one per cent of the total force, thousands of Indian canoes joined the 13 brigantines to barricade Tenochtitlan. Just as the Spanish land forces could not conquer Tenochtitlan alone, so their ships alone could not barricade it. Both Spanish soldiers and brigantines were crucial in their respective roles, although not enough by themselves. Both played essential roles in shock tactics but, without vastly larger native supporting forces to exploit the breaches each made respectively, neither Spanish force could have carried through effectively. Thus, most of the task of barricading Tenochtitlan fell to the thousands of allied canoes that supported the brigantines, and the city was slowly brought to its knees as they cut off the flow of food and water.[118]

The siege was not, however, simply a matter of grinding down the opposition. As the fortunes of war waxed and waned, allies joined and deserted the Spanish side. In one disastrous engagement, 68 Spaniards were captured and publicly sacrificed during the next few days, the skin of their faces and hands being tanned and sent to wavering Aztec tributaries.[119] Following this, many of Cortés's allies departed and he was besieged in his camp for days, able to stave off defeat only because the Aztecs could not maintain a solid front in the face of Spanish arms.[120] Eventually, when Cortés's allies saw that he had not been destroyed, they returned.[121] But, tellingly, no city beyond the Valley of Mexico came to the Aztecs' aid. The two cities the Spaniards claim did so, Malinalco and Matlatzinco,[122] were too small and too distant to be significant threats. Spanish forces were sent against them, although, in all likelihood, these cities were just attacking traditional enemy city-states,[123] not the Spaniards. But, as these cities were already allied with Cortés, they sought Spanish assistance under the pretext that the invaders were supporting the Aztecs. Being dependent upon Indian soldiers, the Spaniards sent aid to avoid losing their allies.

The conquest of Mexico was a campaign fought in fits and starts. The Aztecs mounted clever responses to Spanish tactics, but, in the end, Tenochtitlan fell, not to a handful of Spaniards, but to tens of thousands of Indians.

The Spanish arrival presented groups such as the Tlaxcaltecs with new political opportunities, which they ultimately seized. Cortés unquestionably brought new and effective military technologies to the confrontation — steel swords, metal armour, harquebuses, crossbows, cannons, horses, and ships — but the Aztecs altered their tactics to counter some of these innovations. Horses were attacked from the sides in situations in which they could not respond — from canoes along the causeways and from rooftops in city streets — and courtyards were strewn with stones so they could not gallop. The Aztecs quickly learned that cannons and harquebuses fired only in straight lines and quickly adapted by jumping aside or ducking on discharge. And barricades were built against cannon fire. Native arms could not penetrate steel, but the Aztecs quickly learned to push the heavily armoured Spaniards off the causeways to drown in the lakes, and they even dug pits on either side for the purpose. These tactics could minimize, but not nullify, the effect of European arms.

Spanish weapons made the conquest of Mexico feasible, not because they defeated the Aztecs, but because the Indians recognized the potential of these arms for multiplying their own effectiveness and allowing tens and even hundreds of thousands of Indian soldiers and auxiliaries to execute the conquest. The

Spaniards were so few that their technology alone was not that important; what tipped the balance was the way it was coupled with Indian forces. Spanish arms could disrupt opposing formations in a way that native arms could not, but the victories were won by large numbers of allied Indian troops who exploited these breaches.

The key to the conquest was understanding and manipulating the political organization of Mesoamerican states and empires, the nature of rule and patterns of royal succession, and the individuals and factions involved. Cortés lacked the detailed knowledge or understanding necessary to determine which faction to attack and which to support: only the Indians had this knowledge. The political manipulations that brought in men and materiel were engineered by the Indians in the furtherance of their own factional interests. The Tlaxcaltecs could have destroyed the Spaniards, either in their initial clashes or after their flight from Tenochtitlan, but their leaders recognized the advantages to be gained by an alliance, and it was they, not Cortés, who made the decisions. The conquest was not primarily a conflict between Mexico and Spain, but between the Aztecs and the various Mesoamerican groups who used Cortés for their own purposes. The clash centred on issues internal to Mesoamerica; Cortés neither represented the forces of Spain nor did he have formal Spanish backing. Instead, he fought on his own behalf in hope of eventual Spanish royal recognition and support.

When Tenochtitlan fell, it was not the conquest of the entire Aztec empire, but of the capital, since most Aztec allies did not participate. Generally, when a Mesoamerican empire fell, its constituent cities continued independently, or with new overlords. Much the same would have been expected when the Aztecs fell, and certainly their defeat meant that former tributaries were freed. It also left them vulnerable, however, and they were separated and easily defeated in the subsequent Spanish pacification operations, although much of this was accomplished with the help of Tlaxcaltec soldiers.

Most of Cortés's Indian allies were, however, primarily concerned with local matters. And, however tumultuous an event, the overthrow was seen by the Indians as just another normal piece of political restructuring, a shift in the hierarchy rather than a fundamental change in the system itself.

The goals of Spaniards and Indians overlapped, but differed fundamentally. Both wanted to defeat the Aztecs, but the Indians would also have seen their main purpose as conquering tributaries and making themselves lords, in a continuation of the same system. The Spaniards, by contrast, were intent on conquest in a European sense, and sought to subjugate the Aztecs and everyone else in Mesoamerica, installing new rulers even at the level of city-states and towns, introducing a new religious order, and using the wealth of this new land for their own and Spain's benefit. In short, the Indians sought a change in the regime, whereas the Spaniards sought a change in the system. As long as the battle continued, their goals converged, since both focused on defeating the Aztecs; but once it was over, the Spaniards moved to consolidate their position, while the Indians were content to leave the situation largely as it was.

Why, however, did the Tlaxcaltecs not emerge as the dominant power? One reason was that they were poorly positioned, both geographically and socially. They were the most powerful single group after the conquest, but they were still not as strong as the Aztecs had been, and they lacked the population needed to support an army capable of dominating large areas. Besides, they were not the only power to survive the conquest. Tetzcoco and their subject cities emerged as a power too, though, like Tlaxcallan, they were not overwhelming. Neither the Tlaxcaltecs nor the Tetzcocas were powerful enough to seize control, and neither were the Spaniards. But their post-conquest political manipulations made them seem dominant. Allied with several independent powers, including Tlaxcallan, Tetzcoco, and the Chalcas, the Spaniards could play one group off against the others and keep any one from gaining dominance. Moreover, despite having been allied against a common enemy, many Mesoamerican city-states still regarded each other as enemies, so that no consolidation under the banner of one was likely. None of their allies bore old grudges against the Spaniards, who used that position both to block the rise of any of the indigenous powers and to advance themselves.

Even though they seized nominal control of Mesoamerica by virtue of their occupation of Tenochtitlan, the Spaniards were weak. They knew that they lacked real control, and in the early colonial years armed Spaniards were ordered to Tenochtitlan (now Mexico City) to repel an Indian rebellion that never happened.[124] Only later, with the arrival of more Spaniards, more munitions, and the subversion of native culture and political autonomy, did Spanish control seem assured.

With the fall of Tenochtitlan, and the alliance of the other significant groups in and around the Valley of Mexico, little remained in the Spaniards' way. The object lesson of the Aztecs' destruction was not lost, and even the Tarascan empire surrendered with little struggle.[125] That left few opponents more powerful than city-states, and in the three years following Tenochtitlan's fall virtually every Mexican city came under Spanish control, some by capitulation, others by the sword, but none presenting major problems. The highland Maya cities also fell rapidly but, despite incursions, some Maya cities in the lowland jungle survived, the last surrendering to Spanish domination more than a century and a half later. Elsewhere in the Maya region the Spaniards controlled areas along the coast, as the malaria they introduced ravaged the interior. The Spaniards also expanded into the desert northwards, far beyond the limits of the high cultures of Mesoamerica. Drawn by promises of wealth – some illusory, such as the seven cities of gold, but others realized in silver and land – the Spaniards created a series of armed settlements, yet remained besieged by the many warlike tribes they could fight and kill, but not control.

Thus, Mexico was not conquered from abroad but from within. The Spaniards were important and quickly took full credit, but they served only as the most visible, though not the most crucial, element of the conquest. This was a war fought overwhelmingly by Indians who, while taking full advantage of the Spanish presence, exploited their own unique inside knowledge of Mesoamerican political dynamics to achieve their ends. The Spaniards lacked this intimate understanding of Mesoamerican politics or the pivotal actors to enable them to do the same.

As with the Aztecs, word of Spanish successes smoothed their expansion throughout Mesoamerica, and they controlled conquered cities and provinces by co-opting the local political leadership. They also received tribute in the same fashion, relying on local functionaries to channel the flow from producer to Spaniard. But the Spaniards did not simply remove the Aztecs from the apex of their political and economic system and substitute themselves. Unlike their predecessors, who were content to leave the local political, economic, social, and religious systems intact and merely extract tribute, the Spaniards dismantled these down to the level of the individual town or city. Landed estates were created, giving Spaniards rights to native labour in a manner that rapidly diminished all but the cosmetic rights of the indigenous nobility. Native priests coexisted with Spanish for several decades, but once native schools were displaced by Spanish ones, and intellectual traditions shifted to European notions of song, verse, literacy, religion, technology, and cosmology, the native priesthood and world-views withered, leaving the Spaniards firmly in command of vast numbers of natives, whose ability to organize regionally had been undermined.

The Spaniards had a longer-term view which was based on their experiences in Europe and, to them, the conquest meant the removal of the only significant competing Mesoamerican power, leaving the Indians fully exposed to Spanish control. The Indians could only have assumed that the system which they knew would continue, and could not have anticipated the changes the Spaniards were to impose. The Spaniards focused on the control of all groups in Mesoamerica, the imposition of centralized rule, and the collection of tribute on a very broad scale. But it was the Indians who won the war. What the Spaniards won was the peace and the authorship of the main accounts. How we understand the conquest of Mexico is not a question of wading through histories written by the winners but, instead, of critically assessing the data in order to glean the truth from among the dubious claims of those who took the credit.

225

Notes

1. Where available, I have supplied citations to English translations as a concession to accessibility. For a fuller consideration of the events of the Conquest, see R. Hassig, *Mexico and the Spanish conquest* (London, Longmans, 1994).

2. B. Díaz del Castillo, *The true history of the conquest of New Spain*, A. P. Maudslay (tr.) [5 vols] (London, The Hakluyt Society, 1908–16), I, pp. 8, 11–12; P. Martyr d'Anghera, *De orbe novo: the eight decades of Peter Martyr D'Anghera* [2 vols] (New York: Burt Franklin, 1970), II, p. 6.

3. Díaz del Castillo, *True history*, I, pp. 18, 20–21; Martyr d'Anghera, *De orbe novo*, II, p. 10.

4. J. Díaz, Itinerario, in H. R. Wagner (ed.), *The discovery of New Spain in 1518 by Juan de Grijalva* (Berkeley, Calif., The Cortes Society, 1942), pp. 73–5; G. F. de Oviedo y Valdés, Fernández de Oviedo's account, in H. R. Wagner (ed.), *The discovery of New Spain in 1518 by Juan de Grijalva* (Berkeley, Calif., The Cortes Society, 1942), pp. 99–102, 105–6, 112.

5. Díaz, Itinerario, pp. 76–7, 79–82; Oviedo y Valdés, Account, pp. 114, 125, 130, 132–3.

6. Díaz del Castillo, *True history*, I, p. 70; F. López de Gómara, *Cortés: the life of the conqueror*, L. B. Simpson (tr.) (Berkeley and Los Angeles, University of California Press, 1964), p. 19.

7. Díaz del Castillo, *True history*, I, p. 90; López de Gómara, *Cortés*, pp. 20–1; Martyr d'Anghera, *De orbe novo*, II, p. 26; A. de Tapia, The chronicle of Andrés de Tapia, in P. de Fuentes (ed.), *The conquistadors: first-person accounts of the conquest of Mexico* (New York, Orion Press, 1963), pp. 19–20, 26–7.

8. F. de Aguilar, The chronicle of fray Francisco de Aguilar, in P. de Fuentes (ed.), *The conquistadors: first-person accounts of the conquest of Mexico*, (New York, Orion Press, 1963), pp. 137; H. Cortés, *Letters from Mexico*, A. Pagden (tr.) (New York, Grossman Publishers, 1971), p. 17; Díaz del Castillo, *True history*, I, pp. 100–3; López de Gómara, *Cortés*, pp. 30–2; Martyr d'Anghera, *De orbe novo*, II, pp. 28–31; Tapia, Chronicle, pp. 20–1.

9. Cortés, *Letters*, pp. 18–22; Díaz del Castillo, *True history*, I, pp. 106–10, 118–20, 153; C. Gibson, *Spain in America* (New York, Harper Torchbooks, 1966), pp. 38–9; López de Gómara, *Cortés*, pp. 37–40, 46–7; Tapia, Chronicle, p. 23.

10. Aguilar, Chronicle, pp. 67–8; Cortés, *Letters*, p. 24; Díaz del Castillo, *True history*, I, 137–40; López de Gómara, *Cortés*, p. 56; Martyr d'Anghera, *De orbe novo*, II, p. 38; B. de Sahagún, *Florentine codex: general history of the things of New Spain. Book 12 – The conquest of Mexico*, A. J. O. Anderson and C. E. Dibble (tr.) (Salt Lake City, University of Utah Press, 1975), pp. 5–6; Tapia, Chronicle, p. 25.

11. J. de Acosta, *The natural and moral history of the Indies* [2 vols] (New York, Burt Franklin, 1970–3), II, p. 515; Díaz del Castillo, *True history*, I, pp. 140–2, 145; López de Gómara, *Cortés*, pp. 57–59; Sahagún, *Book 12*, p. 6.

12. Díaz del Castillo, *True history*, I, pp. 151–3; López de Gómara, *Cortés*, p. 61; Martyr d'Anghera, *De orbe novo*, II, p. 59; Tapia, Chronicle, p. 25.

13. Cortés, *Letters*, pp. 25–7; Díaz del Castillo, *True history*, I, pp. 153, 155–7; F. de A. Ixtlilxóchitl, *Obras completas* [2 vols] (Mexico City, Universidad Autónoma Nacional de México, 1975–7), II, p. 202; López de Gómara, *Cortés*, pp. 67–8.

14. Díaz del Castillo, *True history*, I, pp. 166–74; Ixtlilxóchitl, *Obras*, II, pp. 203–4; López de Gómara, *Cortés*, pp. 69, 72–3, 76–80; Tapia, Chronicle, p. 25.

15. Aguilar, Chronicle, pp. 138–9; Cortés, *Letters*, pp. 51–3; Dípaz del Castillo, *True history*, I, pp. 206, 208–9, 211–15; López de Gómara, *Cortés*, pp. 89–90; Martyr d'Anghera, *De orbe novo*, II, p. 62; Tapia, Chronicle, pp. 25–6.

16. Díaz del Castillo, *True history*, I, pp. 140–1, 208–9, 211, 217–18, 268; Ixtlilxóchitl, *Obras*, II, p. 208; López de Gómara, *Cortés*, pp. 91, 93; Martyr d'Anghera, *De orbe novo*, II, p. 61.

17. Díaz del Castillo, *True history*, I, pp. 223, 225–7; López de Gómara, *Cortés*, pp. 97; Martyr d'Anghera, *De orbe novo*, II, p. 66; D. Muñoz Camargo, Descripción de la ciudad y provincia de Tlaxcala, in *Relaciones geográficas del siglo XVI* [10 vols] (Mexico City, Universidad Nacional Autónoma de México, 1982–7), IV, pp. 233–4; G. F. de Oviedo y Valdés, *Historia general y natural de las Indias* [5 vols] (Madrid, Ediciones Atlas, 1959), IV, p. 15.

18. Aguilar, Chronicle, pp. 139–40; Díaz del Castillo, *True history*, I, pp. 228–30; Ixtlilxóchitl, *Obras*, II, p. 208; López de Gómara, *Cortés*, pp. 99–101; Martyr d'Anghera, *De orbe novo*, II, pp. 68–9; Oviedo y Valdés, *Historia general*, IV, p. 16; Tapia, Chronicle, p. 28–9.

19. Díaz del Castillo, *True history*, I, pp. 231–4, 237–9; Martyr d'Anghera, *De orbe novo*, II, p. 69.

20. Díaz del Castillo, *True history*, I, pp. 229–30, 235.

21. Aguilar, Chronicle, p. 142; Díaz del Castillo, *True history*, I, pp. 26–66, 274; López de Gómara, *Cortés*, pp. 117–18; D. Muñoz Camargo, *Historia de Tlaxcala* (Guadalajara, Mexico, Edmundo Aviña Levy, 1966), pp. 187–8; Muñoz Camargo, Descripción, IV, p. 236; Oviedo y Valdés, *Historia general*, IV, p. 20; Tapia, Chronicle, p. 32.

22. Aguilar, Chronicle, p. 143; Díaz del Castillo, *True history*, I, pp. 290–2; Ixtlilxóchitl, *Obras*, II, p. 214; López de Gómara, *Cortés*, pp. 123–4; Martyr d'Anghera, *De orbe novo*, II, pp. 78–9; Oviedo y Valdés, *Historia general*, IV, p. 22.

23. Cortés, *Letters*, pp. 73–4; Díaz del Castillo, *True history*, II, pp. 1–3, 5; Tapia, Chronicle, p. 33.

24. Aguilar, Chronicle, p. 144; S. A. M. Chimalpahin Cuauhtlehuanitzin, S. A. M., *Relaciones originales de Chalco Amaquemecan* (Mexico City, Universidad Nacional Autónoma de México, 1965), p. 234; Cortés, *Letters*, pp. 73–4; Díaz del Castillo, *True history*, II, pp. 4–5, 7, 13, 15; Ixtlilxóchitl, *Obras*, II, p. 216; López de Gómara, *Cortés*, pp. 124, 126–9; Martyr d'Anghera, *De orbe novo*, II, pp. 81–2; Muñoz Camargo, *Historia*, p. 213; Muñoz Camargo, Descripción, IV, pp. 250–1; Oviedo y Valdés, *Historia general*, IV, pp. 22–3; Sahagún, *Book 12*, p. 29; B. de Sahagún, *Conquest of New Spain: 1585 revision* (Salt Lake City, University of Utah Press, 1989), p. 58; Tapia, Chronicle, p. 34–6.

25. Aguilar, Chronicle, p. 145; Chimalpahin, *Relaciones*, p. 234; Cortés, *Letters*, pp. 76–9; Díaz del Castillo, *True history*, II, pp. 28–31; Ixtlilxóchitl, *Obras*, II, p. 217; López de Gómara, *Cortés*, pp. 134–6; Martyr d'Anghera, *De orbe novo*, II, pp. 88–9; Oviedo y Valdés, *Historia general*, IV, pp. 28–9; Sahagún, *Book 12*, p. 37; Sahagún, *Conquest*, pp. 64–5.

26. Acosta, *Natural and moral history*, II, p. 518; Aguilar, Chronicle, pp. 145–6; Alvarado Tezozómoc, *Crónica mexicáyotl* (Mexico City, Universidad Nacional Autónoma de México, 1975), pp. 148–9; Chimalpahin, *Relaciones*, pp. 121, 235; Cortés, *Letters*, pp. 81, 84; Díaz del Castillo, *True history*, II, pp. 35–41; D. Durán, *The history of the Indies of New Spain*, Doris Heyden (tr.) (Norman, University of Oklahoma Press, 1994), pp. 525, 529–30; F. de A. Ixtlilxóchitl, *Ally of Cortes: account 13: of the coming of the Spaniards and the beginning of the evangelical law*, D. K. Ballentine (tr.) (Texas Western Press, El Paso, 1969), pp. 4–5; Ixtlilxóchitl, *Obras*, II, p. 217, 18; López de Gómara, *Cortés*, pp. 136–9; Martyr d'Anghera, *De orbe novo*, II, pp. 89–90, 93–4; Muñoz Camargo, *Historia*, p. 215; Muñoz Camargo, Descripción, IV, p. 251; Oviedo y Valdés, *Historia general*, IV, pp. 30–1; Sahagún, *Book 12*, pp. 37, 43–4; Sahagún, *Conquest*, pp. 65–9; Tapia, Chronicle, p. 38.

27. Acosta, *Natural and moral history*, II, p. 519; Aguilar, Chronicle, p. 146; Cortés, *Letters*, p. 87; Díaz del Castillo, *True history*, II, pp. 43, 54–5; Ixtlilxóchitl, *Obras*, II, p. 218; López de Gómara, *Cortés*, p. 140.

28. Aguilar, Chronicle, p. 145; Cortés, Letters, pp. 83–4; Díaz del Castillo, True history, II, pp. 64–5, 85–6; López de Gómara, Cortés, pp. 152, 159; Tapia, Chronicle, p. 37.

29. Cortés, Letters, p. 87; Díaz del Castillo, True history, II, pp. 87, 89–90; Ixtlilxóchitl, Obras, II, pp. 218–19; Martyr d'Anghera, De orbe novo, II, pp. 97–8; Oviedo y Valdés, Historia general, IV, p. 33.

30. Acosta, Natural and moral history, II, pp. 519–20; Aguilar, Chronicle, p. 148; Chimalpahin, Relaciones, p. 235; Cortés, Letters, pp. 88–91; Díaz del Castillo, True history, II, pp. 87, 93–6; Ixtlilxóchitl, Obras, II, pp. 218–19; López de Gómara, Cortés, pp. 169–71; Martyr d'Anghera, De orbe novo, II, pp. 98–100; Tapia, Chronicle, pp. 38–9.

31. Aguilar, Chronicle, p. 149; Cortés, Letters, p. 91; Díaz del Castillo, True history, II, pp. 97–8; Ixtlilxóchitl, Obras, II, pp. 221–3; López de Gómara, Cortés, pp. 170, 176–7; Martyr d'Anghera, De orbe novo, II, pp. 98–9; Oviedo y Valdés, Historia general, IV, pp. 34–5.

32. Chimalpahin, Relaciones, p. 235; Cortés, Letters, pp. 97–8; Díaz del Castillo, True history, II, pp. 115–16, 121–2; López de Gómara, Cortés, pp. 182–4; Martyr d'Anghera, De orbe novo, II, pp. 103–5; Oviedo y Valdés, Historia general, IV, pp. 40–1; Tapia, Chronicle, p. 40.

33. Aguilar, Chronicle, p. 149; Cortés, Letters, pp. 113–15; Díaz del Castillo, True history, II, pp. 153–4, 157–8; López de Gómara, Cortés, p. 191; Martyr d'Anghera, De orbe novo, II, p. 127; Muñoz Camargo, Historia, p. 215; Oviedo y Valdés, Historia general, IV, pp. 52–3; Tapia, Chronicle, p. 44.

34. Aguilar, Chronicle, p. 150; Cortés, Letters, pp. 81–9; Demanda de Ceballos en nombre de Pánfilo de Narváez contra Hernando Cortés y sus compañeros, in J. García Icazbalceta (ed.), Colección de documentos para la historica de México [2 vols] (Mexico City, Editorial Porrúa, 1971), I, pp. 437–44; Díaz del Castillo, True history, II, pp. 153–220; López de Gómara, Cortés, pp. 192–205; Martyr d'Anghera, De orbe novo, II, pp. 129–31; Muñoz Camargo, Historia, p. 216; Muñoz Camargo, Descripción, IV, p. 251; Oviedo y Valdés, Historia general, IV, pp. 52–60; Tapia, Chronicle, pp. 45–8.

35. Aguilar, Chronicle, p. 151; Díaz del Castillo, True history, II, pp. 171; Ixtlilxóchitl, Obras, II, p. 227; B. de Sahagún, Florentine codex: general history of the things of New Spain. Book 2 – The ceremonies (Salt Lake City, University of Utah Press, 1981), pp. 9–10, 66–77; Tapia, Chronicle, p. 45.

36. Acosta, Natural and moral history, II, p. 520; Chimalpahin, Relaciones, p. 121; Códice Aubin (Mexico City: Editorial Innovación, 1980), p. 85; Díaz del Castillo, True history, II, pp. 219–20; D. Durán, Book of the gods and rites and the ancient calendar, F. Horcasitas and D. Heyden (tr.) (Norman, University of Oklahoma Press, 1971), p. 77; Durán, History, pp. 536–8; Ixtlilxóchitl, Ally of Cortes, pp. 7–9; Ixtlilxóchitl, Obras, II, p. 228; López de Gómara, Cortés, pp. 207–8; Muñoz Camargo, Historia, p. 216; Sahagún, Book 12, pp. 51–7; Sahagún, Conquest, pp. 74–8.

37. Cortés, Letters, pp. 128–30; Díaz del Castillo, True history, II, pp. 220–2; Ixtlilxóchitl, Obras, II, p. 229; López de Gómara, Cortés, p. 206; Oviedo y Valdés, Historia general, IV, p. 60.

38. Aguilar, Chronicle, p. 152; Chimalpahin, Relaciones, p. 121; Cortés, Letters, p. 130; Díaz del Castillo, True history, II, pp. 228–9; López de Gómara, Cortés, p. 211; Martyr d'Anghera, De orbe novo, II, p. 132; Sahagún, Book 12, p. 59.

39. Acosta, Natural and moral history, II, p. 521; Alvarado Tezozómoc, Crónica, p. 149; Códice Aubin, pp. 82, 86; Cortés, Letters, p. 132; Díaz del Castillo, True history, II, pp. 232–8; Ixtlilxóchitl, Obras, II, p. 229; López de Gómara, Cortés, p. 212; Martyr d'Anghera, De orbe novo, II, pp. 135–6; Muñoz Camargo, Historia, p. 217; Muñoz Camargo, Descripción, IV, p. 252; Oviedo y Valdés, Historia general, IV, pp. 62–3.

40. Acosta, *Natural and moral history*, II, pp. 521–2; Aguilar, Chronicle, pp. 151, 153–6; Chimalpahin, *Relaciones*, p. 122; G. R. G. Conway (ed.), *La noche triste. Documentos: Segura de la Frontera en Nueva España, año de MDXX* (Mexico City: Antiguo Librería Robredo de José Porrúa e hijos, 1953), pp. 8, 17, 22, 25, 28, 30; Cortés, *Letters*, pp. 137–8; Díaz del Castillo, *True history*, II, pp. 242, 244–7, 249; Ixtlilxóchitl, *Obras*, II, p. 230; López de Gómara, *Cortés*, pp. 219–22; Muñoz Camargo, *Historia*, pp. 218–20; Muñoz Camargo, Descripción, IV, p. 253; Oviedo y Valdés, *Historia general*, IV, pp. 65, 68.

41. Díaz del Castillo, *True history*, II, p. 250.

42. Aguilar, Chronicle, p. 156; Cortés, *Letters*, p. 142; Díaz del Castillo, *True history*, II, pp. 252–4; Durán, *History*, pp. 545–7; Martyr d'Anghera, *De orbe novo*, II, p. 144; Sahagún, *Book 12*, p. 79; Sahagún, *Conquest*, pp. 96–7.

43. Chimalpahin, *Relaciones*, p. 236; Cortés, *Letters*, pp. 143–4; Díaz del Castillo, *True history*, II, pp. 256–63; Martyr d'Anghera, *De orbe novo*, II, p. 145; Oviedo y Valdés, *Historia general*, IV, p. 71.

44. Cortés, *Letters*, pp. 144–5; Díaz del Castillo, *True history*, II, pp. 263, 269; Oviedo y Valdés, *Historia general*, IV, p. 74.

45. Aguilar, Chronicle, p. 157; Díaz del Castillo, *True history*, II, pp. 269–70; Ixtlilxóchitl, *Obras*, II, p. 238; Martyr d'Anghera, *De orbe novo*, II, p. 146; Muñoz Camargo, *Historia*, p. 236; Muñoz Camargo, Descripción, IV, p. 262.

46. Cortés, *Letters*, p. 146; Díaz del Castillo, *True history*, II, pp. 270–3; Oviedo y Valdés, *Historia general*, IV, p. 75.

47. Cortés, *Letters*, pp. 147–8; Díaz del Castillo, *True history*, II, pp. 273.

48. Cortés, *Letters*, pp. 149–55; Díaz del Castillo, *True history*, II, pp. 278–80; Oviedo y Valdés, *Historia general*, IV, pp. 77–80; Sahagún, *Conquest*, p. 102.

49. Cortés, *Letters*, p. 165; Díaz del Castillo, *True history*, II, pp. 290, 301.

50. Aguilar, Chronicle, p. 157; Cortés, *Letters*, pp. 157, 161; Díaz del Castillo, *True history*, II, pp. 300, 302, 304; Martyr d'Anghera, *De orbe novo*, II, pp. 149–50; Muñoz Camargo, *Historia*, p. 237; Sahagún, *Conquest*, pp. 103–4.

51. Cortés, *Letters*, p. 166; Díaz del Castillo, *True History*, IV, p. 1; Ixtlilxóchitl, *Ally of Cortes*, p. 11; López de Gómara, *Cortés*, p. 239.

52. Aguilar, Chronicle, p. 158; Cortés, *Letters*, pp. 168–70; Díaz del Castillo, *True history*, IV, pp. 3–5; Durán, *History*, p. 550; Ixtlilxóchitl, *Ally of Cortes*, pp. 11–12; López de Gómara, *Cortés*, p. 244.

53. Aguilar, Chronicle, p. 158; Alvarado Tezozómoc, *Crónica*, p. 149; Cortés, *Letters*, p. 172; Díaz del Castillo, *True history*, IV, pp. 7–8; Ixtlilxóchitl, *Ally of Cortes*, pp. 12–13; Ixtlilxóchitl, *Obras*, II, pp. 241–2; López de Gómara, *Cortés*, p. 245; Oviedo y Valdés, *Historia general*, IV, p. 89.

54. Díaz del Castillo, *True history*, IV, pp. 8–9; Ixtlilxóchitl, *Ally of Cortes*, pp. 12–15; Ixtlilxóchitl, *Obras*, II, pp. 390–1; J. A. Offner, *Law and politics in Aztec Texcoco* (Cambridge, Cambridge University Press, 1983), pp. 239–40.

55. Cortés, *Letters*, pp. 173–4; Díaz del Castillo, *True history*, IV, p. 9; López de Gómara, *Cortés*, p. 245.

56. Cortés, *Letters*, pp. 174–5; Díaz del Castillo, *True history*, IV, pp. 10–13; Ixtlilxóchitl, *Ally of Cortes*, p. 13; Ixtlilxóchitl, *Obras*, II, p. 246; López de Gómara, *Cortés*, pp. 246–7; Oviedo y Valdés, *Historia general*, IV, pp. 90–1.

57. Díaz del Castillo, *True history*, IV, pp. 21–3.

58. Cortés, *Letters*, pp. 185–6; Díaz del Castillo, *True history*, IV, pp. 24, 27–8; Durán, *History*, pp. 549–50; Ixtlilxóchitl, *Ally of Cortes*, p. 15; Ixtlilxóchitl, *Obras*, II, p. 391; López de

Gómara, *Cortés*, pp. 249–51; Martyr d'Anghera, *De orbe novo*, II, pp. 172–3; Muñoz Camargo, *Historia*, p. 237; Oviedo y Valdés, *Historia general*, IV, pp. 95–6.

59. Cortés, *Letters*, pp. 186–7; Díaz del Castillo, *True history*, IV, pp. 30–4; Ixtlilxóchitl, *Ally of Cortes*, pp. 15–16; Ixtlilxóchitl, *Obras*, II, p. 247; López de Gómara, *Cortés*, pp. 251–2; Oviedo y Valdés, *Historia general*, IV, p. 98.

60. Cortés, *Letters*, p. 187; Díaz del Castillo, *True history*, IV, pp. 34–5; Ixtlilxóchitl, *Ally of Cortes*, p. 16; Ixtlilxóchitl, *Obras*, II, p. 247; López de Gómara, *Cortés*, p. 252; Oviedo y Valdés, *Historia general*, IV, p. 99.

61. Cortés, *Letters*, pp. 187–8; Díaz del Castillo, *True history*, IV, pp. 35–7; Ixtlilxóchitl, *Ally of Cortes*, p. 16; López de Gómara, *Cortés*, p. 252; Sahagún, *Book 12*, p. 81.

62. Cortés, *Letters*, pp. 191–4, 197–8; Díaz del Castillo, *True history*, IV, pp. 55–6, 58–70; Ixtlilxóchitl, *Ally of Cortes*, pp. 18–19; López de Gómara, *Cortés*, pp. 256–9.

63. Cortés, *Letters*, pp. 198–9; Díaz del Castillo, *True history*, IV, pp. 70–9; Ixtlilxóchitl, *Ally of Cortes*, p. 20; Ixtlilxóchitl, *Obras*, II, p. 252; López de Gómara, *Cortés*, p. 259.

64. Cortés, *Letters*, pp. 202–4; Díaz del Castillo, *True history*, IV, pp. 81–2, 85–6; Ixtlilxóchitl, *Ally of Cortes*, pp. 20–1; Ixtlilxóchitl, *Obras*, II, pp. 252–4; López de Gómara, *Cortés*, p. 261.

65. Aguilar, Chronicle, p. 158; Cortés, *Letters*, p. 206; C. H. Gardiner, *Naval power in the conquest of Mexico* (Austin, University of Texas Press, 1959), pp. 125–6; Ixtlilxóchitl, *Ally of Cortes*, p. 21; López de Gómara, *Cortés*, p. 262; Martyr d'Anghera, *De orbe novo*, II, p. 173. For a fuller consideration of these reconstructions, see Gardiner, *Naval power*, pp. 130–2.

66. Cortés, *Letters*, pp. 207–8; Díaz del Castillo, *True history*, IV, pp. 91–3; Ixtlilxóchitl, *Ally of Cortes*, p. 14; Ixtlilxóchitl, *Obras*, II, pp. 255–6.

67. Cortés, *Letters*, pp. 206–7; Díaz del Castillo, *True history*, IV, pp. 93–4; Gardiner, *Naval power*, p. 125; Sahagún, *Conquest*, p. 104.

68. Aguilar, Chronicle, p. 158; Cortés, *Letters*, p. 208; Díaz del Castillo, *True history*, IV, pp. 99–101; Durán, *History*, pp. 550–1; Ixtlilxóchitl, *Ally of Cortes*, p. 23; Ixtlilxóchitl, *Obras*, II, p. 256; López de Gómara, *Cortés*, pp. 263–4; Oviedo y Valdés, *Historia general*, IV, p. 115.

69. Sahagún, *Book 12*, pp. 86, 114.

70. *ibid.*, pp. 84, 86.

71. Díaz del Castillo, *True history*, IV, pp. 112–16; Ixtlilxóchitl, *Ally of Cortes*, p. 28; López de Gómara, *Cortés*, p. 269; Sahagún, *Conquest*, p. 109.

72. Cortés, *Letters*, p. 215; Díaz del Castillo, *True history*, IV, p. 117; Sahagún, *Conquest*, p. 110.

73. Díaz del Castillo, *True history*, IV, pp. 120–1.

74. Aguilar, Chronicle, p. 159; Díaz del Castillo, *True history*, IV, pp. 140–1, 168; Durán, *History*, pp. 552–3; Ixtlilxóchitl, *Ally of Cortes*, pp. 39–41; López de Gómara, *Cortés*, pp. 281–2; Oviedo y Valdés, *Historia general*, IV, p. 133; Sahagún, *Book 12*, p. 104; Sahagún, *Conquest*, p. 121.

75. Cortés, *Letters*, pp. 241–2; Díaz del Castillo, *True history*, IV, pp. 141, 143–5, 149–51; Ixtlilxóchitl, *Ally of Cortes*, p. 42; López de Gómara, *Cortés*, pp. 281–2; Oviedo y Valdés, *Historia general*, IV, p. 133.

76. Díaz del Castillo, *True history*, IV, pp. 161, 163.

77. Cortés, *Letters*, pp. 242–5; Ixtlilxóchitl, *Ally of Cortes*, pp. 42–3; López de Gómara, *Cortés*, pp. 283–4; Oviedo y Valdés, *Historia general*, IV, pp. 135–6.

78. Aguilar, Chronicle, p. 159; Cortés, *Letters*, p. 248; Ixtlilxóchitl, *Ally of Cortes*, pp. 43–4.

79. Acosta, *Natural and moral history*, II, p. 523; Cortés, *Letters*, pp. 260–4; Díaz del Castillo, *True history*, IV, p. 177; Ixtlilxóchitl, *Ally of Cortes*, pp. 48–51; Sahagún, *Book 12*, p. 117.

80. Cortés, *Letters*, pp. 261–4.

81. Acosta, *Natural and moral history*, II, p. 523; Aguilar, Chronicle, p. 160; Cortés, *Letters*, p. 264; Díaz del Castillo, *True history*, IV, pp. 179–81; Ixtlilxóchitl, *Ally of Cortes*, p. 52; López de Gómara, *Cortés*, pp. 291–2; Oviedo y Valdés, *Historia general*, IV, p. 151; Sahagún, *Book 12*, pp. 119–20.

82. Chimalpahin, *Relaciones*, pp. 236–7; Cortés, *Letters*, p. 265; Díaz del Castillo, *True history*, IV, p. 183; Ixtlilxóchitl, *Ally of Cortes*, p. 52; Muñoz Camargo, Descripción, IV, p. 213; Sahagún, *Book 12*, p. 120; Sahagún, *Conquest*, pp. 134–5.

83. Aguilar, Chronicle, p. 160; Díaz del Castillo, *True history*, IV, pp. 185, 187, 193; López de Gómara, *Cortés*, pp. 291, 293; Sahagún, *Book 12*, p. 85; Sahagún, *Conquest*, pp. 110, 135–7.

84. These accounts are by Hernán Cortés, Bernal Díaz del Castillo, Francisco de Aguilar, Andrés de Tapia, and the Anonymous Conquistador.

85. For example, see the works of B. C. Brundage, *A rain of darts: the Mexica Aztecs* (Austin, University of Texas Press, 1972), pp. 252–90; M. Collis, *Cortés and Montezuma* (London, Faber and Faber, 1972); N. Davies, *The Aztecs: A history* (New York, G. P. Putnam's Sons, 1974), pp. 233–83; Gibson, *Spain*, pp. 24–8; H. Innes, *The conquistadors* (New York, Alfred A. Knopf, 1969); W. W. Johnson, *Cortés: Conquering the new world* (New York, Paragon House, 1987); F. A. Kirkpatrick, *The Spanish conquistadores* (Cleveland, OH., Meridian Books, 1967), pp. 66–100; C. M. MacLachlan and J. E. Rodríguez, *The forging of the cosmic race* (Berkeley and Los Angeles, University of California Press, 1980), pp. 68–76; S. de Madariaga, *Hernán Cortés: Conqueror of Mexico* (Garden City, N.Y., Anchor Books, 1969); J. P. McHenry, *A short history of Mexico* (Garden City, N.Y., Doubleday, 1962), pp. 35–46; R. B. Merriman, *The rise of the Spanish empire in the old world and in the new* [4 vols] (New York, Cooper Square, 1962), III, pp. 458–502; R. R. Miller, *Mexico: A history* (Norman, University of Oklahoma Press, 1985), pp. 66–93; A. Moreno Toscano, El siglo de la conquista, in *Historia general de México* [2 vols] (Mexico City, El Colegio de México); H. B. Parkes, *A history of Mexico* (Boston, Houghton Mifflin, 1969), pp. 39–58; H. Thomas, *Conquest: Montezuma, Cortes, and the fall of old Mexico* (New York, Simon and Schuster, 1993), pp. 289–530; J. M. White, *Cortés and the downfall of the Aztec empire* (New York, St Martin's Press, 1971), pp. 159–262.

86. Brundage, *Rain of Darts*, p. 252; Collis, *Cortés*, pp. 55–60; Davies, *Aztecs*, pp. 239, 258–60; J. H. Elliott, The Spanish conquest and settlement in America, in L. Bethell (ed.), *The Cambridge history of Latin America, volume 1, colonial Latin America* (Cambridge, Cambridge University Press, 1984), p. 181; Innes, *Conquistadors*, p. 116; Kirkpatrick, *Conquistadores*, pp. 71–2; M. Leon-Portilla, *The broken spears: the Aztec account of the conquest of Mexico* (Boston, Beacon Press, 1966), p. 13; MacLachlan and Rodríguez, *Cosmic race*, p. 69; Madariaga, *Hernán Cortés*, pp. 16, 118–19; McHenry, *Short history*, pp. 35, 40, 41; Merriman, *Spanish empire*, III, pp. 475, 478; Miller, *Mexico*, p. 78; Moreno Toscano, El siglo, p. 313; R. C. Padden, *The hummingbird and the hawk: Conquest and sovereignty in the valley of Mexico, 1503–1541* (New York, Harper Colophon Books, 1967), pp. 118, 122–5; Parkes, *History*, p. 50; T. Todorov, *The conquest of America: the question of the other* (New York, Harper and Row, 1984), pp. 118–19.

87. Davies, *Aztecs*, p. 251; Madariaga, *Hernán Cortés*, p. 177; Merriman, *Spanish empire*, III, p. 478.

88. D. Carrasco, *Quetzalcoatl and the irony of empire: Myths and prophecies in the Aztec tradition* (Chicago, University of Chicago Press, 1982), pp. 150–1, 200–3; Elliott, Spanish conquest, pp. 181–2; MacLachlan and Rodríguez, *Cosmic race*, p. 72; Padden, *Hummingbird and the hawk*, pp. 205–7; G. C. Vaillant, *Aztecs of Mexico: Origin, rise, and fall of the Aztec nation* (Baltimore, Md., Penguin Books, 1966), p. 238.

89. Elliott, Spanish conquest, p. 175; Madariaga, *Hernán Cortés*, pp. 185–6; Merriman, *Spanish empire*, III, p. 479; Vaillant, *Aztecs of Mexico*, p. 238.

90. Davies, *Aztecs*, p. 252; J. H. Elliott, *Imperial Spain, 1469–1716* (New York, Mentor Books, 1966), p. 65, Spanish conquest, pp. 175, 180.

91. Collis, *Cortés*, p. 91; Davies, *Aztecs*, pp. 250–1; Elliott, *Imperial Spain*, p. 65; Elliott, Spanish conquest, p. 175; Gardiner, *Naval power*; Kirkpatrick, *Conquistadores*, p. 67; MacLachlan and Rodríguez, *Cosmic race*, p. 70; Merriman, *Spanish empire*, III, p. 478; Padden, *Hummingbird and the hawk*, p. 156; Todorov, *Conquest of America*, p. 61; Vaillant, *Aztecs of Mexico*, pp. 238–9; White, *Cortés and the downfall*, pp. 169, 171; E. R. Wolf, *Sons of the shaking earth* (Chicago, University of Chicago Press, 1970), p. 154.

92. Elliott, Spanish conquest, p. 183; Wolf, *Shaking earth*, pp. 154–5.

93. D. Baxby, *Jenner's smallpox vaccine: The riddle of vaccinia virus and its origin* (London, Heinemann Educational Books, 1981), p. 13; Elliott, Spanish conquest, p. 182; D. R. Hopkins, *Princes and peasants: Smallpox in history* (Chicago, University of Chicago Press, 1983), pp. 205–6; Innes, *Conquistadors*, p. 179; W. H. McNeill, *Plagues and peoples* (Garden City, N.Y., Anchor Books, 1977), p. 183; Padden, *Hummingbird and the Hawk*, p. 206; Todorov, *Conquest of America*, p. 61.

94. Todorov, *Conquest of America*, pp. 118–19.

95. For a recent translation of the major indigenous accounts in Nahuatl, see J. Lockhart, *We people here: Nahuatl accounts of the conquest of Mexico* (Berkeley and Los Angeles, University of California Press, 1993).

96. Díaz, Itinerario, pp. 76–7, 79–80; G. F. de Oviedo y Valdés, Fernández de Oviedo's account, in H. R. Wagner (ed.), *The discovery of New Spain in 1518 by Juan de Grijalva* (Berkeley, Calif., The Cortes Society, 1942), p. 114; Oviedo y Valdes, *Historia general*, II, pp. 135–6.

97. Acosta, *Natural and moral history*, II, p. 513; Ixtlilxóchitl, *Ally of Cortes*, p. 3; Sahagún, *Book 12*, pp. 5–6; Sahagún, *Conquest*, pp. 34–6.

98. Acosta, *Natural and moral history*, II, p. 513; Durán, *History*, p. 503; Sahagún, *Conquest*, p. 37.

99. Acosta, *Natural and moral history*, II, p. 514; Sahagún, *Book 12*, pp. 5, 9; Sahagún, *Conquest*, pp. 37–8, 41.

100. For a fuller consideration of the Aztec imperial system and its social implications, see R. Hassig, *Trade, tribute, and transportation: The sixteenth-century political economy of the valley of Mexico* (Norman, University of Oklahoma Press, 1985).

101. For a fuller consideration of Aztec warfare and Mesoamerican warfare generally, see R. Hassig, *Aztec warfare: Political expansion and imperial control* (Norman, University of Oklahoma Press, 1988) and R. Hassig, *War and society in ancient Mesoamerica* (Berkeley and Los Angeles, University of California Press, 1992).

102. Díaz del Castillo, *True history*, I, pp. 262, 265–6; Muñoz Camargo, *Historia*, pp. 187–8; Muñoz Camargo, Descripción, IV, p. 236.

103. Aguilar, Chronicle, p. 143; Díaz del Castillo, *True history*, I, pp. 290–2; Ixtlilxóchitl, *Obras*, II, p. 214; López de Gómara, *Cortés*, pp. 123–4; Martyr d'Anghera, *De orbe novo*, II, pp. 78–9; Oviedo y Valdés, *Historia general*, IV, p. 22.

104. H. R. Wagner, *The rise of Fernando Cortés* (Berkeley, Calif., The Cortes Society, 1944), p. 175.

105. Díaz del Castillo, *True history*, II, pp. 10–11.

106. Aguilar, Chronicle, p. 145; Chimalpahin, *Relaciones*, p. 234; Cortés, *Letters*, pp. 76–9; Díaz del Castillo, *True history*, II, pp. 28–31; Ixtlilxóchitl, *Obras*, II, p. 217; López de Gómara, *Cortés*, pp. 134–6; Martyr d'Anghera, *De orbe novo*, II, pp. 88–9; Oviedo y Valdés, *Historia general*, IV, pp. 28–9; Sahagún, *Book 12*, p. 37; Sahagún, *Conquest*, pp. 64–5.

107. e.g., see Díaz del Castillo, *True history*, I, pp. 90–1, 206–7, IV, pp. 88–91.

108. Alvarado was elevated to the position of one of the three main commanders (Aguilar, Chronicle, pp. 156–8; Cortés, *Letters*, p. 208; Díaz del Castillo, *True history*, IV, pp. 99–101; López de Gómara, *Cortés*, pp. 263–4; Oviedo y Valdés, *Historia general*, IV, p. 115).

109. Chimalpahin, *Relaciones*, p. 236; *Códice Aubin*, pp. 82, 86; Durán, *History*, pp. 540–1; Ixtlilxóchitl, *Ally of Cortés*, p. 9; Ixtlilxóchitl, *Obras*, II, p. 229; Sahagún, *Book 12*, pp. 65–6; Sahagún, *Conquest*, pp. 84–5.

110. Aguilar, Chronicle, p. 153; Chimalpahin, *Relaciones*, p. 236; Cortés, *Letters*, p. 132; Díaz del Castillo, *True history*, II, pp. 237–8; Durán, *History*, pp. 540–1; Ixtlilxóchitl, *Ally of Cortés*, p. 9; López de Gómara, *Cortés*, p. 212; Sahagún, *Book 12*, pp. 65–6; Sahagún, *Conquest*, pp. 84–5.

111. Díaz del Castillo, *True history*, II, pp. 260–2; Durán, *History*, pp. 546–7; Información recibida en Mexico y Puebla. El ano de 1565. A solicitud del gobernado y cabildo de naturales de Tlaxcala, sobre los servicios que prestaron los Tlaxcaltecas a Hernan Cortes en el conquista de Mexico, siendo los testigos algunas de los mismos conquistadores, in *Biblioteca histórica de la Iberia* [20 vols] (Mexico City, I. Escalante, 1870–75), XX, pp. 17, 21, 140, 145; Muñoz Camargo, *Historia*, pp. 236; Muñoz Camargo, *Descripción*, IV, p. 261; Sahagún, *Book 12*, p. 80.

112. Aguilar, Chronicle, p. 159; Alvarado Tezozómoc, *Crónica*, p. 160; *Códice Aubin*, p. 86; S. F. Cook and W. Borah, *Essays in population history: Mexico and the Caribbean. Volume one* (Berkeley and Los Angeles, University of California Press, 1971), pp. 80–2; Díaz del Castillo, *True history*, II, pp. 218–19, 273; F. Fenner *et al. Smallpox and its eradication* (Geneva, World Health Organization, 1988), pp. 236–7; Hopkins, *Princes and peasants*, pp. 204, 207; Ixtlilxóchitl, *Ally of Cortés*, p. 11; Ixtlilxóchitl, *Obras*, II, p. 236; López de Gómara, *Cortés*, p. 204; Sahagún, *Book 12*, p. 83; Sahagún, *Conquest*, p. 102.

113. Aguilar, Chronicle, p. 157; Cortés, *Letters*, p. 146; Díaz del Castillo, *True history*, II, pp. 269–73; Ixtlilxóchitl, *Obras*, II, p. 238; Martyr d'Anghera, *De orbe novo*, II, p. 146; Muñoz Camargo, *Historia*, p. 236; Muñoz Camargo, *Descripción*, IV, p. 262; Oviedo y Valdés, *Historia general*, IV, p. 75.

114. Díaz del Castillo, *True history*, II, pp. 218–19, 273; López de Gómara, *Cortés*, pp. 238–9; Sahagún, *Conquest*, p. 103.

115. Cortés, *Letters*, pp. 150–5; Díaz del Castillo, *True history*, II, pp. 279–80; Oviedo y Valdés, *Historia general*, IV, pp. 78–80; Sahagún, *Conquest*, p. 102.

116. Aguilar, Chronicle, p. 158; Alvarado Tezozómoc, *Crónica*, p. 149; Cortés, *Letters*, p. 172; Díaz del Castillo, *True history*, IV, pp. 7–8; Ixtlilxóchitl, *Ally of Cortés*, pp. 12–13; Ixtlilxóchitl, *Obras*, II, pp. 241–2; López de Gómara, *Cortés*, p. 245; Oviedo y Váldes, *Historia general*, IV, p. 89.

117. Díaz del Castillo, *True history*, IV, pp. 8–9; Ixtlilxóchitl, *Ally of Cortés*, pp. 12–15; Ixtlilxóchitl, *Obras*, II, pp. 390–1; Offner, *Law*, pp. 239–40.

118. Aguilar, Chronicle, p. 158; Cortés, *Letters*, p. 209; Díaz del Castillo, *True history*, IV, pp. 103–5; Hassig, Famine; Ixtlilxóchitl, *Ally of Cortés*, p. 26; Ixtlilxóchitl, *Obras*, II, p. 258; Sahagún, *Book 12*, pp. 82–4.

119. Aguilar, Chronicle, p. 159; Cortés, *Letters*, pp. 241–2; Díaz del Castillo, *True history*, IV, pp. 140–1, 143–5, 149–51, 168; Durán, *History*, pp. 553–4; Ixtlilxóchitl, *Ally of Cortés*, pp. 39–42; López de Gómara, *Cortés*, pp. 281–2; Oviedo y Valdés, *Historia general*, IV, p. 133; Sahagún, *Book 12*, p. 104; Sahagún, *Conquest*, p. 121.

120. Díaz del Castillo, *True history*, IV, pp. 152–7.

121. *ibid.*, IV, pp. 161, 163.
122. Cortés, *Letters*, pp. 242–5; Hassig, *Aztec warfare*, pp. 184–5, 190; Ixtlilxóchitl, *Ally of Cortes*, pp. 42–3; López de Gómara, *Cortés*, pp. 282–4; Oviedo y Valdés, *Historia general*, IV, pp. 134–6.
123. Durán, *History*, p. 290.
124. I. Bejarano, (comp), *Actas de cabildo de la ciudad de México* [54 vols] (Mexico City, 1889–1916), I, p. 12 (26 May 1524).
125. J. Benedict Warren, *The conquest of Michoacán* (Norman, University of Oklahoma Press, 1985), pp. 24–80.

Further reading

For first-hand Spanish accounts of the conquest of Mexico, see:

H. Cortés, *Letters from Mexico*, A. Pagden, tr. (New York, Grossman Publishers, 1971).
P. De Fuentes, *The Conquistadors: first-person accounts of the conquest of Mexico* (New York, Orion Press, 1963).
B. Díaz del Castillo, *The true history of the conquest of New Spain*, A. P. Mauslay, tr., 5 vols (London, The Hakluyt Society, 1908–16) (or any of a number of abridged versions currently available).

For indigenous accounts of the Conquest in English translation, see:

D. Durán, *The history of the Indies of New Spain* (Normal, University of Oklahoma Press, 1994).
F. de Alva Ixtlilxochitl, *Ally of Cortes: Account 13: of the coming of the Spaniards and the beginning of the evangelical law* (El Paso, Texas Western Press, 1969).
B. de Sahagún, *Florentine codex: general history of the things of New Spain. Book 12 – The conquest of Mexico* (Salt Lake City, University of Utah Press, 1975).
B. de Sahagún, *The war of conquest: how it was waged here in Mexico: the Aztecs' own story* (Salt Lake City: University of Utah Press, 1978).

For an account of Cortés's life, see:

S. de Madariaga, *Hernán Cortés: Conqueror of Mexico* (Garden City, NY, Anchor Books, 1969).

For a general background of the Aztecs, see:

N. Davies, *The Aztecs: A History* (New York, G. P. Putnam's Sons, 1974).

For the Aztecs and their military situation, see:

R. Hassig, *Trade, Tribute, and Transportation: The Sixteenth-Century Political Economy of the Valley of Mexico* (Normal, University of Oklahoma Press, 1984).
R. Hassig, *Aztec Warfare: Political Expansion and Imperial Control*, (Norman, University of Oklahoma Press, 1988).
R. Hassig, *War and Society in Ancient Mesoamerica* (Berkeley and Los Angeles, University of California Press, 1992).
R. Hassig, *Mexico and the Spanish Conquest* (London, Longmans, 1994).

For accounts of the Aztec situation after the Conquest, see:

C. Gibson, *The Aztecs Under Spanish Rule: A History of the Indians of the Valley of Mexico, 1519–1810* (Stanford, Stanford University Press, 1964).

J. Lockhart, *The Nahuas After the Conquest: A Social and Cultural History of the Indians of Central Mexico, Sixteenth Through Eighteenth Centuries* (Stanford, CA, Stanford University Press, 1992).

For the Spanish military situation, see:

R. B. Martínez and T. M. Barker (eds), *Armed Forces and Society in Spain Past and Present* (Boulder, CO, Social Science Monographs, 1988).

L. P. Wright, The Military Orders in Sixteenth and Seventeenth Century Spanish Society: The Institutional Embodiment of a Historical Tradition, *Past and Present*, 1969, 43, pp. 34–70.

Chapter Ten

European–Native American warfare in North America, 1513–1815

Armstrong Starkey

Military contact between European and native American cultures in North America began with the 1513 Florida expedition of Juan Ponce de Leon. A veteran of Columbus' 1493 voyage and the conqueror of Puerto Rico, Ponce de Leon arrived on the east Florida coast in search of treasure. He found the fierce Calusa people whose archers drove off the Spanish invaders. Despite such technological advantages as firearms, crossbows, metal armour, and horses, the Spanish gained no easy victories over the native peoples of southeastern North America. Other Spanish expeditions followed in the sixteenth century: Lucas Vasquez d'Ayllon in 1526, Panfilio de Narvaez in 1527, Hernando de Soto in 1539, and Tristan de Luna y Arellano in 1559. De Soto's expedition cut a wide swath across the southeast, but the rest did not prosper. There were only four survivors of Narvaez's ill-conceived foray into Florida. Disease, hunger, shipwreck, and fierce resistance by Indians, whose bows often proved superior to Spanish missile weapons, turned Florida (a term which then embraced much of what is now the southeastern United States) into a graveyard for Spanish adventurers. Spain did not establish a permanent presence in eastern North America until the construction in 1565 of the first in a series of forts at St. Augustine. Ponce de Leon's expedition was thus only the first step in the European "invasion" of North America, one which the native peoples of the eastern portion of the continent resisted militarily until 1815.[1]

European settlements were confined to the margins for much of the period. English settlements were founded at Jamestown in 1607 and Plymouth in 1620, the Dutch founded New Amsterdam in 1614 and Albany (Fort Orange) in 1624, Samuel de Champlain launched the French colony of Quebec in 1608, and New Sweden was established in 1638. Some European settlements provoked almost immediate native military resistance. Others were too weak to be perceived as a threat by their Indian neighbours. Plymouth and Albany, for example, were dependent on the goodwill of Indian neighbours for survival. Although Quebec's geographic situation provided excellent water communications with the interior of the continent, its small population precluded the establishment of a formal empire in the west. During the seventeenth century the French fought a prolonged war with the Iroquois of northern New York for control of the western fur trade, but achieved victory only with the support of other Indian peoples. French penetration of the west depended on diplomacy, trade, and missionary activity rather than on force. On the other hand, the land hunger of English settlers contributed to major Indian wars in Virginia and New England in the seventeenth century. English settler penetration of the Allegheny mountain barrier began in earnest only after 1763, and turned the area today encompassed by the states of Tennessee, Kentucky, Ohio, Indiana, Illinois, Michigan, and Wisconsin into dark and bloody lands. The Indian hold upon the "Old Northwest" was broken only by the defeat of an Indian confederacy army by United States General Anthony Wayne at the Battle of Fallen Timbers in 1794. Even so native resistance continued throughout the period covered by this chapter, led by the great Shawnee chief Tecumseh who sought to unite all eastern Indians into an anti-United States alliance. His death, fighting alongside a British army at the Battle of the Thames in 1813, deprived Indian resistance fighters of their greatest leader.

Scholars continue to debate the number of people living in North America in 1492. Estimates have been revised upward during the twentieth century as new methodologies have been applied. American history textbooks in the early 1990s have provided estimates ranging from one to twelve million with most inclining toward the middle or higher range.[2] Scholars also agree that the native population went into steep decline in the decades following contact with Europeans. Indians were exposed to numerous European epidemic diseases for which they had no immunity, and the results were often as severe as the outbreak of the bubonic plague in fourteenth-century Europe. Some communities were virtually wiped out. The French colonists found the St. Lawrence valley, formerly inhabited by an Iroquoian people, deserted in 1608. Plymouth Colony was established in an area whose native inhabitants, the Wampanoags, had been devastated by disease in the preceding decade. Some settlers saw this the hand of Providence at work. Other tribes, however, such as the Wampanoags' neighbours the Narragansetts seem to have been unaffected by epidemics. Nevertheless, scholars estimate that the pre-colonization population of New England ranged from 72,000 to 144,000. By 1670, on the eve of New England's greatest Indian war, the native population may have been as few as 8,600.[3] Other European settlements such as Jamestown occurred amid more significant Indian populations, and in initial military encounters the Europeans were frequently outnumbered.

Europeans also suffered high mortality rates from disease, food shortages, and war in the early decades of settlement. But, while native American populations were in decline, European settlements could draw upon a stream of European immigration and external resources. Thus, the fragile English settlements of New England increased to around 50,000 by 1670. Demographic trends were definitely in favour of Europeans, with significant implications for European–Indian power relationships.[4]

Disease was not the only factor which undermined Indian resistance to European military conquest. By the mid-seventeenth century much of eastern North America had been integrated into a trans-Atlantic economy. Hitherto subsistence farming, hunting, gathering native American economies were revolutionized by the European market for furs. Indians became dependent on a wide variety of European trade goods including firearms and ammunition, and they competed with one another for control of the fur trade. The most baleful by-product of the Indians' contact with European commerce was a plague of alcoholism which also ravaged many Indian communities. The impact of European commerce varied from tribe to tribe and by region. One scholar argues that the fur trade was an unequal relationship, extracting wealth from the Indian margin of the trans-Atlantic economy to the benefit of the European centre. Other historians have argued that native Americans knew how to hold their own in trading relationships and that, in the case of Indians of the Great Lakes region, European goods possessed symbolic rather than material value in Indian eyes.[5] Indian economies which were deeply integrated into the fur trade were vulnerable to market changes. Demand for beaver pelts collapsed after 1660 causing a decline in the value of wampum, a fur-backed shell currency. Southern New England Indians were now under pressure to sell land to pay their debts to European merchants. Tensions over land sales were a principal cause of the outbreak of King Philip's War in 1675.

Historians have also described a European assault on native American cultures as an instrument of conquest. Missionary activity undermined traditional cultural values and religious beliefs. Denys Delage has painted a bleak picture of the consequences of the Jesuit missions among the powerful and prosperous Hurons who inhabited modern-day Ontario. Not only did the Jesuits introduce murderous epidemic diseases among the Hurons, but their success in converting a proportion to Christianity caused deep divisions in the Huron society, rendering it vulnerable to attack by rival Iroquois. Protestant missionary effort in New England has received harsh treatment from revisionist historians such as Francis Jennings, who portrays such figures as John Eliot, the "Apostle to the Indians", as unscrupulous hypocrites.[6] In both cases the missionaries succeeded among people weakened and demoralized by epidemic disease. Stronger, self-confident native communities such as the seventeenth-century Narragansetts remained faithful to their religious traditions. Religious conversions divided native peoples and provided allies for Europeans in their conflicts with other Indian peoples. Twenty per cent of the native population of southern New England had converted to Christianity by 1675. Most supported the English during King Philip's War.

Politically, therefore, the native peoples of eastern North America did not present a united front to European conquest. There were scores of different tribal and language groups, many of which were historically antagonistic. Many Indian "nations" consisted of village societies, loosely organized into confederacies based on language and kinship. Central authority was usually weak, with power divided between religious leaders, chiefs or elders who guided the community in peacetime, and younger more aggressive war leaders whose influence increased in times of war. Indian communities relied upon discussion and consensus to arrive at decisions and could be fractured by an immediate crisis. Some confederacies recognized the hereditary authority of paramount chiefs (this was true of the Wampanoag sachem Massasoit and his sons Wamsutta and Metacom [Philip]), but no Indian leader possessed the authority of a king, although, as in the case of Philip, Europeans attributed such a role to prominent individuals. Native communities, therefore, found it difficult to unite against a European threat. Non-Christian Indians sometimes found it in their interest to co-operate with Europeans against other Indian rivals. Philip's war against the English settlers of New England received a serious setback when his followers were routed by their old Mohawk enemies in the winter of 1676. Attempts by New England Indians to unite against the English consistently failed to bear fruit. During the great imperial wars of the latter part of the eighteenth century a greater sense of pan-Indian identity appears to have emerged. Indians seem to have become more reluctant to kill one another in white men's wars. Nativist religious revivals preached the message of a return to traditional ways of life and religious belief as a means of restoring lost power.[7] These movements merged with efforts to unite against the pressure of white settlement. Pontiac's war of resistance in 1763, which involved a number of Midwestern peoples, was partially inspired by the Delaware prophet, Neolin. Tecumseh's appeal for pan-Indian unity was anchored in the religious revival movement led by his brother, the prophet Tenskwatawa. Such movements generated Indian military efforts that shook European dominion. However, while Europeans themselves made war upon one another and thus could be exploited by Indian diplomacy, among Indians the lack of the political unity achieved by centralized European states translated into serious military weakness.

In addition to the vulnerabilities described above, the native Americans faced European powers which possessed decided military advantages. Sixteenth- and seventeenth-century European invaders were seldom professional soldiers, but they were beneficiaries of European "military revolutions". The timing and nature of such revolutions remain matters of historical debate, but during the sixteenth century the war-making powers of European societies were transformed in relation to the capacities of American Indians.[8] Central to this change was naval power in the form of long-distance sailing ships, floating castles which could support the establishment and maintenance of settlements on the North American seaboard and which in many cases could penetrate its bays and rivers. Second to this was the new European reliance on gunpowder weapons in preference to bows and catapults. The introduction of infantry firearms occurred slowly and at an uneven pace over the sixteenth century: the English trained bands, the elite units of the militia, did not complete the exchange of bows for muskets until the end of the century, and it is debatable whether the musketeers of the day, equipped with slow and cumbersome matchlock weapons, were superior to trained archers. English conversion to firearms may have been more the consequence of the decline in English archery standards than of a commitment to modernization. However, whatever the limitations of sixteenth-century military power in hindsight, when weighed in the balance against the resources available to Indian peoples, it seems formidable indeed. This power increased in the seventeenth and eighteenth centuries, particularly with the professionalization of European armies in the eighteenth. Nevertheless, Indian forces throughout the period inflicted numerous defeats upon well-equipped European armies, and wars between the two peoples were often fought to a standstill. Considering the clear imbalance of power between the two societies, why was the final Indian defeat so long in coming?

Victory in war is not achieved by imbalance of resources alone. Battlefield performance counts in the end. Leadership, training, skill, and motivation can reverse apparent imbalances of power. In the Indians the Europeans encountered martial peoples whose mastery of forest warfare provided them with tactical advantages which frequently reversed strategic imbalances. Given the vast size and remoteness of the territory, relative to the settler population, this tactical skill was sufficient to delay European conquest for centuries. Indeed, not until Europeans could adapt to the Indian way of war could they achieve the military conquest of eastern North America.

European soldiers who fought alongside Indian warriors often complained of their lack of discipline and their inconstancy in battle. James Smith, an eighteenth-century veteran of frontier war and a former Indian captive, scoffed at "the British officers" who

call the Indians undisciplined savages, which is a capital mistake – as they have all the essentials of discipline. . . . Could it be supposed that undisciplined troops could defeat Generals Braddock, Grant [generals defeated by

Indians in attempts to capture the French Fort Duquesne at the forks of the Ohio River] . . . ?[9]

Smith's description of Indian military discipline stands in sharp contrast to that of British armies which might lead to victory on the fields of Flanders, but was useless in the woodland terrain of North America. Indian discipline manifested the qualities advocated by eighteenth-century British military reformers, particularly those interested in the development of light infantry. "Is it not the best discipline that has the greatest tendency to annoy the enemy and save their own men?"[10] Unlike European practice, Indian discipline was founded on individual honour rather than corporal punishment; leaders were chosen according to merit based upon courage and experience, instead of on privilege or purchase. Commanders were concerned to save their men's lives and believed that victory did not justify unnecessary sacrifice. There was no disgrace in retreating to await a more favourable occasion for battle. Indian leaders taught their men to move in scattered order to take advantage of the ground, to surround the enemy, and to avoid being surrounded. They practised running and marksmanship, and were accustomed to endure hunger, inclement weather, and hardship with patience and fortitude. Although they avoided unnecessary casualties, they were prepared to sell their lives dearly in defence of their homes. Smith believed that these were moral qualities which provided the Indians with the ability to oppose enemies possessing seemingly overwhelming advantages in numbers, material, and state power.[11]

The Indian warrior's moral advantage was enhanced by physical endurance which only the hardiest Europeans could equal. Captives who survived Indian raids often perished on the brutal marches to Indian villages. They were expected to maintain the pace of Indian warriors who could march 30–50 miles in a day, frequently without food. Mrs Mary Rowlandson, taken in a raid on Lancaster, Mass. on February 16 1676, was forced to carry a wounded child through the snow. An Indian threatened to kill the child if she did not keep pace with the party. The only food available on this march was broth made from a horse's leg. She found that Indians could exist on diets at least as demanding as those of modern military survival courses: acorns, groundnuts, horse guts and ears, skunks, tree bark, rattle snakes, and extracts from old bones. Her comment on her captivity experience says at least as much about Indian values as it does about her own religion: "It is good for me that I have been afflicted. The Lord has shown me the vanity of these outward things."[12]

Robert Rogers, the famous frontier commander of the Seven Years' War, observed that the Indians

> have no stated rules of discipline, or fixed methods of prosecuting a war; they make attacks in as many different ways as there are occasions on which

they make them, but generally in a very secret skulking, underhand manner, in flying parties that are equipped for the purpose, with thin light dress, generally consisting of nothing more than a shirt, stockings and mogasins, and sometimes almost naked.[13]

Indians required no "stated rules" such as those provided in European military handbooks. The ability to exploit particular situations was a hallmark of experienced Indian warriors trained in the Indian way of war from the age of twelve. The rigid and inflexible discipline of European armies was a means by which inexperienced and unmartial peasants might be transformed into soldiers. This was unnecessary for Indian warriors, possessing as they did the skills and self-discipline of modern commandos or special forces, and capable of adapting to unique circumstances. They were masters of the "secret, skulking" way of war: the raid, the ambush and the retreat. Their clothing is indicative of their practicality. Many whites came to prefer Indian dress to European uniforms and shoes. Frontier rangers such as Rogers, George Rogers Clark, and Daniel Boone clothed themselves in Indian fashion. General John Forbes, leader of the successful British march on Fort Duquesne in 1758, ordered many of his men to adopt Indian dress: "I must confess in this country, wee must comply and learn the Art of Warr, from Ennemy Indians or anyone else who have seen the Country and Warr carried on in it."[14]

In addition to clothing, Europeans adopted many native crafts for use in frontier warfare. Light birchbark canoes were excellent vessels for men moving quickly on inland waterways interrupted by frequent portages. The seventeenth-century Massachusetts Indian superintendent, Daniel Gookin, observed that one man could carry a five-passenger canoe on his back for several miles.[15] Snowshoes made possible long-distance wintertime raids; easily-portable maize rations helped sustain them.[16] Indians seem to have been able to apply any material to practical use in an emergency. Mary Rowlandson's captors eluded their English pursuers by crossing a river on rafts made from brush. Her would-be rescuers were forced to give up the chase. On the other hand, Indians prized the products of European ironworking industries. These trade goods, which transformed the Indian way of life, included tools such as knives, chisels, drills, and hammers. Iron hatchets were valued both as tools and weapons. In addition, woollen blankets provided warmth unmatched by any Indian materials. But it was the introduction of firearms which was to transform fundamentally the native American way of war.

Samuel de Champlain is generally credited with being one of the first to introduce the Indians of northeastern North America to the use of firearms in a battle against the Mohawks in 1609. By the end for the seventeenth century the Indians of the region were well supplied with muskets. The Indian preference for the musket over the bow and arrow requires some explanation.[17] Early seventeenth-century matchlock guns, fired when the powder was ignited by a slow burning fuse or match, were unreliable, inaccurate, cumbersome and slow. In wet weather they were useless. Indeed, sixteenth-century Spanish troops continued to rely upon crossbowmen and swordsmen in battles with Indian opponents. Indians preferred the self-igniting flintlock musket, introduced during the seventeenth century. However, one modern expert who has tested the flintlock against the bow has found the latter to be superior in almost every respect.[18] Flintlock muskets were also inaccurate, single-shot weapons which were difficult to load in any position other than standing. While the musket's discharge produced a frightening noise, the sound and the smoke emitted by black gunpowder was inconsistent with a "skulking" way of war. Europeans may have been converted from bows to early firearms because it was easier to train new recruits to become musketeers rather than archers. But Indian boys were accustomed to bows from an early age. Patrick Malone believes that native Americans saw that bullets travelled faster than arrows and took a more direct route to the target, thus making a musket easier to aim. Bullets were less likely to be deflected by brush and were more damaging on impact. Indians were skilled at dodging arrows, which was almost impossible in the case of bullets. Muskets could be loaded to fire several small bullets with one shot, making it easier to strike targets.[19]

During the eighteenth century lighter and more practical weapons became available for hunting and woodland warfare. European officers noted the Indian preference for the short-barrelled and lightweight fusil. In the latter half of the century rifle barrelled muskets with increased accuracy and range became common on the frontier. European soldiers often scorned rifles because they were slower to fire and more fragile than the standard-issue, smoothbore muskets which could also support a bayonet. But rifles were marksmen's weapons suitable for hunting and Indian military tactics. One officer present at General Edward Braddock's defeat in 1755 attributed the slaughter of the British troops to the Indians' effective use of rifles. By the mid-1760s, the veteran frontier commander Colonel James Bradstreet became so concerned about the large number of rifles acquired by Ohio and Great Lakes Indians that he "submitted if it would not be a public benefit to stop making and vending of any more of them in the colonies, nor suffer any to be imported".[20] Indians did not entirely abandon bows. They had value as stealth weapons and could be resorted to in ammunition shortages, but by the end of the seventeenth century firearms were the principal weapons of the Indians of eastern North America.

Indians soon demonstrated skill in the use of firearms which was superior to their European opponents. Since they made no distinction between hunting and warfare, they trained to achieve accurate marksmanship in both. From an early age Indian men spent their lives acquiring these skills and they became second nature. In contrast, the peasantry were disarmed by law in most European countries. When recruited as soldiers, they were trained to fire rapid but unaimed volleys rather than to aim at marks. Destructive enough at close quarters on European battlefields, this method of fire was ineffective in the woods. European settlers in North America brought their military training with them. While they possessed firearms for self-defence, they remained for the most part an agrarian people with no special skill in hunting or marksmanship. As Malone observes,

> Unfortunately, our popular image of the sharp-shooting frontiersman is questionable even for the early nineteenth-century settlers of Kentucky and is far removed from the reality of the seventeenth-century colonists of New England.[21]

Ironically, the North American Indians not only adapted firearms to their own use, but became the most formidable marksmen of the seventeenth- and eighteenth-century world. The challenge that this skill presented to European soldiers cannot be overestimated. The Indian commitment to firepower is even more striking when placed in the context of the eighteenth-century, European, theoretical debate about *shock* versus *fire*. Many European officers believed that infantry firearms did relatively little damage, and expressed a preference for attacks with cold steel. Generals such as Maurice de Saxe and, early in his career, Frederick the Great advocated advancing on the enemy with shouldered muskets. The Sieur de Folard urged the reintroduction of the pike and the revival of something resembling the Macedonian phalanx. Folard had many disciples: his advocacy of the column in preference to the line (the natural formation for volley fire) would influence French military thought through the Napoleonic wars and beyond. There were examples of shock prevailing over fire in the eighteenth century, but it appears that Indian tactics based on aimed fire represented an advance over much of the best in European military thought and practice.[22]

Indian conversion to firepower meant a dependence on European suppliers for arms and ammunition. If Indian–European warfare had been a simple conflict between two monolithic blocks, this would have been a fatal dependency. Colonial governments often sought to prevent arms sales to Indians, but such regulations were seldom effective. Not only did French, Dutch, and English governments pursue different arms-sale policies, the English colonies themselves often failed to co-operate. Arms were an economic as well as a security issue, and an important commodity of exchange in the fur trade. Furthermore, while it was clearly desirable to deprive hostile Indians of firearms, it was equally desirable to equip one's allies. Indeed, failure to provide arms and ammunition could drive an Indian ally into the hands of the enemy. These complex economic and political conditions ensured that the Indians of eastern North America were equipped with firearms by the end of the seventeenth century.[23]

Firearms required extensive maintenance and repair, which presented the Indians with new technological challenges. On the whole, native artisans adapted well. During the seventeenth century New England Indians acquired the art of casting bullets and making gunflints. There is evidence that Indian blacksmiths became proficient in the repair of muskets and in assembling them from parts. Gunpowder manufacture, however, required concentrations of capital and technological expertise beyond the capacity of Indian societies. While weapons could be repaired and re-used, gunpowder was an expendable commodity which only Europeans could supply. Ammunition shortages could contribute to the sudden collapse of promising Indian military efforts, such as King Philip's War in New England in 1676 and the Pontiac uprising in the Midwest in 1764.[24]

Artillery remained a virtual European monopoly, although the Swedes provided the Susquehannock Indians of the Delaware Valley with cannon in the 1660s. They used them to beat off an attack by an army of Five Nations Indians, and later to defend a fort against a siege by the Virginia and Maryland militia.[25] Palisaded Indian villages were rendered defenceless against European troops equipped with cannon. Indians learned that their forts could easily turn into death traps, and often abandoned their villages on the approach of a European army. European commanders had to content themselves with burning the villages and the crops. Slender food reserves might force the Indians to make peace, but such hardships usually did not impair the Indians' ability to retaliate by ambushes and raids against white settlements. Indians were seldom prepared to risk casualties in assaults on fortified positions. Settlers fortunate to gain the security of a blockhouse or stockade were relatively safe from attack by Indian raiders. However, it was difficult for settlers to watch their homes and fields go up in smoke and often, as in the case of the celebrated Wyoming Valley "massacre" in Pennsylvania in 1778, they sallied forth into disastrous ambushes. Without cannon the Indians could seldom overcome forts. Often they employed fire arrows, carts loaded with combustibles, and sometimes mining against fortifications. They were skilled at seizing posts by ruses, as at Michilimackinac in 1763 when they gained entrance to the fort in pursuit of a lacrosse ball.

Firearms seem to have transformed inter-Indian warfare in the seventeenth century. Pre-European contact warfare was often characterized by hand-to-hand encounters between large forces, which resulted in relatively few casualties. Indians were able to dodge arrows and sometimes wore wooden or leather armour which provided a measure of protection. Indian success in war was frequently measured by captives taken rather than deaths inflicted. The seventeenth-century Iroquois, their population levels under stress from epidemic disease and the rising level of violence associated with the fur-trade wars, placed a high value on captives, whom they adopted in order to sustain their numbers. Despite their fearsome reputation, Iroquois warriors did not take unnecessary risks and were prepared to yield an apparent victory on the field if the cost in life was too high. Indians appear to have been shocked by the level of violence introduced by European soldiers. During the New England Pequot War of 1637, Connecticut troops and their Indian allies surrounded a palisaded Pequot village on the Mystic River. The Connecticut men overwhelmed the defenders by musket fire, burned the houses, and killed all of the inhabitants, including women and children. Many of the English Indian allies departed rather than participate in such an atrocity, and those who remained denounced the unnecessary slaughter. European arms and methods altered Indian styles of warfare. They could ill afford to compete in the open field against the murderous volley fire of European musketeers. During the seventeenth and eighteenth centuries Indian warriors discarded armour as useless against musket balls and avoided hand-to-hand combat unless the enemy was in disarray. The skulking way of war was a logical response to new conditions, and was employed by parties of warriors whose numbers might range from a handful to several hundred.[26]

Native American warfare is often portrayed as being marked with special cruelty or savagery. Indian warriors were not constrained by European military codes, and did not draw the same distinctions between combatant and non-combatant or between war and murder. Their style of war was equivalent to that of the modern commando or guerrilla fighter, one which even today cannot be easily waged according to the principles of international law and military codes. For example, commandos may find themselves in possession of prisoners whom they cannot safeguard and whose liberty would endanger them. Would they be justified in killing the prisoners in such circumstances? While military lawyers generally answer in the negative, some officers believe that necessity must prevail.[27] The eighteenth century ranger, Robert Rogers, killed prisoners in such circumstances, and it would be surprising if Indians showed greater scruples. In fact Indians probably had greater motivation for keeping prisoners alive than Rogers did.[28] The Indian "skulking" way of war included many practices that Europeans regarded as unfair or inhumane: ambushes, surprises, attacks on civilians, and cruel treatment of prisoners. Aimed fire was a controversial issue in itself. Indian sharpshooters had no scruples about firing at sentries and officers, a practice which many European regulars regarded as tantamount to murder.

The Indian way of war paralleled the male Indian's life as a hunter. One European observer concluded that the Indian warrior "uses the same stratagems and cruelty as against the wild beasts...."[29] Some aspects of Indian cruelty towards captives – including torture, scalping, beheading, and cannibalism – may be explained by the close relationship between warfare and hunting. Indian cosmologies did not award humans a position superior to other creatures. Hunters believed that animals deserved respect: they could be killed for food, but possessed a spiritual nature that requires ritual attention. Similarly, many Indians do not seem to have regarded non-members of their tribal group as fully human. Many captives could expect nothing better than death nor torture, but others passed through adoption rituals which gave them full membership in the tribal family. Thomas Gist was captured near Fort Duquesne in 1758 and was fortunate to be adopted into an Indian family as a replacement for a dead member. He recalled that:

> I was led into the house where I was to live, there strip'd by a female relation and then led to a river. There she wash'd me from head to foot. . . . As soon as this ceremony was over I was clad from head to foot; then there was an interpreter brought to tell me which of my kin was the nearest to me. I think they re[k]onded from brother to seventh cousin.[30]

The purposes of the brutal torture and cannibalism are not clear. In some cases torture seems to have been rooted in tribal rituals. In others the motive was revenge for an injury suffered at the hands of the enemy. For example, the brutal torture of Colonel William Crawford after his defeat by the Delawares at Sandusky, Ohio in 1782 was a response to the massacre earlier in the year of a peaceful village of Moravian mission Indians by undisciplined frontiersmen. Not all Indians engaged in cannibalism and some rejected torture. The Delawares were never cannibals and expressed contempt for Mohawk "man-eaters". By the mid-eighteenth century eastern tribes had generally abandoned the practice. The Ottawa resistance leader, Pontiac, was criticized by his Indian allies for cannibalism and later became known for his "lenity and gentleness" with prisoners. The great Shawnee chief Tecumseh was well-known for his anti-torture views.[31]

Scalping was the most notorious Indian rite of war. However, it paled in comparison with beheading and other cruelties, and many scalping victims survived to tell of their experience. While there have been allegations that scalping was introduced by Europeans, it now seems firmly established that it was a widespread, pre-Columbian custom among North American Indians.[32] In the seventeenth century European frontier fighters also began to scalp their opponents, and the practice continued throughout the period. European authorities began to offer bounties for scalps, which transformed the practice into a financial transaction and encouraged its spread. Experienced frontier diplomats warned that bounties prompted indiscriminate killings that only inflamed the frontier. By the mid-eighteenth century some leaders worried about the moral, or at least the "public relations", consequences of scalp bounties, but that did not stop the practice. Scalp bounties created a kind of war by body count, which played havoc with attempts to establish good Indian relations.[33]

These good relations were crucial to successful frontier military efforts. European commanders found Indian allies to be indispensable in the wilderness. Successful ranger leaders such as Benjamin Church and Robert Rogers included a large number of Indians in their commands, while generals such as Edward Braddock and John Forbes lamented their absence. Few Europeans could equal the Indians' woodcraft, scouting ability, and marksmanship. At the very least, it was best to seek them as allies rather than to confront them as enemies. Indians allied themselves with Europeans for a variety of reasons. Some sought advantages against rival Indian nations. Christian Indians were prepared to ally with Europeans as a means of accommodation. The mission Indians of Canada supported the French partly as the result of the influence of Jesuits, who sometimes accompanied their raids. Christian or "praying" Indians sided with the New England settlers during King Philip's War. In the late seventeenth century, New England authorities recruited Indian mercenaries, whose pay was an important source of income at a time when they were losing their lands.[34] Economic decisions sometimes dictated alliances. During the seventeenth century the French allied with the Hurons against the Iroquois because of the former's strategic position in the fur trade. This ignited a period of prolonged war, which devastated the Hurons. The Iroquois continued to contest the control of the fur trade with western Indian tribes and the French in the latter part of the seventeenth century. Although the small Quebec colony suffered heavily in these conflicts, the Iroquois were defeated by an alliance of French and Great Lakes Indians, who now matched the Iroquois in firearms. The failure of New York to honour commitments to support the Iroquois in these wars caused the latter to retreat into a policy of neutrality during the first half of the eighteenth century. Indian economic dependence on European trade goods, including arms and ammunition, often formed the basis of political alliances. During the American War of Independence, the inability of impoverished Revolutionary authorities to supply friendly Indians undermined the efforts of American diplomats to secure frontier alliances.

The cardinal mistake made by some white authorities was the assumption that Indians could be forced into alliances or dependent roles against their interests. Indian tribes did not regard themselves as subject peoples, and often rejected commitments made by their own chiefs which they believed ran counter to their wellbeing. Richard White has demonstrated that French influence in the Great Lakes region during the eighteenth century rested upon diplomacy and commerce rather than force. The Indians of the region referred to the Governor of Quebec as Onontio, the great mountain, the keeper of peace and harmony.

When the French sent an expedition into the Ohio country in 1747 to claim formally the area for the French king, it was met with hostility. Subsequent construction of French forts led the Indians to explore an alliance with British authorities. Only when British leaders proved unwilling or incapable of protecting Indian lands from English settlers, did the Native Americans reluctantly ally themselves with the French.[35] British General, Jeffrey Amherst, who led the Anglo-Americans to victory over France in North America, developed an Indian policy that was a prescription for disaster. He scorned the ability of Indian warriors, and was determined to secure by force the Great Lakes region, ceded by France in 1763, without consulting its Indian inhabitants. On the one hand, he severely reduced expenditures for presents to the Indians, which they considered to be the tangible sign of good will; on the other, he spread a number of inadequately garrisoned forts across the region, which provoked Indian hostility without overawing them. The result was the 1763 uprising known as Pontiac's rebellion, which shook Britain's grip on the region. In two years of war the Indians fought the British Empire to a draw.[36]

Some eighteenth-century military commanders, such as John Burgoyne and Barry St. Leger, blamed their Indian allies unfairly for their lack of success. Some modern historians have also disparaged the Indians as unreliable allies and useless fighters. Often these writers fail to appreciate the qualities of Indian warriors, who had no interest in fighting in the European style. These critics also assume that the Indians were passive clay who could be "used".[37] American Indians seldom served as mercenaries; they were not sepoys. Instead they fought for motives of their own and in their own way. They had to be convinced that their ally's cause justified their participation. The Western Abenakis of Vermont were thus prepared to fight English settlers during the Seven Years' War, whether or not the French Governor wanted them to. But they were not enthusiastic about participating in the American War of Independence. A few hundred were coerced into joining General John Burgoyne's march from Canada to New York in 1777, but deserted him as his prospects dimmed.[38] On the other hand, the Shawnees of Ohio, determined to protect their lands from American settlement and to drive settlers from their Kentucky hunting grounds, were at the forefront of a British–Indian alliance that retained the military initiative in the Midwest until the conclusion of peace between Britain and the United States.[39] The Indians were thunderstruck when they learned that Britain had ceded the region to the new American government. Not until 1795, after a series of military humiliations, were the Americans able to impose their claims upon the Indian peoples.

Although they were expected to see to their own defence, few of the Spanish, English, French and Dutch who came into conflict with North American Indians during the sixteenth and seventeenth centuries were "professional" soldiers.

Sixteenth-century Spanish soldiers were warlike military volunteers and adventurers. They came from the strong martial tradition of the Reconquista, but are not to be confused with the professionals of the *tercios* which projected Spanish power in Europe. English settlers brought with them their native militia institutions and methods of warfare. The Iroquois war prompted the French government to send professional troops to Canada in 1665, but the regulars achieved limited success. The Quebec militia, many of whom gained experience of the Indians' way of life by participating in the fur trade to the interior, proved to be more effective in frontier warfare than any of the regulars dispatched from home. The latter were usually best assigned to garrison duty.[40] British regulars did not make a significant appearance in North American warfare until the 1750s. Their first campaign, Braddock's march to the Monongahela, was an unmitigated disaster. Some British regular officers such as Forbes and Bouquet adapted well to frontier warfare. Others, such as Amherst, never bothered to learn.

English colonists arriving in Virginia based their defence on an ancient institution: the militia which had its roots in the Anglo-Saxon *fyrd*. As feudalism became militarily obsolete and politically suspect during the Tudor period, the militia gained renewed significance for the defence of the realm. Elizabeth I's government gave increased attention to the training and equipment of the militia, and established elite trained bands to provide a well-trained and well-armed core. By the end of her reign the trained bands had exchanged bows for firearms and began to be trained in the volley-fire techniques common to European battlefields. This militia organization and the adoption of firearms were the two important elements of English military life which the first settlers brought to Jamestown. They were crucial to the salvation of the colony when war erupted with the Powhatan Indian confederacy in 1609. Even so, the colony was almost abandoned before a new governor arrived with reinforcements, including experienced soldiers, and imposed strict military discipline upon the inhabitants. The new commanders included men who had served in Elizabethan wars in the Netherlands and in Ireland. One expert concludes that "at present there is little evidence to permit an evaluation of the tenuous but indisputable relationship between English military experiences in Ireland and developments in Virginia".[41] But there are clear parallels. The Irish used guerrilla tactics against the English successfully, winning most of their victories by ambush. They were also better shots. The English responded with a strategy that was to be the staple of their wars against North American Indians: to seek out and destroy the enemy in open battle; to seek aid from the Irish themselves; to hem in the enemy with fortifications; and, in the last resort, to devastate the countryside so that the hostile force could not live upon it.[42]

The English defeated the Powhatan confederacy by a similar strategy. The Powhatans lived in a region penetrated by numerous navigable waterways. The

English exploited this geographical feature by confining the Indians with lines of fortifications and sailing into their homelands on heavily-armed ships to burn their villages and crops. A central weakness of Indian societies was slender food reserves and the inability to replace lost provisions by imports. The English sought to force them to choose between an open-field battle against armoured musketeers or starvation. Naval power gave the English the opportunity to strike deeply and unexpectedly. In the Pequot War of 1637 the Connecticut troops exploited their ability to move by sea to carry out their devastating surprise attack against the Pequots' village at Mystic.

Continued challenges by the Powhatan Indians forced Virginia to maintain vigorous militia institutions during the first half of the seventeenth century. As the threat waned and social tensions increased in the second half of the century, the militia became smaller, excluding slaves and servants. The militia had become an agency of domestic order, and the colony now relied on imperial forces or diplomacy for external defence. The middle colonies, insulated until the mid-eighteenth century from threats from Canada, also allowed their militias to decay. South Carolina's militia remained active in the face of a threefold threat: Spanish and Indian enemies on the frontier and a large slave population within the colony's borders. Indian fighting during the eighteenth century influenced the partisan war carried out by militia veterans against British and loyalist forces during the War of Independence. However, in normal circumstances, South Carolina's unique situation made it difficult to assemble a large force, since militiamen were reluctant to leave their homes unguarded against potentially rebellious slaves. The militia's military potential was neutralized by the demands of domestic order.[43]

The New England militia, recruited from towns governed by elected officials and faced with a long-term threat from hostile Indians and their French allies, remained a vigorous institution throughout most of the colonial period. During King Philip's War the militia provided adequate local defence, but was continually outmatched by an enemy skilled in the use of firearms and in woodcraft. Trained in close order and volley fire, the militia suffered a series of stinging defeats against an enemy who seemed always to have the advantage of surprise.[44] Massachusetts Bay experienced a wave of anti-Indian hysteria, which led colonial authorities to confine even friendly Christian Indians to an island in Boston harbour, thus depriving the English of allies skilled in forest warfare. Connecticut, by contrast, employed non-Christian Pequot and Mohegan warriors and its forces fared much better in the woods. The most famous English soldier in this war was Benjamin Church, who formed a ranger force that ultimately killed the Wampanoag leader, Philip. Church's command included a company of Indians, some of whom were recruited from prisoners. He adopted Indian skulking tactics and proved capable of pursuing hostile Indians in the forest.[45] Church's success occurred while the Indian war effort was in decline. After a successful offensive against Massachusetts and Plymouth settlements in the spring of 1676, the Indian effort collapsed. Food and ammunition shortages, Indian disunity, battle casualties, disease and exposure made it impossible for the Indians to continue. Indian losses were horrific. One estimate is that out of a southern New England Indian population of 11,600 in 1675, 7,900 were dead, enslaved or homeless by the end of 1676. The English probably lost at least 1,000 dead out of a population of 50,000. Of 52 towns, 17 had been destroyed and 25 pillaged. The New England economy was virtually bankrupt at war's end.[46]

By the end of the eighteenth century, English–Indian conflicts in New England merged with the great imperial struggles between Britain and France. These wars presented a new dimension of challenge for New Englanders. Having destroyed Indian independence in southern New England, English settlers now encountered warlike new enemies in the Abenakis of the more remote regions of Vermont, New Hampshire, and Maine. For decades the Abenakis were able to mount destructive raids against English settlements and retire into the remote fastnesses of the north. While New Englanders destroyed the eastern Abenaki settlement at Norridgewick, their punitive expeditions could not even find the villages of the elusive western Abenakis of Vermont. French support for the Abenakis provided them with reliable supplies and ammunition and Canadian sanctuaries for their families. They, therefore, were able to conduct their war against English settlers from a more secure base than had Philip's followers. However, the Abenakis fought to protect their land and homes, not as French mercenaries. Even during the period of Anglo-French peace in the 1720s, the western Abenaki chief, Grey Lock, waged an independent and successful frontier war against English settlers.[47]

English militia performed poorly in these campaigns. They lacked adequate training and tactics to match Abenaki warriors in the forest. Furthermore, as part-time soldiers they could not afford to desert their fields for lengthy campaigns fought at a long distance. New sources of manpower and new measures were needed to meet the challenge. Colonial governments turned to the recruitment of volunteers, who would serve for pay or the promise of loot. Volunteers came from elements of the population not represented in the militia: Indians, free Blacks, white servants and apprentices, and others who lacked deep ties with settler communities. By the eighteenth century most frontier warfare was conducted by these soldiers, while the militia constituted a part-time home guard with limited training. The New England strategic response to the challenge of border raids was to launch major naval–military expeditions against the Canadian sanctuary. This allowed the English to exchange unconventional border wars in which they were weak for conventional campaigns in which they possessed advantages in ships, men, and materials. However, the strategy did not bear fruit until the fall of Quebec in 1759.

The tactical superiority of their Indian opponents and their French allies thus required a major imperial response. British naval forces participated in early campaigns against Quebec or its outlying defences at Louisbourg and Port Royal. Unsuccessful expeditions were launched against Quebec in 1690 and 1711 before it fell in 1759. Port Royal was captured in 1710 and Louisbourg twice in 1745 and 1758. But British regulars did not play a significant role in Indian warfare until 1755 when Braddock's army arrived to drive the French from the Ohio Valley. Braddock's campaign was compromised from the beginning when colonial authorities failed to secure him Indian allies who could protect his column in the woods. Braddock may have sealed his fate when he spurned a Delaware chief who asked that the British guarantee the Ohio Indians possession of their lands.[48] The Delawares would be among his opponents on the Monongahela. Although Braddock followed the standard march discipline employed against light troops in Europe, his mixed force of regulars and Virginia militia were almost totally without forest experience. When they encountered a numerically inferior party of French and Indians near Fort Duquesne, they were quickly surrounded on three sides by enemy marksmen and shot to pieces. Out of Braddock's defeat came the myth that colonials understood woodland combat better than the regulars, but it was not founded on reality. A few weeks later a colonial commander, Colonel Ephraim Williams, led New England troops into an Indian ambush near Lake George without taking even Braddock's precautions.[49]

European commanders learned the value of rangers trained in forest warfare. Many ranger units included Indian scouts. All great frontier commanders including the English Benjamin Church and Robert Rogers and the French La Corne St. Luc and Chaussegros de Lery, gained success because of their ability to lead mixed forces of European partisans and Indians. British general, John Forbes, lamented his lack of Indian support in his march on Fort Duquesne. He experimented with what he called the Indians "cousins", the Highlanders, as light troops to screen his army, but his able subordinate, the Swiss professional Henry Bouquet, later complained that Highlanders became lost as soon as they stepped off the path.[50] Forbes and Bouquet avoided Braddock's fate by exercising great caution. Forbes moved carefully from one fortified post to another but, even so, Colonel James Grant carelessly led an advance party into a defeat at the hands of the Indians. Bouquet also had to command a relief expedition to Fort Duquesne in 1763. He fought a bloody, two-day battle with Indians at Bushy Run, in which he succeeded in beating off the enemy with a surprise bayonet attack, but suffered such severe losses that he was unable to continue his campaign after the fort was relieved. Bouquet seems to have believed that regular troops could not match the Indians in loose-order, woodland fighting. His plans for an advance on the Ohio Indian towns in the following year called for the troops to form square and engage in volley fire if attacked.[51]

During the 1770s English settlers west of the Appalachian mountains adopted styles of warfare similar to those practiced by Indian opponents. Frontiersmen such as George Rogers Clark and Daniel Boone, wore Indian dress and fought as mounted riflemen. Clark did not hesitate to scalp Indian prisoners. However, they were still unable to outmatch the Indians in this sort of war. Frontiersmen were plagued by what has been called "fool bravery", which led them into ambushes set by more cautious Indians. The most famous example of this flaw was the defeat of a party of 180 experienced Kentucky woodsmen including Boone, who rushed heedless into an Indian ambush at the Battle of Blue Licks in 1782.[52] This incident counters the myth of the natural superiority of the frontier partisan over regulars such as the unfortunate Braddock.

During the American War of Independence American authorities were unable to protect the frontier from raids by Indian warriors supplied from British bases at Niagara and Detroit. American armies launched punitive expeditions against Indian homelands in 1778, most notably General Sullivan's campaign against the Iroquois. Sullivan invaded Iroquoia with an army of 4,000 men, including Oneida scouts and troops drawn from Daniel Morgan's famous rifle corps. Sullivan wreaked great destruction on the towns and fields of the enemy Senecas and Cayugas, but fought only one inconclusive action against native Americans and Tory Rangers. The expedition was forced to withdraw because of its own logistical problems and the onset of cold weather. The western Iroquois had been rendered dependents of the British, but were still formidable enemies in the field. The inability of the Americans to capture Niagara and Detroit meant that the western Indians retained the military initiative until the end of the war.[53]

The Anglo-American peace treaty presented the western Indians with a situation similar to the one which they had encountered in 1763. Even though they had not been defeated, their ally had surrendered title to their homeland without consultation. British officers on the scene were humiliated by this betrayal of those whom they had encouraged to pursue the war. While the new government of the United States looked upon the Ohio lands as a solution to its financial problems, it did not want an Indian war. Its hand was forced by a stream of settlers determined to establish themselves in lands north of the Ohio River. This led to the new republic's first major war in which two American armies were defeated by an Indian confederacy determined to defend its rights by force of arms. General Anthony Wayne's decisive victory at Fallen Timbers in

1794 owed as much to divisions among the Indians and British failure to provide timely aid as it did to American military prowess. Fallen Timbers led to Indian recognition of American claims north of the Ohio.[54]

Native American resistance to American expansion revived, however, after 1809 in the wake of the imposition of new treaties which resulted in additional land cessions. Tecumseh and his brother, the Shawnee Prophet, combined nativist spiritualism with an appeal for a great north–south Indian alliance. Tecumseh's attempt to rally the southern Indians met with little success, and the Prophet's followers were dispersed by Indiana Governor, William Henry Harrison, at the Battle of Tippecanoe in 1811. The outbreak of the War of 1812 breathed new life into native resistance. During 1812 the British and their Indian allies swept all before them in the Northwest, capturing Michilimackinac and Detroit. Indians made up the majority of the allied forces and, under Tecumseh's leadership, they retained the initiative in forest warfare. However, American fortunes revived in the following year when the American fleet gained control of Lake Erie. Fearing isolation in upper Canada, the British commander, General Procter, abandoned the Northwest and his Indian allies. Overtaken by William Henry Harrison in his retreat, Procter made a stand in what became known as the Battle of the Thames. The British troops were routed by Harrison's mounted riflemen and Tecumseh was killed while leading Procter's remaining Indian allies. With Tecumseh's death, the dream of united Indian resistance to American expansion was extinguished.[55]

Notes

1. I. Steele, *Warpaths: invasions of America* (New York, Oxford University Press, 1994), pp. 3–35; J. L. Wright, Jr., *The only land they knew: the tragic story of the American Indians in the Old South* (New York, The Free Press, 1981), pp. 27–52.

2. J. D. Daniels, The Indian population of North America in 1492, *William and Mary Quarterly*, 49, 1992, pp. 298–320.

3. F. Jennings, *The invasion of America: Indians, colonialism and the cant of conquest* (Chapel Hill, University of North Carolina Press, 1975), p. 31; N. Salisbury, *Manitou and providence: Indians, Europeans and the making of New England, 1500–1643* (New York, Oxford University Press, 1982), 24–30.

4. This issue is developed by G. Raudzens, Why did Amerindian defences fail? Parallels in the European invasions of Hispaniola, Virginia and beyond, *War in History*, Vol. 3, No. 3, 1996, 331–52.

5. D. Delage, *Bitter feast: Amerindians and Europeans in Northeastern North America, 1600–64*, tr. J. Brierly (Vancouver, UBC Press, 1993), pp. 78–102.

6. Jennings, *The invasion of America*, pp. 212–13; J. Axtell, *The invasion within: the contest of cultures in colonial North America* (New York, Oxford University Press, 1985), p. 273; N. Salisbury,

Red Puritans: the praying Indians of Massachusetts Bay and John Eliot, *William and Mary Quarterly*, 3rd ser., **31**, 1974, pp. 27–54.

7. See G. E. Dowd, *A spirited resistance: the North American struggle for Indian unity 1745–1815* (Baltimore, Johns Hopkins University Press, 1992).

8. M. Roberts, *The military revolution 1560–1660. An inaugural lecture delivered before the Queen's University of Belfast* (Belfast, 1956); G. Parker, *The military revolution: military innovation and the rise of the West* (Cambridge, Cambridge University Press, 1988); J. Black, *A military revolution? Military change and European society 1550–1800* (Atlantic Highlands, N.J., Humanities Press International, 1991).

9. *Scoouwa: James Smith's Captivity Narrative* (Columbus, Ohio, Ohio Historical Society, 1978), p. 161.

10. *ibid.*, p. 167.

11. Smith's account of the Indian way of war is supported by many informed observers including the ranger commander Robert Rogers. See his *A Concise Narrative of North America* (London, 1753), pp. 229–35. Also the comments of the experienced frontier diplomat Conrad Weiser in P. A. W. Wallace, *Conrad Weiser 1696–1760, friend of colonist and Mohawk* (Philadelphia, University of Pennsylvania Press, 1945), p. 201.

12. *Narratives of the Indian wars 1675–1695*, ed. C. H. Lincoln (New York, Scribner's, 1913), p. 167.

13. Rogers, *Concise narrative*, p. 229.

14. *Writings of General John Forbes pertaining to his service in North America*, ed. A. P. James (Menosha, Wisc., Collegiate Press, 1938), p. 125.

15. Daniel Gookin, Historical collections of the Indians in New England, *Massachusetts Historical Society Collections*, 1st Ser., **I**, 1792, p. 153.

16. My discussion of Indian technology is based primarily upon P. Malone, *The skulking way of war: technology and tactics among the New England Indians* (Lanham, Md., Madison Books, 1991).

17. In addition to Malone on this point, see also T. B. Abler, European technology and the art of war in Iroquoia, *Cultures in Conflict: Current Archeological Perspectives*, ed. D. C. Tkaczuk and B. C. Vivian, Proc. of the 20th Ann. Conf. of the Archaeological Ass. of the University of Calgary (1989), pp. 273–82; and B. Given, The Iroquois and Native Firearms, *Native peoples, native lands. Canadian Indians, Inuit and Metis*, Carleton Library Series No. 142, ed. B. A. Cox (Ottawa: Carleton University Press, 1987), pp. 3–13. The standard work on firearms for the period is M. L. Brown, *Firearms in colonial America: the impact on history and technology 1492–1792* (Washington, Smithsonian Institution Press, 1980).

18. Abler, p. 10.

19. Malone, p. 31. Both Malone and Abler reached their conclusions by comparative tests of the musket against the bow.

20. See numerous references to fusils in the *Writings of General John Forbes*. Also Military Affairs; Colonel Bradstreet's thoughts on Indian Affairs, *Documents relative to the colonial history of New York*, ed. E. B. O'Callaghan, **VII**, 1856, p. 692.

21. Malone, p. 60.

22. Maurice de Saxe, *Reveries on the art of war*, tr. T. R. Phillips (Harrisburg, 1944), p. 32; Frederick the Great, *Instructions for his generals*, tr. T. R. Phillips (Harrisburg, 1960), p. 92; Sieur de Folard, *Nouvelles Découvertes sur la Guerre* (Paris, 1726), 83, 253–74. The best discussion of eighteenth-century military thought is A. Gat, *The origins of military thought from the Enlightenment to Clausewitz* (Oxford, 1989).

23. Malone, pp. 42–51.

24. *ibid.*, pp. 71–72; J. West, *Gunpowder, government and war in the mid-eighteenth century* (The Royal Historical Society, The Boydell Press, 1991).

25. Steele, *Warpaths*, p. 53.

26. J. Axtell, *Beyond 1492: encounters in colonial North America* (New York and Oxford, Oxford University Press, 1992), 141–2; I. Steele, *Warpaths: invasions of North America* (New York, Oxford University Press, 1994), pp. 92–3; A. Hirsch, The collision of military cultures in seventeenth-century New England, *The Journal of American History*, Vol. 74, 1987–1988, pp. 1187–1212; N. Salisbury, *Manitou and providence: Indians, Europeans, and the making of New England, 1500–1643* (New York, Oxford University Press, 1982), pp. 221–5; D. Richter, War and culture: The Iroquois experience, *The William and Mary Quarterly*, Ser. 3, Vol. 40, 1983, pp. 528–59.

27. T. Taylor, *The anatomy of the Nuremberg trials: A personal memoir* (New York, A. Knopf, 1992), p. 253.

28. R. Rogers, *Journals of Major Robert Rogers* (Readex Microprint, 1966), pp. 128, 145; Rogers, Journal of a Scout, Jan. 25, 1757, Huntington Library, San Marino, Ca., Loudon Papers, LO 2704 A&B.

29. W. Smith, *An historical account of the expedition against the Ohio Indians in the Year MDCCLXIV under the Command of Henry Bouquet. . . .* (Philadelphia, 1766), p. 38. Smith based this account on information provided by Bouquet.

30. H. Peckham, Thomas Gist's Indian captivity narrative 1756–1759, *The Pennsylvania Magazine of History and Biography*, Vol. 80, No. 3, July, 1956, p. 299. For the Indian "Rites of War" see G. E. Dowd, *A spirited resistance: The North American struggle for Indian unity 1745–1815* (Baltimore, Johns Hopkins University Press, 1992), pp. 9–22.

31. Jennings, *The invasion of America*, pp. 160–3; White, *The middle ground*; Great Britain, Scottish Record Office, Edinburgh, Journal of a detachment of the 42nd Regiment going from Fort Pitt down the Ohio to the country of the "Illenoise". . . . , Hunter, Harvey, Webster and Will Collection, G.D. 296\196, pp. 144–5; R. D. Edmunds, *Tecumseh and the quest for Indian leadership* (Boston, Little Brown, 1984), p. 44.

32. J. Axtell and W. C. Sturtevant, The unkindest cut, or who invented scalping?, *The William and Mary Quarterly*, 3rd Ser., Vol. 37, No. 3, July, 1980, pp. 451–72.

33. Wallace, *Conrad Weiser*, p. 434; *Frontier advance on the upper Ohio, 1778–1779*, ed. L. P. Kellogg (Madison, 1916), p. 385; *Frontier retreat on the upper Ohio, 1779–1781*, ed. L. P. Kellogg (Madison, 1917), pp. 183–4.

34. R. C. Johnson, The search for a usable Indian: an aspect of the defense of colonial New England, *The Journal of American History*, Vol. 64, 1977, pp. 623–51.

35. R. White, *The middle ground: Indians, empires, and republics in the Great Lakes region, 1650–1815* (Cambridge, Cambridge University Press, 1991), pp. 199–232; M. N. McConnell, *A country between: the upper Ohio Valley and its Peoples, 1724–1774* (Lincoln, University of Nebraska Press, 1992), pp. 61–120.

36. Steele, *Warpaths*, pp. 234–7; White, *The middle ground*, pp. 256–61; McConnell, *A country between*, pp. 147–81.

37. Those who fail to appreciate the abilities of Indian warriors and thus the value of Indian allies include R. L. Yaple, Braddock's defeat: the theories and a reconsideration, *Journal of the Society for Army Historical Research*, 46, 1968, pp. 194–201 and H. Swiggett, *War out of Niagara: Walter Butler and the Tory Rangers* (New York, Columbia University Press, 1933; repr. Port Washington, N.Y., Ira J. Friedman). Those who conclude that the British did not properly "use" the Indians in the American War of Independence include J. M. Soison, *The revolutionary frontier 1763–1783* (New York, Holt, Rinehart and Winston, 1967), p. 105; and H. S.

Commager and R. B. Morris, eds, *The spirit of Seventy-Six: The American Revolution as told by participants* (Indianapolis and New York, 1958), 2 vols., **II**, p. 999.

38. C. G. Calloway, *The American Revolution in Indian country: crisis and diversity in native American communities* (Cambridge, Cambridge University Press, 1995), p. 72.

39. *ibid.*, p. 39.

40. W. J. Eccles, *The Canadian frontier 1534–1760* (New York, Holt, Rinehart, and Winston, 1969), pp. 122–4.

41. W. Shea, *The Virginia militia in the Seventeenth Century* (Baton Rouge, Louisiana University Press, 1983), p. 140. For Elizabethan military institutions and practices see C. G. Cruikshank, *Elizabeth's army*, 2nd edn (Oxford, Oxford University Press, 1966); L. Boynton, *The Elizabethan militia* (London, 1967); and J. S. Nolan, The militarization of the Elizabethan state, *The Journal of Military History*, Vol. 58, No. 3, July, 1994, pp. 391–420.

42. C. Falls, *Elizabeth's Irish wars* (New York, Barnes and Noble, 1970); N. P. Canny, *The Elizabethan conquest of Ireland: a pattern established 1565–1576* (New York, Harper and Row, 1976), p. 160.

43. J. Shy, A new look at the colonial militia in *A people numerous and armed, reflections on the military struggle for American independence* (New York, Oxford University Press, 1976), Ch. 2. For the Quebec militia see W. J. Eccles, The French Forces in North America during the Seven Years War, *The Dictionary of Canadian biography*, **III**, *1741–1770*, ed. Francis G. Halpenny (Toronto, University of Toronto Press, 1974), p. xvii.

44. D. Leach, *Flintlock and tomahawk: New England in King Philip's War* (New York, Macmillan, 1958), particularly Ch. 6. See also the same author's The military system of Plymouth colony, *The New England Quarterly*, **XXIV**, 1951, pp. 342–64.

45. See B. Church, *Diary of King Philip's war 1675–1676*, ed. A. and M. Simpson (Chester, Conn., Pequot Press, 1975).

46. Axtell, *Beyond 1492*, p. 239; R. Bourne, *The red king's rebellion: racial politics in New England 1675–1678* (New York, Athenaeum, 1990), p. 36.

47. C. Calloway, *The Western Abenakis of Vermont, 1600–1800* (Norman, University of Oklahoma Press, 1990), pp. 113–15.

48. McConnell, *The middle ground*, pp. 119–20.

49. For reports of the Battle of Lake George see *Documents relative to the colonial history of New York*, ed. E. B. O'Callaghan, **VI**, pp. 1003–13, and **X**, pp. 316–99, 422–3.

50. *Writings of General John Forbes*, pp. 117, 191, 198; D. Brymer, *Report on the Canadian archives*, 1889, Note D (Ottawa, 1890), 61–61.

51. Disposition for march and to receive attack, Sept. 15, 1764, Bouquet Papers, British Museum, Add. Mss. 21,653, pp. 316–20.

52. J. M. Faragher, *Daniel Boone: the life and legend of an American pioneer* (New York, Henry Holt, 1992), pp. 214–24.

53. *Journals of the military expedition of Major General John Sullivan against the Six Nations of Indians in 1779*, ed. F. Cook (Auburn, NY., Knapp, Peck and Thomson, 1887); Calloway, *American Revolution*, pp. 51–1; Swiggett, *War out of Niagara*, pp. 194–9.

54. W. Sword, *President Washington's Indian war: the struggle for the Old Northwest, 1790–1795* (Norman, University of Oklahoma Press, 1985).

55. For biographies of Tecumseh and his brother, see R. D. Edmunds, *The Shawnee prophet* (Lincoln, University of Nebraska Press, 1983), and *Tecumseh and the quest for Indian leadership* (Boston, Little Brown, 1984). The combination of spiritualism and resistance is best explored by G. E. Dowd, *A spirited resistance: the struggle for North American unity, 1745–1815* (Baltimore, Johns Hopkins University Press, 1992). For the War of 1812, see R. Horsman, *The War*

of 1812 (New York, Knopf, 1969), and H. L. Coles, *The War of 1812* (Chicago, University of Chicago Press, 1965).

Further reading

R. Allen, *His Majesty's Indian Allies: British Indian Policy in the Defence of Canada, 1774–1815* (Toronto, Dundurn, 1992).

J. Axtell, *European and Indian: Essays in the Ethnohistory of Colonial America* (New York, Oxford University Press, 1981).

J. Axtell, *The Invasion Within: The Contest of Cultures in Colonial North America* (New York, Oxford University Press, 1985).

J. Axtell, *Beyond 1492: Encounters in Colonial North America* (New York, Oxford University Press, 1992).

R. Bourne, *The Red King's Rebellion: Racial Politics in New England, 1675–1678* (New York, Atheneum, 1990).

C. Calloway, *The Western Abenakis of Vermont, 1600–1800* (Norman, University of Oklahoma Press, 1990).

C. Calloway, *The American Revolution in the Indian Country: Crisis and Diversity in Native American Communities* (Cambridge, Cambridge University Press, 1995).

B. Church, *Diary of King Philip's War, 1675–1676*, eds A. and M. Simpson (Chester, Conn., The Pequot Press, 1975).

H. L. Coles, *The War of 1812* (Chicago, University of Chicago Press, 1965).

D. Delage, *Bitter Feast: Amerindians and Europeans in Northeastern North America, 1660–1664*, tr. Jane Brierly (Vancouver, UBC Press, 1993).

G. Dowd, *A Spirited Resistance: The North American Struggle for Indian Unity, 1745–1815* (Baltimore, Johns Hopkins University Press, 1992).

W. J. Eccles, *Frontenac: The Courtier Governor* (Toronto: McClelland and Stewart, 1959).

W. J. Eccles, *The Canadian Frontier, 1534–1760* (New York, Holt, Rinehart and Winston, 1969).

R. D. Edmunds, *The Potawatomis: Keepers of the Fire* (Norman, University of Oklahoma Press, 1978).

R. D. Edmunds, *The Shawnee Prophet* (Norman, University of Oklahoma Press, 1983).

R. D. Edmunds, *Tecumseh and the quest for Indian leadership* (Boston, Little, Brown, 1984).

L. V. Eid, A kind of running fight: Indian battlefield tactics in the late eighteenth century, *The Western Pennsylvania Historical Magazine*, **LXXI**, 1988, pp. 147–71.

J. M. Faragher, *Daniel Boone: the life and legend of an American pioneer* (New York, Henry Holt, 1992).

J. Ferling, *A wilderness of miseries: war and warriors in early America* (Westport, Conn., Greenwood Press, 1980).

G. Fregault, *Canada: the war of the conquest*, tr. M. M. Cameron (Toronto, Oxford University Press, 1969).

L.H. Gipson, *The British Empire before the American revolution*, 15 vols (Caldwell, Id., Caxton Printers, 1936–1970).

B. Graymont, The Six Nations Indians in the Revolutionary War, *The Iroquois in the American Revolution* (Rochester, Rochester Museum and Science Center, 1981).

R. Horsman, *Expansion and American Indian policy, 1783–1812* (East Lansing, Michigan State University Press, 1967).

R. Horsman, *The War of 1812* (New York, Knopf, 1969).

R. D. Hurt, *The Ohio frontier: crucible of the Old Northwest, 1720–1830* (Bloomington, Indiana University Press, 1996).

F. Jennings, *The invasion of America: Indians, colonialism, and the cant of conquest* (Chapel Hill, University of North Carolina Press, 1975).

F. Jennings, *The ambigious Iroquois empire* (New York, Norton, 1984).

F. Jennings, *Empire of fortune: crowns, colonies, and tribes in the Seven Years War* (New York, Norton, 1988).

I. Kelsay, *Joseph Brant, 1743–1807: man of two worlds* (Syracuse, Syracuse University Press, 1984).

R. Kohn, *Eagle and sword: The Federalists and the creation of the military establishment in America, 1783–1802* (New York, the Free Press, 1975).

P. Kopperman, *Braddock at the Monongahela* (Pittsburgh, University of Pittsburgh Press, 1977).

D. Leach, *Flintlock and tomahawk: New England in King Philip's War* (New York, Macmillan, 1958).

P. Malone, *The skulking way of war: technology and tactics among the New England Indians* (Lanham, Md., Madison Books, 1991).

M. McConnell, *A country between: the upper Ohio Valley and its peoples, 1724–1774* (Lincoln, University of Nebraska Press, 1992).

J. Merrell, *The Indians' new world: Catawbas and their neighbors from European contact through the era of removal* (Chapel Hill, University of North Carolina Press, 1989).

P. Nelson, *Anthony Wayne: Soldier of the early republic* (Bloomington, Indiana University Press, 1985).

J. O'Donnell, *Southern Indians in the American Revolution* (Knoxville, University of Tennessee Press, 1973).

S. Pargellis, *Military affairs in North America, 1748–1765* (1936, repr. Archon Books, 1969).

F. Parkman, *France and England in North America*, 2 vols (New York, 1983).

H. Peckham, *Pontiac and the Indian uprising* (Princeton, Princeton University Press, 1947).

H. Peckham, *The Colonial Wars 1689–1762* (Chicago, University of Chicago Press, 1964).

F. Prucha, *The Sword of the republic: The United States army on the Frontier, 1783–1846* (Toronto, Collier-Macmillan, 1969).

D. Richter, *The ordeal of the longhouse: peoples of the Iroquois League in the era of European colonization* (Chapel Hill, University of North Carolina Press, 1992).

N. Salisbury, *Manitou and providence: Indians, Europeans and the making of New England, 1500–1643* (New York, Oxford University Press, 1982).

W. Shea, *The Virginia militia in the seventeenth century* (Baton Rouge, Louisiana State University Press, 1983).

J. Shy, *A people numerous and armed; reflections on the military struggle for American independence* (New York, Oxford University Press, 1976).

R. Slotkin, *Regeneration Through violence: mythology of the American frontier, 1600–1860* (Middletown, Conn., Wesleyan University Press, 1973).

J. Soison, *The revolutionary frontier, 1763–1783* (New York, Holt, Rinehart and Winston, 1967).

I. Steele, *Guerrillas and grenadiers, the struggle for Canada, 1689–1760* (Toronto, Ryerson Press, 1969).

I. Steele, *Betrayals: Fort William Henry and the "Massacre"* (New York, Oxford University Press, 1990).

I. Steele, *Warpaths: invasions of North America* (New York, Oxford University Press, 1994).

H. Swiggert, *War out of Niagara: Walter Butler and the Tory rangers* (New York, Columbia University Press, 1933).

W. Sword, *President Washington's Indian war: The struggle for the Old Northwest, 1790–1795* (Norman, University of Oklahoma Press, 1985).

B. Trigger, *The children of Aataentsic: a history of the Huron people to 1660*, 2 vols (Montreal, McGill-Queen's University Press, 1976).

A. Vaughn, *The New England frontier: Puritans and Indians, 1620–1675* (Boston, Little, Brown, 1965).

R. White, *The middle ground: Indians, empires, and republics in the Great Lakes region, 1650–1815* (Cambridge, Cambridge University Press, 1991).

J. L. Wright, Jr., *Britain and the American frontier, 1783–1815* (Athens, University of Georgia Press, 1975)

J. L. Wright, *The only land they knew: the tragic story of the American Indians in the Old South* (New York, The Free Press, 1981).

Index

263